PRAISE FOR
Overdo$ed America

"The strength of *Overdo$ed America* is in these close readings of the research. Abramson walks the reader through the contradictions he's discovered between the exorbitant claims made for the products and the actual study data. . . . Enlightening."

—*Washington Post Book World*

"A powerful and coherent case that American medicine has gone badly astray and needs a new paradigm—one untainted by profits."

—*Publishers Weekly*

"[R]eaders who might be inclined to view *Overdo$ed America* as simply another in the growing number of diatribes against drug companies should be aware that this book makes its arguments in a detailed, well-referenced manner. Moreover, responsibility for the overdosing of America goes far beyond the drug industry, resting equally with the nation's physicians. I beg all of my physician colleagues to read this book and to think deeply about how we are practicing our chosen profession."

—Thomas Bodenheimer, M.D., *Health Affairs*

"Required reading for all medical students and doctors."

—*Journal of the American Medical Association*

"Some of the nation's worst drug dealers aren't peddling on street corners, they're occupying corporate suites. *Overdo$ed America* reveals the greed and corruption that drive health care costs skyward and now threaten the public health. Before you see a doctor, you should read this book."   —Eric Schlosser, author of *Fast Food Nation*

"I have taught with Dr. Abramson for several years; he is a superb family doctor, researcher, and communicator. In *Overdo$ed America* he uses all of these skills to present a clear and concise explanation of how American medicine has gone astray and what you can do to optimize your health. This book is a must-read for both patients and doctors concerned about health and the quality of medical care."

—Herbert Benson, M.D.,
author of *The Relaxation Response* and *The Breakout Principle*

"*Overdo$ed America* fulfills all of the criteria for high quality in health services: the right diagnosis and the right prescription at the right time. It is required reading for everyone: Americans will learn about the perverse incentives in their health care system, and those abroad will learn of the perils of importing what the United States is now trying to sell them."   —Barbara Starfield, M.D., M.P.H., University Distinguished Professor, Johns Hopkins University and Medical Institutions

"Most Americans assume that the scientific information provided to patients and physicians is accurate, that clinical practice is guided by science, and that as a result—more medical care means better medical care. *Overdo$ed America* provides a compelling and well-documented analysis of why each of these assumptions is wrong. It is a book every American should read."   —Elliott Fisher, M.D., M.P.H., Professor of Medicine, Dartmouth Medical School

Lahey Clinic

About the Author

JOHN ABRAMSON, M.D., has worked as a family doctor in Appalachia; inner-city Cleveland, Ohio; and in Hamilton, Massachusetts. He has served as chairman of the department of family practice at Lahey Clinic. Abramson was a Robert Wood Johnson Fellow and is on the clinical faculty of Harvard Medical School, where he teaches primary care.

OVERDO$ED AMERICA

The Broken Promise of
American Medicine

JOHN ABRAMSON, M.D.

HARPER
PERENNIAL

HARPER ⬤ PERENNIAL

A hardcover edition of this book was published in 2004 by Harper-Collins Publishers.

HarperCollins books may be purchased for educational, business, or sales promotional use. For information please write: Special Markets Department, HarperCollins Publishers Inc., 10 East 53rd Street, New York, NY 10022.

FIRST HARPER PERENNIAL EDITION PUBLISHED 2005.

Designed by Barbara Balch

The Library of Congress has catalogued the hardcover edition as follows:

Abramson, John.
    Overdo$ed America : the broken promise of American medicine / John Abramson.
        p.   cm.
    Includes bibliographical references and index.
    ISBN 0-06-056852-6
        1. Medicine—United States.   2. Medical care—United States.
    3. Pharmaceutical industry—United States.   I. Title.

R151.A23 2004
610'.973—dc22   2004047421

ISBN-10: 0-06-056853-4 (pbk.)
ISBN-13: 978-0-06-056853-5 (pbk.)

06   07   08   09   ❖/RRD   10   9   8   7   6

DEDICATION

As I complete this manuscript, my 84-year-old father is hospitalized, fighting for his life. The surgery he had yesterday was successful, and if he is strong enough, he will have another in four days. It is not clear whether he will survive the removal of the stones that are blocking his right kidney and seeding his bloodstream with life-threatening bacteria.

Many people have contributed to his medical care, giving him a chance to recover from this illness: from the nurse's aide who, like an angel, entered his life in his darkest moments and helped to rekindle his will to get well by reminding him that kindness is its own reward; to the nurses, nurse practitioner, and physician's assistant who worked hard and often behind the scenes to provide and coordinate his care; to the primary care doctors who managed the multisystem medical problems that have arisen; to the radiologist who saved his life by coming in late at night to insert a tube into his side to drain his blocked and infected kidney; to the world-class specialists who have the technical skills to remove these complex stones; to the researchers who pushed the limits of our knowledge enough to make all of this care possible.

This book is dedicated to my dad, come what may, and to all of the wonderful people who have participated in his care. It is dedicated to my former patients, whom I left to write this book. I thank you for the trust we shared and the lessons that I learned from you. Finally, it is dedicated to all of the hardworking and committed Americans working in health care—finding expression of their highest values in the kindness, skill, and dedication they bring to their work every day.

If at times I seem too hard on American medicine in these pages, it is because I know its potential and its importance. My hope in writing this book is that it will play a constructive role in helping to redirect American medicine back toward its highest ideals.

It is no limitation upon property rights or freedom of contract to require that when men receive from government the privilege of doing business under corporate form . . . they shall do so upon absolutely truthful representations. . . . Great corporations exist only because they are created and safeguarded by our institutions; and it is therefore our right and duty to see that they work in harmony with these institutions.

Theodore Roosevelt

CONTENTS

PREFACE TO THE
PAPERBACK EDITION

When *Overdo$ed America* was first published, I expected the book to generate immediate excitement. After all, the book exposes many of the drug companies' well-kept secrets, such as the misrepresentation of their own research on Vioxx and Celebrex in our most respected medical journals and the pushing of cholesterol-lowering drugs on millions of Americans, unsupported by the scientific evidence. I had spent nearly three years documenting the undue influence of the drug and other medical industries on American health care and was sure that the response to my findings would be explosive.

During the first week after publication the silence was deafening. Maybe doctors were not ready to accept that much of the "scientific evidence" upon which they base their medical decisions is more like infomercials than disciplined science. Maybe the American public was not ready to swallow this bitter, but critically important, pill.

Then, just one week after the book hit the stores, Merck stunned the medical world with its announcement that it was withdrawing its $2.5 billion a year arthritis remedy Vioxx from the market. This was the biggest drug recall ever(about one out of ten American adults had taken Vioxx in the previous five years.

Initially Merck was credited with acting responsibly and decisively when it learned that its blockbuster drug doubled the risk of serious cardiovascular problems in a study designed to determine whether Vioxx reduces the recurrence of non-cancerous polyps of the colon. But the real news was not that Merck had done the right thing in September 2004 (which it had). Rather it was that American doctors had prescribed $7 billion worth of Vioxx, causing an estimated tens of thousands of heart attacks and deaths, *after* both Merck and the FDA had become aware (in 2000) that Vioxx was significantly more dangerous and no more effective than an older and far less costly anti-inflammatory drug, naproxen (Aleve).

Suddenly it was as if the waters had parted or the code of silence lifted. Americans wanted to know how a non-essential drug that turned out to be so dangerous had become so widely used. The media responded. Instead of being ignored, I was invited to explain to millions of Americans how this had happened on NBC's *Today* show, CNN's *American Morning, Lou Dobbs Tonight*, and on all the other major networks.

In the following three months an unprecedented string of drug company failures and embarrassments came to light. Just one week after the Vioxx recall, Americans learned that half of our supply of flu vaccine, 46 million doses, would not be arriving as planned from a manufacturing plant in Liverpool, England. The plant, which sends 90 percent of the flu vaccine it makes to the United States, had been abruptly shut down. Bacterial contamination of four million doses of flu vaccine was the initial sign of trouble, but the underlying problem was the inadequacy of the manufacturing safety systems. With most of the flu vaccine being produced in this plant headed for the United States, one might assume that the FDA had been actively monitoring the safety of these imported medicines-especially given its oft-expressed concern about the potential danger to individual citizens of importing drugs from abroad. But it wasn't the FDA that shut down the plant in England. In fact, FDA officials were taken by surprise when they were informed that the British drug authorities had shut the plant down to protect Americans from unsafe flu vaccine being produced by an American company's plant in the United Kingdom. This debacle was an accident that had been waiting to happen, at least in part the result of having transferred more than one thousand FDA employees into the department that approves new drugs (like Vioxx) and out of the department that oversees drug safety (like inspecting manufacturing plants).

This was not all. The following week the FDA issued a strong warning about the use of antidepressants in young patients: "Antidepressants increase the risk of suicidal thinking and behavior (suicidality) in children and adolescents." British drug authorities had mandated a similar warning a year and a half earlier, based upon the same information that had been available to the FDA. Eight months before the warning was issued in the United States, an FDA Advisory Committee met to discuss the potential danger of these drugs. But the FDA's own epidemiologist, who had been heading up this investigation, was removed from the agenda and not allowed to present his report.

Although the six studies involving young patients that had been published in medical journals showed that antidepressants are safe and effective, nine studies showing just the opposite had not been published. Doctors, trusting their medical journals, were being misled. Instead of taking protective action based on a clear and present danger, the FDA asked an independent panel of researchers to review the data. When the outside experts agreed with its own, the FDA belatedly mandated the highest level of caution: a "black box warning" on the drug label and a patient information sheet to accompany the medication. In other words, the drug companies had maintained sales of largely ineffective drugs by not publishing results from their own studies showing that the new antidepressants increase suicidal behavior in youngsters, thus leaving doctors uninformed about these negative studies. When confronted with this situation, the FDA's reaction was first to protect the drug companies rather than our children. (This brings to mind the maxim that the best measure of a society is how it treats its most vulnerable members.)

This rapid-fire series of events may have brought us to a watershed in American medicine, dispelling the illusion that what's good for the drug companies is good for Americans and helping us to understand that we are not getting commensurate value for the enormous cost of our health care. Probably the greatest cause for optimism is the Senate Finance Committee hearing called by Sen. Grassley (R-Iowa) to investigate whether the FDA and Merck had adequately monitored the safety of Vioxx. Americans were given the opportunity to witness academic researchers and public employees describing how drug companies wield influence and suppress information. Most of the senators on the committee appeared to care deeply about protecting Americans from the unnecessary dangers of potentially harmful drugs and seemed to understand that the FDA is not now providing adequate monitoring of drug safety.

As the litany of previously undisclosed risks of some of our most widely used drugs grows ever longer, most of the attention is being focused on the FDA. Certainly reform at the FDA is necessary to improve the safety and effectiveness of our medical care, but this is in no way sufficient to achieve all our goals. Like a dentist not drilling all the way to the bottom of a cavity, we are still not getting to the bottom of the problem, and anything less is going to squander this extraordinary opportunity.

The over-use of Vioxx, Celebrex, and cholesterol-lowering drugs in adults, and antidepressants in children and adolescents all show that at the heart of the crisis in American medicine is a crisis in the quality of our medical knowledge. As you will learn in the pages to follow, the corruption of that knowledge extends far beyond the reach of the FDA. *Overdo$ed America* tells this story without protecting any of the vested interests, which is how we need to approach the crisis in American medicine if we truly want to restore its broken promise.

—February 2005

INTRODUCTION

For more than 20 years I practiced family medicine in a small town about 45 minutes north of Boston. During those years I often marveled at how lucky I was to have found my calling, balancing the science of medicine with the art of caring for people. I got enormous satisfaction out of watching children grow and families mature, assisting them through daily worries and occasional tragedies. I treasure the lessons I learned from my older patients as they met the challenges of their senior years with dignity and humor. I have had no greater sense of accomplishment than helping people preserve their health, recover from illness, and, when recovery was not possible, provide comfort.

Just before I left my practice to write this book, one of my longtime patients, Mrs. Francis, came in for a last visit. I always enjoyed seeing Mrs. Francis, a widow then in her in mid-eighties. Her greeting was warm and her presence made the exam room feel comfortable—an oasis in the midst of daily time pressures, multiple tasks, and complex patient challenges. During this visit, Mrs. Francis asked why I was leaving. This wasn't just a casual question, nor did I feel that she was prying. Over the years, we had enjoyed many conversations, and I felt as if she genuinely wanted to understand what had gone into my decision. I did my best to explain.

I told her that over the last few years a profound shift had been taking place in the culture of American medicine. I explained that tests unlikely to improve patient care were being routinely ordered and expensive drugs that had not been shown to be any more effective or safer than the older drugs they were replacing were being routinely prescribed. I told her that the research I had been doing at night and on weekends was confirming my sense that much of the "scientific evidence" on which we doctors must rely to guide our clinical decisions was being commercially spun, or worse; and that many of the articles published in even the most respected medical journals seemed more like infomercials whose purpose was to promote their sponsors' products rather than to search for the best ways to improve people's health.

I told her that many of my patients were being drawn in by the growing number of drug ads and medical news stories; that patients were increasingly arriving for their visits with a firm (if not fixed) idea of the outcome they wanted instead of the expectation that the best medical care would emerge from open discussion of their symptoms, concerns, and exam, and then mutual consideration of the options. I told her that when I tried to refocus patients on interventions proved to be safe and effective, many were reacting as if I were purposely trying to withhold the best treatment, making me choose between providing the best care and yielding to their demands in order to maintain the healing potential of our relationship. Finally, I told her that I had come to the conclusion that the best way I could help people to achieve better health was to find out what the scientific evidence really shows and explain this to the public—in much the same way that she and I had talked over the years—and to other medical professionals.

That was the best answer I could give Mrs. Francis at the time. I wasn't sure what I was going to find when I turned my full attention to these issues. But it was becoming clear that American medicine was like a runaway train picking up speed, fueled by the commercially generated belief that ever-increasing medical spending is necessary to achieve good health. It was also becoming clear that the train's brakes were failing. It seemed to me that, despite a few clear and brave voices, there was no effective counterbalance to the influence of commercially sponsored research. Nor was there even a way to determine whether all this expensive new care actually led to better health. And it was also clear that this crisis would soon come to a head when the burden of relentlessly increasing medical costs became more than many Americans could bear.

What I found over the next two and a half years of "researching the research" is a scandal in medical science that is at least the equivalent of any of the recent corporate scandals that have shaken Americans' confidence in the integrity of the corporate and financial worlds. Rigging medical studies, misrepresenting research results published in even the most influential medical journals, and withholding the findings of whole studies that don't come out in a sponsor's favor have all become the accepted norm in commercially sponsored medical research. To keep the lid sealed on this corruption of medical science—and to ensure its translation into medical practice—there is a complex web of corporate influence that includes disempowered regulatory agencies, commercially sponsored medical education, brilliant advertising, expensive public relations campaigns, and manipulation of free media coverage. And last, but not least, are the financial ties between many of the most trusted medical experts and the medical industry. These relationships bear a remarkable resemblance to the conflicts of interest the Securities and Exchange Commission recently brought to a halt after learning that securities analysts were receiving bonuses for writing reports that drove up stock prices with the intent of bringing in more investment banking business.

As a result of all this, the pharmaceutical industry is raking in unheard-of profits—more than three times the average of the other Fortune 500 industries, even after accounting for all its research and development costs. At the same time, the average yearly out-of-pocket health care costs for employees of large corporations (including payroll deductions for health insurance, co-pays, and non-covered drugs and services) increased by more than $1000 between 1998 and 2003. To put the magnitude of this growing "health tax" in perspective, the much ballyhooed middle-class tax cut amounts to $469 for the average American family. In 2004, out-of-pocket health care costs for that same family are projected to increase by another 22 percent, coincidentally costing exactly an additional $469 per year. While the drug and medical-device industries are enjoying their enormous profits, hardworking Americans are struggling to keep up with their health insurance premiums and medical bills, 44 million Americans are without any health insurance at all, and half of all personal bankruptcies in the United States are caused by medical expenses.

Worse, many of the mechanisms that Americans trust to protect their health and resources have been dismantled by political pressure from doctors and medical industry lobbyists, while others have become absurdly dominated by people with financial ties to the pharmaceutical companies—a situation that no impartial observer would ever conclude was designed to represent anything other than corporate interests. The shocking news is that this is now commonplace at even the most trusted of American health institutions, the National Institutes of Health and the Food and Drug Administration.

The bottom line is this: There has been a virtual takeover of medical knowledge in the United States, leaving doctors and patients little opportunity to know the truth about good medical care and no safe alternative but to pay up and go along. The ugliest truth of all is that these enormous costs do not come close to producing commensurate improvements in our health—the health of Americans is actually losing ground to that of the citizens of the other industrialized countries, which are spending far less and at the same time providing health care to all of their citizens.

Over the past 28 years as a physician I have had the privilege of observing the transformation of American medicine from a number of vantage points. My first experience as a primary care doctor was in Appalachia, with the National Health Service Corps (then a part of the U.S. Public Health Service). There I worked in a rural health clinic where I got an excellent introduction to the basics of clinical medicine—including working alongside an exceptional nurse practitioner, who showed me the importance of a team approach to patient care. Later, as a Robert Wood Johnson Fellow, I spent two years studying research design, statistics, epidemiology, and health policy and then researching the consequences of providing medical care to low-income inner-city residents through an innovative health maintenance organization (HMO). I was able to continue my academic interest in health policy at Brandeis University's Heller School of Social Policy, participating in a project designed to tailor local health care expenditures to local health needs. I witnessed the evolution of HMO coverage from the inside during my seven years as a part-time associate medical director in an early HMO in Massachusetts. In the mid-

1990s, I merged my practice into Lahey Clinic, a large, doctor-run multi-specialty group practice. Lahey Clinic showed its commitment to primary care by setting up a department of family practice, in which I served as chair for seven years.

Teaching has also been an important lens through which I have observed the changes in medicine. I began teaching Harvard Medical School students in my office after I had been in practice for about 10 years and enjoyed supporting and supervising them as they progressed during these clerkships through the stages of becoming doctors. My first task was to help the students learn to apply the medical science they were learning to the patients they were seeing in my office. As they became comfortable with the nuts and bolts of disciplined primary care, I especially enjoyed helping them develop their skills in the art of medicine—understanding that the person-to-person connection they were making with their patients was not just a pleasant amenity but an integral part of medical care. I hoped to help them add this essential dimension of good doctoring to the technically oriented medicine they were learning while caring for very sick patients in university hospitals, where they spent most of their time.

As an outgrowth of this focus on the fundamental importance of healing relationships in good medical practice, I taught a course for several years at Harvard Medical School with Dr. Herbert Benson of the Mind/Body Medical Institute. My goal was to provide medical students with an intellectual framework to support ("protect" may be a better word) their humanistic ideals while they struggled to learn the scientific basis of medicine.

But by far the most important vantage point from which I observed the changes taking place in American medicine was caring for my patients. I enjoyed keeping up to date on the latest developments by reading the medical journals and occasionally using my research skills to check analyses and conclusions. I took great pleasure in working with specialist colleagues on patients who required more care than I could provide alone.

As I think back on my practice and patients over the years, I recall with particular clarity the moment before each visit when I would lift the patient's chart out of the holder on the exam room door, pause for a moment to think about the person I was about to see, and refresh my memory with a quick look at the chart. As I entered the exam room, I would make a mental note of anything that might help me better tune in to my patient and then would begin the visit with either an open-ended question or a continuation of a conversation from the last visit (a recent change in medication, grandchildren, a job change, a sporting event, a marital problem, a school report, and so on). Visits of this kind gradually build the healing relationships that establish the foundation of good medical care. In the final analysis, it was both the loss of trust in medical science and the weakening of doctor-patient relationships that led me to write this book.

Mrs. Francis listened carefully to my explanation, but she had a hard time understanding what I was saying—not because she didn't believe me but because the changes in American medicine that I was telling her about were so vastly different from the world of medicine and the values that she had grown up with and that had served her so well. Nonetheless, she sincerely wished me well, and we ended the visit making clear to each other that we would miss our relationship.

This book approaches the crisis in American medicine from the radical center—the simple ideal that unbiased medical science and strong doctor-patient relationships ought to define optimal medical care and serve as the basis of medical practice.

My research has shown me how easily this could be achieved simply by restoring the integrity of medical science and refocusing its mission on improving health. I have come to understand that the system we now have is far from the best way to advance medical knowledge and pay for health care, but is probably the best of all possible ways to transfer massive amounts of wealth from the American people to the drug industry and other medical industries.

Popular wisdom, even among health policy experts, is that there is no good solution to this crisis of rising health care costs. As long as the validity of our medical science and method of translating it into medical practice remain unquestioned, this is true. But our medical science has become deeply flawed, manipulated to serve corporate interests. What appears to be a crisis in the cost of medical care is really a crisis in the quality of American health care. Fixing the distortions in our medical knowledge will not only lead to far better health and health care, but at the same time save hundreds of billions of dollars a year.

Obviously, one person and one book cannot present an exhaustive discussion of all the issues that need to be considered to resolve this crisis. But by beginning to lift the veil of scientific authority, commercial spin, and outright deception, I hope I can improve public understanding about the contribution of commercial distortion to the crisis in American medicine.

This book is presented in three parts. The first, "A Family Doctor's Journey of Discovery," describes the changes that were taking place in my own practice and the commercial influence that was starting to appear in respected medical journals that made me want to delve deeper. Discovering the hidden truth about Celebrex and Vioxx and, later, understanding the debacle of hormone replacement therapy showed me how profoundly disordered American medical research and practice had become.

The second part, "The Commercialization of American Medicine," presents a brief history of the commercial takeover of medical knowledge and the techniques used to manipulate doctors' and the public's understanding of new developments in medical science and health care. One example of the depth of the problem was presented in a 2002 article in the *Journal of the American Medical Association,* which showed that 59 percent of the experts who write the clinical guidelines that define good medical care (the standard to which doctors are often held in malpractice suits) have direct financial ties to the companies whose products are being evaluated. The exaggerations and distortions of the 2001 cholesterol guidelines that are responsible for millions of Americans' being treated with cholesterol-lowering statin drugs (despite the lack of scientific evidence of benefit for such widespread use) is presented as a case in point.

The final part, "Taking Back Our Health," proposes a broader paradigm of medical care than the one learned by doctors during their medical training and reinforced by the medical industry's commercial interests. Part III examines what the research really shows about the most common chronic diseases—from osteoporosis to heart disease—

explaining that much of what is called "scientific evidence" is really disease mongering designed to sell more drugs. The final chapter shows that restoring the integrity of medical science is the best way to finance universal health care and still save hundreds of billions of dollars a year.

This book tells the hidden story of American medicine. If you or your doctor ignore its findings, it could be hazardous to your health.

PART I

A FAMILY DOCTOR'S
JOURNEY OF DISCOVERY

CHAPTER 1

MEDICINE IN TRANSITION

CARING FOR PATIENTS AT THE CROSSROADS

The air was hot and muggy even by Amazon standards. It was the end of an exhausting but very satisfying day of doctoring indigenous people of all ages in a two-room school building temporarily transformed into a clinic for this small medical mission. We were putting the medical equipment and records away, and I was thinking about how nice a cool shower was going to feel, when our interpreter approached me with a look of concern and asked if I would make a house call to a woman who was too sick to come to our makeshift clinic.

Several villagers led me across an open field and down a narrow dirt path to the sick woman's open cabin. As we approached, I could see her lying still in a hammock. Her husband was sitting nervously by her side, and her four young children were darting playfully in and out of the cabin, pausing for just a moment to check on their sick mother. As I sat down next to her, I could tell from her detached, pained, and frightened look that she was seriously ill. Even the subtle facial expression she mustered to greet me seemed to cause her pain.

I was introduced to the sick woman and her husband by our interpreter, and learned that she had had a spontaneous miscarriage several days before. The pain in her belly and vomiting had been getting worse for the past two days. I asked if I could examine her. She responded with a minimal nod and looked over to her husband to make sure that he agreed. Her temperature was now 103 degrees. Her abdomen was stiff and exquisitely tender to even the slightest touch. Most likely she had developed a uterine infection as a consequence of an incomplete miscarriage, and the infection had spread throughout her abdominal cavity, causing peritonitis. She needed to be hospitalized for intravenous antibiotics and fluids, and she needed dilatation and curettage of her uterus—a D and C—to remove the infected tissue.

Her husband and several other villagers listened attentively as I explained my diagnosis. But their expressions changed from hope to despair when I told them that she needed to be treated in a hospital. They said that she couldn't go to the hospital because they did not have any money. I suggested that they take her there anyway and that someone would care for her. They said that wouldn't work, that she would be ignored, left to die on the hospital steps. I asked how much it would cost for her to get hospital care. They said $160. The two other Americans present and I glanced at one another and agreed, without a word being spoken, that we would get the money together. Fortunately, a boat soon came by, headed in the right direction, and off she went, accompanied by our capable interpreter, who could help her with travel and hospital arrangements. The woman returned to the village three days later, weak but much improved. Her look of fear was gone. Her husband and children stared in happy disbelief when they first saw her and realized she would recover.

When I got back home, I went to my office the Sunday before resuming my normal schedule to go through the paperwork that had accumulated while I was away. Among the several 3-foot-high stacks of patients' charts, test results, consultants' notes, medical journals, and junk mail was the latest issue of the *Journal of the American Medical Association* (JAMA), from November 24, 1999. I noticed an article about Celebrex and one about Vioxx, the latest drugs for arthritis pain. Each article presented the results of a study sponsored by the drug's manufacturer claiming that the drug was significantly safer than older anti-inflammatory medication, which was available in much less costly generic form.

The accompanying editorial—these are typically included in medical journals to provide expert perspective on the most noteworthy articles published in each issue—reported with unusual candor (especially since both authors had financial ties to at least one of the manufacturers of the new drugs) that neither of the new anti-inflammatory drugs provided better relief of symptoms than the older alternatives. The editorial also explained that the highly touted safety benefits of the new drugs appeared minimal in people who were not at high risk of developing serious gastrointestinal side effects. So minimal, the editorial said, that 500 such people would have to be treated for one full year with the new drugs instead of the older anti-inflammatory drugs to prevent just one serious but nonfatal stomach ulcer. Based on the difference in price between the new and older anti-inflammatory drugs, the editorial calculated that the cost of each serious ulcer thus prevented was $400,000.

Still moved by my experience in the Amazon, I wondered how many lives like that of the woman to whom I had made the house call might be saved for the cost of preventing a single nonfatal stomach ulcer by using Celebrex or Vioxx. I took out my calculator to see how many times $160 goes into $400,000. I could feel myself change when I saw the figure "2500" on the display and realized the injustice of that equation. Though I didn't realize it at the time, this book was conceived in that moment.

This incident sensitized me to the intense marketing of these two drugs. Advertisements for them suddenly popped up everywhere. At first the ads seemed inappropriate, but quickly they claimed their place as normal fixtures of the American cultural landscape. The implication of the ads was that the (unspecified) superiority of the new drugs allowed people to enjoy activities that they had previously been unable to enjoy because of arthritic pain—though no such superiority had been found in any of the major research.

The marketing campaigns were certainly successful. In the year following the JAMA editorial, Celebrex and Vioxx were two of the four drugs with the greatest increase in sales. Many, if not most, of the orthopedists and rheumatologists in my community began prescribing them enthusiastically, despite the reservations expressed in the JAMA editorial. My patients were not immune to the effect of all this advertising. They increasingly requested and occasionally demanded these expensive new drugs for their arthritis symptoms and various other aches and pains, and many interpreted my reluctance to prescribe the new drugs as simply a primary care doctor's lack of expertise or inability to keep up with the latest medical therapies. Even after I carefully explained the details of the best available scientific evidence about these drugs, not all of my patients could be convinced otherwise.

THE NEW MEDICAL CONSUMERISM

Mr. Black's visit provides a typical example. A successful small-business owner in his mid-forties and an avid intermediate tennis player, Mr. Black came to see me because of nagging pain in his right elbow. A brief exam revealed tenderness on the outside of his elbow at the point where the tendon that extends the wrist into a backhand tennis shot attaches to the bone. I explained that the problem was epicondylar tendonitis, more commonly known as tennis elbow, which is caused by the repetitive impact of the tennis racquet hitting the ball. I made a series of recommendations that would allow the tendon to heal: use a forearm band when playing tennis to partially protect the point of insertion of the tendon into the bone from the impact of the tennis ball hitting the racquet; ice the area after playing tennis to prevent the inflammatory reaction from progressing; decrease the tension in the racquet strings and perhaps change to a more flexible racquet frame to lessen the impact of its hitting the ball; and talk to his tennis pro about possible grip or swing changes that might improve his tennis elbow (and perhaps his tennis game at the same time). Finally, if there was still no improvement after doing all of these things, I warned Mr. Black that he might have to temporarily decrease the amount of tennis he was playing to give his arm time to heal.

Mr. Black listened patiently to all my suggestions. When I was done, he said, "My friends are getting good relief from Celebrex. Would you write me a prescription for that?" I explained that, despite what the ads implied, Celebrex would not provide him with any better relief than the other anti-inflammatory drugs (commonly referred to as "nonsteroidal anti-inflammatory drugs," or "NSAIDs" for short) and was a lot more expensive. He replied that the additional cost was not a problem, "because my insurance covers it." Mr. Black's belief that Celebrex would solve his problem made him unwilling, or perhaps unable, even to consider my suggestions. And he made it very clear that if I would not prescribe Celebrex, he would find a doctor who would.

I quickly thought through the possible responses to Mr. Black's ultimatum. I didn't want to permanently weaken our relationship of many years over a single prescription for a drug that was unnecessarily expensive but unlikely to do him harm. I wrote the prescription.

A couple of weeks later Mr. Black called my office to report that his elbow pain had not improved and to request a referral to an orthopedic surgeon. I was frustrated that he was still unwilling to do the simple things necessary to protect his elbow from the consequences of more stress than it had been designed to withstand, but I did not want to put either of us through a repeat of the last visit. If I wanted to preserve the potential of our relationship's being helpful in the future, my only option was to acquiesce, once again. The orthopedist confirmed the obvious diagnosis of tendonitis with an MRI and sent Mr. Black for physical therapy. His elbow pain improved slowly

AN OLD-FASHIONED DOCTOR-PATIENT RELATIONSHIP

In stark contrast, my relationship with Sister Marguerite is an example of the potential of doctor and patient working together toward the same goals. I first met Sister Marguerite after she had been brought to the emergency room by ambulance, desperately short of breath. She could barely talk as she struggled to get enough air into her lungs. Her heart was beating irregularly, at about 170 times per minute. She was in atrial fibrillation—chaotic electrical activity in the upper chambers of her heart was overriding her heart's own natural pacemaker. Her chest x-ray showed pulmonary edema, fluid in her lungs, as a result of her heart not being able to pump blood effectively when beating so fast. All I knew about Sister Marguerite was from her chart: she was in her mid-eighties and had recently retired to the local convent after teaching school for 55 years.

At first I thought she would not survive this episode without intubation and mechanical ventilation. Fortunately, she responded quickly to intravenous medications that slowed down her heart and made her kidneys excrete much of the excess fluid in her body. Within 24 hours her breathing was almost back to normal. Blood tests showed that Sister Marguerite had suffered a small heart attack, which probably had set off the atrial fibrillation.

After she was out of the hospital, Sister Marguerite required frequent office visits to monitor her fragile medical condition. Our visits would often start with her saying, "You must be so sick of seeing me. Other people must need your attention more than me." She was wrong on both counts. The dose of her diuretics (fluid pills) needed to be adjusted frequently to maintain the proper fluid balance. Retention of extra fluid could have caused her to go back into pulmonary edema, and even a small amount of fluid buildup in her feet and ankles for just a few days caused her unusually thin skin to break down, leaving painful skin ulcers that took months to heal. In the opposite direction, pulling too much fluid out of her body with diuretics would have prevented her kidneys from functioning properly. Her other medicines needed to be monitored closely as well: digoxin to control her heart rate; supplemental potassium to replace the potassium that the diuretics caused her kidneys to excrete; and a blood thinner, coumadin, to prevent small blood clots from forming in her irregularly beating heart that could cause a stroke. I saw Sister Marguerite every two to four weeks when things were going smoothly, and even more often when they were not.

As I attended to the technical details of her medical care, we would talk about her religious and spiritual life, her colleagues and activities in the convent, and her family, especially her grandniece, the apple of her eye. She would tell me about her former students, always with affection. She was proud of the convent where she lived with other retired nuns, and invited me to visit her there. I accepted.

When I arrived at the convent, Sister Marguerite particularly wanted to show me the chapel where she attended mass every morning and meditated every afternoon. As we entered the chapel, the sunlight was filtering through the beautiful stained-glass windows. We sat down and shared a couple of minutes of silence together. She then showed me her tidy room and gave me a tour of the grounds.

The next time she came for an office visit I built up all my courage and asked, "Sister, when you are in your chapel meditating and I am alone reflecting on the larger issues of life, do you think that we are having similar experiences?" She responded without a moment's hesitation, "Of course we are." Sister Marguerite's acknowledgement of our common experience, though approached from different directions, felt like the most genuine of blessings.

The recurring focal point of Sister Marguerite's medical care—especially the troublesome skin ulcers—became getting her well enough to participate in special activities at the convent and enjoy her next trip to her grandniece's home. (Of all the attention that I and other doctors gave those ulcers, it was the skin care provided by a well-trained and very determined visiting nurse that helped the most.) As fragile as her health was, Sister Marguerite continued to live quite happily—albeit receiving more frequent medical care than she would have preferred—for seven years after the emergency room visit that originally brought us together.

One day, the nurse at the convent called to tell me that Sister Marguerite had died and to ask if I would come to "pronounce" her, a last rite of the medical sort. I found Sister Marguerite in her recliner, ashen and still. The nurse and one of her closest friends were already there, and soon others arrived. I felt privileged, if a little ill at ease, to be included in this sad and beautiful scene. I wanted to share with her friends just how important my relationship with Sister Marguerite had been to me, and I began to tell the story of my chapel visit. When I got to the point in the story when Sister Marguerite acknowledged our spiritual connection, all of the nuns nodded their heads, letting me know that they agreed with Sister Marguerite's assessment. It was a beautiful conclusion to our relationship.

PRACTICING MEDICINE AT THE CROSSROADS

The contrast between the care of my two patients, Mr. Black and Sister Marguerite, could not have been greater. Of course the relationship that evolved between Sister Marguerite and me was special, but still it serves as an example of the importance of shared values in the challenge of providing good medical care. Visiting her family, attending mass, meditating in the chapel, and being an active part of her community—these were the things that gave Sister Marguerite a sense of meaning. And these were the things that motivated her to be the recipient of a lot more medical care than she ever expected or wanted. Sister Marguerite and I were partners in her care, working together on the same project, optimizing her health so that she could continue to be active and independent. And our partnership became all the more rewarding because she was so open about the deeper values that made the project worthwhile for her.

On the other hand, the influence of the medical industry, especially the drug companies, was starting to make this kind of medical care seem antiquated. Increasingly my patients were looking to pills to keep them well instead of making the changes in their lives that evidence showed to be far more beneficial. Engaging patients in constructive dialogue about their health risks and habits—a big part of what I think is good doctoring—was becoming more difficult, and occasionally impossible. Too many visits were turning into nonproductive contests of wills, like my visit with Mr. Black, instead of evolving therapeutic alliances, like my relationship with Sister Marguerite.

The illusion that newer is better and consumer autonomy is more important than a relationship with a trusted physician is leading to medical care that is often less effective and, at the same time, more expensive. Mr. Black's Celebrex cost about $90 per month, while offering little if any advantage over drugs that cost one-third to one-seventh as much (as we'll see in Chapter 3). In contrast, the four medications that kept Sister Marguerite alive for seven years cost a total of $38 per month at today's prices. Nonetheless, the best way to serve my patients within this disordered medical system often called for me to accede to seemingly unreasonable demands, like Mr. Black's.

As it happened, about a year after Mr. Black came in to request Celebrex for his elbow pain, he returned for another visit. As I walked into the exam room, I noticed that he looked tired and sad. When I asked him how he was doing, he said he was having trouble sleeping and asked if I would prescribe a sleeping pill. I asked him what was going on. With an uncharacteristic demeanor of defeat, he told me about a series of business setbacks that might force him to lay off several of his longtime employees. He shared his frustration and fears about the future. Just to be sure, I asked him if he was thinking about ending his life. He said no, but I sensed that he was relieved that I was taking his distress seriously.

I suggested a low dose of trazodone, an older, non–habit-forming antidepressant drug that has a side effect of sleepiness—just what Mr. Black needed. I reminded him how important it was to resume his regular exercise, which he had given up. I also made sure that he had at least one person with whom he was sharing his real feelings. I asked him to make an appointment to come back in two weeks so I could check on his progress, and to call me in the interim if he felt worse. At the end of the visit, Mr. Black thanked me for listening to his problems.

I was glad that Mr. Black had not simply demanded one of the expensive new antidepressant drugs or sleeping pills, neither of which would have unburdened him of his real-world problems. Mostly he needed to be heard and understood—and he needed more sleep and exercise and time to work through his business difficulties. I was glad that he trusted me enough to let me help. The difference between this visit and his earlier one illustrated the difference between commercially distorted medical care and old-fashioned (yet up-to-date) primary care.

When the history of this era of American medicine is fully written, there is no doubt that many of the scientific and technological advances will stand as great achievements. But I hope that the erosion of the healing alliance between doctors and patients will be looked back upon as a cultural aberration, a consequence of the unrealistic belief that good health is primarily a product of medical science rather than primarily the natural consequence of a healthy lifestyle and environment. Often the breakthroughs and sophisticated technology themselves weaken doctors' ability to help their patients by drawing attention away from real encounters between real people working together to arrive at the best approach to each situation. As these relationships become less important, not only are we spending inordinate amounts of money on therapies that don't provide commensurate value, but our health is actually suffering. This was the biggest surprise for me as I began to understand the real truth about the "scientific evidence" upon which I was basing my medical decisions.

CHAPTER 2

SPINNING THE EVIDENCE

EVEN THE MOST RESPECTED MEDICAL JOURNALS ARE NOT IMMUNE

By the time all the morning patients had been seen, phone calls returned, nurses' questions about patient care answered, and administrative issues addressed, I would be ready for some time alone to eat lunch and relax. I enjoyed reading through the current medical journals during my short break, looking for articles that might be relevant to my practice.

In August 2000, I was reading the *New England Journal of Medicine* (NEJM) over a typical lunch in my office when I noticed an article titled "Pravastatin Therapy and the Risk of Stroke." This caught my attention because stroke is a fairly common problem among my elderly patients, and though most strokes are minor, some are tragic, leaving patients trapped in a permanent state of severe disability. I remembered one patient in particular, Mrs. Rose, who had spent the last year and a half of her life in a nursing home, wheelchair-bound, unable to feed herself or take care of her basic needs independently. Even though the stroke had left Mrs. Rose with garbled, almost incomprehensible speech, she managed to make it painfully clear to me each time I went to see her in the nursing home that she would much rather have died from her stroke than be stuck living that way.

I was certainly interested in decreasing other patients' risk of suffering the same fate. But as I started to read the abstract (a brief summary of the study's design, findings, and conclusions that precedes most articles in medical journals), I became a bit suspicious when I realized that the title itself was misleading. The study did indeed examine the effect of pravastatin, a cholesterol-lowering statin drug (more commonly known by its brand name Pravachol), in decreasing the risk of stroke, but it only included people who had already suffered a heart attack or unstable angina (chest pain that may precede a heart attack). The reduction in the risk of stroke reported in the study did not apply to Mrs. Rose or to other patients who did not already have heart disease, as might be reasonably assumed from the article's title. Still, the abstract went on to report a statistically significant reduction in the risk of strokes among post–heart attack patients given Pravachol compared with those given a placebo, and concluded that "pravastatin has a moderate effect in reducing the risk of stroke."

THE DEVIL IS IN THE (STATISTICAL) DETAILS

In the few minutes I had left before it was time to see my afternoon patients, I noticed that when the pre-study differences in conditions that predisposed a person to stroke (such as diabetes, high blood pressure, smoking, atrial fibrillation, and previous strokes) were taken into account, the reduction of stroke in the people who took Pravachol was not even large enough to be statistically significant.* This was the first time I had seen an article published in a major journal that reported

---

*The standard way to determine whether a treatment has a significant effect is to calculate the probability that the observed difference in outcome (improvement or side effect) between the patients in the group that received the new treatment and the group that received the old treatment (or placebo) would have happened by chance if, in fact, the treatment really had no effect whatsoever. The conventional cutoff for determining statistical significance is a probability (p) of the observed difference between the groups occurring purely by chance less than 5 times out of 100 trials, or $p < .05$. This translates to: "the probability that this difference will occur at random is less than 5 chances in 100 trials." The smaller the p value, the less likely it is that the difference between the groups happened by chance, and therefore the stronger—i.e., the more statistically significant—the finding.

results that did not reach statistical significance. I paused for a moment to register this fact and then read on.

The NEJM article reported an impressive-sounding 19 percent reduction in the risk of stroke in people who had taken Pravachol compared with those who had been given the placebo. This came down to 16 percent when the results were corrected for pre-study differences in factors that predispose to stroke. This way of expressing the effect of taking Pravachol is called the "relative risk reduction." But *relative* risk tells only part of the story and often conveys an exaggerated impression of the benefit of the new drug or therapy. The far more important result is the amount of disease that is prevented by a given drug or therapy, called the "*absolute* risk reduction."

The research skills I had learned as a Robert Wood Johnson Fellow served me well in critically reading articles in medical journals. Occasionally I would take out a pencil and calculator to do the arithmetic when the findings were confusing or their importance was not clear. And that is what I did with this study.

Over the course of this six-year study, 4.5 percent of the patients who took the placebo had strokes, compared with 3.7 percent of the patients who took Pravachol. The ratio between 4.5 percent and 3.7 percent provides the relative risk reduction of 19 percent. However, the actual number of strokes prevented by taking Pravachol, or the absolute risk reduction, is calculated by subtracting 3.7 percent from 4.5 percent. So over the six years of the study there were 0.8 percent fewer strokes among the people who took Pravachol. In other words, if 1000 post–heart attack patients took Pravachol for a year, there would be about one less stroke. This didn't sound to me like a major finding. I called the local pharmacy to find out the cost of Pravachol 40 mg per day (the dose used in the study) and calculated that the cost of each stroke thus prevented was $1.2 million, not even including the cost of the extra blood tests and doctor visits to monitor for potentially dangerous side effects of the medication.

My curiosity about the rest of this article was now piqued, but it was time to start the afternoon clinic session. I took the article home to continue the time-consuming process of careful analysis. One of the benefits of a faculty appointment at Harvard Medical School is access to the school's digital library, which provides access to virtually all the important medical journals. I wanted to dig around a little to see if I could find more information about statins and strokes.

STUDYING THE WRONG PEOPLE

The better I understood the details of this article, the more misleading its conclusion appeared to be. The biggest problem was the disparity between the people included in the study and the people most at risk of stroke. The people in the study averaged 62 years of age, but the age at which most strokes occur in the general population is much older: half of the men who have strokes are 71 or older, and half of the women who have strokes, like Mrs. Rose, are 79 or older. This is important because the patients in the study age 70 and older who had been treated with Pravachol actually had 21 percent *more* strokes than the patients given a placebo.

I kept going.

Eighty-three percent of the people included in the study were men, but three out of five stroke victims in the general population are women. The fact that only one out of six people in the Pravachol study were women turns out to be important because the women in the study who were given Pravachol experienced 26 percent *more* strokes than the women who were given a placebo.

And five out of six patients in the study were taking aspirin routinely to decrease their risk of having more heart trouble. But in the general population, the vast majority of people, like Mrs. Rose, do not take aspirin routinely. This is important because among the people in the study who were not taking aspirin, those taking Pravachol had 20 percent *more* strokes than those taking placebos.

My patient, Mrs. Rose, was a typical stroke victim: female, in her early eighties, and not taking aspirin. According to the results of the study, her risk of stroke would have been increased, not decreased, by treating her with Pravachol. It seemed to me that the only conclusion that could be reasonably drawn from the data presented was that men under the age of 70 who had suffered a heart attack and were taking aspirin might lower their risk of stroke by taking Pravachol.

When I finished analyzing the article and understood that the title didn't tell the whole story, that the findings were not statistically significant, and that Pravachol appeared to cause *more* strokes in the population at greater risk, it felt like a violation of the trust that doctors (including me) place in the research published in respected medical journals. More than anything else in medical training, doctors are taught that good medical care is based upon a foundation of scientific evidence. I can remember well as a medical student, intern, and resident the daily exchange of photocopied journal articles as we went from patient to patient on hospital rounds. The latest articles from respected journals were accepted as the undisputed authority, defining good medicine and defending the decisions that had been made. A big part of becoming a doctor is learning to trust this scientific evidence enough to let it guide decisions that can have profound effects on vulnerable patients.

The Pravachol article seemed likely to have the effect of exploiting this deeply ingrained trust. Had the purpose of the study truly been to assist doctors in reducing their patients' risk of stroke, it certainly would have mentioned other proven approaches to achieve that goal. Even taking at face value the article's claimed 19 percent reduction in the risk of stroke—just to make this point—other more effective ways to decrease the risk of stroke had been well documented at the time the article was published. For example, simply eating fish once a week reduces the risk of stroke by 22 percent. Controlling high blood pressure reduces the risk of stroke by 35 to 45 percent. And even moderate exercise for less than two hours a week reduces the risk of stroke in an elderly population by about 60 percent.

The purpose of this article seemed incontrovertible: to establish "scientific evidence," legitimized by the prestige of the *New England Journal of Medicine,* that would lead doctors to believe that they were reducing their patients' risk of stroke by prescribing Pravachol. The collateral damage in establishing this belief is the diversion of doctors' and patients' attention away from far more effective ways to prevent stroke and achieve better health. But there is no profit to be made from these nondrug approaches, and therefore they receive much less attention than profitable and expensive drugs.

COLLABORATION IN THE ACADEMY

My instinct was to write an article for a medical journal explaining to doctors how to avoid being misled by the pro-drug spin in the pravastatin article and others like it that might appear in the future. I was confident of my analysis but thought that teaming up with an academic expert would make an even more powerful paper. I went over the problems I had identified in the article with a recognized authority. He found no fault with my analysis. I asked if he would be interested in writing the article with me, assuming that a university-based expert would welcome the opportunity to help correct the commercial bias that was creeping into the medical literature. He politely declined, explaining that he did "some consulting for the drug companies." Stunned by his response, I quickly realized how naive I had been about the growing commercial influence in academic medicine. Nonetheless, this expert had generously taken the time to go over the article with me, so I did my best not to show my dismay.

I came away with a whole new understanding of how behind-the-scenes financial relationships between the drug companies and the academic experts (who write the articles in medical journals that are then received as "scientific evidence") can neutralize potential criticism. I was starting to understand that these issues were all of a piece: the changes in my own practice, the disordered priorities, and the growing commercial influence in clinical research and medicine. I went back to my day-to-day practice with the sense of having lost my innocence and with a new wariness about the research findings presented in the medical journals.

STATINS AND STROKE REDUX

In June 2001 another article reporting the results of a study about stroke prevention appeared, this time in the *Journal of the American Medical Association* (JAMA). The stated purpose of the study was to examine the association between ischemic strokes and the three commonly measured forms of cholesterol—HDL (good), LDL (bad), and total cholesterol.

(Ischemic strokes, the most common kind, are caused by loss of blood supply to an area of the brain, resulting in cell death and irreversible brain injury.) By examining hospital records, the study identified cases of ischemic stroke among racially and ethnically diverse residents of Harlem. Each case was then matched with two similar control patients from the same community who had not suffered a stroke.

The cases and controls were then compared for significant differences in cholesterol levels, as well as other lifestyle, medical, and demographic factors, to identify risk factors associated with ischemic stroke. The study found that the people with low levels of HDL (good) cholesterol were at increased risk of suffering a stroke. On the basis of this finding, the authors recommended checking HDL cholesterol levels routinely and suggested that people with low levels consider treatment with a statin drug to increase their "good" cholesterol. From a quick read of the abstract, this recommendation made sense, but as with the Pravachol and stroke article, as I carefully went through the details I realized that the data led to a very different conclusion. And as in the case of the Pravachol article, the direction of the spin would lead doctors to prescribe more statins. I took out my pencil again.

Not mentioned in the article's abstract, and mentioned only once in passing in the text, were the unexpected findings that the lower (that is, what we think of as healthier) the total and LDL (bad) cholesterol, the *greater* was the risk of stroke. (More on cholesterol later, but generally total cholesterol and more specifically LDL cholesterol play a role in blocking arteries, and HDL cholesterol partially counteracts this effect.) Buried within the tables included in this article were statistics showing that lower levels of total cholesterol and lower levels of LDL cholesterol were both significantly correlated with a *higher* risk of stroke ($p < .001$ and $p = .04$, respectively). As I read on, I was completely baffled by the authors' statement that "we found no relation between total cholesterol levels and stroke risk." How could they say there was no relationship between total cholesterol and stroke when their own data showed that the odds were greater than 1000 to 1 that lower total cholesterol levels were associated with a higher risk of stroke? A follow-up letter to the editor of JAMA from a doctor employed by the U.S. Department of Health and Human Services (expressing his own views) pointed out that the authors had "neglected to discuss these findings," but once the cows are out of the barn such a letter has very little effect in correcting the misperception created by the original article.

The article got even stranger when it argued that its data supported the use of statins to prevent strokes in patients with low HDL cholesterol levels. Statins raise HDL cholesterol only half as much as the article found would be necessary to significantly reduce the risk of stroke. But statins lower total and LDL cholesterol at least three times more on a percentage basis, far more than enough to significantly *increase* the risk of stroke, according to the data from the study. Nevertheless, the article concluded that treatment of low HDL cholesterol with statin drugs could significantly decrease the risk of stroke—ignoring its own findings that the overall effect on cholesterol would be associated with increased risk of stroke.

I started to wonder why the article focused on cholesterol at all. The study found that other factors were just as significant as low HDL cholesterol in increasing the risk of stroke: untreated blood pressure, lack of exercise, cigarette smoking, heavy drinking, not graduating from high school, and being uninsured or on Medicaid. In fact, the authors of this article had used data from the same case-control study in an article published in 1998 to show that even light to moderate physical activity reduced the risk of stroke in the same people by 61 percent and that heavy exercise reduced the risk of stroke by 77 percent. The benefit of exercise documented by these authors certainly overshadows the 19 percent reduction in stroke associated with an increase in HDL of 5 mg/dL*—almost twice as much as is achievable with statins. Curiously, the authors' earlier findings about the important role of exercise were not even mentioned in the current article. And, though the authors did cite the earlier NEJM article about Pravachol and stroke, they failed to mention that that article found no relationship between low HDL levels and increased risk of stroke.

---

*The blood levels of all three kinds of cholesterol (total, LDL, and HDL) are expressed as "mg/dL," meaning the number of milligrams of cholesterol present in one-tenth of a liter of serum (the clear liquid that remains after the cells have been removed from a blood sample).

It was hard for me to believe that the *Journal of the American Medical Association* would have published an article that had strayed so far from its own data and the medical literature, and so far from recommending what seemed like the best approach to helping patients avoid strokes. Thinking that it would probably not be a good idea to go back to the same research expert to review the article, I asked a well-respected cardiologist who had published more than 50 papers to look over my critique and make sure I had it right. He saw no problems with my analysis.

COMMERCIAL GOALS OR HEALTH GOALS?

The JAMA study focusing on the increased risk of stroke in people with low HDL cholesterol levels was done in a community with many more risk factors and health problems than most. The life expectancy of a black man in Harlem is only 60 years, less than the life expectancy of a man in Bangladesh. So why did this article ignore the much more powerful anti-stroke effects of positive lifestyle changes and blood pressure control? And why did it focus on raising HDL cholesterol with statins, while ignoring its own findings that the more powerful effect of statins on total and LDL cholesterol would increase, not decrease, the risk of stroke?

At the time the study was published, there were two potential changes coming that could have provided commercial incentive to do so. Pfizer had a new "HDL-elevator" drug that was well along in the pipeline of drug approval, and already being tested in clinical trials. It was also becoming clear that senior citizens would soon get some kind of assistance with prescription drug coverage from the federal government. Lower-income minority communities like Harlem represent relatively unpenetrated markets for expensive drugs with purported widespread benefits. A generous prescription drug benefit would make statin drugs affordable to many residents in this community who could not previously afford them. It seemed sinful to me to be recommending that more than $1000 per patient be spent each year—in a community with a 34 percent poverty rate—on treating people with statins with at best shaky scientific justification, while ignoring proven interventions such as increasing participation in exercise, smoking cessation programs, nutritional counseling, blood pressure control, and other medical outreach. These could have a much stronger impact not only on stroke reduction but on overall health and quality of life.

These two articles about using statins to prevent strokes, appearing in the two most influential American medical journals, seemed to approach stroke not as a human tragedy but as a commercial opportunity. Both appeared to spin research results to provide "scientific evidence" that justified more use of expensive drugs. The article in the NEJM presented findings from a study done on an unrepresentative group of patients, findings that were not even statistically significant. The article in JAMA ignored its own data showing that treatment with a statin drug was more likely to increase the risk of stroke. Both articles focused almost exclusively on drug therapy rather than inexpensive lifestyle changes that have been shown to be far more effective.

Why was all of this so important to me? For the elderly, a debilitating stroke is one of the worst possible fates. Both of these articles seemed off-key, particularly as I reflected back on Mrs. Rose's suffering and what I hoped to accomplish as a doctor. Remembering my own medical training and watching the medical students whom I was teaching struggle to learn how to base their care on the scientific evidence in the medical journals, I could see that doctors' trust in the literature was being skillfully exploited by commercial interests. But my colleagues and students were skeptical when I tried to show them that the material they were trying so hard to keep up with could not always be trusted.

I had always thought of myself as a disciplined mainstream practitioner grounded in medical science, caring, and common sense. But I was losing my faith in the knowledge that guides medical practice, and there was no going back.

In retrospect I can see that these two articles on stroke reduction, for all their flaws, had at least presented enough data to allow the commercial sleight of hand to be uncovered by careful analysis. I was soon to learn that this is not always the case.

CHAPTER 3

FALSE AND MISLEADING

THE MISREPRESENTATION OF CELEBREX AND VIOXX

In April 2001 I noticed on my desk what looked like a piece of routine junk mail from Pharmacia, the manufacturer of Celebrex. When I opened it, the first thing I saw was the following headline, in large capital letters: "IMPORTANT CORRECTION OF DRUG INFORMATION." This was clearly not ordinary junk mail.

The letter continued:

> *Dear Healthcare Provider,*
>
> *This letter is being sent to you at the request of the U.S. Food and Drug Administration. The FDA's Division of Drug Marketing, Advertising, and Communications has notified Pharmacia Corporation that it considered . . . promotional statements and actions by or on behalf of Pharmacia [concerning Celebrex] to be false or misleading and therefore in violation of the Federal Food, Drug, and Cosmetic Act.*

I recalled the unusually forthright editorial about Celebrex and Vioxx that I had read in the *Journal of the American Medical Association* about a year and a half earlier, when these drugs were first approved. Since then, the marketing blitz for these drugs—both to doctors and to the public— had been unprecedented.

By the time the "Dear Healthcare Provider" letter arrived, most people considered Celebrex to be a breakthrough anti-inflammatory drug. Though the advertising was doing a spectacular job of making the drug seem "better" than the older nonsteroidal anti-inflammatory drugs (NSAIDs), its single claim to superiority rested on its lower risk of causing stomach problems. Nonetheless, Celebrex was selling like hotcakes, racking up well over $3 billion in sales in its first two years on the market. The drug was being widely prescribed for every kind of ache and pain. Rarely did a day go by when I didn't hear the word "Celebrex" from a patient, a fellow doctor, or an ad on TV. The new drug was now accounting for one-third of all arthritis drug sales in the United States.

I read on, but the letter was vague. It mentioned several routine warnings, including a potentially dangerous drug interaction with the blood thinner coumadin and allergic reactions, and then went on to say that the FDA objected to marketing that "promoted Celebrex for unapproved uses, and made unsubstantiated comparative claims." This was followed by several warnings in bold print, including the following admonition:

Serious gastrointestinal toxicity such as bleeding, ulceration or perforation of the stomach, small intestine, or large intestine, can occur . . . in patients treated with NSAIDs, including Celebrex.

I read the letter several times, trying to understand exactly what the important message was that the FDA had instructed Pharmacia to get out to all health care providers. It seemed to be saying that Celebrex had just about the same risk of serious GI complications as other anti-inflammatory drugs. But this didn't jibe with the results of the large Celecoxib Long-Term Arthritis Safety Study that had been published in JAMA in the fall of 2000. This study, informally known as CLASS, had made a strong case that Celebrex was safer. I wondered if new evidence had become available to the FDA in the interim. Suspecting that this was not the last I would hear of the matter, I filed the letter away.

THE NEJM "DRUG THERAPY" ARTICLE

Four months after receiving the letter from Pharmacia, I noticed an article in the influential Drug Therapy section of the NEJM, "The Coxibs, Selective Inhibitors of Cyclooxygenase-2." It was a review article primarily about Celebrex and Vioxx, both members of this new class of arthritis drugs. (Review articles are designed to provide practicing doctors with expert and up-to-date overviews of important and evolving therapies.) While studies published about each of these drugs in the fall of 2000 had concluded that both were safer than the older alternatives, there were still some outstanding questions, and I assumed that this review article would answer them. Perhaps, I thought, the article would also explain the FDA-mandated letter about Celebrex.

It did nothing of the sort. The article started with the basic science: Celebrex and Vioxx were the first two selective cyclooxygenase-2 (COX-2) inhibitors approved by the FDA. COX-2 molecules participate in the inflammatory process within joints that causes the symptoms of arthritis. COX-1 molecules, on the other hand, protect the lining of the stomach from developing erosions and ulcers. The older nonselective NSAIDs (pronounced "en-sades"), such as ibuprofen (Motrin, Advil), naproxen (Aleve), and diclofenac (Voltaren), reduce inflammation by blocking the activity of COX-2 inside joints. The problem is that they also inhibit the activity of COX-1, which can lead to irritation of the lining of the stomach. The theoretical advantage of the new selective COX-2 inhibitors is that they can block inflammation without causing irritation of the stomach lining.

As I got into the review of the scientific evidence, I became increasingly puzzled. The authors praised both drugs, stating that they cause "significantly fewer serious gastrointestinal adverse events than does treatment with non-selective NSAIDs." I pulled the "Dear Healthcare Provider" letter out of my files to make sure that my recollection of its wording was accurate. It was. After going over the language very carefully, I realized that this review article had taken drug salesmanship into new territory. This supposedly authoritative review article in the *New England Journal of Medicine* seemed to be stating as fact one of the "unsubstantiated comparative claims" that the FDA had forbidden the manufacturer of Celebrex to make on its own behalf.

The review article also seemed to be trying too hard to present a favorable picture of Vioxx. The results of the Vioxx Gastrointestinal Outcomes Research (VIGOR) study, published in the NEJM in the fall of 2000, had raised the possibility of Vioxx increasing the risk of heart attack and other cardiovascular complications. The NEJM review article published in August 2001 reported that people who took Vioxx had twice as many heart attacks, strokes, and cardiovascular deaths and four times as many heart attacks as the people who took naproxen ($p < .05$ and $p < .01$, respectively). But then, rather than addressing these serious complications, the authors dismissed them with a most unusual statement: "The difference in major cardiovascular events in the VIGOR trial [of Vioxx] may reflect the *play of chance*" (italics mine) because "the number of cardiovascular events was small (less than 70)." The comment that a statistically significant finding "may reflect the play of chance" struck me as very odd. Surely the experts who wrote the review article knew that the whole purpose of doing statistics is to determine the degree of probability and the role of chance.

Anyone who has taken Statistics 101 knows that p values of .05 or less ($p < .05$) are considered statistically significant. In this case it means that if the VIGOR study were repeated 100 times, more than 95 of those trials would show that the people who took Vioxx had at least twice as many heart attacks, strokes, and death from any cardiovascular event than the people who took naproxen. And in more than 99 out of those 100 studies, the people who took Vioxx would have at least four times as many heart attacks as the people who took naproxen. This "play of chance" caveat seemed like a not very well camouflaged attempt at damage control. Then I noticed that the two authors of the review article had financial ties to the manufacturers of Celebrex and Vioxx, even though financial relationships between authors of review articles and drug companies were prohibited by the *New England Journal of Medicine* at the time the article was published.[*]

---

[*]Less than a year after the review article was published, the NEJM loosened its editorial policy so that authors of review articles and editorials were allowed to have relationships, but not "significant" relationships, with the companies that could be affected by what they wrote.

I went back to the NEJM article that presented the results of the VIGOR study from the fall of 2000. The article mentioned that the differences in cardiovascular complications between the patients who had taken Vioxx and naproxen had been measured. But, curiously, the article did not report what those differences were; purportedly they were to be included in a later article. The NEJM article claimed, "A separate analysis of these events, however, was not specified in the study design."

I became even more suspicious when I noticed that the total number of serious gastrointestinal complications that occurred in the patients in the VIGOR study was only 53. Wait a minute. The authors of the VIGOR study (as well as the authors of the review article) declared that a total of 53 serious GI complications was the most important finding in the study, and reason alone to prescribe Vioxx instead of a far less expensive NSAID. How could the authors of the review article then dismiss the reported cardiovascular risk with Vioxx on the grounds that there were "less than 70" cardiovascular events? Moreover, as I searched through the original VIGOR article, I couldn't find the number 70 anywhere, suggesting that the authors of the review had another source of information.

Now I was determined to find out the real story. The articles about statins and strokes had shown me how effectively the drug companies can spin their "scientific evidence." As I was about to find out, the articles about Celebrex and Vioxx went a step further.

A SEARCH FOR THE REAL DATA

One might assume that anyone who was willing to go to the trouble of verifying conclusions presented in medical journals could do so. This is not the case at all. Drug companies often keep the results of their studies secret, even from their own researchers, on the grounds that such results are "proprietary information" of economic value. Getting to the bottom of the Celebrex and Vioxx stories would be difficult, but I had already done enough of this kind of research to know that it was usually worth poking around online.

I started with Harvard Medical School's digital library, but couldn't find any new research or more complete data. Next I tried the government-sponsored "Pub-Med" website, a database of several thousand scientific journals; but a comprehensive search there didn't yield any new information either. Then I went to the FDA website to see if I could find any unpublished data the agency had used in its decision to mandate Pharmacia's "Dear Healthcare Provider" letter. Not knowing what I was looking for, I came blindly upon reports from the FDA's Arthritis Advisory Committee meeting of February 7–8, 2001, which had been held specifically to go over the FDA reviewers' analyses of the data from the CLASS and VIGOR studies in order to consider the manufacturers' requests to remove warning labels about the risk of ulcers from Celebrex and Vioxx.

As I started to go through these reports, I realized that they were the actual FDA reviewers' internal analyses of the research data that the manufacturers of Celebrex and Vioxx had submitted to the FDA from the CLASS and VIGOR studies. I could not believe what I was seeing. The FDA reviewers' reports contained a treasure trove of "not-yet-spun" data, revealing a very different picture of the safety of these two drugs than had been presented in the JAMA and NEJM articles.

Based on the data from the manufacturers' own studies and the FDA reviewers' analyses, the conclusions that had been presented in the Celebrex CLASS and Vioxx VIGOR articles seemed to be encouraging physicians to prescribe drugs that provide few benefits and possibly even cause harm. The amazing thing is that the conclusions presented in these articles were based upon exactly the same data that the manufacturers had sent to the FDA. I couldn't believe that these data—clearly illustrating the magnitude of the scientific distortion presented in our two most respected medical journals—were publicly available and yet nobody seemed to be aware of the problem.

I proceeded to spend nights and weekends comparing the data available on the FDA website with those presented in the journal articles in the fall of 2000. Meanwhile, sales of the two drugs kept growing, bolstered by an advertising blitz featuring a still graceful former Olympic figure-skating champion and a strikingly happy older woman in an outdoor tai chi class. And my patients kept requesting and demanding that I prescribe these "better" new drugs for their aches and pains.

THE CLASS STUDY: CELEBREX

The results of the CLASS study were published in the September 13, 2000, issue of JAMA. CLASS is what's known as a Phase 4 postapproval study, which was required by the FDA. Before any drug is approved, manufacturers have to submit data to the FDA that demonstrate the drug's safety and effectiveness. These preapproval clinical trials are expensive, and as a result usually include a relatively small number of people. Occasionally, a drug that seems safe in preapproval trials is later found to cause unexpected side effects when used more widely. Therefore, the FDA often requires that drug companies conduct postapproval Phase 4 studies on a much larger group of people to make sure the drug is as safe and effective as it appeared to be in the earlier, smaller trials.

CLASS, which included over 8000 people with rheumatoid and osteoarthritis, compared the risk of gastrointestinal problems in people taking Celebrex with the risk in those taking ibuprofen (Motrin, Advil) and diclofenac (Voltaren). The article in JAMA concluded that Celebrex, "when used for 6 months . . . is associated with a lower incidence of clinical upper GI events than comparator NSAIDs (ibuprofen and diclofenac)." The accompanying editorial supported this conclusion: "The results of this important study . . . provide promising data to suggest that [Celebrex is] . . . effective in reducing, but not eliminating, the risk of symptomatic [minor] ulcers and [major] ulcer complications in the enormous number of individuals who might benefit from these drugs . . ."

There was, however, one very large problem. The manufacturer's original research plan, as submitted to the FDA, had defined the duration of the CLASS study that compared Celebrex with ibuprofen as 12 months, and that of the study comparing Celebrex with diclofenac as 16 months. And, indeed, the combined study had run for a full 12 months. The authors, however, submitted only the first 6 months for the article in JAMA. Left unreported (and unmentioned) in the JAMA article were the data from the *second* 6 months of the study, during which time, as shown in the data on the FDA's website, six of the seven serious gastrointestinal complications that occurred were in patients taking Celebrex.

Pharmacia, the manufacturer of Celebrex, presented a statistical argument to the FDA justifying its omission of the data from the second half of its study. The company claimed that since a higher percentage of people taking diclofenac dropped out of the study because of minor symptoms like heartburn, the data from the second half of the study were invalid because of what is called "informed censoring." The manufacturer argued that these dropouts would have gone on to develop serious gastrointestinal complications, and their dropping out of the study artificially minimized the risk of serious complications from taking diclofenac. The FDA flatly rejected this argument. It countered that there was no proof that the people with heartburn would have developed more serious gastrointestinal problems. Further, if minor symptoms caused people in the study to stop taking diclofenac, people in the real world would similarly stop taking the drug if it caused heartburn and would similarly protect themselves from going on to develop serious gastrointestinal complications.

The FDA's opinion of the manufacturer's decision to publish only half of the data from its study was clear: "the sponsor's presentations of 6-month data . . . are not statistically valid or supportable." The FDA's gastroenterology reviewer concluded that the first 6 months of data— which had been presented in the JAMA article as if they were a report of the entire study—were not worthy of separate consideration: "Based on the lack of adequate rationale, these post-hoc analyses will not be further discussed or presented in this review." Looking at the data from the entire year of the study, the FDA's gastroenterology reviewer concluded that "the sponsor has failed to demonstrate a statistically significant lower rate" of serious GI complications in the people who took Celebrex compared with the people who took the other NSAIDs. When the reviewer looked at only the second six months of data (i.e., the data that had not been published in the JAMA article), he concluded that the risk of serious GI complications appeared to be higher in the people who took Celebrex "compared to both ibuprofen and diclofenac" (FDA's underscore). This was hardly an endorsement for a drug whose only advantage (besides the convenience of a once-daily dosing) was that it caused fewer serious GI problems.

This didn't entirely escape public notice. While I was delving into FDA data, I came across a story that had been published in the *Washing-*

ton Post about Pharmacia's having provided only the first half of the data to the editors of the *Journal of the American Medical Association.* "I am furious. . . . I looked like a fool," Dr. Michael Wolfe, coauthor of the JAMA editorial supporting Celebrex, told the reporter when he learned of this deception. JAMA editor Dr. Catherine D. DeAngelis said, "I am disheartened to hear that they had those data at the time that they submitted [the manuscript] to us. . . . We are functioning on a level of trust that was, perhaps, broken." I could find no other major media that reported this story.

The disparity between the CLASS article published in JAMA and the information in the FDA's files by no means stopped there. The primary question that the CLASS study had been designed to answer had been changed, producing results that were far more favorable to the manufacturer. The original research design submitted to the FDA by the manufacturer of Celebrex had stated: "The primary objective of this study is to compare the incidence of clinically significant [major] upper gastrointestinal events . . . in patients taking Celebrex to patients taking other NSAIDs." The term "clinically significant" refers to complications that would generally require hospitalization: active bleeding, perforation of the stomach or duodenum requiring surgery, or obstruction of the outlet of the stomach. The research plan specifically called for the less serious gastrointestinal side effects to "be categorized and analyzed separately." Indeed the FDA's gastroenterology reviewer specifically commented that the plan to identify the "truly significant" serious gastrointestinal complications alone was a "major strength of the current study."

But when the results of the study were published in JAMA, the incidences of major and minor gastrointestinal complications were combined. Why the change? The results of the study as originally designed failed to show that the people who took Celebrex developed significantly fewer major gastrointestinal complications than the people who took ibuprofen or diclofenac, even for just the first six months. Only by combining the minor GI symptoms with the more serious gastrointestinal complications could the article conclude that Celebrex caused a statistically significant decrease in gastrointestinal complications compared with the other NSAIDs. As noted above, when the FDA looked at the results of the CLASS study in terms of the research question that had *originally* been posed, Celebrex was not significantly safer than the other NSAIDs.

Finally, the most important measure of safety is the overall frequency of serious side effects—including but not limited to gastrointestinal side effects. For the full 12 months of the study, the people in the CLASS study who took Celebrex experienced 11 percent more serious complications (in all body systems combined) than the people who took the older and less expensive anti-inflammatory drugs. This difference did not reach statistical significance but certainly is significant in countering Pharmacia's claim that Celebrex is better than older NSAIDs because it's safer.

These findings contributed to the FDA's decision to send one of its rare Warning Letters to the CEO of Pharmacia in February 2001. The letter cites repeated unsubstantiated marketing claims that Celebrex is the preferred NSAID for people taking a blood thinner and that it is safe and effective for the treatment of acute pain—a use for which it is not approved—and points out that Pharmacia's marketing material fails to warn of the possibility of serious GI complications caused by the drug. The Warning Letter concludes by saying:

> *Your promotional activities described above raise significant health and safety concerns in that they minimize crucial risk information and promote Celebrex for unapproved new uses. In two previous untitled letters dated October 6, 1999, and April 6, 2000, we objected to your dissemination of promotional materials for Celebrex that ... contained unsubstantiated comparative claims, and lacked fair balance. Based upon your written assurances that this violative promotion of Celebrex had been stopped, we considered these matters closed. Despite our prior written notification, and notwithstanding your assurances, Pharmacia has continued to engage in false or misleading promotion of Celebrex.*

Also included in the Warning Letter was the requirement that Pharmacia send out the "Dear Healthcare Provider" letter that had landed on my desk. Of course, the letter sent out by the manufacturer was not quite as specific as the FDA's Warning Letter. Few doctors, even if they had bothered to wade through the difficult language, had the time or inclination to find out the story behind the letter. As a result, doctors continued to prescribe Celebrex for their patients based on the scientific evidence published in

JAMA, scientific evidence that I now understood was more than just biased in the manufacturer's favor. It was incomplete and presented an inaccurate picture of the so-called safety advantage of Celebrex over other far less expensive NSAIDs. The NEJM review article didn't even mention the Warning Letter issued to Pharmacia or the mandated "Dear Health Care Provider" letter, which had been sent six and four months, respectively, before the review article was published.

THE VIGOR STUDY: VIOXX

Two months after the CLASS study appeared in JAMA, the results of the Vioxx Gastrointestinal Outcomes Research study, VIGOR, were published in the November 23, 2000, issue of the *New England Journal of Medicine*. This Phase 4 study, which included over 8000 people with rheumatoid arthritis, compared the risk of serious gastrointestinal problems in people treated with Vioxx against those treated with naproxen. Treatment with Vioxx, the article concluded, "resulted in significantly fewer clinically important [major] upper gastrointestinal events than did treatment with naproxen." The case for Vioxx appeared to be even stronger than the case for Celebrex.

But when I read the NEJM article carefully I noticed that, as with the Pravachol and stroke study described in the last chapter, the people included in the VIGOR study were very different from the vast majority of people for whom doctors prescribe NSAIDs. More than half of the people in VIGOR were taking steroids, such as prednisone, in addition to an NSAID for their arthritis. Only a small percentage of the people for whom Vioxx is prescribed in the general population, however, take steroids at the same time. This turns out to be an important detail, because buried in the text of the article is the finding that among the people in the study who were *not* taking steroids, the reduction in the risk of serious gastrointestinal complications was not large enough to be statistically significant. This may have been the most important finding in the study, but it remained hidden in plain sight and is still virtually unknown.

Next I looked at the data in the FDA files comparing the risk of serious cardiovascular complications in the people who took Vioxx with the risk of those who took naproxen. The original research plan for the VIGOR study had acknowledged the possibility that naproxen users might develop fewer serious cardiovascular complications than those who took Vioxx. The reasoning was that the COX-1 inhibiting activity of naproxen makes platelets less "sticky" (like aspirin, but not to the same extent), potentially decreasing the risk of unwanted blood clots—a property not shared by Vioxx, which is a selective COX-2 inhibitor. Because of this possibility, the research plan called for serious "cardiovascular thrombotic or embolic" complications* to be examined by an independent committee to make sure that the study results were accurate and unbiased.

It turns out that the increased number of serious cardiovascular complications in Vioxx users more than offset the highly touted GI benefit of this drug. In the VIGOR study the people who took Vioxx experienced 21 fewer serious GI complications than those who took naproxen, but they experienced 27 *more* serious cardiovascular complications. These were the results that the November 2000 NEJM article on the VIGOR study acknowledged had been assessed, but did not report.

The more closely I scrutinized these data on the cardiovascular complications in the VIGOR study, the more I learned about how data can be manipulated to color the "scientific evidence" that is so trusted by doctors and the public. The November 2000 NEJM article focused most of its discussion about cardiovascular risk on heart attacks alone, although heart attacks had not been identified in the research plan as a specific cardiovascular complication to be monitored by itself. Considering heart attacks alone, however, allowed the authors to claim that Vioxx significantly increases risk only in people who should have been taking aspirin because of a previous cardiovascular problem (but had been prevented from doing so by the design of the study). The NEJM review article reported the frequency of a broader but still incomplete list of cardiovascular complications (increased risk of heart attacks, strokes, and sudden death), once again minimizing the extent of the problem.

---

*Serious cardiovascular complications include: sudden cardiac death, heart attack, stroke, unstable angina, transient ischemic attack, arterial blood clot, and venous blood clot.

However, when all of the serious cardiovascular complications documented in the manufacturer's own data are included, the picture that emerges is different from and much more troubling than the picture presented in either of the NEJM articles. Overall, the people in the VIGOR study who took Vioxx were 2.4 times more likely than those who took naproxen to experience a serious cardiovascular complication. The statistical significance of this finding ($p = .0016$) means that there are less than two chances out of a thousand that this increase in the risk of developing serious cardiovascular complications is simply due to chance. In absolute terms, for every 100 people treated with Vioxx instead of naproxen for one year there was one additional serious cardiovascular complication. Indeed when the FDA statistical reviewer independently analyzed all serious cardiovascular events from the study, she found that the risk of cardiovascular complications was more than double in the people who took Vioxx, and that the likelihood that this difference was simply due to chance was 1 in 10,000 ($p = .0001$).

Even for people without a history of cardiovascular problems (the people for whom the NEJM VIGOR article reported no significant increase in the risk of heart attacks) taking Vioxx instead of naproxen almost doubled the risk of developing a serious cardiovascular complication (1.9 times the risk, $p = .041$). An FDA reviewer commented that the greater risk of cardiovascular problems in the people who took Vioxx "could lead one to conclude that naproxen . . . would be the _preferred_ drug" (FDA's underscore).

Both of the NEJM articles warned that, because of an increased risk of heart attack or cardiovascular complications, patients with a history of cardiovascular disease taking Vioxx should also take prophylactic low-dose aspirin. Neither of the articles, however, gave doctors any idea of the magnitude of this increased risk. The results of the VIGOR study show that for every 100 people with a history of cardiovascular disease treated with Vioxx instead of naproxen there were between _seven and 11 additional serious cardiovascular complications each year_.*

---

*This much risk may seem hard to believe, but I urge you to check the FDA cardiology reviewer's report posted on the FDA website.

No mention was made in either of the NEJM articles about the single most important finding of the VIGOR study. Overall, including GI, cardiovascular, and all other serious complications, the people who took Vioxx had 21 percent more "serious adverse events," complications that usually lead to hospitalization or death, than did the people who took naproxen (p = .013). This translates to an absolute risk of 2.5 more serious complications for every 100 people who took Vioxx instead of naproxen each year. Something is very wrong with a system that leads patients to demand, and doctors to prescribe, a drug that provides no better relief and causes significantly more serious side effects. (Vioxx *might* be the drug of choice for a patient with arthritis who is taking steroids, who requires an anti-inflammatory drug, and who has no history of cardiovascular disease but a history of GI bleeding or complications from other NSAIDs. But even for this patient, there might be other, older drugs that would be safer to try first.) Adding insult to injury, Vioxx costs $100 to $134 a month, compared with $18.19 a month for prescription naproxen, or $7.50 for over-the-counter naproxen.*

Just one month after publication of the NEJM review article that dismissed the increased cardiovascular risk of Vioxx as a "play of chance" and failed to mention the significantly increased risk of serious complications in people who took Vioxx, the FDA sent a warning letter to Merck citing it for marketing that was "false, lacking in fair balance, or otherwise misleading." The letter pointed specifically to Merck's "promotional campaign for Vioxx that minimizes the potentially serious cardiovascular findings that were observed in the . . . VIGOR study." "Simply incomprehensible" is what the FDA's letter says about a press release issued by Merck on May 22, 2001, titled, "Merck Confirms Cardiovascular Safety Profile of Vioxx." The warning letter adds: "Your misrepresentation of the safety profile for Vioxx is particularly troublesome because we have previously, in an untitled letter, objected to promotional materials for Vioxx that also misrepresented Vioxx's safety profile."

---

*The dose for over-the-counter tablets is slightly lower than that for prescription tablets: 440 mg (in two tablets) compared with 500 mg twice daily.

CAN WE TRUST OUR MOST RESPECTED
MEDICAL JOURNALS?

Surely authors who are expert enough to have written the "Drug Therapy" review article about Celebrex and Vioxx in the *New England Journal of Medicine* were aware (or should have been aware) of the manufacturers' unprocessed data from the VIGOR and CLASS studies—even if the manufacturers hadn't volunteered these data on their own. The data had been available on the FDA's website for 6 months prior to the publication of the article. And surely they had an obligation to inform their readers just how much the FDA's interpretation of the data from these two studies differed from the articles published in our two most respected and influential medical journals.

Rather than presenting a balanced view of the scientific evidence, the NEJM review article repeats the "unsubstantiated claim" that Celebrex causes significantly fewer serious gastrointestinal complications than other NSAIDs—completely ignoring the FDA's Warning Letter to Pharmacia and the "Dear Healthcare Provider" letter mandated by the FDA. Likewise, the NEJM review article did exactly what the FDA's Warning Letter cited Merck for doing: minimizing the cardiovascular risk and the unfavorable safety profile of Vioxx.

The FDA reviewers' reports posted on the Internet provide an unusual opportunity to compare the unprocessed data from the manufacturer-sponsored CLASS and VIGOR studies with the medical journal articles and "medical knowledge" that they subsequently became. Unlike the articles about statins and strokes that I investigated, this went beyond spin.

One of the most surprising (and frightening) parts of this story is that even though all this information was (and is) publicly available, that knowledge has done little to correct doctors' and patients' beliefs that these drugs are superior. How had we gotten to a place where expensive new drugs could become "blockbusters" when there was little scientific evidence to justify their routine use? And why hadn't the FDA spoken up more publicly about the misleading journal articles?

At a 2002 faculty medical ethics seminar at Harvard Medical School, I had the opportunity to ask Dr. Janet Woodcock, Director of the FDA's Center for Drug Evaluation and Research, why the FDA had not intervened in JAMA's publication of the Celebrex study. I pointed out that the FDA was aware that publication of the CLASS article in JAMA would lead to greatly increased use of Celebrex under false pretenses. Dr. Woodcock said the FDA could not "constrain communication" in a scientific journal, and that this was "a First Amendment right of commercial speech issue." Then Dr. Marcia Angell, former editor of the *New England Journal of Medicine,* asked Dr. Woodcock, "Do you ever write a letter to the editor if you feel that an article has misrepresented the results of a study that the FDA has reviewed?" Dr. Woodcock said that this had been done in the past, but the FDA did not do so in this case, adding, "I don't know why."

The pressure from my patients to prescribe Celebrex and Vioxx did not let up, intruding into alliances that had been built up over many years. I tried to explain that these drugs offered no better relief than the older, less expensive anti-inflammatory drugs. I actually started to enjoy the challenge of trying to refocus my patients' attention back onto their underlying issues and medical problems, trying to reengage them in the search for constructive solutions. I did my best to help them understand that their beliefs about these drugs were being masterfully manipulated by the drug companies' multipronged marketing efforts, and that these efforts were being driven far more by the goal of improving the drug companies' sales than improving patients' health or comfort.

I realized how little even the best doctors understood the risks of Vioxx when a colleague, a prominent cardiologist, underwent arthroscopic surgery on his knee. His surgeon prescribed Vioxx for his postoperative pain, no doubt convinced that he was treating his VIP patient with "the best." My colleague subsequently developed deep-vein thrombophlebitis, a blood clot, in the leg that had been operated on. Neither one of these very well informed doctors had been aware of the significant cardiovascular risk associated with Vioxx.

By the end of 2001, 57 percent of all the money spent on prescription arthritis medication in the United States was spent on Celebrex and Vioxx, and both were among the top 10 selling drugs in the United States. My research into statins, and now Celebrex and Vioxx, was showing that what was being presented by the most trustworthy sources as the best medicine was often quite the opposite, and that the commercial distortion of our medical knowledge had become a major impediment to good medical care.

CHAPTER 4

THE MYTH OF EXCELLENCE

One sunny spring day in the mid-1990s, Ms. Fletcher stopped me on the brick walk outside my office just as I was opening the front door. With only a few minutes before the start of afternoon office hours, I was feeling pulled by a couple of phone calls that still needed to be returned. She asked if I was Dr. Abramson. When I said yes, she said that the HMO she had just enrolled in had required her to choose a primary care doctor. Ms. Fletcher wanted to know if she could list me as her doctor because she had heard that I was interested in alternative medicine. I said that was partially true; I am interested in any kind of treatment that helps. But I also made it clear that I was interested only in therapies—alternative or not—that were supported by good scientific evidence.

Ms. Fletcher, who appeared to be a healthy though harried woman in her mid- to late forties, then told me that she had breast cancer. The pressure I was feeling to get to the telephone faded. She quickly added that the only therapy she had received, or wanted to receive, was alternative therapy—no surgery, no radiation, and no chemotherapy.

My mind flashed back to Ms. Card (who had insisted I call her by her first name, Wendy), a woman I had taken care of several years before who had made the same decision. By the time I got involved in her care, the tumors in her breast and under her arm were growing quickly, and actually eroding through the skin. I prescribed medication to control her pain and the local infection around the tumors, but there was little chance that any therapy could control her underlying disease. As her physical condition deteriorated over the next few weeks, I made several house calls. We talked about what could be done to make her more comfortable; she told me about her friends and her spiritual practice, both of which were very important to her; and we talked about her family. She had been estranged from her parents for several years and was struggling with the decision about whether to let them back into her life. She invited her parents to visit for a couple of days. During their visit she decided to go home to New York with them, to let them take care of her in her last few weeks. I arranged for hospice to get involved as soon as she got to her parents' home. Wendy's capacity to heal the wounds in her life as best she could in preparation for her death brought a sense of hope to the tragedy of her situation.

My attention returned to Ms. Fletcher. I suspected that in this seemingly casual conversation—interrupted as it was by office staff, patients, and the Fed Ex guy walking between us on their way into the office—she was asking for my approval of her decision to use only alternative therapy. After visualizing what Wendy's upper chest and underarm had looked like before she left for New York, I wanted to be careful not to leave Ms. Fletcher with the impression that I supported her decision to forgo conventional therapy. I told her that I would be happy to be her doctor, and that she should make an appointment so that we could get to know each other and discuss her options.

Ms. Fletcher did sign up as my patient, but she never came in for an appointment. I think she knew that I would try to engage her in a discussion about her medical situation and that I had reservations about her approach. Sometimes just the process of engaging in a doctor-patient relationship is the most effective alternative medicine—using the safety and trust of the doctor-patient encounter as an opportunity to connect with deeper concerns, to be able get these issues out on the table so that they can be addressed and progress made: physical, emotional, or both. But I also thought it was her right to choose not to engage in this kind of relationship with me.

I had not heard from Ms. Fletcher for about a year, when I got a message that she had called my office requesting a referral to see an oncologist in Boston. To avoid creating an uncomfortable telephone encounter, I suggested through a nurse that she come in to see me first. She declined. I approved the consultation.

The oncologist soon called to inform me that Ms. Fletcher's breast cancer had metastasized widely throughout her body and asked for my approval, as Ms. Fletcher's primary care physician, for her to receive high-dose chemotherapy followed by bone marrow transplantation. The goal of this treatment is to administer an otherwise lethal dose of chemotherapy—enough to destroy all of the rapidly dividing cells in the body, including the blood-forming cells in the bone marrow—in the hope of destroying all of the cancer cells in the process. Before the therapy, bone marrow cells from Ms. Fletcher would be "harvested." After the chemotherapy, Ms. Fletcher would then be "rescued" by "reseeding" her marrow with her own bone marrow cells, thereby restoring her ability to make red and white blood cells. The procedure required about two weeks in a sterile room, to avoid infection while her immune system was suppressed, and up to a month in the hospital. This was a rough ride, with the volume turned all the way up on all the discomfort and risks of chemotherapy: hair loss; nausea and vomiting; ulcers on the inside of the mouth and the gut; possible damage to the heart, kidneys, and nerves; and the risk of serious infection until the immune system recovers.

Knowing how sick Ms. Fletcher would become from the therapy itself and sadly aware of how advanced her breast cancer was, I asked the oncologist if she was sure this was the right thing to do. She said that high-dose chemotherapy and bone marrow transplantation was the best therapy for women like Ms. Fletcher, that is, women with advanced breast cancer. I had little experience with this and had to trust the oncologist's opinion. I certainly wanted my patient to get the best therapy available.

As this conversation was going on, I was thinking about the contrast between Ms. Fletcher's complete rejection of conventional medicine and her abrupt return to the most aggressive therapy in the face of her advancing disease. Even though she had eschewed conventional therapy early on, now it seemed that she may have been taking comfort in the belief that modern medicine could rescue her if her disease got out of control. I also thought about her unwillingness (or inability) to engage in a doctor-patient relationship with me, and wondered whether she had been able to explore with anybody the important issues in her life. And I wondered whether her oncologist thought of death as the final defeat against which all-out war must be waged, even though there was no real hope of winning.

Although the decision to go forward had already been made and the oncologist seemed to be calling more as a courtesy than for a real discussion, I still regret that in that rushed moment on the telephone I was so deferential. I feared that Ms. Fletcher and her oncologist were, each for her own reasons, grasping at straws, and I hoped I was wrong. In the end I kept my doubts to myself, approved the procedure, and got back to the patient I had left to take the phone call.

In retrospect, I realize that there was something else going on. Ms. Fletcher, her oncologist, and I were all emboldened by our implicit trust in the efficacy of the most advanced medical care that was to be provided in a top-notch academic medical center. Most Americans share this great faith in the superiority of American medicine. It is easy to see why. During the twentieth century alone longevity in the United States increased by 30 years. During the last 50 years medical science has made tremendous progress in improving health and the quality of our lives.

A HALF-CENTURY OF MEDICAL BREAKTHROUGHS

The elimination of polio, the most feared disease of my childhood, is a perfect example of the triumph of American ingenuity. In 1953 about one out of every 100 Americans below the age of 20 had experienced some degree of paralysis caused by polio. Then, with well-deserved fanfare, the Salk vaccine was launched for use on April 12, 1955, exactly 10 years after the death of our most famous polio victim, President Franklin Delano Roosevelt. The vaccine was immediately put into widespread use. I remember lining up in the elementary school gym as a third-grader to get my first polio shot, my childhood fear eased (mostly) by the understanding that I would no longer have to worry about getting polio.

Huge strides have also been made in biomedical engineering and surgical techniques in the last 50 years. The cardiopulmonary bypass machine, which pumps blood through an artificial lung, replacing carbon dioxide with fresh oxygen, and then back into the body, allows surgeons to perform intricate heart surgery. The first successful surgery using cardio-pulmonary bypass was done in Sweden in 1953, on an 18-year-old girl with a congenital heart defect. By 1960, surgery to bypass blockages in the arteries that supply the heart muscle with blood (coronary arteries) could be performed with relative safety. Surgical replacement of poorly func-tioning heart valves soon followed. By the time I was in medical school, in the mid-1970s, these operations had become routine.

Dialysis, to filter the blood of people with chronic kidney failure, became a reality in the 1960s. In 1972 the Social Security Act was amended to extend Medicare coverage to all patients with end-stage renal disease, covering all the costs of chronic dialysis. About 250,000 Ameri-cans are alive today because they have access to ongoing dialysis. Success-ful transplantation of hearts, lungs, and livers have been lifesaving. Transplantation of kidneys and corneas allows people to live normal lives. Hip and knee replacements have restored comfort and function to millions of Americans.

There has been great progress with new drugs, too. Tagamet first became available when I was just starting my two years in the National Health Service Corps of the U.S. Public Health Service, in 1977. I remem-ber the first patient I treated with Tagamet: a state policeman who had already had one stomach operation because of an ulcer and was develop-ing the same symptoms again. He thought he was headed for a second and more extensive operation, but Tagamet suppressed the acidity enough for the lining of his stomach to heal. Zantac was perhaps a slight improvement, reputedly causing fewer side effects. The vast majority of people with ulcers and ulcerlike symptoms improved with these drugs. In 1989 Prilosec came on the market, the first of the proton-pump inhibitors, suppressing acid formation many times more powerfully than Tagamet or Zantac.

The mortality rate from AIDS in the developed countries has gone way down as new drugs have been developed that control HIV infection. Gleevac is a true miracle of modern medical science. This treatment for a slow-acting form of leukemia (chronic myelogenous leukemia) specifically blocks the body's production of an enzyme that causes white blood cells to become malignant. (Unfortunately it's priced at $25,000 per year of treatment.)

The introduction of magnetic resonance imaging (MRI) into clinical practice in the mid-1980s is rated, in a survey of well-respected primary care doctors, as the most important development in clinical medicine over the last 25 years. In the early 1980s, when the chief radiologist at my local hospital first explained how this soon-to-arrive technology produced its images, I thought he was joking. (Nuclei of the body's hydrogen atoms are aligned by a powerful magnet. FM radio beams are focused on the area to be scanned, causing "resonance" of the aligned nuclei. Minute amounts of energy are emitted as the radio beam is turned off and the nuclei return to random orientation. This energy is measured by sensors and sent to a computer, which produces exquisite three-dimensional pictures of the human body.) Now these scans are commonplace.

A number of my patients are alive only because of recent medical advances: massive heart attacks completely reversed by "clot-busting" drugs, exquisitely delicate lifesaving cancer surgery on a child, successful liver transplantation, and an implanted cardiac defibrillator that senses and automatically treats several episodes of potentially fatal cardiac arrhythmia, to name just a few of the more dramatic examples. After the satisfaction of providing good medical care based on ongoing trusting relationships with my patients and the pleasure of working with an incredibly dedicated group of people in my office, my greatest satisfaction as a doctor has been working with my specialist colleagues to ensure that my patients get the full benefit of the most up-to-date care available.

THE AMERICAN PARADOX

Clearly these medical breakthroughs have contributed to increased longevity and improved quality of life; this is why I, too, believed that Americans received the best medical care in the world. Then I saw an article in the *Journal of the American Medical Association*, in July 2000, claiming that "the U.S. population does not have anywhere near the best health in the world." On first read, I thought that surely the author was overstating the case.

In a comparison of 13 industrialized nations that will surprise most Americans—and certainly most American physicians—Dr. Barbara Starfield, University Distinguished Professor at Johns Hopkins School of Public Health, found that the health of Americans is close to the worst on most measures and overall ranked second to last. Contrary to common wisdom, the poor ranking of the United States cannot be attributed to our rates of smoking, drinking, or consumption of red meat. Surprisingly, Americans rank in the better half of the 13 countries on these measures, and have the third lowest cholesterol level. (Deaths due to violence and car accidents were not included in the data.)

The low ranking of Americans' health reported in this article was so disparate from what I had believed that I started to look for other sources of comparative data to see if this was right. An extensive comparison of the health of the citizens of industrialized countries done by the Organisation for Economic Co-Operation and Development (OECD) confirmed the conclusions presented in Dr. Starfield's article. The United States again ranked poorly, with 18 industrialized countries having greater life expectancy.*

One of the best single indicators of a country's health was developed by the World Health Organization (WHO); it is called "healthy life expectancy." This measure represents the number of years that a child born now can expect to live in good health (i.e., total life expectancy minus years of illness adjusted for quality of life). Children born in the

---

*The United States ranks a lowly 24 among 39 developed countries on infant mortality. There is, however, a problem with international comparisons of infant mortality. Resuscitation is more likely to be attempted on extremely premature babies born in the United States than in many other countries. The extremely premature babies on whom resuscitation is unsuccessful are then counted as infant deaths, whereas they are counted as fetal deaths when resuscitation has not been attempted. A way around this problem is to look at mortality rates only after one day or one week of life. On that measure the United States' position improves only from 24 to 20.

United States today can expect to live the equivalent of about 69.3 healthy years of life, while children born in the other 22 industrialized countries can expect an average of 2.5 additional years of healthy life. And children born in Japan can expect almost six more years of good health than Americans. Americans' healthy life expectancy ranks 22 out of 23 industrialized countries, better only than the Czech Republic.

The World Health Organization also developed several broader measures of health system performance, providing more in-depth comparisons between countries. On "overall achievement,"* the health care system in the United States ranks 15 in the world. "Overall performance" measures the efficiency of a health system by taking into account the per-person health expenditures required to reach its level of achievement. On this measure the U.S. health care system ranking falls to 37. Finally, "performance on the level of health" measures the efficiency with which health care systems improve their citizens' overall health. On this measure, the United States' ranking drops to a lowly 72 in the world.

Despite the poor performance of the American health care system, our health care costs are simply staggering. In 2004, health expenditures in the United States are projected to exceed $6100 for every man, woman, and child. How does this compare with other countries? The United States spends more than twice as much per person on health care as the other industrialized nations. Even taking into account our higher per-person gross domestic product, the United States spends 42 percent more on health care per person than would be expected, given spending on health care in the other OECD nations. The excess spending on health care in the United States is like a yearly tax of more than $1800 on every American citizen. (And still the United States is the only industrialized country that does not provide universal health insurance, leaving more than 43 million Americans uninsured.)

The U.S. health care system is clearly alone among the industrialized countries. The following chart shows that Japan and Switzerland stand

---

*Includes level of health (25 percent), distribution of health (25 percent), fairness of financial contribution (25 percent), level and distribution of responsiveness of health care system (25 percent).

FIGURE 4-1. HEALTHY LIFE EXPECTANCY AND PER PERSON MEDICAL EXPENDITURES FOR 23 OECD COUNTRIES

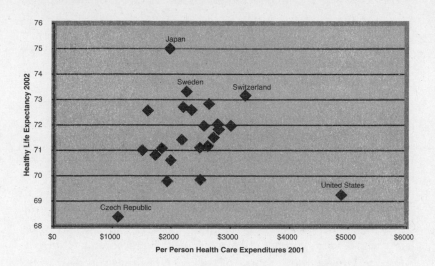

Per Person Health Care Expenditures 2001

out for their good health, and the Czech Republic stands out for its low cost and poor health. The United States, however, is almost off the chart with its combination of poor health and high costs (see Fig. 4-1).

Notwithstanding the tremendous progress and the enormous cost of American medicine, over the last 40 years the health of the citizens of the other industrialized countries has been improving at a faster pace. According to researchers from Johns Hopkins, "On most [health] indicators the U.S. relative performance declined since 1960; on none did it improve." One of the most telling statistics is the change in the years of life lost below the age of 70, before death due to natural aging starts to become a factor. In 1960, Americans ranked right in the middle of 23 OECD countries on this measure. But despite all of the extra money being in spent on health care in the United States, the health of the citizens in the other OECD countries is improving more quickly. By 2000, men in the United States were losing 21 percent more years of life before the age of 70 than men in the other OECD countries, and American women were losing 33 percent more.

THE ROOTS OF THE MYTH

All this does not add up. The United States' emergence as the world leader in medical research, combined with seemingly bottomless pockets when it comes to health care, does not square with the comparatively poor health of Americans.

One explanation for this paradox is that the United States foots the bill for a disproportionate share of medical innovation, from which the rest of the world then benefits. And indeed, this argument is often used to explain why brand-name prescription drugs cost about 70 percent more in the United States than in Canada and western Europe. But at least with respect to pharmaceutical innovation, the facts tell a different story. From 1991 to 1999, pharmaceutical companies in the United States did not develop more than their share of new drugs on a per capita basis compared with western Europe or Japan. Furthermore, according to the U.S. Food and Drug Administration, of the 569 new drugs approved in the United States between 1995 and 2000, only 13 percent actually contain new active ingredients that offer a significant improvement over already available drugs and therapies.

Another reason why Americans believe they get better health care than any other nation may be that it *appears* as though we do. According to surveys done by the World Health Organization for its *World Health Report 2000*, patients in the United States are provided with the best service in the world. These surveys evaluated seven nonmedical aspects of health care—dignity, autonomy, confidentiality, prompt attention, quality of basic amenities, access to family and friends during care, and choice of health care provider. The WHO aggregated these results into a measure called "health system responsiveness," on which the United States ranks first.

The myth of excellence is also sustained by the assumption that advances in medical care are responsible for most of the gains in health and longevity realized in the United States during the twentieth century. I admit that I was dubious when I first read that this was not the case. According to the U.S. Centers for Disease Control and Prevention, "Since 1900, the average lifespan of persons in the United States has lengthened by greater than 30 years; 25 years of this gain are attributable to advances in public health." These include improvements such as sanitation, clean food and water, decent housing, good nutrition, higher standards of living, and widespread vaccinations.

The CDC's report was based on a 1994 article in the prestigious *Milbank Quarterly*, written by researchers from Harvard and King's College, London. They found that preventive care as recommended by the U.S. Preventive Services Task Force report—including, for example, blood pressure screening, cancer screening, counseling about smoking, routine immunizations, and aspirin to prevent heart attacks—adds only 18 to 19 months to our lives. Medical care for illness (heart attacks, trauma, cancer treatment, pneumonia, appendicitis, etc.) increases our life span by 44 to 45 months. The overall effect of medical care, then, has been to increase longevity by only about 5 years and 3 months during the twentieth century. (It is also important to remember that many medical interventions—like joint replacement and cataract removal—can produce benefits in the quality of life without improving longevity. These improvements are included in the World Health Organization's calculation of "healthy life expectancy," discussed above.)

By looking at the leading causes of death during the twentieth century, we can see just how limited the role of advances in medical care has been in extending life expectancy. In 1900, tuberculosis was the leading cause of death in the United States. Over the next 50 years, the death rate from TB fell by 87 percent.

This dramatic decrease in the tuberculosis death rate may appear to be a great triumph for American medicine, but in truth it was entirely due to improvements in the social and physical environment, such as healthier living and working conditions, better nutrition, more education, and greater prosperity. The first effective *medical* therapies for tuberculosis, the antibiotics isoniazid and streptomycin, were not even introduced until 1950, well after death rates for tuberculosis had plummeted. Throughout the twentieth century, similar patterns occurred in the death rates from many other infectious diseases, such as measles, scarlet fever, typhoid, and diphtheria. As with tuberculosis, the vast majority of the decline in mortality occurred before the introduction of effective medical therapy, antibiotics, or vaccines—polio and HIV/AIDS being the notable exceptions.

René Dubos, a French-born microbiologist who discovered the first two commercially manufactured antibiotics, wrote in his classic book *The Mirage of Health*, "The introduction of inexpensive cotton undergarments easy to launder and of transparent glass that brought light into the most humble dwelling, contributed more to the control of infection than did all the drugs and medical practices."

Our experience with cancer during the twentieth century proves the point in reverse. Despite an enormous investment in cancer research, the age-adjusted death rate for cancer in the United States actually *increased* by 74 percent from the beginning to the end of the twentieth century. And by the end of the twentieth century, the age-adjusted death rate for cancer was the same as for tuberculosis at the beginning of the century: it had become the number one killer among people below of the age of 75.

In 1971 Congress launched a war on cancer by passing the National Cancer Act. President Nixon boasted, "This legislation—perhaps more than any legislation I have signed as President of the United States—can mean new hope and comfort in the years ahead for millions of people in this country and around the world." In 1984 the director of the National Cancer Institute told Congress that the death rate from cancer could be cut in half by 2000. But two years later, an article published in *New England Journal of Medicine*, coauthored by a statistician from the National Cancer Institute, concluded just the opposite: Cancer death rates were going up, and "we are losing the war against cancer."

There have been a few tremendous successes in this war, notably with some of the childhood cancers, testicular cancer, Hodgkin's disease, and leukemia. Notwithstanding the barrage of news about major breakthroughs in the diagnosis and treatment of cancer, the overall death rate from cancer was exactly the same in the year 2000 as it had been in 1971, when "war" was declared.

THE PRICE OF BLIND FAITH

In 1998, the President's Advisory Commission on Consumer Protection and Quality in the Health Care Industry provided a concise statement of the proper goal of a nation's health care system: "The purpose of the health care system is to reduce continually the burden of illness, injury, and disability, and to improve the health status and function of the people of the United States." About 70 percent of the health care in the United States is directed toward meeting this goal.* The other 30 percent is commercially driven health care activity without demonstrable health benefits. The problem for doctors and the public is that there is no clear line of demarcation between these two fundamentally different health care activities, and as the commercial influence on medical practice grows, the line between the two becomes ever more blurred.

This brings us back to the decision about how to treat Ms. Fletcher's advanced breast cancer. It turns out that in 1996, when I had the conversation with Ms. Fletcher's oncologist, only one small randomized trial, done in South Africa, showed that women who received high-dose chemotherapy and bone marrow transplants did better than women who received conventional therapy. Nonetheless, bone marrow transplantation had become an accepted therapy (covered by insurance), and big business. A superb article in the *New York Times* explained that at $80,000 to $200,000 per procedure, the service was a great lure for doctors and hospitals. A for-profit chain of cancer treatment centers, Response Oncology, grossed $128 million in revenues in 1998, mostly from bone marrow transplants. For-profit hospitals were advertising, competing for patients, and even offering to reimburse patients for their transportation costs. Academic medical centers got in on the action. One breast cancer expert told the *New York Times*, "Bone marrow transplanters are kings. They usually get a higher salary, they usually get more money. And more important, they have security and power." Even community hospitals started offering the procedure. All this when nobody really knew whether the more aggressive treatment was worth the additional suffering and cost.

The *Times* article described the dramatic meeting of the American Society of Clinical Oncology that took place in 1999, three years after Ms.

---

*Based on health care spending in the United States being 42 percent higher than predicted by the median per-person expenditures in the other OECD countries (corrected for per-person GDP). Even 70 percent is an overstatement, though, because Americans' health is inferior to the health of the citizens of the other OECD countries.

Fletcher received her treatment. The much-awaited results of five randomized trials of bone marrow transplantation for women with advanced breast cancer were presented. The four largest trials reported no benefit. Only the smallest study, done by the same researcher in South Africa, reported a survival advantage.

The response to this bad news provides a peek into how American health care is shaped. A press release issued by the American Society of Clinical Oncologists (including oncologists who perform transplants) said that the studies "report mixed early results." The president of the society recommended that the therapy continue to be offered. The president of the National Breast Cancer Coalition, Fran Visco, said, "How can anybody look at these data and think this is something we should continue doing or that [the results of the studies] are inconclusive?" But Dr. William H. West, the chairman of the for-profit Response Oncology, said that it was "an oversimplification" to consider discontinuing this therapy.

One year after the American Society of Clinical Oncology meeting, American researchers made a site visit to the South African researcher's laboratory and found that his data were fraudulent. The researcher's article was retracted by the *Journal of Clinical Oncology,* and he was fired from his university post. Finally, in 2000, this unfortunate chapter in medical history was brought to an end when the results of a study published in the *New England Journal of Medicine* failed to show any benefit from high-dose chemotherapy followed by bone marrow transplantation. The accompanying editorial laid the issue to rest: "this form of treatment for women with metastatic breast cancer has been proved to be ineffective and should be abandoned. . . ." But this was four years too late to save Ms. Fletcher from her horrific experience. She never fully recovered from the procedure, and died several months later.

Ms. Fletcher's experience is not an isolated case. Every day wasteful diagnostic tests and therapies, from the serious to the mundane, are prescribed in the name of "state-of-the-art" health care: heart surgery for which no benefit has been shown; treatment with expensive brand-name medications when drugs costing only one-fifteenth as much are more effective; MRIs performed simply to satisfy patients' or consultants' curiosity (and often leading to erroneous diagnostic assumptions); expensive drugs when lifestyle changes would be far more effective at protecting health; tests and consultations that are very unlikely to lead to better outcomes. Multiplied countless times, these tests and therapies show how the U.S. health care system can be so expensive, yet not produce better results.

When I first read of the poor performance of the U.S. health care system I was incredulous. But as I confirmed these findings with data from multiple sources and began to understand the underlying causes, my skepticism gave way to a sense of vindication. I had been trained to believe that carefully reading the medical journals, following experts' recommendations, and keeping up with continuing education would ensure that I was bringing the best possible care to my patients. I had been practicing mainstream medicine, along with a few clearly effective alternative remedies, but over the last few years, I had become increasingly aware that this wasn't good enough.

Now I knew why. My discoveries about the myth of excellence in American health care led me to realize that the commercialization of medicine wasn't just causing doctors to prescribe unnecessary drugs and procedures. It was actually subverting the quality of medical care. I must respectfully disagree with President George W. Bush's comments about American health care in a speech made to the Illinois Medical Society in June 2003: "One thing is for certain about health care in our country, is that we've got the best health care system in the world and we need to keep it that way." The only thing that appears to be certain about health care in our country is that we aren't getting the health we're paying for.

CHAPTER 5

A CASE IN POINT: THE SAGA OF HORMONE REPLACEMENT THERAPY

Mrs. Clark had been coming to me for her nongynecological primary care for about 10 years. She was a cheerful, attractive, and well-dressed woman in her early sixties with stylishly short brunette hair who exuded confidence and positive energy. For about 15 years, since her periods had started to become irregular, Mrs. Clark had been going to her trusted female gynecologist for annual pelvic and breast exams, PAP smears, and mammograms, and to monitor her hormone replacement therapy (HRT). When we first met, Mrs. Clark let me know that she felt more comfortable discussing personal issues with her gynecologist, so at her annual exams I would make only general inquiries and therefore did not get to know her as well as most of my other patients. I knew that her family was doing well, her lifestyle was unusually healthy, and she had no significant medical problems.

When Mrs. Clark's elderly father moved into the area, I became his doctor as well. As I observed her deft handling of her father's needs and demands, I began then to get a sense of Mrs. Clark's unusual competence. She shared with me how difficult her childhood relationship with her father had been. I could see that he still had the potential to be difficult—

especially with her. She worked hard to get things right. Her requests of me and my office were reasonable, and she advocated well on behalf of her family and herself.

Then she was diagnosed with breast cancer. Mrs. Clark told me that within a day or two after she first felt a lump in her left breast, she had seen her gynecologist, who arranged for a needle biopsy. The lump was malignant. A surgeon removed the tumor, leaving the rest of her breast intact, but biopsies done at the time of her lumpectomy showed that cancer cells had already spread to several lymph nodes. She went on to have a complete mastectomy, including removal of the lymph nodes under her arm.

During our next 15-minute appointment, she brought me up to date on the details of her care. She had recovered well from her surgeries and was about to begin chemotherapy. She was very happy with the care provided by a local cancer specialist. This positive attitude would serve her well in meeting the challenge of this illness, yet I worried that it might make it difficult for her to come to grips with the inevitable sadness and fear that accompany cancer.

Toward the end of the appointment, I asked if she would like to talk more in depth about her situation. She said that she would. At the time, I was teaching a course at Harvard Medical School about the role of the doctor-patient relationship in the healing process, and I asked Mrs. Clark if I might tape our conversation so my students could get an idea of what this experience was like for her. I sensed that the opportunity to contribute to the education of medical students would make it easier for her to get "down and dirty" with her feelings.

When Mrs. Clark returned several days later, she expressed confidence that her treatment would be successful. She told me that her illness had brought her even closer to her husband and children, and that her church was a great source of personal support and spiritual comfort. The only time she cried was when she spoke about the prospect of losing her hair during chemotherapy. But she laughed later as she recounted the banter with her husband as they had contemplated different "looks" when shopping for a wig.

Yet Mrs. Clark was upset about two issues related to her medical care. She described her discomfort with an encounter she'd had with an oncologist at one of the major teaching hospitals in Boston. She recalled how the doctor had remained standing while she and her husband were seated, trying to persuade her to enroll in an experimental trial of aggressive chemotherapy. She said he did not seem interested in her as a person, and after she declined his offer, he appeared to lose all interest in her care as well. She and her husband were left with the sense that the oncologist's only interest was to enroll another body in his chemotherapy study.

More troubling to Mrs. Clark was the fact that there was about a 50-50 chance that the hormones she had been taking for 12 years, ostensibly to protect her health, had actually caused her breast cancer. Mrs. Clark was aware, as was I, of the finding published in JAMA almost a year before her cancer had been diagnosed that a woman's risk of breast cancer increases by 8 percent for each year that she takes combined hormone replacement therapy (HRT). Mrs. Clark could not understand why her trusted gynecologist had prescribed HRT 12 years earlier when, with only very mild hot flashes, she had entered menopause. Nor could she understand how her gynecologist could have been so confident that she should remain on the hormones indefinitely. Why, she asked, didn't the JAMA article have more of an impact on doctors' opinions about the routine treatment of postmenopausal women with HRT?

Mrs. Clark had only minimal side effects from the chemotherapy administered by her local oncologist, but she did lose her hair. She came through this phase of her treatment very well, and was proud to show me when her hair had grown back enough so that she could stop using her wig. When I next spoke with her local oncologist, I asked if by refusing to participate in the clinical trial Mrs. Clark had passed up an opportunity to receive more effective therapy. The oncologist answered that the best evidence we have to date shows that this aggressive therapy was very unlikely to be more effective than the more mild chemotherapy regimen that Mrs. Clark had chosen. Perhaps Mrs. Clark had trusted her gynecologist too much, but she did not make the same mistake again.

Mrs. Clark had done the best that she could with the information she had at the time. She is a well-educated person who takes excellent care of herself, seeking the best medical care and following her trusted gynecologist's advice. Yet she ended up profoundly disappointed with the medical system that had urged her to receive hormone replacement therapy, ostensibly to protect her health, that could very well have caused her cancer.

Mrs. Clark, as we all know, is not alone. Over the last several decades, millions of healthy women entering menopause were urged to take HRT. Doctors, researchers, and newspaper and magazine articles all told the same story: The scientific evidence is overwhelming that HRT will protect postmenopausal women's health and improve the quality of their lives. Hormone pills became the top-selling drugs for several years running—until it became clear that all the compelling science supporting the use of HRT was nothing but a house of cards. HRT not only doesn't decrease the risk of heart disease, strokes, or Alzheimer's disease—it *increases* these risks.

In this era of modern, evidence-based medicine, how could so many women have been placed on drugs that turned out to be bad for their health?

MEDICALIZING MENOPAUSE

Menopause, the end of menstruation, is the second most significant biological transition in a woman's life, the first being the onset of menstruation. The high levels of reproductive hormones necessary for childbearing shift down to the lower levels needed during the post-reproductive part of a woman's life. In 1997, Dr. Susan Love, a nationally recognized breast surgeon and women's health advocate, wrote a courageous and what turned out to be right-on-the-mark book about menopause and hormones. *Dr. Susan Love's Hormone Book* explains that in menopause, "The hormonal dance doesn't end; the band just strikes up another tune." Estrogen production does not cease entirely after menopause. The cells that maintain the internal structure of the ovary (the stroma), as well as the adrenal glands and fat tissue, combine to produce about one-tenth as much estrogen after menopause as was produced before.

Estrogen levels do not, however, decline steadily as women go through menopause. They fluctuate as the body adjusts to its new "tune." Hot flashes and night sweats are caused by the hypothalamus (the part of the brain that controls body temperature) responding to fluctuating levels of estrogen in the blood.

On a personal and social level, menopause is the time when women are able to shift their focus beyond the needs of young children. Dr. Christiane Northrup, in her book *The Wisdom of Menopause*, talks of menopause as a time when many women rekindle their "concerns with social injustices, the political interests, and the personal passions that were sublimated in the childbearing years," and explore new interests and sources of meaning.

With change, however, also comes vulnerability. Much like the acute sense of vulnerability that so many adolescent girls experience, the transition into the post-reproductive years—especially in our youth-oriented society—also creates anxiety. Medicalization of this transition often increases many women's fears about aging and chronic disease and at the same time makes them vulnerable to commercial exploitation—especially by the drug companies.

Premarin (brand name for estrogen) was approved by the FDA in 1942 for the treatment of symptoms associated with menopause, prima rily hot flashes, night sweats, and vaginal dryness. Wyeth-Ayerst, the manufacturer of Premarin, still holds the patent for the manufacturing process. Premarin was named for its source: PREgnant MARes' urINe. During pregnancy, mares increase their production of estrogen several hundredfold. Most of this extra estrogen is excreted by the kidneys into the urine. Horse estrogen is similar to human estrogen, a fact that led Wyeth-Ayerst to an inexpensive source for Premarin: pregnant mares. Wearing a urine collection bag and kept in a small stall, each mare produced enough estrogen to treat about 150 women.

Only a minority of women have menopausal symptoms that are severe enough to require medical therapy. As Dr. Love points out, only one out of six women going through menopause experiences "really bothersome" hot flashes; one out of three rates her hot flashes as "somewhat bothersome"; one out of eight experiences "really bothersome" night sweats; and fewer than one in 30 experiences "really bothersome" vaginal dryness. Half of the women going through menopause have no hot flashes at all. Symptoms usually last no more than two to five years— only about one out of 20 women has troublesome symptoms that persist long after the transition through menopause is complete. Clearly, restricting the use of Premarin to women with troublesome menopausal

symptoms limited its potential market greatly. If more drugs were to be
sold, new reasons to take estrogen would have to be found.

What better way to inaugurate the modern era of pharmaceutical
marketing than to promise women protection from the ravages of age? In
a 1962 article published in JAMA, Dr. Robert Wilson, a gynecologist,
reported the results of a study in which 304 women had been treated with
estrogen. Though 18 cancers were predicted over the time that the
women had been taking estrogen, none developed. Wilson concluded
that hormone pills "are prophylactic to breast and genital cancer." In his
best-selling book, *Feminine Forever,* published in 1966, Wilson wrote
with the authority of a medical scientist, communicating a message of
unbridled fear that untreated menopause marked the beginning of a
rapid decline in appearance, sexuality, health, and overall quality of life.
Dr. Wilson wrote poetically of the tragedy of menopause:

> *The transformation, within a few years, of a formerly pleasant,
> energetic woman into a dull-minded but sharp-tongued caricature
> of her former self is one of the saddest of human spectacles. The suf-
> fering is not hers alone—it involves her entire family, her business
> associates, her neighborhood storekeepers, and all others with
> whom she comes into contact. Multiplied by millions, she is a focus
> of bitterness and discontent in the whole fabric of our civilization.*

Perhaps Wilson's own tongue had been sharpened by the support his
foundation was receiving from several drug companies, including the
manufacturer of Premarin. In 1965 the Wilson Research Foundation
received $34,000 (the equivalent of about $175,000 in 2004 dollars) in
contributions from drug companies, enough to cover Wilson's expenses
while he was writing his book. In total, Wilson's foundation received
$1.3 million from drug companies.

The rhetoric was toned down just a bit in an article coauthored by
Wilson and his wife, Thelma, a registered nurse, published in the *Journal
of the American Geriatrics Society* in 1972 and titled "The Basic Philosophy of Estrogen Maintenance." The article offered both carrot—"Estrogen produces beauty, the allure which attracts the male. This can no more
be resisted than the moth can resist the flame"—and stick: "Breasts and

genital organs will not shrivel. Such women will . . . not become dull and unattractive." The Wilsons described female aging as a disease caused by the failure of postmenopausal women's ovaries to produce estrogen. They hypothesized that this medical condition could be treated with estrogen, the same way that diabetes, caused by the failure of the pancreas to produce adequate insulin, is treated with insulin.

It's easy to be angry about the harm done to so many women as a result of Dr. Wilson's work. Yet his harsh rhetoric becomes understandable—even evokes compassion—when seen as his attempt to transform his own personal trauma into a positive contribution to medicine. According to his son Ron, Wilson's own mother had been "the shrew of all shrews." Ron says that Wilson believed that his mother's condition "was due to a chemical imbalance, and it was that belief that led him to do his research. He did indeed wish to help women. . . . So I suppose the real thanks for the beginning research must go back to dear ol' grandma, for if she hadn't been such a witch, medical 'progress' might well have been delayed. I can respect his efforts for women at the time even if his thinking was flawed."

This personal history set the stage for Wilson to become a well-paid manservant of the drug industry, believing all the while that he was saving the world from the misery that his mother went through and, in turn, had caused. According to his son, Wilson was motivated not by the money he received from the drug companies, but by a desire to help the "cause." So much so that when Thelma Wilson, who had been taking hormone replacement therapy, developed breast cancer, this fact was hidden even from her son, Ron.

Ron Wilson's mother's breast cancer may not have been the only fact that was changed. Ron went on to say, "It is my opinion that some of the original research findings are flawed to downright false. Much of that opinion came out of the mouth of my father, who was not above changing a few figures to help the cause." Ron says that his father "was used by the various drug firms and when no longer needed he was quickly and quietly cast aside, leaving him with no office practice, no foundation, little family life and few friends." Wilson turned to alcohol and drugs, and took his own life in 1981. It may be hard to believe that Wilson's exaggerated claims about Premarin were so effective, but in no small measure owing to his efforts, Premarin became the most frequently prescribed brand-name drug in the United States in 1966. It remained one of the five most frequently prescribed drugs through 1975. Wilson's book promoting the use of estrogen for women who had reached menopause, and the hundreds of newspaper and magazine articles that followed, had accomplished their mission.

A DRUG IN SEARCH OF A DISEASE

It was not, however, all smooth sailing in the business of selling eternal youth and femininity. In December 1975, two articles published in NEJM showed that estrogen therapy increased the risk of cancer of the lining of the uterus (endometrial cancer), up to 14-fold after seven years of treatment. This fear was quashed when, four years later, in 1979, an article published in *The Lancet* showed that adding another hormone, progestin, for about 10 days each month to estrogen therapy prevented the changes in the lining of the uterus that predisposed to cancer. Several other studies soon confirmed that progestin protected women on estrogen therapy from developing endometrial cancer. Still, HRT had been linked with cancer in the public's mind, and sales plummeted. Only half as many prescriptions for Premarin were filled in 1980 as had been filled in 1975.

An aggressive drug rehabilitation program was needed. "Marketing a disease is the best way to market a drug," notes Dr. Love. And osteoporosis, or thinning of the bones, was a perfect disease to market: There are no symptoms until you develop fractures, so no postmenopausal woman could be sure she was safe. And the criteria were set so that one quarter of all women over 65, and more than half over 75, would be diagnosed with the "disease" if they had bone density tests. There was, however, a lot of work to be done to turn osteoporosis from part of the normal spectrum of skeletal aging into a feared disease. To educate the doctors, according to Dr. Love, "the pharmaceutical companies started placing ads in the medical journals showing wheelchairs, x-rays of crooked spines, and pathetic-looking women with dowager's humps. They funded medical meetings and lectures about osteoporosis."

The next step was to "educate" the public. In 1985, only 23 percent of women had heard of osteoporosis. But, according to *US News and World Report*, that changed quickly as the result of the efforts of Burson-Marsteller, the public relations firm hired by Wyeth-Ayerst. The campaign was successful in increasing public concern (some would say unnecessary fear), generating many articles in women's magazines and culminating in National Osteoporosis Week. The National Osteoporosis Foundation was started with drug company support in 1986. Doctors (including me) and patients came to fear that undiagnosed osteoporosis would lead to hipbones' suddenly snapping with minimal trauma, though in more than 20 years as a busy family doctor I never saw such a thing.

Coinciding with the public's "education" about osteoporosis was a 1985 report in NEJM about the positive effect of estrogen on the risk of heart disease. More than 30,000 postmenopausal women participating in the Nurses' Health Study, which followed the women for more than three years, showed that nurses who were currently using estrogen had 70 percent less risk of developing coronary heart disease than women who had not used hormones—a dramatic finding.

This was exactly the boost that Wyeth-Ayerst needed to rehabilitate Premarin sales. Who would worry about a modest increase in the risk of breast cancer when you could take a pill to beat the odds against osteoporosis, the silent disease; and heart disease, the number one killer? (Much less attention was given to results from the Framingham Heart Study, published in the same issue of the *New England Journal of Medicine*, showing that women who had taken estrogen were 50 percent *more* likely to develop heart disease.)

By 1992, Premarin sales were topping their 1975 peak. One out of five postmenopausal women in the United States was taking hormones. The prestigious American College of Physicians issued guidelines to practicing physicians recommending that "all women . . . should consider preventive hormone therapy," and that 10 to 20 years of therapy were recommended for "maximum benefit." The American College of Obstetrics and Gynecology also recommended that all postmenopausal women, barring a medical contraindication like breast cancer, should take HRT for life. Bolstered by the recommendations of these professional organizations, Premarin use increased another 40 percent over the

next three years. In 1995 Premarin once again became the most frequently prescribed brand-name drug in the United States. Perhaps the
strongest evidence supporting routine HRT was presented in a 1997 article published in NEJM showing that "mortality among women who use
postmenopausal hormones is lower than among nonusers," again overriding continuing concerns about the link to breast cancer.

HOW DID SO MANY PEOPLE GET IT SO WRONG?

It helps to take a step back and look at the methods used in medical
research. The two most common types of medical studies are randomized controlled trials (RCTs) and observational studies. A simple example
demonstrates how these types of studies differ and illustrates the inherent strengths and weaknesses of each. Imagine that researchers want to
study the impact that running a 10-kilometer road race has on women's
health over a one-year period.

The simplest way to do this would be to set up an observational
study. Researchers would wait at the finish line of a local 10K race and
ask women if they would be willing to participate in the study. Let's say
100 women sign up. These women would then complete a questionnaire
that would include health habits, personal and family health history, and
other personal characteristics that might have an impact on their health,
such as marital status, educational level, and family income. This group
of women, called the treatment group, would then be compared with a
"control group," also including 100 women, matched as closely as possible on all characteristics—except that they didn't run in the race. This
control group of women would then fill out the same questionnaire.

One year after the race, all the women in the study would be queried
about their health. Rates of illness that occurred in the women who ran
in the race and in the control group would be calculated. These results
would then be statistically "adjusted" for preexisting differences between
the groups that might have had an impact on health: If, say, the women
who ran in the race were more likely to have a college education or keep
up with their preventive health care, the impact of such differences on
health could be adjusted for in the statistical analysis. Once all these fac-

tors were taken into account, the researchers would then be able to postulate whether running a 10K race had an effect on overall health.

The advantage of this observational study design is that it is inexpensive and can include large numbers of people. Participants don't have to do anything different from what they are already doing, except fill out the questionnaires. Observational studies take advantage of the differences that occur naturally, without any experimental intervention, such as some women choosing to run in the 10K race and others not.

The disadvantage of this type of study, of course, is that we can never be sure that all the differences between the groups are adequately included in the statistical adjustment. For example, maybe the runners share a strong commitment to investing time and energy in maintaining their health. But perhaps when the researchers designed the questionnaire, they weren't smart enough to include a question that identified this belief, which could be the real reason why the runners were healthier one year after the race. Without being aware of this difference between the groups, the researchers might incorrectly attribute the runners' better health to their having participated in the race.

The other way to do this study is a randomized controlled trial, the gold standard of medical research. This study design provides a much more precise way to identify the factors that contribute to a particular outcome. Continuing with the example of the 10K race, researchers would find 200 women who agreed to participate in a study about the health effects of running such a race. The women would then be randomly assigned to the treatment group (to run in the race) or the control group (not to run in the race). The same questionnaire would be filled out at the beginning of the study, and the same inquiry about health events would be made at the end of the year. The differences in health experienced by the women in each group during the year following the race would then be calculated, including statistical adjustments to correct for randomly occurring preexisting differences between the two groups that might have an impact on their subsequent health.

The obvious advantage of this study design is that the differences that make some women more likely than others to run in the race are neutralized by random assignment to the two groups. This greatly reduces the probability that an unidentified preexisting factor is responsible for any differences in health outcome. For this reason, an RCT would be much more likely to identify the true effect of having run in the race. The problem with this kind of study is that it takes more time and is more expensive to do.

It is amazing that before 1998, not one of the claims supporting the benefits of HRT had been substantiated by large RCTs. There were good reasons why the drug companies had not undertaken such studies: these studies are expensive, and when sales are proceeding well, there is little motivation to risk an unfavorable outcome. The Nurses' Health Study— the source of much of the information about HRT that came out in the 1990s—is an observational study (funded by the National Institutes of Health) designed to reveal the relationship between diet, lifestyle, and hormone therapy (both birth control pills and HRT).

The Nurses' Health Study was the source of the data for the 1997 NEJM article showing a lower mortality rate among women taking HRT. This benefit of HRT lasted for up to five years after women stopped taking the therapy, but after five years they had a 16 percent *increase* in their death rate compared with women who had never taken hormones. These contradictory findings deserved a lot more attention than they got at the time. Why did the nurses experience a lower death rate while they were taking hormones, and for five years after they stopped? And why did they then go on to experience a significantly higher death rate than women who had never been on HRT?

As the study published in the NEJM concluded, the lower mortality rate among nurses taking hormones could have been due to the "survival benefit" of the hormones. In other words, women had a lower mortality rate because they took hormones. The reverse could also have been true: the women who were already going to have a lower mortality rate might have been more likely to take hormones. In other words, perhaps it was their greater propensity toward health or the absence of disease that led them to take the hormones, and not the reverse. The third possibility is that the women who took the hormones believed that they were doing something that would protect their health and that this placebo effect played a role in keeping them healthier.

The Nurses' Health Study researchers statistically adjusted their results for many potentially confounding factors: body weight, cigarette smoking, high blood pressure, high cholesterol, early heart attack in a parent, history of breast cancer in mother or sister, previous use of birth control pills, number of children, age of onset of period, diet, alcohol use, multivitamin use, vitamin E use, aspirin use, and regular exercise. Despite this meticulous statistical caution, however, the most elegant aspect of the Nurses' Health Study may also have been its tragic flaw. The study purposely included only registered nurses to minimize the impact of differences in "socioeconomic status and access to health care." But the researchers may have trusted this assumption too much.

It turns out that several important confounding factors had not been adequately taken into account, precisely the kinds of variables that the researchers thought that their study design—by including only registered nurses—had eliminated. Women who chose to take hormones tended to be wealthier and better educated, were twice as likely to be white than black, and received more preventive health care. Dr. Elizabeth Barrett-Connor, a professor at the University of California, San Diego, points out that while the observational studies of HRT were going on, doctors across the country knew, from Premarin product labeling (included in the *Physicians' Desk Reference*), that women with a history of heart disease, high blood pressure, or diabetes should not be treated with estrogen. This would certainly contribute to the spurious finding in the observational studies that women who took hormones had less heart disease. Of course they did: Not only were they the type of women who were going to be healthier; the women taking hormones had already been screened to exclude those with heart disease, high blood pressure, and diabetes. The observational studies that found that Premarin decreased the risk of heart disease had not, according to Dr. Barrett-Connor, adequately adjusted for this.

In 1998 the results of the first randomized controlled clinical trial of HRT were published. The Heart and Estrogen/Progesterone Replacement Study (HERS), published in JAMA, had been designed to determine whether HRT decreased the risk of recurrent heart disease in women who already had heart problems (so-called secondary prevention). The results came as a huge surprise. This manufacturer-sponsored study showed that despite significantly lowering LDL (bad) cholesterol and raising HDL (good) cholesterol, HRT *increased* women's risk of heart disease by 50 percent in the first year. And over the four years of the study, treatment with hormones provided no reduction in the risk of developing cardiovascular disease. In fact, this study showed that the overall death rate was not lower in the women who took hormones; it was slightly higher.

Why had Wyeth-Ayerst, the manufacturer of Premarin, agreed to do this study, taking a chance that the results would come out against the company's interests? The answer is simple: the insatiable quest to expand its market for hormones. In 1990, Wyeth-Ayerst had requested that the FDA approve Premarin for the prevention of heart disease in postmenopausal women, notwithstanding the lack of evidence from randomized controlled trials documenting such a benefit. Cynthia Pearson, of the nonprofit, independent National Women's Health Network, pointed out in an FDA hearing that the evidence supporting this claim was weak: "You couldn't approve a drug for healthy men without a randomized clinical trial. Even aspirin [to prevent heart disease] had to have a randomized controlled trial with healthy men."

Ms. Pearson's argument—that the standard for the gander ought to apply to the goose—prevailed. The FDA ruled that a randomized controlled trial was necessary to justify the claim that HRT decreased a woman's risk of heart disease. Wyeth-Ayerst agreed to perform the requisite study, confident that the results would come out in their favor. Eight years later, when the results became available, we learned that combined HRT (estrogen plus progestin) does not prevent heart disease.

THE DEMISE OF ROUTINE HRT

The truth about HRT came out very slowly and was difficult for most doctors to accept. Even after the article appeared in JAMA in 2000 showing the 8 percent per year increase in the risk of breast cancer in women taking combined hormone therapy, most experts continued to recommend, and most doctors continued to prescribe, routine hormone replacement for postmenopausal women. In 2001, Premarin was still the third most frequently prescribed drug in the United States.

In July of 2002, everyone found out that it was not Mother Nature but the American College of Physicians and the American College of Obstetrics and Gynecology that had made the big mistake. The newspapers were full of articles about the government-sponsored Women's Health Initiative study, which had been specifically designed to determine whether routine HRT was beneficial for postmenopausal women. The 16,000 women in the study had been randomly assigned to take either combined (estrogen and progestin) HRT or a placebo. The study had been scheduled to run through 2005, but the women received letters instructing them to stop taking the study medication because the risk (increase in breast cancer, heart attack, stroke, and blood clots) associated with combined HRT had been found to be significantly greater than the benefit (decrease in hip fractures and colon cancers). The study found a statistically significant increase (15 percent) in the overall frequency of adverse events in the women taking HRT compared with the women who took a placebo. This translated into about one adverse event for every 100 women who took hormones for five years. The data and safety monitoring board of the study determined that the increased frequency of complications in the women who had taken HRT instead of a placebo had "crossed the designated boundary . . . of a finding of overall harm," and that it was no longer ethical to continue the study knowing that the women taking HRT were going to be harmed more than helped.

Two more defeats for routine combined HRT (other than for treatment of menopausal and postmenopausal symptoms) followed soon thereafter. In May 2003 more results from the Women's Health Initiative were published showing that combined HRT not only did not prevent Alzheimer's disease, but actually doubled the risk of developing dementia (primarily Alzheimer's disease) in women aged 65 and older, causing about 1 additional case of dementia for every 100 women treated with HRT for five years.

Just three months later came the final nail in the coffin, when the results of probably the biggest study of all time, the Million Women Study, were published in *The Lancet*. One million women in the United Kingdom completed questionnaires about their personal health, sociodemographic information, whether they had reached menopause, and whether they had ever taken or were currently taking hormones. Over the following four years, the local cancer registries reported when women participating in the study developed or died from breast cancer. The results showed that women who were currently taking hormones had a 66 percent higher chance of getting breast cancer (30 percent for those taking only estrogen, and 100 percent for those taking both estrogen and progestin) than the women who were not taking hormones. The women taking hormones were also significantly more likely to die of breast cancer than the women not taking hormones. To put the risk into perspective, the researchers calculated that there had been about 20,000 extra cases of breast cancer caused by HRT in the United Kingdom over the previous 10 years. Based on the difference in population size alone, even at the same rate of hormone use, there would have been an extra 94,000 cases of breast cancer in the United States in the previous 10 years as a result of women's taking HRT. The total number of American women who developed breast cancer because of taking HRT was likely to be much higher than this, though, because women in the United States were about four times more likely to take HRT than women in the United Kingdom.

There is yet another disturbing finding from the Million Women Study: Starting in the early 1980s, progestins were added to estrogen to reduce the risk of uterine cancer in women who had not had a hysterectomy. The risk of uterine cancer was reduced to near zero, but nobody evaluated the overall effect of adding progestin to routine HRT. The Million Women Study confirmed that the taking of estrogen without progestin caused 10 extra uterine cancers and 5 extra breast cancers, a total of 15 extra cancers per 1000 women over 10 years. Adding progestin did, in fact, eliminate the risk of uterine cancer but caused an extra 19 breast cancers per 1000 women over 10 years. In other words, the problem of uterine cancer was "solved" by adding a drug that *increased* a woman's overall risk of getting other types of cancer.

The estrogen-only part of the Women's Health Initiative Study was ended prematurely, in February 2004. Researchers concluded that after almost seven years, the women taking estrogen had more strokes and fewer broken hips than the women taking placebos. The most important finding was that there was no overall benefit to taking estrogen and that, therefore, it "should not be recommended for chronic disease prevention in postmenopausal women."

Twenty million American women have taken HRT not only to relieve symptoms such as hot flashes and vaginal dryness but also believing that hormones would protect their hearts, decrease Alzheimer's and Parkinson's disease, prevent tooth loss and diabetes, strengthen their bones, preserve sexual function and urinary continence, improve the quality of their lives, and increase their longevity. The women who took HRT had access to the best care that American medicine had to offer: Compared with the population at large, they were more likely to have graduated from college, were wealthier, and were more likely to have received preventive health care. Despite this, they unwittingly exposed themselves to increased risks of breast cancer, heart attack, stroke, Alzheimer's disease, and blood clots.

In the end, the 26 percent increase in the risk of breast cancer caused by HRT found in the Women's Health Initiative study was deemed by the National Institutes of Health "too high a price to pay, even if there were a heart benefit." This risk had been known a decade earlier, when the American College of Physicians made its recommendation that all women without unusual risks should consider taking HRT, but was not of enough concern at the time to invoke the principle "First do no harm." Far more than 100,000 unnecessary cases of breast cancer resulted.

The important lessons from this chapter of American medical history will be lost if we simply attribute the debacle of routine HRT for healthy postmenopausal women to the vagaries of medical progress. Failure to understand how this mistake occurred commits us (doctors and patients alike) to being naively swept up by each new cycle of exaggerated claims about the effectiveness and safety of ever more expensive medical therapies—that is, until even newer "medical knowledge" is produced that supports even costlier drugs. The fundamental lesson to be learned from the HRT debacle is that therapeutic decisions must be based on solid and unbiased scientific evidence. The trend, however, is going in exactly the opposite direction. The ideals and personal goals that had brought me to medicine and then to family practice now called me to investigate, full-time, just how the fundamental mission of American medicine was being undermined—and how we might begin to fix it.

PART II

THE COMMERCIALIZATION
OF AMERICAN MEDICINE

CHAPTER 6

AMERICAN MEDICINE'S PERFECT STORM

A BRIEF HISTORY

In 1982, the National Governors Association sponsored a conference in New Orleans to explore innovative ways for states to control their unsustainably increasing health care costs. I presented research that I had done as a Robert Wood Johnson Fellow showing the benefit of offering inner city of Cleveland families covered by Medicaid the option of enrolling in a health maintenance organization that would give them access to private primary care doctors. For families who opted to join the HMO, hospital admissions and emergency room visits had plummeted, immunization rates and well-child care visits had improved, and costs had gone down. All the pilot programs being presented at this conference were variations on the same theme, and all came to the same conclusion: establishing a relationship between each Medicaid patient and a primary care doctor responsible for providing and coordinating all medical care improved the quality of care and, at the same time, decreased costs.

Several weeks later, I moved from Cleveland to Massachusetts to begin my career as a family doctor. Initially, the health insurance that most of my patients had, besides those with Medicare and Medicaid, did not cover my services in the office. A few people had very expensive "Cadillac" health insurance that paid for all of their medical care and drugs. An equally small number were insured by the sole, recently started HMO in eastern Massachusetts, and were charged only a $3 co-payment for office visits. The people who had chosen to enroll in this plan agreed to access nonemergency medical care through their primary care (or covering) doctor only.

Over the next two decades, of course, all this changed: HMOs and managed care plans swept the country. Each year, more and more patients enrolled in these programs. It wasn't long before nearly all of my patients who weren't on Medicare or Medicaid were covered by some form of HMO or managed care plan.

What happened to health care costs? Per-person health care expenditures, adjusted for inflation, more than quadrupled over the following 20 years. Starting in 2001, premiums rose a whopping 43 percent over the next three years alone. Health care costs now account for one-seventh of the total GNP, up from 9 percent in 1980 to an estimated 15.5 percent in 2004. What seemed like a major crisis in 1982 now looks trivial. And as we have seen, all the while our health outcomes are lagging further and further behind those of the other wealthy industrialized countries.

How is it that those sweeping changes, adopted to control health care costs and improve the quality of care, had precisely the opposite effect? People tend to point a finger at one of two culprits: Many blame the HMOs and managed care companies for wresting control of medical decisions away from doctors and unreasonably restricting care in order to save money. Others blame the excessive power of the medical industries and particularly the drug companies, with their exquisitely honed marketing techniques, for the commercialization of medical practice.

Looking for *the* single cause of the poor performance of the American health care system is futile. The truth is closer to Pogo's discomforting epiphany: the enemy is us. We all have a relationship to the health care system: patients and potential patients, doctors and other health care professionals, researchers, workers in health care industries, health policy experts, government officials, lawmakers, and investors. We have all been pulled into this enormous and complex system by our hopes and fears, our myths and ideologies, our dedication and pursuit of scientific knowledge, and our personal and institutional aspirations. As the interests and energies of all these elements keep merging into an ever larger and more powerful system, a perfect storm is gathering that is producing enormously expensive and disturbingly ineffective health care, American style.

THE GOLDEN AGE OF HMOS AND MANAGED CARE

Nothing has had more impact on the practice of medicine in the United States than the rapid transition from traditional indemnity insurance to HMOs and managed care plans. And nothing could have produced more profound unintended consequences.

Prior to the era of managed care, indemnity insurance simply paid a contracted percentage of the bills for covered services, which rarely included office visits or prescription drugs. HMOs, on the other hand, offered to provide virtually complete health care coverage for a predetermined price. In return for this more complete coverage, patients who were enrolled in HMOs agreed to access medical care only through the HMO, usually through their primary care doctor. The burden of cost control is placed on the health care providers, whose responsibility, in addition to providing medical care, is to keep the cost of care within a defined budget. Managed care plans differ from HMOs in that the burden of cost control is not put directly on health care providers. Doctors are not prepaid and do not work on a fixed budget, but agree to accept a fee schedule for their services and participate in oversight of the quality and utilization of care—thus "managing" the care.

HMOs and managed care plans quickly came to dominate health insurance in the United States. They appealed to employers because of their promise of holding down insurance costs, which were increasing between 10 percent and 18 percent per year in the late 1980s and early 1990s. And they were attractive to patients because, unlike indemnity insurance, HMOs covered most medical services and drugs with relatively small co-pays—similar to the very expensive Cadillac indemnity plans. In addition, by paying for primary care and preventive services, and with long-term incentives that favored illness prevention, these plans held out the promise of actually improving people's health. The prospect of a win-win insurance arrangement providing better care for less money, like the early HMO I studied in Cleveland, catalyzed the rapid change in U.S. health insurance. In the late 1970s, almost all employer-sponsored health insurance (95 percent) was the traditional indemnity type. By the end of the 1990s, HMO and managed care plans accounted for 92 percent of employer-based health insurance.

The period of the late 1980s and early 1990s was the golden era of HMOs and managed care plans. They appeared to have solved the problem of rising health insurance costs in a uniquely American way. Health care spending budgets that would have been unacceptable coming from the government were created by competing independent health plans, with employers choosing which to offer and employees usually (but not always) given a choice of several from which to choose. Positive coverage of the new plans by the media contributed to the enthusiasm. In 1990, stories about the new types of health insurance were twice as likely to be positive than negative. This market-based approach successfully tamed the double-digit percentage increases in health insurance premiums of the late 1980s and early 1990s, bringing the annual rate of increase down from a peak of 18 percent in 1989 to less than 2 percent by 1996.

PATIENTS BECOME CONSUMERS

Almost all of my patients welcomed the new plans. The broader insurance coverage meant that they no longer had to pay for their office visits or go through a lot of paperwork to collect from their indemnity insurance. And because family doctors take care of a broader range of problems than other primary care physicians, most of my patients already expected to discuss most of their medical problems with me before going to a specialist anyway. Besides the additional administrative burden of processing referrals to specialists, the added responsibility of functioning as the medical gatekeeper had little impact on my practice.

Despite the discounted fees, I preferred taking care of my patients on the new insurance plans. I could provide better care because patients were more willing to come in for routine exams and follow-up visits. Money was removed as an impediment to the doctor-patient relationship. True, the low co-pay for office visits contributed to some nonessential patient-generated visits, but most of these served to increase the patients' trust and enhanced my ability to provide good care.

Patients were also grateful for the prescription drug coverage that was usually part of the new insurance plans. In 1965, prior to the advent of managed care, 93 percent of the cost of prescription drugs was paid directly by patients; by 1998 this was down to 25 percent. Between 1990 and 1997, out-of-pocket expenditures for prescription drugs by people who were covered by employer-based health insurance went down by 8 percent. During those same years, the actual per-person inflation-adjusted cost of prescription drugs in employer-based insurance plans tripled.

At the same time that the patients' out-of-pocket medical costs were going down, Americans' faith in the benefits of the latest medical science was high. Surveys done between 1992 and 2000 showed that half again as many Americans as Europeans described themselves as "very interested" in new medical discoveries (66 percent versus 44 percent), and almost twice as many Americans over the age of 65 were "very interested" in new medical discoveries as were European seniors (79 percent versus 42 percent). Almost half of Americans believed that health insurance or the government should "pay for all new medical technologies." One-third of Americans believed that "modern medicine can cure almost any illness for people who have access to the most advanced technology and treatment." And given their strong interest and faith in medical progress, Americans were overwhelmingly of the opinion that more rather than less money should be spent on "improving and protecting the nation's health," by an 11-to-1 margin.

Medical information was becoming available on the Internet, and the increasing media coverage of the latest "breakthroughs" in medical science further heightened public enthusiasm about the latest developments. (There was little awareness that most of this information had been made available to serve commercial interests; one study showed that the focus of 80 percent of Internet sites that address back pain is advertising, and only 12 percent of the sites were rated as "high-quality.")

The stage could not have been set more perfectly for prescription drug advertising to become a major force in American medicine. And so it did. In 1991 the drug companies spent a paltry $55 million on advertising drugs directly to consumers. Over the next 11 years, this increased more than 50-fold to over $3 billion in 2003. The ads appeal to viewers as independent decision makers—capable of forming their own opinions about which drugs they need—and resonate with the growing concern that HMOs and managed care plans tend to withhold the best care to save money.

Largely freed of concerns about out-of-pocket costs, enticed by advertising and media coverage of developments in medicine, and emboldened by a sense of autonomy, patients began requesting, and then demanding, specific tests, drugs, and procedures. Indeed, it became nearly impossible to convince many patients that more medical care was not necessarily better. Rather than adopting lifestyle changes that could prevent illnesses, many people began to believe that the latest "medical breakthroughs" were all that was needed to keep them healthy. Ethicist Daniel Callahan in his book *False Hopes* sums this up beautifully: "The market sells dreams and hopes as well as things." To exactly the same extent that a person is seduced by the false hopes and dreams offered by the medical industry's marketing efforts, the ability to trust his or her doctor, especially a primary care doctor, is eroded.

BACKLASH

It wasn't long, however, before the enthusiasm about HMOs and managed care plans started to wane. News stories about HMOs unreasonably withholding care became a dominant theme, and by 1997, critical stories were outnumbering positive ones by a seven-to-one margin. The health insurance industry added grist to the mill by imposing one-day obstetric hospitalizations for normal deliveries, selectively contracting with doctors so that long-standing doctor-patient relationships were disrupted, and trying to save money by avoiding high-cost patients like those with HIV/AIDS. Patients' rights legislation emerged as a major political issue as the public focused on restricted access to care. The public's esteem for managed care companies plummeted. In 1997, 51 percent of those surveyed said that managed care companies were serving patients well; that figure was down to 29 percent just four years later.

The data about the actual effect of managed care tell a very different story. The quality of care neither improved nor deteriorated under managed care. The stories about patients being rushed through doctors' offices turned out not to be true (like the myth of the estate tax causing the loss of the family farm). An article published in the *New England Journal of Medicine* showed that between 1989 and 1998, the frequency with which people saw their doctors did not change. There was no shortening of visits for managed care patients for either primary or specialty care visits; in fact, the duration of doctor visits actually increased by one to two minutes. Even the public anger at the withholding of care by overly aggressive or financially greedy "gatekeepers" turned out to be largely a myth: a study conducted by a nationwide managed care company, United Healthcare, showed that fewer than one in 100 requests for referrals were being denied, leading the insurer to drop its requirement for primary care approval of referrals. Still, as an American researcher observed in a Canadian medical journal, "Regardless of the evidence, there is a strong sentiment among both physicians and patients that managed care is harming quality of care." So what was the real problem?

Initial cost savings had come fairly easily. Doctors, hospitals, and other health care providers had little choice but to accept discounted fees in order to be included in the newly formed networks of health care providers; otherwise they risked losing access to their patients. These so-called volume discounts controlled prices during the transition to managed care, but the apparent solution was short-lived. Once the discounts had been factored in, this apparently exquisite solution to controlling costs—local health care budgets set by the marketplace instead of the government—became the problem. When there were no more cost savings to be squeezed out of the fees paid to health care providers, HMOs and managed care companies had only one avenue open: they had to start to really "manage" care, that is, control costs by eliminating unnecessary or wasteful care. (Of course, cutting down on advertising, executive salaries, and profits would have helped, too.)

Almost overnight, the hyperbolic hopes for managed care and appreciation of the greater coverage quickly turned into hyperbolic vilification. In one survey, 59 percent of the people expressed negative feelings about HMOs and managed care in general, but 69 percent of the same people were satisfied with the actual care they were receiving from their own HMO or managed care plan. Of course there were abuses and mistakes on the part of the health insurers, but why the change in public opinion?

Each of the constituents of this complex system felt threatened by the limitation on medical expenditures. Though I have no proof, I strongly suspect that the parties that had the most to lose financially— the drug, medical equipment, and hospital industries; and the specialty care doctors—played the biggest role in fanning the flames of public disgruntlement. When public opinion turned so strongly against the measures necessary to control health care costs, the insurance companies had no choice but to loosen their management of care. Yearly increases in health insurance premiums once again started to balloon out of control, rising steadily from a low 2 percent annual increase in 1996 to 13.9 percent in 2003.

Ironically, the move into managed care created a historic opportunity for the medical industry. The cost-containment potential of HMOs and managed care plans was, initially, a serious threat to drug companies and medical device manufacturers. But the broader coverage offered by the new plans turned out to have the most profound unintended consequences: Instead of containing health care costs, HMOs and managed care plans facilitated the almost unrestrained increases in health care spending that followed. The captains of the drug and other medical industries certainly hadn't planned this, but they knew how to take advantage of opportunity when it came knocking on their door. After a brief period of clear skies, dark clouds could be seen gathering on the horizon.

THE DIMINISHING ROLE OF PRIMARY CARE DOCTORS

Comparisons both within the United States and between countries show that access to comprehensive, family-oriented primary care service is the distinguishing characteristic of health care systems that are both effective at producing good health and efficient at controlling costs. Nonetheless, American medicine has become heavily dominated by specialty care over the past 40 years. In 1965 there were as many primary care doctors as specialists in the United States. Since then, the ratio of primary care doctors to the U.S. population has remained about the same, while the ratio of specialists has more than doubled.

Most health policy experts recommend that between 42 percent and 50 percent of doctors in the United States should be primary care doctors. Instead 31 percent of doctors in the United States practice primary care and 69 percent are specialists. In order to correct this imbalance, the Council on Graduate Medical Education (a body established by Congress to make recommendations about the supply and distribution of doctors to the U.S. Department of Health and Human Services) recommended training at least 50 percent of physicians as primary care doctors. In 1998, this goal was not being met. Only 36 percent of U.S. medical students that year reported that primary care was their first choice of specialty. And to show how quickly the medical environment is changing, only four years later, interest in primary care among U.S. medical students plummeted by 40 percent, so that only about one out of five students (21.5 percent) identified primary care as his or her first choice.

A number of factors turn medical students away from careers in primary care. The intellectual culture within the academic medical centers where students are trained is dominated by specialists, whose ideals of "good" and "real" medicine are very different from the kinds of challenges faced by primary care doctors. A survey of medical students showed that only three out of 1000 thought that good students were encouraged to go into primary care fields. Most doctors are in their late twenties or early thirties when they finish their training. They finish with an average debt of over $100,000, at just about the time they want to start a family and get on with their lives. The starting salary for many specialties is more than twice that of primary care doctors. And to make this choice even more difficult, the boundary between professional responsibilities and personal time is often more blurred in primary care than in other specialties.

Nobody can blame these young doctors for not choosing primary care—it takes a tremendous amount of commitment and idealism to choose a career that is not supported by role models in training, carries less prestige among peers, intrudes more into one's personal life, and pays far less than most other specialties. A bright and concerned Harvard Medical School student lamented to me that he really wanted to become a pediatrician and take care of children in a community-based practice, but his enormous debt was forcing him into a more lucrative subspecialty. The same story is heard over and over.

In addition to the growing imbalance between primary care doctors and specialists, the ever-present threat of malpractice litigation is also increasing the cost of American medical care. This threat may provide some protection to patients and allow recourse for substandard care, but the justice meted out is inconsistent. In a *New York Times* op-ed piece, Philip K. Howard, author of *The Collapse of the Common Good: How America's Lawsuit Culture Undermines Our Freedom,* commented that most of the doctors who do commit malpractice are not sued, and most of the lawsuits brought against doctors are about situations in which malpractice was not committed. Nonetheless, the current medical malpractice system consistently distorts our medical care. Doctors are aware of the risk of a malpractice suit lurking in every patient visit. Three-fifths of doctors in the United States admit that they do more diagnostic testing than is necessary because of the threat of litigation. And why not? The risk of ordering an extra test is nil, but the threat of a lawsuit because of a test not ordered is ever present—even when the likelihood of serious disease is very low and reasonable professional judgment would say the test was not necessary.

These extra tests can and often do set off a cascade effect, requiring even more tests to follow up on abnormal results, many of which then turn out to be normal. With the specter of malpractice looming, doctors feel justified in ordering almost any test, including tests in which they have a financial interest.

The rising cost of malpractice insurance is causing a rebellion among doctors forced to pay the price for our litigious culture (and a few bad doctors) regardless of their own track record and commitment to quality care. Some, caught between the ever-present fears of litigation and the mounting costs of insurance, are shielding their assets and practicing without insurance, while others are leaving the practice of medicine altogether.

At the same time that all of this is happening, the medical information available to doctors (and to their patients) is increasingly dominated by commercial interests. The skies are darkening.

DRUGGING THE WATCHDOGS

Within the FDA, the doctors, scientists, and statisticians are dedicated to making sure the data about drugs and medical devices presented by manufacturers justify their claims of safety and efficacy. But the FDA is understaffed, underfunded, and under pressure, according to its own employees. Even worse, the FDA has fallen under the influence of the drug and medical-device industries, so much so that it was labeled "a ser vant of industry" by Dr. Richard Horton, the editor of the British journal *The Lancet.*

The FDA used to be famous for moving at a glacial bureaucratic pace. In 1980, the General Accounting Office of Congress reported that the FDA was inadequately staffed to keep up with its workload. In 1988, political action by AIDS activists drew attention to the very real need for quicker access to potentially lifesaving drugs. The ensuing political crisis resulted in the 1992 passage of the Prescription Drug User Fee Act, otherwise known as PDUFA. The drug companies agreed to pay a $300,000 fee for each new drug application; in return, the FDA's Center for Drug Evaluation and Research promised to adhere to a speedier timetable for the new drug approval process. According to a 2002 GAO report, a little more than half the cost of reviewing new drug applications was funded by user fees from the drug industry.

New-drug approval certainly became quicker. With PDUFA funds, the FDA was able to increase the staff at the Center for Drug Evaluation and Research, or CDER, from 1300 to 2300, all assigned to expedite new-drug applications for patented (not generic) drugs. In the four years following the enactment of PDUFA, the median length of time the FDA took to decide on priority new-drug applications dropped from 20 months down to six months. At the same time, the average number of new drugs approved doubled.

Funding by drug companies may have seemed like a good idea for the cash-strapped FDA, but what about protecting the consumer from the drug companies' influence? How unbiased can CDER be when half its budget comes from the drug companies themselves? An anonymous survey done by Public Citizen in 1998 revealed that FDA review officers felt that standards had declined as pressure to approve new drugs increased. The FDA medical officers who responded to the survey identified 27 new drugs that had been approved within the previous three years that they felt should not have been. A similar report on CDER by the inspector general of the U.S. Department of Health and Human Services, published in March 2003, found that 58 percent of the medical officers said that the six months allotted for review of priority drugs is not adequate, and that one-third of respondents did not feel comfortable expressing their differing opinions. In the FDA's own *Consumer Magazine,* Dr. Janet Woodcock, director of CDER since 1994, wrote that tight deadlines for drug approval were creating "a sweatshop environment that's causing high staffing turnover."

The most dangerous consequence of these changes was that the number of drugs approved by the FDA but later withdrawn from the market for safety reasons increased from 1.6 percent of drugs approved between 1993 and 1996 to 5.3 percent between 1997 and 2000. Seven drugs that had been approved by the FDA after 1993 were withdrawn from the market because of serious health risks. The *Los Angeles Times* reported that these drugs were suspected of causing more than 1000 deaths (though the number of deaths could actually be much higher because reporting of adverse drug events to the FDA is voluntary). Even though none of these seven drugs was lifesaving, according to the *Los Angeles Times,* "the FDA approved each of those drugs while disregarding danger signs or blunt warnings from its own specialists." All told, 22 million Americans, one out of every 10 adults, had taken a drug that was later withdrawn from the market between 1997 and 2000.

The blood sugar–lowering diabetes drug Rezulin is one of the drugs that was approved in haste by the FDA—and later withdrawn, but much too late for many Americans. The details of the story were first presented in 2000 in a Pulitzer Prize–winning series of investigative reports by David Willman of the *Los Angeles Times.* Remarkably, as quickly as medical news travels, this story had no "legs" and went largely unheeded. Three years later David Willman wrote a similar story showing that the same problems were still there.

Dr. Richard Eastman was the director of the NIH division in charge of diabetes research, and in charge of the $150 million Diabetes Prevention Program study. This large study was designed to determine whether diabetes could be prevented in people at high risk (overweight and with mildly elevated blood sugar levels) by drugs or by lifestyle interventions. In June 1996 Dr. Eastman announced that Rezulin had been selected as one of the two diabetes drugs to be included in the study—a real victory for Warner-Lambert, the manufacturer of Rezulin.

Also in 1996 Warner-Lambert submitted Rezulin to the FDA for approval, and it became the first diabetes drug to be given an accelerated review. The medical officer evaluating the new drug application, Dr. John L. Gueriguian, was a 19 year veteran of the FDA. His review recommended that Rezulin not be approved: the drug appeared to offer no significant advantage over other diabetes drugs already on the market, and it had a worrisome tendency to cause inflammation of the liver. Warner-Lambert executives "complained about Gueriguian to the higher-ups at the FDA." Dr. Gueriguian was then removed from the approval process for this drug. When the Advisory Committee met to decide on the approval of Rezulin, they were not informed of Dr. Gueriguian's concerns about liver toxicity. The FDA approved Rezulin in February 1997, and brisk sales soon earned it "blockbuster" status.

However, reports of fatal liver toxicity due to Rezulin soon started to appear. Notwithstanding reports of deaths in the United States as well as in Japan, and the withdrawal of the drug from the United Kingdom because of liver toxicity in December 1997, Dr. Eastman and his colleagues decided to continue treating volunteers in the Diabetes Prevention Program study with Rezulin. Only after Audrey LaRue Jones, a 55-year-old high school teacher, died of liver failure in May 1998 did Rezulin stop being given to the volunteers in the study. Warner-Lambert maintained that Rezulin was not responsible for the liver failure that led to her death.

Despite the mounting reports of liver problems in the United States, Rezulin was not withdrawn from the U.S. market until March 2000. By that time, $1.8 billion worth of the drug had been sold. The *Los Angeles Times* reported that, all told, Rezulin was suspected in 391 deaths and linked to 400 cases of liver failure. Looking back on his experience, Dr. Gueriguian told the *Los Angeles Times,* "Either you play games or you're going to be put off limits . . . a pariah."

Another FDA medical officer and former supporter of Rezulin, Dr. Robert I. Misbin, was threatened with dismissal by the FDA. His offense? He provided a copy of a letter to members of Congress from himself and other physician colleagues at the FDA expressing concern about the FDA's failure to withdraw Rezulin from the market after the FDA had linked it to 63 deaths due to liver failure. Dr. Janet B. McGill, an endocrinologist who had participated in Warner-Lambert's early studies of Rezulin, told the Los Angeles Times that Warner-Lambert "clearly places profits before the lives of patients with diabetes."

In retrospect one wonders why the NIH and FDA continued to support Rezulin long after it was known to be associated with so many deaths. One particularly troubling aspect of Rezulin's seemingly privileged treatment was provided by David Willman's series in the Los Angeles Times: Dr. Eastman, while in charge of diabetes research at the NIH and overseeing the $150 million study in which Rezulin was included, was receiving $78,455 from Warner-Lambert on top of his $144,000 annual salary from the NIH. Between 1991 and 1997, Dr. Eastman had received, according to the Los Angeles Times, "at least $260,000 in consulting-related fees from a variety of outside sources, including six drug manufacturers." None of this was part of the public record, but the financial relationship with Warner-Lambert had been approved by two of Dr. Eastman's superiors. And Dr. Eastman was by no means alone. In fact, the Los Angeles Times reported that no fewer than 12 of the 22 researchers who were overseeing the $150 million government-sponsored diabetes study as "principal investigators" were receiving fees or research grants from Warner-Lambert.

One would think that, once these drug companies' lucrative consulting contracts with high-ranking NIH officials with direct responsibility for the companies' products had been brought to the light of day, a firewall would have been quickly erected. Hardly. In December 2003, David Willman wrote an article titled "Stealth Merger: Drug Companies and Government Medical Research," in which he identified multiple examples of NIH officials receiving payments of hundreds of thousands of dollars from drug companies.

"Subject No. 4" died while participating in a drug study at the National Institutes of Health on June 14, 1999. She was Jamie Ann Jackson, a 42-year-old registered nurse, married and a mother of two. Mrs. Jackson was the second person who had died while participating in NIH studies of a drug named Fludara, marketed by Berlex Laboratories. This drug, which had been used to treat leukemia since 1991, was being tested to see if it helped patients with autoimmune diseases. No more patients were enrolled in the study after the second death, but the study continued with the patients already enrolled for another nine months, and terminated only when five of the remaining 12 patients developed abnormalities in their blood tests. Dr. Stephen I. Katz was the director of the NIH's National Institute of Arthritis and Musculoskeletal and Skin Diseases, which was conducting the study. According to the *Los Angeles Times*, between 1996 and 2002 Dr. Katz received more than $170,000 in consulting fees from the German drug manufacturer Schering AG. (It was during this time period that the fatal study of Berlex's drug Fludara was being conducted.) These details are important because Berlex is a wholly owned subsidiary of Schering AG, described as its "U.S. business unit." Dr. Katz told the *Los Angeles Times* that he had been "unaware of any relationship between Berlex and Schering AG," and therefore unaware of a potential conflict of interest. But, according to the *Los Angeles Times*, "Katz declined to identify when he learned that Berlex was the U.S. affiliate of Schering AG."

Drs. Eastman and Katz were certainly not the only high-ranking officials at the NIH to receive consulting fees from the drug industry. Another official had accepted $1.4 million plus stock options over an 11-year period, while at least one of the companies for whom he was consulting was involved with the work of the laboratory he directs at the National Institute of Allergy and Infectious Diseases.

The financial conflicts of interest at the NIH are by no means isolated examples of drug company influence on the government oversight of the drug industry. Because crucial recommendations about drug approval and drug labeling are made at the FDA's Advisory Committee meetings, federal law "generally prohibits" the participation of experts who have financial ties to the products being presented on these committees. An article in *USA Today* in September 2000 shows, however, that the FDA granted so many waivers—800 between 1998 and 2000—that 54 percent of the experts on these all-important Advisory Committees had "a direct financial interest in the drug or topic they are asked to evaluate." And this 54 percent figure does not take into account that FDA rules do not even require an Advisory Committee member to declare receipt of amounts less than $50,000 per year from a drug company as long as the payment is for work not related to the drug being discussed.

The storm clouds grew even darker as the government institutions responsible for protecting the public's interest became dependent on drug company largesse.

THE GREAT AMERICAN DRUG LOBBY

None of this would have been possible, of course, without the insatiable appetite of politicians for industry dollars. Lobbying efforts on behalf of the drug industry are unrivaled. It spent $177 million on lobbying in 1999 and 2000, $50 million more than the next closest industry, insurance. The drug industry hires 625 lobbyists, more than one for each member of the House and Senate. The drug industry's $20 million in campaign contributions for the 2000 election seems downright stingy compared with the insurance industry's $40 million. (Could this be playing any role in President Bush's desire to privatize Medicare?) The $20 million, however, doesn't include the approximately $65 million for so-called issue ads aired by Citizens for Better Medicare. Though this organization appeared to be a grassroots movement, it was in fact funded primarily, if not exclusively, by the drug industry, and its ads tended to benefit candidates who supported the drug industry's legislative goals.

Money from the drug industry has been pouring into politics, with the balance of support tipping progressively more toward the Republicans, who received about 76 percent of the drug industry's financial largesse in the 1999–2000 election cycle. It's not often that we get to see what this money actually buys, the actual quid pro quo laid out in black and white. But a letter from Jim Nicholson, the chairman of the Republican National Committee, to Charles Heimbold, chairman and CEO of Bristol-Myers Squibb, made public as a result of legal challenges to the constitutionality of the McCain-Feingold campaign finance reform law, shows how this can work. The letter, written in April 1999, was delivered at a time when pressure for a bill to provide prescription drug benefits to senior citizens was beginning to mount. The drug industry was jockeying for a bill that would enhance its bottom line by providing Medicare funds to purchase its drugs, while at the same time blocking the federal government from using purchasing power to negotiate lower prices (as Medicare has done so successfully with payments to doctors and hospitals).

In the letter, Nicholson expresses his approval of "forming a pharmaceutical coalition" that will provide the "perfect vehicle for the Republican Party to reach out to the health care community and discuss their legislative needs." The letter goes on to say, "We must keep the lines of communication open if we want to continue passing legislation that will benefit your industry." The penultimate paragraph describes just how to keep those lines open, including a request for a $250,000 donation from Bristol-Myers Squibb to the Republican National Committee. With tens of billions of dollars a year on the line for the drug industry, what was a mere $250,000?

Perhaps the storm clouds were being actively seeded.

Drug companies, government, doctors, patients, insurers. Health care costs keep rising, with no end in sight, and despite the myths about the excellence of our medical care, we are not realizing commensurate improvements in our health. The American health care system keeps edging ever closer to the breaking point. Many factors are contributing, but in the eye of the storm is a single factor: the transformation of medical knowledge from a public good, measured by its potential to improve our health, into a commodity, measured by its commercial value. This transformation is the result of the commercial takeover of the process by which "scientific evidence" is produced. How this takeover occurred, and how it affects the quality of the medical information that well-informed, dedicated doctors rely on to make clinical decisions, is the subject of the next chapter.

CHAPTER 7

THE COMMERCIAL TAKEOVER OF MEDICAL KNOWLEDGE

From their first day of training, medical students are taught to trust the research published in peer-reviewed medical journals. They learn to take for granted that publication of research findings in these journals ensures that the principles of rigorous science have been followed: that the research has been properly designed to answer the question in a way that can be translated into clinical practice; that the data have been analyzed fairly and completely; that the conclusions drawn are justified by the research findings; and that the scientific evidence that has been published constitutes our best medical knowledge. This medical literature then serves as the source that enables doctors to keep current with new developments in medicine.

As part of my fellowship in the early 1980s, I spent many hours with some very smart people, meticulously analyzing and critiquing scientific articles. Of course there were flaws and limitations in virtually every study, but I can't remember a single instance when the validity of a study was called into question because of manipulation of the data or compromise of the rules of science to gain commercial advantage. That vision of the medical literature now seems as quaint as Norman Rockwell's painting of the boy standing on a chair, bending forward slightly, about to get an injection in his backside from his trusted doctor.

It's not news that medical research has become big business, often with billions of dollars on the line. The problem is that the search for scientific truth is, by its very nature, unpredictable, and this uncertainty is hardly optimal from a business point of view. There is far too much at stake to leave this process to the uncertainties of science. In this context, the role of the drug and medical-device companies has evolved so that their most important products are no longer the things they make. Now their most important product is "scientific evidence." This is what drives sales. In this commercial context, the age-old standards of good science are being quietly but radically weakened, and in some cases abandoned. Here's how it works.

THE MEDICAL INDUSTRY STARTS TO CALL THE SHOTS

Prior to 1970, medical researchers had relatively little problem obtaining funding from the National Institutes of Health, and few medical studies were sponsored solely by drug companies. An article published in the journal *Science* in 1982 describes medical scientists thumbing "their academic noses at industrial money" in the 1970s. But as government support for medical research started to decline, scientists and universities were forced to look for alternative sources of support for their research. The medical industry was more than willing to step in and lend a helping hand. Universities had no choice, and researchers' attitudes about commercial funding changed. Government funding continued to decline so that by 1990 almost two-thirds of requests for research funds from the NIH were not granted. Meanwhile, between 1977 and 1990, drug company expenditures on research and development increased sixfold, and much of the money went to support university-based clinical research.

This shift in the source of funding set the stage for what was to follow. In 1991, four out of five commercially sponsored clinical drug studies were still being conducted by universities and academic medical centers. Academic researchers still played key roles in all phases of the research, from designing studies to recruiting patients to analyzing data to writing the articles and submitting them for publication. This may have been good for medical science and good for universities, but it was certainly not optimal for the drug and medical-device companies. Research done in university medical centers cost more and involved more administrative hoops and delays. Most important, the checks and balances present in an academic environment could be sidestepped if the research dollars were taken elsewhere.

As drug and biotech industries assumed an ever-larger role in funding clinical trials (reaching 80 percent by 2002), they increasingly exercised the power of their purse. Control over clinical research changed— quietly at first, but very quickly, and with profound effects on medical practice. The role of academic medical centers in clinical research diminished precipitously during the 1990s as the drug industry turned increasingly to new independent, for-profit medical research companies that emerged in response to commercial funding opportunities. These companies could gain access to patients for clinical research through community-based doctors, or play a larger role in research design, data analysis, and even writing up the findings and submitting complete articles to journals for publication. By 2000, only one-third of clinical trials were being done in universities and academic medical centers, and the rest were being done by for-profit research companies that were paid directly by the drug companies.

Increased reliance on private research companies allowed the drug industry to kill two birds with one stone: It could now call the shots on most of the studies that were evaluating its own products without having to accept input from academics who were grounded in traditional standards of medical science. And the increasing competition for commercial research dollars put academic centers under even more pressure to accept the terms offered by the commercial sponsors of research, threatening the independence and scientific integrity that had been the hallmark of the academic environment. In 1999 Dr. Drummond Rennie, deputy editor of the *Journal of the American Medical Association*, characterized the response of academic institutions to this changing climate: "They are seduced by industry funding, and frightened that if they don't go along with these gag orders, the money will go to less rigorous institutions. It's a race to the ethical bottom."

AN ALARM IS SOUNDED

In September 2001 an unprecedented alarm was sounded. The editors of 12 of the world's most influential medical journals, including the *Journal of the American Medical Association,* the *New England Journal of Medicine, The Lancet,* and the *Annals of Internal Medicine,* issued an extraordinary joint statement in their publications. In words that should have shaken the medical profession to its core, the statement told of "draconian" terms being imposed on medical researchers by corporate sponsors. And it warned that the "precious objectivity" of the clinical studies that were being published in their journals was being threatened by the transformation of clinical research into a commercial activity.

The editors said that the use of commercially sponsored clinical trials "primarily for marketing . . . makes a mockery of clinical investigation and is a misuse of a powerful tool." Medical scientists working on corporate-sponsored research, the editors warned, "may have little or no input into trial design, no access to the raw data, and limited participation in data interpretation."

Commercial influence on medical research raises two kinds of concerns: First, what is being studied? Those who pay the piper get to call the tune. The drug companies' funding buys them the right to set the research agenda. The result of commercial sponsorship is that medical knowledge grows in the direction that maximizes corporate profits, in much the same way that plants grow toward sunlight. The questions that do get answered, and thus become our medical knowledge, are often not the ones that will contribute most to improving our health.

Second, is commercially sponsored research "disinterested," or neutral, enough to stand as good science? There is mounting evidence that it is not. One would have expected that, after the editors' extraordinary warning of the mounting threat to the integrity of clinical research, scientific business would not just go on as usual; that this public airing of concern about the health of our medical science would have created a stir in the media and alerted doctors across the country to the commercial bias in their most trusted source of medical knowledge. But it didn't, and most doctors still hold fast to the basic tenet of their training: that the scientific evidence reported in respected peer-reviewed medical journals is to be trusted and serve as the basis of good medical care.

Studies repeatedly document the bias in commercially sponsored research, but the medical journals seem powerless to control the scientific integrity of their own pages. In 2003, separate studies were published in JAMA and the *British Medical Journal* showing that the odds are 3.6 to 4 times greater that commercially sponsored studies will favor the sponsor's product than studies without commercial funding. And in August of 2003 a study published in JAMA found that among the highest-quality clinical trials, the odds that those with commercial sponsorship will recommend the new drug are 5.3 times greater than for studies funded by nonprofit organizations. The authors noted that the lopsided results of commercially sponsored research may be "due to biased interpretation of trial results." They cautioned that readers should "carefully evaluate whether conclusions in randomized trials are supported by data." In other words, doctors are warned that the conclusions of even the best research published in the best journals *cannot* be taken at face value: Caveat lector—let the reader beware. This is the sorry state of the "scientific evidence" on which medical practice is based in the United States today.

Although many doctors have a gut feeling that there is a pro-industry bias in the scientific evidence that guides their care, almost all of the information that comes their way, including the opinions of the experts they trust, reinforces the validity of this "knowledge." Plus, the findings are made to appear so overwhelmingly compelling and contain such enormous hope to provide ever more effective care to their patients that it is hard not to be a believer. There is a magical quality to all this progress that causes us to suspend our better judgment and seduces us into believing that what we are hearing and seeing is really true.

The techniques used by world-class magicians are nearly impossible to spot, but once their methods are exposed, the magic quickly fades. The rest of this chapter explores the techniques used by the most talented masters of commercial medicine to brilliantly skew and slant their findings in the production of their "scientific" illusions.

BROADENING THE MARKET:
WHO NEEDS A DEFIBRILLATOR?

After new drugs and medical devices are introduced to the market, the manufacturers go to great lengths to convince health care professionals that their products should be used for an ever-expanding range of symptoms. The case for implantable defibrillators is a perfect example. A patient of mine, Mr. Peters, is a 78-year-old easygoing retired mechanic who has been living alone since his wife passed away. A few years ago he was hospitalized for what turned out to be a small heart attack. While he was resting peacefully in his hospital bed, without warning his heart suddenly went into ventricular fibrillation (a rapidly fatal arrhythmia in which the heart's ventricular contractions become chaotic and ineffective). The nurses saved his life by responding to the alarm set off by his heart monitor, immediately initiating cardiopulmonary resuscitation (CPR) and successfully shocking his heart back into a normal rhythm with defibrillator paddles applied to his chest.

The risk of this lethal arrhythmia recurring over the next two years was high, making Mr. Peters a perfect candidate for an implantable cardiac defibrillator. Just like U.S. Vice President Cheney, Mr. Peters had a defibrillator—an electrical device slightly smaller than a pack of cigarettes—surgically inserted underneath the skin of his chest.

About two months later, Mr. Peters was standing in his kitchen when, with absolutely no warning, he was suddenly knocked to the floor. Lying there, he realized that the jolt must have come from the cardiac defibrillator, and indeed, the recorder built into the device showed that his heart had once again gone into ventricular fibrillation. This episode probably would have been fatal without the defibrillator. When Mr. Peters told me this story, he was clearly grateful that his life had been saved by the device. And he chuckled about having been knocked to the floor.

The cost of the defibrillator is another story—about $25,000 for the device and another $5,000 to $15,000 for the doctor and hospital charges. Medicare covers the costs, and the therapy is, literally, lifesaving. But the number of people who survive ventricular fibrillation to become candidates for implantable defibrillators is limited. After its initial success with patients such as Mr. Peters, Guidant, the manufacturer, set its sights on a much larger group of patients.

Guidant turned its attention to the 400,000 Americans whose hearts are weakened each year by heart attacks, but who, unlike Mr. Peters, have not experienced life-threatening disturbances of their heart rhythm. These patients have a much higher risk of dying than do heart attack victims whose hearts remain strong: about 20 percent die in the 20 months following their heart attacks. Guidant hit a grand slam when a study was published in the NEJM showing a significant benefit of implanted defibrillators in this population. The patients who were randomly assigned to receive a defibrillator had 31 percent less risk of dying over the next 20 months than the patients in the control group. The article concluded that "prophylactic implantation of a defibrillator [in patients with hearts weakened by heart attacks] improves survival and should be considered as a recommended therapy."

On the surface, this appears to be the best of all worlds: private enterprise motivated by the prospect of greater earnings discovering new ways to save lives. But let's look at the results of this study from a slightly different perspective. For the first nine months of the study there was no difference between the death rate in the people who got the defibrillator and those who did not. Over the next 11 months, 5.6 percent fewer people who received defibrillators died. Based on these results, if 1000 heart attack patients with weakened hearts received defibrillators, a total of 56 would be alive at the end of 20 months who would otherwise have died. The other 944 patients would derive no benefit. In fact, there would be a downside for them: for each life saved by the defibrillator, there would be one additional hospitalization for congestive heart failure among the people who got defibrillators, compared with the control group.

The cost per year of life saved? Between $1.1 and $1.5 million, without including the cost of the additional hospitalizations required for the people who developed congestive heart failure.* Though it may sound

---

*Defibrillators for 1000 patients would cost $30 million to $40 million. A total of 308 months of life were saved among the 1000 patients over the last 11 months of the 20-month study. So each month of life extended by defibrillators in heart attack patients with weak hearts costs $100,000 or more, according to the company's data.

callous, around $100,000 per year of life saved is considered the upper limit of cost-effectiveness for routine medical interventions. Although this number may be drifting upward as new, more expensive technologies are introduced, more than $1 million per year of life saved is clearly a staggering sum for any nation, even the richest in the world.

The NEJM article failed to mention that there is good evidence that there are other, much less expensive ways to prevent many more deaths among these high-risk patients. Only three years before the NEJM study, *Circulation*, the journal of the American Heart Association, published an article in which a group of Italian researchers looked at the effects of exercise training on a similar group of people with weakened hearts. This study randomized patients to receive either exercise training three times a week for eight weeks and then twice a week for one year, or to be in the control group and receive no exercise training. The results were dramatic: The risk of death was reduced by 63 percent in the exercise group (more than twice the benefit of the defibrillator); the risk of hospitalization for congestive heart failure went down by 71 percent (instead of up by 33 percent in the patients who received implanted defibrillators); and both exercise capacity and quality of life improved significantly in the exercise group and remained improved for the 40 months of the study ($p < .001$ for both).

The patients in this study were not exactly the same as those in the defibrillator study, but they did have similar mortality rates (about 20 percent per 20 months for the control groups). In absolute terms, twice as many lives were saved by exercise (22.8 percent over 40 months) as were saved by implanted defibrillators (5.6 percent over 20 months).

The study sponsored by Guidant made no mention of changes in exercise capacity and quality of life in the heart attack patients who received implanted defibrillators. Nor did it reference the Italian study in *Circulation* showing the dramatic benefits of exercise in a similar population of patients.

There is another effective and inexpensive tool to help these patients that was overlooked: smoking cessation. Eighty percent of the patients in the defibrillator study were either "current or former smokers." How many of those patients were still smoking? The NEJM article does not tell us, but we do know from a review article in the *Archives of Internal Med-*

icine that smoking cessation after heart attack is associated with 1.5 to 2 times as much benefit as a defibrillator. The NEJM article reporting the benefits of implanted defibrillators did not venture beyond the interests of the study's sponsor; there was no mention of exercise, smoking cessation, or other lifestyle changes.

While there were no technical violations in Guidant's defibrillator study, sleight of hand was at work: the study was presented as if its purpose were to determine the best treatment for heart attack patients with weakened hearts. Closer inspection suggests that its real purpose was to create scientific evidence that would support sales of Guidant's product. The study of defibrillators could easily have been designed to include lifestyle interventions, but, like the vast majority of commercially sponsored studies, it didn't. Such a study might well have shown that defibrillators do play a role in the optimal treatment of some heart attack patients with weakened hearts. If so, that finding would have provided invaluable information to doctors. Instead, we are left not knowing the appropriate role of this potentially remarkable device in post–heart attack patients. Such research issues will not be addressed by the drug and medical-device companies as long as sales are rolling along. Why would the company that makes implantable defibrillators risk doing a study that might show that lifestyle changes were more effective than its expensive devices? That's not its job.

TINKERING WITH DOSAGES

The first step in a clinical trial is to decide what the drug or medical device will be compared with. The researchers then decide upon the doses for both the new and comparison drug(s). Companies can design studies in which the doses of the drugs being compared are not equivalent.

For example, Nexium, the "purple pill" for gastroesophageal reflux disease (GERD), is chemically almost identical to the acid-blocking drug Prilosec. Both are manufactured by AstraZeneca. In 2001, the patent was about to expire on Prilosec. This basically means that a drug's "recipe" enters the public domain, and other companies can manufacture generic equivalents of it that sell for a small percentage of the price of the brand-name drug. So AstraZeneca sponsored "head-to-head" studies between Prilosec and Nexium, whose patent would remain in effect for several more years. One such study, done at the Cleveland Clinic, concluded that Nexium "demonstrates significantly greater efficacy than [Prilosec] in the treatment of GERD patients with erosive esophagitis." It sounds as though doctors should abandon Prilosec and start prescribing the newer Nexium. The catch is that the dose of Nexium used in the study was 40 mg, but the dose of Prilosec was only half of that. Would 40 mg of Prilosec daily work as well as 40 mg of Nexium daily? The drug company never bothered to find out. Does 20 mg of Nexium work better than 20 mg of Prilosec? Not according to AstraZeneca's own research. Nonetheless, Nexium 20 mg costs $4.90 per dose, while Prilosec 20 mg without a prescription costs about one-eighth as much.

COMPARING SOMETHING WITH NOTHING

One might think that a new drug earns its place among preferred therapies only after it has been shown to be superior, or at least equal, to the best available therapies. Often this is not the case. Expensive brand-name drugs are frequently tested against a placebo (meaning no therapy) even when effective alternative therapies are already in use. Evidence of being significantly more effective than no treatment is sufficient for the FDA to approve new drugs and for doctors to prescribe them in place of older, established, and usually less expensive treatments. A study of OxyContin, a long-acting form of oxycodone (commonly known as Percocet), provides a particularly dramatic example.

The study was designed to test OxyContin's ability to provide relief to patients who were having "moderate to very severe" pain following knee replacement surgery. Patients were randomized into two groups: those assigned to the treatment group received OxyContin twice daily as "preemptive" pain medication, in a dose equal to six Percocet tablets over each 24-hour period. The patients assigned to the control group (also having moderate to very severe pain) were given twice-daily preemptive doses of a placebo. Patients in both groups could request a single Percocet tablet every four hours if they were uncomfortable, and the preemptive doses of pain medication were adjusted based on patients' requests for additional medication—meaning that the patients in the treatment group who were having breakthrough pain received a higher dose of OxyContin and those in the control group received a higher dose of an inert pill. Can you guess which group had more pain? A hint: the people in the OxyContin group averaged the equivalent of more than 10½ Percocet tablets per day, while the people in the control group averaged 2½ Percocet tablets per day. The results of this study, published in the *Journal of Bone and Joint Surgery*, concluded: "Preemptive use of controlled-release oxycodone [OxyContin] during rehabilitation following total knee arthroplasty [replacement] leads to improved pain control, more rapid functional recovery, and a reduced need for inpatient rehabilitative services."

In other words, treatment of moderate to very severe pain after knee replacement surgery with preemptive doses of OxyContin is superior to treatment with preemptive doses of nothing. Based on this study, the drug manufacturer earned the right to claim that treating post–knee replacement surgery patients with OxyContin significantly decreases their pain, facilitates their rehabilitation, and shortens the time spent in rehabilitation centers. Does this mean that routine "preemptive" treatment with OxyContin is more effective than routine "preemptive" treatment with other shorter-acting (and much less expensive) pain medication? This study leaves that question unanswered.

STUDYING THE WRONG PATIENTS

The next step in designing a clinical trial is to determine the characteristics of the people to be included in the study. Ideally, people included in a trial reflect the population of patients to whom the results will be applied—those most likely to use the drug or device being tested. But this is not always the case, as we've seen with the studies supporting the use of both Vioxx and Pravachol. Many studies choose a population that is younger and fitter than the target population, and therefore less likely to show side effects. An editorial in the *Canadian Medical Association Journal* pointed out that only 2.1 percent of all patients in studies of anti-inflammatory drugs are over the age of 65; yet senior citizens, the editorial points out, "are among the largest users" of these drugs and are more likely to have serious complications from them. The editorial also indicts research on drugs for Alzheimer's disease: A study to determine the effectiveness of one such drug, Aricept, restricted the range of patients to age 65 to 74 and excluded people with other medical problems besides Alzheimer's disease, thus minimizing the likelihood of side effects. The problem is that the vast majority of patients for whom this drug will be prescribed are older than this, and therefore the results of the study do not apply to them. As the editorial pointed out, "If frail older patients are going to be targeted for dementia therapy we need to study this group in clinical trials to ensure the safe administration of the drug."

Studies of cancer drugs are similar. Nearly two-thirds of all cancer patients are 65 or older, but only one-quarter of the people in cancer studies have reached 65. Most of these studies exclude older patients by requiring that participants be able to take care of themselves independently or be able to work. Conducting research on only the strongest subset of cancer patients is not a good way to find out how to treat most cancer patients. Perhaps older people will have more severe reactions or derive less (or possibly more) benefit from the cancer therapies being tested. In any event, the systematic inclusion of unrepresentative patients in clinical studies may be good for the profits of the commercial sponsors of the studies (at least in the short term), but it is not good for the people who will receive care based on this distorted "science."

GETTING OUT WHILE THE GETTING IS GOOD

Even when studies are designed to enroll the right mix of patients, make fair comparisons between drugs, and measure valid end points, there is still no guarantee that they won't be prematurely stopped. That's what happened in a study sponsored by Pharmacia, ironically titled CON-VINCE. The study compared Pharmacia's blood pressure drug Covera, a long-acting reformulation of an older calcium channel blocker, with far less expensive standard therapies, a beta blocker (atenolol) and a diuretic (hydrochlorothizide). This huge study included 16,600 patients and was planned to continue for five years, yet it was stopped two years early. The results up to that point showed that the sponsor's more expensive drug was slightly less effective at preventing the complications of high blood pressure than the less expensive drugs. According to an editorial in JAMA, the decision to stop the study went against the recommendation of its own data and safety-monitoring board. Ignoring its own experts, the CONVINCE study quit while it was behind. What rationale did the sponsor give for stopping the drug trial? According to the JAMA editorial, "business considerations." What were they? We may never know, but I'd hazard a guess that it had something to do with the fact that the sponsor's drug, costing about $1.50 per day, was proving to be no better than the generic drugs that cost as little as 15 cents per day. Nonetheless, doctors continue to prescribe calcium channel blockers for hypertension more than any other drugs, believing them to be in some way better. The marketing is evidently still "convincing," even if the scientific evidence is not.

KEEPING THE REAL DATA HIDDEN

Often the medical researchers who carry out company-sponsored studies are not even allowed to see all of the data from the studies they are working on. These researchers are left in the position of analyzing and including in their articles only the data that the drug or device manufacturers have allowed them to see. In May 2000, Dr. Thomas Bodenheimer brought many of these issues to light in an important article in the *New England Journal of Medicine* titled "Uneasy Alliance: Clinical Investigators and the Pharmaceutical Industry." One researcher quoted in the article explained that controlling access to the data allows drug companies to "provide the spin on the data that favors them."

The September 2001 joint statement issued by the editors of major medical journals weighed in heavily on this important issue: "we strongly oppose contractual agreements that deny investigators the right to examine the data independently. . . . Such arrangements not only erode the fabric of intellectual inquiry that has fostered so much high-quality clinical research, but also make medical journals party to potential misrepresentation." Practicing doctors count on the articles in medical journals to present and interpret the complete data, thus providing the "scientific evidence" that they trust to guide their patient care decisions. If even the researchers who write the articles have access to only the data that the corporate sponsors allow them to see, how can anyone have confidence in the "scientific evidence" published in the medical journals? And how can anyone have confidence in the medical care that is based upon results that have been censored to serve commercial interests?

The editors revised the guidelines of the International Committee of Medical Journal Editors to make explicit the recommendation that researchers have control over their data, analysis, and publication of their work. A follow-up study was done a year later to see if the new guidelines were being honored in university-based research contracts. It turns out that, despite their highly unusual public statement, the medical editors might as well have been whispering into the wind. The study found that their recommendations had not been implemented, and concluded that "academic institutions rarely ensure that their investigators have . . . unimpeded access to trial data."

Before any medical article is accepted for publication in a respectable journal, it is peer-reviewed. Independent experts are called upon to evaluate the study's data, and to concur (or not) with the authors' analyses and conclusions. Most doctors believe that this peerreview process guarantees the integrity and completeness of the scientific evidence presented. But peer reviewers see only the data that have been included in the article—not all of the data the authors had access to and certainly not all of the data from the study. Readers of medical journals cannot assume that the process of peer review ensures fair and impartial presentation of research results.

USING GHOSTWRITERS AND RUBBER STAMP EXPERTS

Yet another way that drug companies can make sure that research results are written to best represent their interests is to hire ghostwriters to write the original draft of the article after a clinical trial is completed. As described by Melody Petersen in the *New York Times,* the ghostwriter submits his or her draft to the drug company, which then passes it along for final approval to the authors of record—often busy doctors who are happy not to have to labor over the first draft. The problem with this system is that the drug companies get to infuse their perspective into the results from the very beginning. Dr. Linda Logdberg, a former medical ghostwriter, explained that drug companies "will drop a doctor if they don't think he will be particularly malleable." The *New York Times* article says, "The result . . . is marketing masquerading as science." According to a study published in JAMA, 11 percent of the articles published in peer-reviewed medical journals are written by "ghost authors." (And 19 percent of the articles named "honorary authors" who had not contributed enough to the research and writing to justify being listed as authors.)

CONTROLLING THE DAMAGE

Even when studies that do not support the use of a sponsor's product are published in medical journals, there is still a chance that well-funded marketing and public relations efforts will be able to protect drug sales. The Antihypertensive and Lipid-Lowering Treatment to Prevent Heart Attacks Trial (ALLHAT) study,* for instance, compared the effectiveness of four drugs in preventing complications from high blood pressure. The study had been designed to measure important outcomes (heart attack and the broader category of cardiovascular disease—heart disease, stroke, other vascular disease, and the need for cardiac procedures to open blocked arteries). The study was to continue for four to eight years, but a part of it was stopped prematurely because the people who had been assigned to take one of the brand-name blood pressure drugs, Cardura—manufactured by Pfizer—were developing significantly more cardiovascular complications (particularly congestive heart failure) than the people taking a diuretic. At the time the results were published in JAMA, in April 2000, about $800 million worth of Cardura was being

---

*Sponsored by the National Heart, Lung, and Blood Institute, part of the U.S. National Institutes of Health.

sold worldwide each year. The diuretic that was proving more effective than Cardura at preventing the complications of high blood pressure cost about one-seventh as much.

According to a report in the *British Medical Journal,* as soon as they learned of the disastrous results for their drug, Pfizer hired damage-control consultants. The consultants discovered that most doctors simply weren't aware of this research, and weren't aware that Cardura ought not to be their first choice for the treatment of high blood pressure. So Pfizer simply kept quiet.

The American College of Cardiology (ACC), however, responded to the findings published in the JAMA article by issuing a press release, posted on its website, recommending that doctors "discontinue use" of Cardura. But within hours, the ACC downgraded its warning, recommending only that doctors "reassess" their use of Cardura. What happened? A confidential memo from Pfizer to the ACC requested a "clarification" of the ACC's original press release. Bear in mind that Pfizer contributes more than $500,000 each year to the ACC.

The next round of results from the ALLHAT study came out two years later and contained more bad news for the manufacturers of brand-name blood pressure medicines. Again the low-cost diuretic was shown to be equal to or better than the higher-cost drugs—this time a calcium channel blocker (Norvasc) and an angiotensin-converting enzyme (ACE) inhibitor (Zestril and Prinivil). If medical practice were truly "evidence-based," these results would have been a major problem for the manufacturers of the far more expensive but not as effective brand-name drugs. But not such a problem if the game is really hardball dressed up as evidence-based medicine. A strategic marketing consultant for the pharmaceutical industry was quoted in the *British Medical Journal* as saying, "So you've got one study that says yes, you should [use a diuretic], then starting the day after, you've got a $10 billion industry . . . and 55 promotional events . . . for an ACE inhibitor coming back in and saying 'Here's why my ACE inhibitor is safe and here's why you should be using this.' I mean, it's promotion. Can ALLHAT stand up to that?" Almost certainly not.

Research results cannot always be hidden when studies don't come out in the drug company's favor, but that doesn't mean drug companies don't try to influence researchers to minimize the damage. Dr. William

Applegate, then from the University of Tennessee, was a principal investigator in a study of a new blood pressure pill, DynaCirc, sponsored by the drug maker Sandoz (now Novartis). Not long before a dramatic meeting at which researchers were going to be shown the results of their study, Applegate was offered a $30,000-a-year consulting position with the drug company. He turned down the offer. Then, when he saw the data, he told the *Baltimore Sun,* "I thought the company was trying to buy my favor and my opinion." It was simple. Sandoz's new blood pressure drug had a higher rate of complications than the older drug with which it had been compared. The company twice made offers of research grants to Applegate's research center, each time asking whether he had reconsidered his conclusions about the study.

Applegate eventually resigned from the project along with three of his colleagues. In a letter to JAMA, explaining the reason for their departure, the investigators stated: "We believed that the sponsor of the study was attempting to wield undue influence on the nature of the final paper. This effort was so oppressive that we felt it inhibited academic freedom and led to substantial differences . . . with regard to the ultimate presentation and interpretation of the results." Dr. Applegate and his three colleagues endorsed the ultimate presentation of the study in JAMA, but most likely their willingness to resign on principle in the face of drug-company pressure played an important role in the publication of a fair report.

As the function of medical research in our society has been transformed from a fundamentally academic and scientific activity to a fundamentally commercial activity, the context in which the research is done has similarly changed: first in universities funded primarily by public sources, then in universities funded primarily by commercial sources, then by independent for-profit research organizations contracting directly with drug companies. And most recently, the three largest advertising agencies, Omnicom, Interpublic, and WPP, have bought or invested in the for-profit companies that perform clinical trials. These advertising agencies are now full-service operations, as an executive for one of the biggest health care marketing companies told the *New York Times:* "We provide services that go from the beginning of drug development all the way to the launch of your products." The dialectic of the market rolls along.

There is nothing illegal or unethical about these commercial arrangements, but both the public's interest and the commercial sponsor's interest cannot always be served simultaneously: Either a study is designed to maximize sales or it is designed to determine the best way to prevent or treat a particular health problem. Certainly commercially sponsored research has produced important findings. But at best, the medical knowledge produced by commercial interests is restricted to the medical problems that are most profitable to study. And at worst, research is manipulated, misrepresented, or withheld, with the goal of maximizing sales. The most visible consequence of this is ignoring diseases like malaria, which causes millions of unnecessary deaths each year but has little appeal to industry because the disease occurs in the third world, where there are relatively few paying customers. Much less obvious is the extent to which it has become accepted as "normal" to sacrifice the well-known standards of medical science to achieve commercial goals.

The drug companies pour billions of dollars each year into medical research, and they need to have a number of successes in order to stay in business. Nonetheless, as Drs. Bruce Psaty and Drummond Rennie said in a JAMA editorial, "Medical research, even if it is conducted by the pharmaceutical industry, is not solely a commercial enterprise designed to maximize personal gain or company profits. The responsible conduct of medical research involves a social duty and a moral responsibility that transcends quarterly business plans or the changing of chief executive officers."

CHAPTER 8

THE SNAKE
AND THE STAFF

DUPING THE DOCTORS

If it weren't so important, my struggle to keep up with all the new developments in medicine that came across my desk would bring to mind the hilarious scene from *I Love Lucy* when Lucy and Ethel struggle in vain to package the chocolates flying by them on a conveyor belt. The sheer volume of new material is overwhelming. Perhaps if doctors had the time to critically analyze each article before adopting its conclusions and recommendations, they would see through the commercial bias; but there are not enough hours in the day. Even the most disciplined practitioner cannot keep up with more than one or two medical journals, let alone with all of the new drugs and developments in all of the different fields of medicine. Since few doctors have the time to figure out which new drugs or procedures are real improvements—and for which patients—it should come as no surprise that the medical industry, well aware that doctors are responsible for about 80 percent of all health care expenditures, is more than willing to lend a helping hand.

From the moment doctors enter medical school to the moment they retire, drug companies and medical-device manufacturers attempt to influence their medical decisions. Armed with their industry-generated

medical research, marketing and sales departments rarely miss an opportunity to persuade doctors to incorporate new drugs and products into
their practices. Medical students and residents are treated to free lunches
while they listen to subtle and not so subtle infomercials. Company salespeople schmooze and muscle their way into doctors' offices, leaving
behind a trail of freebies emblazoned with their products' names. Doctors are invited to learn about new medical breakthroughs at free suppers
and conferences in tropical paradises. And most pernicious: companies
lure doctors into becoming paid consultants, staff experts, or lecturers,
leveraging their relationships and prestige to hawk the companies' products to their peers.

Doctors tend to believe that they are immune to drug company
influence. They don't realize that at every step of the way, at every
moment of information transfer, and with nearly unimaginable skill, the
medical industry insinuates itself into their medical decision making.
And often this influence is invisible. Even if a doctor wants to avoid these
entanglements and relationships, the culture of American medicine is
such that he or she has to make a special effort to maintain what appears
to colleagues as an outsider, holier-than-thou code of ethics. Doctors finish their training at about age 30, with enormous medical school debts
and in many cases young families. Accepting freebies or financial support
from industry sponsors seems like a reasonable reward for their efforts.
The practice is so pervasive and looks like such standard operating procedure that many doctors believe that it doesn't adversely affect their
patient care. Unfortunately, they are wrong.

TRUSTING THE MEDICAL JOURNALS, TOO MUCH

According to the editor of the *British Medical Journal*, Dr. Richard Smith,
"The major journals try to counterbalance the might of the pharmaceutical industry, but it is an unequal battle—not least because journals
themselves profit from publishing studies funded by the industry."

The journals benefit from the publicity gained from publishing large
drug company–sponsored studies. This increases the value of their
advertising and enables them to sell back to the drug companies reprints

of articles, which the drug companies then distribute as marketing tools to doctors. According to Dr. Smith, this can amount to more than $1 million for a single article. At the same time that medical journals are given incentives to please the drug companies, they are also given strong disincentives to go against drug company interests. According to Dr. Marcia Angell, former editor of NEJM, editors of medical journals exercise self-censorship—trying to avoid offending their chief advertisers, the drug companies.

Dr. Robert Fletcher learned about this firsthand. In 1992, he was editor of the *Annals of Internal Medicine* when it published an article reporting that 44 percent of the drug ads in medical journals were written in a way that would lead doctors with no other source of information to prescribe improperly. The article also reported that 92 percent of these ads were in some violation of FDA rules. Writing in *The Lancet* in 2003, Dr. Fletcher said that as punishment for publishing this article, the pharmaceutical industry "withdrew many adverts" and showed that it was "willing to flex its considerable muscles when it felt its interests were threatened." This is a price that medical journal editors would prefer not to pay.

NOT TELLING THE WHOLE TRUTH: PUBLICATION BIAS

Even if a doctor could keep up with all the studies that were published, he or she would still have a limited and skewed view of the real evidence. Notwithstanding all the potential ways that research can be tipped in favor of a sponsor's product, clinical trials still tend to reveal the truth about whether a new therapy is effective—or not. The problem is that research that shows that a product is not effective or safe can be hidden away, that is, the "knowledge" can be filtered to let through findings that favor the sponsor's product, making it difficult for even the most fastidious doctors to discover the truth. Positive studies tend to get published quickly, so sales of expensive drugs and new technologies get a jumpstart. Negative studies have a much higher likelihood of not being published at all or being published only after a lag time that protects the company's profits—the public's health be damned.

These words may sound too harsh; surely no drug company would ever go that far. But when the truth finally comes out about how doctors' access to the scientific evidence has been manipulated, we find that this is exactly what happens. One example stands out above all the rest for me because in this case I was seriously misled in the care of so many of my patients. In the 1980s, cardiologists had a low threshold for recommending 24-hour ambulatory heart monitor ("Holter monitor") tests. The purpose of these tests was to identify heart patients who were having irregular heartbeats that put them at increased risk of fatal arrhythmias—like the one Mr. Peters almost suffered. The criteria for starting an antiarrhythmic drug to suppress extra heartbeats were well established, and the degree to which the particular drug and dose had succeeded in suppressing each patient's extra heartbeats could be evaluated by repeating the 24-hour heart monitor test. Few diagnostic tests and therapeutic interventions seemed as important as decreasing these patients' risk of sudden death.

These so-called class I antiarrhythmic drugs* were routinely prescribed into the 1990s. It turned out that even though these drugs do effectively decrease the frequency of extra heartbeats, they *increase* the risk of death. One study documenting a higher death rate in people treated with these drugs was completed in 1980. The results, however, weren't published until 1993. According to a 2003 article in JAMA, had doctors been aware of these findings earlier, their use might have been stopped sooner. The JAMA article then presents a frightening calculation: "There are estimates that 20,000 to 75,000 lives were lost each year in the 1980s in the United States alone from inappropriate administration of [class I] antiarrhythmic drugs." I wonder if any of those were my patients, taking medications that I had prescribed. And I wonder how much more money the drug company made as a result of the 13-year delay in the publication of these findings.

The mistakes of medicine are always easier to see through the "retrospectoscope." What we think we now know about the new antidepressants provides a current example. In a recent survey, respected primary care doctors ranked the new antidepressants as the eighth most impor-

---

*Brand names are Quinaglute, Norpace, and Pronestyl.

tant medical innovation of the past 25 years. And well they should; the scientific evidence available to them left little doubt about the benefit of these drugs. There is, however, a lot of evidence that they couldn't have known about.

When application was made to the Swedish Drug Authority for approval of five new antidepressant drugs, 28 separate clinical trials evaluating the drugs' effectiveness had been published in medical journals. The results were overwhelmingly positive: Twenty-two studies showed that the new drugs were significantly more effective than a placebo, and only 6 showed no difference. In Sweden, drug applications must include *all* known studies—published or not—relevant to the new drug. When researchers from the Swedish Drug Authority went through the new drug applications for the five new antidepressants, they found that a total of 42 studies had been completed. It turned out that exactly half of these showed that the new antidepressants are more effective than the placebos and half found that they are not. The 22 positive articles that had been published represented 19 of the positive studies (three were published twice). In contrast, only six of the 21 studies with negative or inconclusive findings had been published. Even the most conscientious doctor could know only the results of the studies that had been published and would reasonably conclude that the weight of the evidence about the new antidepressants was overwhelmingly positive.

The Swedish researchers commented that their finding that 40 percent of the studies that had been completed on these drugs remained unpublished (as independent studies, not pooled with others) was consistent with the findings of other such reviews. In their conclusion, they warned that "for anyone who relies on published data alone to choose a specific drug, our results should be cause for concern. . . . Any attempt to recommend a specific drug is likely to be based on biased evidence." What else can a practicing physician rely on but the published data? In an understated way, these researchers were telling doctors that they could not trust the published scientific evidence about antidepressants to be complete and unbiased.

In another study, researchers in the United States obtained data under the Freedom of Information Act from all of the studies (both published and unpublished) that the FDA had reviewed in the process of approving seven new antidepressants (Prozac, Zoloft, Paxil, Effexor, Serzone, Remeron, and Wellbutrin SR) between 1987 and 1997—a total of 5200 pages of documents. The results of all of the "pivotal" studies (those deemed to be of high enough quality to be used in the FDA's determinations) for these seven antidepressants were then put together to assess the overall effect of the new drugs. By looking at all the studies, the researchers avoided the distortion of "publication bias" and were able to determine whether or not the scientific evidence really showed that the new antidepressants are more effective and safer than the older ones.

When all the evidence is considered, it turns out that the new antidepressant drugs are no more effective than the older tricyclic antidepressants (the classic being amitriptyline, brand name Elavil). More important, the new antidepressants were found to be not even 10 percent more effective than the placebos: Symptoms of depression improved by 30.9 percent in the people who took the placebos; by 40.7 percent in the people who took the newer antidepressants; and by 41.7 percent in the people who took the older antidepressants. Most doctors will be surprised to know that, for people with less severe depression (in my experience, the majority of patients treated with the new antidepressants by primary care doctors), nine out of 10 studies showed that the new drugs are no more effective than placebos.

One of the disadvantages of the older tricyclic antidepressants is that they are much more dangerous when taken as an overdose. But a very well-kept secret, revealed by considering all the research, is that the actual rate of death from suicide is higher in patients who take the new antidepressants than in those who take the older tricyclics. Even more important, twice as many people taking the new antidepressants successfully committed suicide than did the people who took placebos. The results of all the studies—published *and* unpublished—showed that of every 1000 people with depression treated with one of the new antidepressant drugs, 4.6 more committed suicide each year than would have if they had been treated with a placebo.

Another, more specific example of bias in the research results available to doctors is the "evidence" showing that Paxil is safe and effective for depressed adolescents. A study published in 2001 showed that depressed adolescents were significantly more likely to improve when treated with Paxil than when treated with a placebo. But in May 2003, when the British drug authorities reviewed all nine studies that had been done on Paxil for the treatment of adolescents under the age of 18—only one of which had been published—a very different picture emerged. The patients were no less depressed after taking Paxil than after taking placebos, and the incidence of emotional lability (including suicidal thoughts) was twice as high (3.2 percent versus 1.5 percent). The United Kingdom Medicines and Healthcare Products Regulatory Agency promptly advised that Paxil no longer be prescribed for patients under the age of 18.

When all of the evidence is considered, "breakthrough" is not exactly the first word that comes to mind to describe the effectiveness and safety of the new antidepressant drugs. The one advantage of the new drugs is that they cause about 12 percent fewer side effects, but that hardly justifies using them routinely for all depressed patients, considering the possibility of increased suicide risk and the increased cost.

With only selective reporting of commercially sponsored clinical trials, doctors reading their journals are led to believe that newer drugs are more effective and less dangerous than older drugs, even when the actual scientific evidence points in the other direction. Based on the best information available, antidepressants (almost exclusively the newer ones) were the best selling class of drugs in the United States between 1999 and 2001, and ranked number three behind cholesterol-lowering statins and acid-suppressing drugs in 2002 and 2003. All told, in 2001, Americans spent a total of $12.5 billion on antidepressants. That amounts to $43.85 for every man, woman, child, and infant.

COMMERCIALIZING DOCTORS' CONTINUING EDUCATION

Virtually all doctors keep abreast of developments in their field by regularly attending educational lectures and courses. For most doctors this is mandatory; participation in continuing medical education (CME) is required to maintain their state medical licenses. Lectures and conferences about the latest breakthroughs and state-of-the-art care are presented by experts with impressive academic credentials and are often held at prestigious academic medical centers.

Drs. Arnold Relman and Marcia Angell have publicly lamented the changes in doctors' continuing education meetings over the years: "To many senior physicians who have watched the atmosphere at these meetings decline in quality from the sober professionalism of a few decades ago to the trade-show hucksterism of today, it is a dispiriting spectacle."

I am a little younger. By the time I entered private practice, the drug industry was already playing a significant role in "educating" doctors about new drugs. I had been in practice two years when I attended grand rounds at the local hospital, which was a lecture on pain control given by a faculty member from one of the Boston medical schools. I knew that his talk was drug company–supported, but given his academic position, I didn't think this would influence the content of his presentation. Toward the end of his informative talk he turned his attention to the benefits of a relatively new drug called Zomax, a non-narcotic pain reliever that purportedly provided as much pain relief as codeine, a claim my patients were telling me was really true. The only problem was that Zomax had a propensity to cause serious allergic reactions, some of which had been fatal. The FDA had taken the drug off the market the week before the professor's talk. My recollection is that the manufacturer of Zomax had sponsored the talk, and evidently the terms of the professor's contract had not been updated.

I was well aware of the problems Zomax could cause, because one of my patients, with whom I had enjoyed a particularly good relationship, was at the time suffering from a severe and unrelenting allergic reaction to Zomax. She left my practice because of this drug reaction and threatened to sue me as well. (Fortunately she did not.) Had the FDA not withdrawn this dangerous drug from the market the week before, the professor's talk would have persuaded many doctors in the audience to prescribe Zomax for their patients as well, if they weren't doing so already.

Commercial support for doctors' continuing education courses has been increasing at a rapid clip, doubling between 1996 and 2000. The medical industry (and in particular the drug companies) funded more than three-fifths of doctors' continuing education in 2001. Industry spending on doctors' continuing education then increased by another 30 percent in 2002. By 2003, the drug companies were spending more than $1500 per year on CME for every doctor in the United States, funding 70 percent of all continuing education for doctors. At first glance, this may not appear to be a bad arrangement: Drug companies do busy doctors the service of providing easy access to up-to-date research findings, distilling the information down to concise operational points, all usually within one or two hours. But it's not so simple.

The drug companies understand precisely what it takes to persuade doctors to change their prescribing habits. They know that we have been taught in medical school and during our residencies to accept information that modifies our practice only after it has been "blessed" by doctors farther up the chain of command. In training, these authority figures are the residents, fellows, and attending physicians, depending on where you are in the hierarchy. Practicing physicians in turn look to recognized experts, usually with prestigious academic affiliations.

Marketing mavens call these doctors "thought leaders" or "key opinion leaders" (KOLs)—whether local or national—because they command enough respect to influence the medical decisions made by other doctors. These are the experts chosen to make CME presentations. The medical industry goes to great lengths to cultivate relationships with these experts, in the same way that athletes are recruited for product endorsements. For example, Pfizer, the manufacturer of the best-selling cholesterol-lowering statin drug Lipitor, sponsored a special meeting of leaders in the field of cardiology—doctors who could influence other doctors' prescribing patterns. The meeting was held in Sydney, Australia, and happened to coincide with the 2000 Olympic games. With tactics like this, it is hardly surprising that companies manage to gain the allegiance of influential doctors.

Besides the talks and formal lectures, drug companies also work hard to draw doctors into an environment where they are predisposed to be agreeable—be it a convenient lunch or a luxury resort. In an article published in the *American Journal of Bioethics* titled "All Gifts Large and Small: Toward an Understanding of the Ethics of Pharmaceutical Industry Gift Giving," the authors point out that "food, flattery, and friendship are all powerful tools of persuasion, particularly when combined." It is very difficult to maintain an objective perspective about a particular drug—much less take an opposing point of view—while eating a delicious salmon and wild rice lunch provided by attractive and friendly marketing folks.

I've turned down more offers than I can count for "educational" dinners, sporting events, golf and ski outings, and even weekends in the best hotels plus $500. And I must confess to having given in to temptation on several occasions.

A couple of months after the Boston Celtics were defeated by the Los Angeles Lakers in the historic 1987 NBA world championship series (the last great Larry Bird–versus–Magic Johnson showdown), the manufacturer of the latest anti-inflammatory drug sponsored a weekend outing. The educational courses consisted of the Celtics' team doctors and therapists reviewing the team's injuries: viewing the x-ray of Kevin McHale's heel fracture after game four and seeing how much farther the fracture had extended two games later; learning that another star's back would go out many times each game and needed to be manipulated into place. The conference, I must admit, was fascinating.

The quid pro quo, of course, ranges from subtle pressure to prescribe the company's product to the threat of withdrawing any future funding for research and, of course, to being cut off from future freebies. The expensive new NSAID touted at the conference did not seem to offer any real advantage, and I cannot recall writing many prescriptions for it. The manufacturer offered me no further invitations.

GETTING THEIR MONEY'S WORTH FROM DOCTORS

Does it work? The evidence is quite clear. Notwithstanding doctors' steadfast belief in their resistance to commercial pressure, the drug companies know better: doctors who attend sponsored lectures significantly increase their prescribing of the sponsor's drug. A study followed the prescribing habits of 20 doctors who attended CME seminars sponsored by the manufacturers of two different drugs. Though all but one doctor denied that attendance at the seminars had affected their prescribing habits, all but one of the doctors increased their use of the two drugs in comparison with other doctors at their institutions and in comparison with the national average. Clearly, the doctors had been influenced by education sponsored by drug companies, and it was all the more effective because they naively believed themselves impervious to such influence.

There seems to be no end to the medical industry's influence over CME. Nearly half of the members of the task force that establishes the guidelines for drug industry involvement with CME are directly employed by the drug companies or are their paid consultants. Some drug and medical-device companies actually own their own educational subsidiaries to ensure that the right "educational" message gets communicated.

A report written by the health research group of Public Citizen describes the new industry that has emerged, called medical education and communication companies (MECCs). What are the guiding principles of these MECCs? One of the largest of these companies, Concepts in Professional Education and Communications, representing 14 drug companies, states its purpose succinctly in its marketing materials: "Medical education is a powerful tool that can deliver your message to key audiences, and get those audiences to take action that benefits your product. Whatever combination of audiences you need to motivate in order to exert maximum leverage on the marketplace, we can help you identify them, reach them, and influence their behavior." (What's health got to do with it?)

Purdue Pharma, the maker of the expensive painkiller OxyContin, went one step further. The company gave $3 million to the prestigious Massachusetts General Hospital in return for, among other things, the hospital's renaming its current pain center the MGH Purdue Pharma Pain Center. According to a news release from Massachusetts General, the money will be used to support educational activities, including continuing medical education courses. Part of the agreement, according to the *Boston Globe,* includes MGH pain specialists conducting continuing education seminars on pain control "using Purdue-designed curriculum written, in part, to encourage wary doctors and pharmacists to prescribe pain-killers such as OxyContin." A medical ethicist from Boston University, George Annas, commented: "You don't let outside people write your curriculum. You don't put your name on their curriculum. There's the

potential for that being a curriculum run by the drug companies." Doctors coming to the prestigious Massachusetts General Hospital for continuing education have every reason to believe that the content of the
lectures will be guided by the sole mission of improving patient care. Most
will be unaware of the underlying commercial agenda of the program.

Occasionally, the drug industry pays lip service to complaints of its
marketing excesses. In 2002, Pharmaceutical Research and Manufacturers
of America (PhRMA), the drug industry's trade association, voluntarily
changed its guidelines regarding CME. Permissible offerings are now limited to meals that are "modest as judged by local standards" and occur "in
a venue and manner conducive to informational communication and
provide scientific or educational value." A study done over the following
six months monitored CME for doctors during their residencies (the
most formative years for establishing patterns of interaction with the
drug industry) to determine whether the drug industry's self-imposed
guidelines were being followed. The study concluded: "Findings at our
institution suggest poor compliance with the spirit of the PhRMA guidelines in the first 6 months of their inception. Dinners were frequently held
at high-priced restaurants that are known to be among the best."

The president of PhRMA, Alan Holmer, claims that the drug industry provides a much-needed service to doctors: "Industry-supported
conferences, seminars, and symposia are helping physicians to provide
the best, most appropriate, and most up-to-date health care to their
patients. They help to ensure the widespread adoption of new medicines
and technologies that save lives, cure disease, relieve pain, and allow individuals to lead longer, healthier, and more productive lives." He's
certainly right about one thing: Industry-supported CME definitely
accelerates widespread adoption of new developments in medicine. The
net effect on Americans' health, however, is not so clear.

Who's to blame for the commercial takeover of the education that
keeps doctors up to date on the latest in medical science? It's too easy to
lay all the blame on the drug and medical-device companies and the
medical education and communication companies. Doctors who allow
their reputations and academic positions to be leveraged by drug companies for commercial purposes provide a crucial link in the chain of corporate influence. Most insist that these financial relationships do not

color their opinions, but a review article published in JAMA titled, "Physicians and the Pharmaceutical Industry: Is a Gift Ever Just a Gift?" shows that drug company–sponsored lectures are two-and-a-half to three times more likely to mention the sponsor's drug in a positive light and the competitors' drugs in a neutral or negative light. Doctors who receive honoraria for speaking and research support from a drug company are four and nine times more likely, respectively, to support the use of that company's drug in their hospital. Meanwhile, doctors practicing on the front lines of medicine, drilled to believe new information when it comes from sources they've been taught to accept as legitimate, are unwittingly and effectively influenced by the underlying commercial agenda of the majority of their continuing "education."

Doctors in training are gradually eased into the process so that it seems like a normal part of their educational environment. The gifts and meals start in medical school, but really come into play during residency training, when doctors are developing their prescribing and information-gathering habits. An editorial in *The Lancet* sheds light on how this process evolves: "It starts slowly and insidiously, like an addiction, and can end up influencing the very nature of medical decision-making and practice. It first appears harmless enough: a textbook here, a penlight there, and progresses to stethoscopes and black bags, until eventually come nights 'on the town' at academic conventions and all-expenses-paid 'educational symposia' in lovely locales." It doesn't take long before doctors and drug reps are on a first-name basis.

A 2001 study published in the *American Journal of Medicine* looked at residents' interactions with drug salespeople and their opinions about accepting gifts and attending drug company–sponsored educational activities. Eight out of 10 medical residents saw the inclusion of such sponsored education and interaction with drug reps as "appropriate." This shows how seamlessly drug company infomercials have become integrated into medical training, even in the very best medical centers, just as soft drink and snack machines gradually have become accepted as a normal part of the public school environment. The study commented on the "ubiquity of the [drug] industry's presence" in the residents' environment and on the lack of formal education for residents about the effect of relationships with drug industry salespeople. Eighty-four percent of residents in the study thought that their colleagues were influenced by drug-company promotions, but only 39 percent felt that the same could be said of themselves. A 2003 article in the *British Medical Journal* succinctly summarized these issues: "Twisted together like the snake and the staff, doctors and drug companies have become entangled in a web of interactions as controversial as they are ubiquitous."

INVADING THE DOCTOR'S OFFICE

Anyone who has spent any time in a doctor's office will have noticed the constant parade of attractive and well-dressed drug company sales representatives giving away trinkets to the staff and trying desperately to get a moment of the doctor's time. The number of reps making sales pitches in doctors' offices has *tripled* over the past 10 years. There is now one full-time drug rep for every four and a half office-based doctors. In 2001, drug companies spent $4.7 billion "detailing" ("industry speak" for drug reps' sales calls) to the 490,000 office-based doctors in the United States, or about $10,000 for each doctor per year. And that doesn't include the cost of the drug samples the reps left.

It is difficult for doctors to avoid dealing with sales reps. They are usually pleasant people who are convinced that they are providing a useful service. They are also experts in the art of getting doctors' attention: finding a place to sit or stand from which eye contact with the doctor cannot be avoided, starting their sales pitch when the doctor comes within view, and skillfully creating situations in which the only way to contain their influence is to be uncomfortably and blatantly impolite—often in front of patients. They come bearing free drug samples and many enticing gifts.

I, too, have accepted some of their offerings. A Swiss Army penknife bearing the name of a now forgotten antihistamine was irresistible. Drug companies were very generous in donating medicine for my medical trip to the Amazon, with no strings attached. Once, I accepted a $1000 grant to fund a small trial of alternative healing in my office. (I wanted to see if these services would help my patients, but I didn't feel right charging for therapies that I wasn't sure would be effective.) The quid pro quo for this grant was that I agreed to listen to the drug reps' sales pitches three times. They lost interest after the first meeting took a contentious turn: I asked if they honestly believed that I should use their powerful antibiotic for routine infections or if they were just trying to persuade me to do this because it was their job.

The rule in my office was that the drug reps could talk to the nurses to find out if we needed samples, but not to me. Looking back, I think that the drug reps were quite supple—if not brilliant—in accommodating my anticommercial bias and actually leveraging it to their advantage. We doctors tend to remember the dose, timing, and side effects of only two or three drugs in each class. The drug companies knew this, of course, and were willing to give me a steady supply of samples in order to make sure that I was familiar with their drug instead of a competitor's. With free samples to give out to people who needed them, I felt like Robin Hood. And they (I now realize) felt like very effective drug reps.

You may wonder why 80 to 90 percent of doctors—with all their training and clinical experience—are willing to listen to drug reps at all. Moreover, you may wonder how self-respecting doctors could possibly allow themselves to be influenced by the sales pitches from people with so much less understanding of the complexities and pitfalls of medical practice, and with such obvious commercial motives. The drug reps provide what can seem to busy doctors like a useful service. Along with their trinkets, doughnuts, and free lunches, they arrive with reprints of articles from medical journals and the drug company's own educational materials summarizing the latest medical research. Like CliffsNotes, the drug reps provide doctors with easy-to-read versions of the latest research (that supports their product), allowing the doctors to feel up to date. How accurate is this so-called educational material? According to an article in the *Journal of General Internal Medicine* published in 1996, 42 percent of the material given to doctors by drug reps made claims that were in violation of FDA regulations, and only 39 percent of the material provided scientific evidence to support its marketing claims.

Most doctors firmly believe that their opinions about drugs and scientific evidence are not compromised by these interactions. The research shows otherwise. A review of doctor–drug company interactions, published in JAMA, shows that these interactions have a mostly negative

effect on the quality of medical care. For example, more interaction with
pharmaceutical company marketing people, as well as having drug samples on hand, increases the likelihood that doctors will prescribe newer,
more expensive drugs and fewer generic drugs. The more a doctor sees a
sales rep, the less likely the doctor is to identify false claims about the
drug, and the greater the doctor's tendency to prescribe more drugs
overall. Doctors who interact with drug companies are also about 15
times more likely to request that drugs manufactured by specific companies be stocked in hospital pharmacies.

How do the drug reps and their bosses know that their sales pitches
are working? It's easy to keep track of how many doctors meet with each
rep; how many offices accept samples; how many offices load up on trinkets (pens, notepads, coffee cups, calenders, clocks, and wall posters that
broadcast the message that commercialism is okay); and how many docs
can be rounded up for an "educational" dinner meeting.

But most important, the drug companies purchase from local pharmacies individual doctors' prescribing information, so they know exactly
what we prescribe, and can precisely measure the effect of their reps'
office calls and enticements. (I am happy to report that the small-town
family-owned pharmacy near my office has not succumbed to the temptation to sell this information.)

The upshot is that the drug companies now know much more about
doctors' prescribing habits than doctors know themselves. They also
understand that it doesn't really matter that drug reps don't know as
much about medicine, or that their materials fail to present the whole
truth. The only thing that matters is how to influence doctors. Clearly,
that's the one thing drug reps have down to a science. This raises an
important question: Is that the way you want your doctor to keep
informed about the best medical care for you?

There is one area that has been neglected in all the education provided to doctors by the drug companies: doctors have surprisingly little
awareness of the cost of drugs. Nine out of 10 doctors think that brand-
name drugs cost less than they actually do, and an equal proportion think
that generic drugs cost more than they actually do. Most important, in
terms of the cost of health care, the drugs for which doctors are most
likely to underestimate the cost are those that are most widely prescribed.

DICTATING DOCTORS' ORDERS

Recognizing that no doctor can keep up with the deluge of medical research about all of the different clinical conditions, the medical profession regularly develops clinical practice guidelines to establish the standards that define good medical care. These guidelines are created by panels of nationally recognized clinical experts, and are usually sponsored by nonprofit organizations (such as the American Heart Association, the National Osteoporosis Foundation, or the National Stroke Association), professional societies (such as the American Colleges of Gastroenterology, Psychiatry, or Rheumatology), or governmental agencies.

Clinical guidelines provide expert review of the research and allow doctors to be confident that their decisions regarding patient care reflect the best available scientific evidence. Guidelines also provide benchmarks by which the quality of a doctor's care can be evaluated, and (always lurking in the background of a doctor's thoughts) they are admissible as evidence of the accepted standards of care in medical malpractice cases.

A study published in JAMA in 1999 evaluating the quality of the guidelines showed, ironically, that they often fall short of established standards. The following year *The Lancet* published a report that found that only one out of 20 clinical guidelines examined met established standards of quality for three simple criteria: description of the professionals involved in formulating the guidelines; description of the sources of information used to find the relevant scientific evidence; and grading of the evidence used to support the main recommendations.

In 2000, Canadian researchers from the British Columbia Office of Health Technology Assessment evaluated the quality of the guidelines that addressed the testing of cholesterol levels. They found that four out of five of these guidelines did not reflect the best scientific evidence available. The Canadian researchers also found that "the greater the involvement of clinical experts in the development process of the clinical practice guidelines, the less the recommendations reflected the research evidence."

Then, in 2002, JAMA published the most damning study of all. The study found that four out of five experts who participate in the formulation of clinical practice guidelines have financial relationships with drug companies, averaging more than 10 such relationships each. A whopping *59 percent* of the experts "had relationships with companies whose drugs were considered in the guideline they authored." This would be the equivalent of a judge's having an ongoing financial relationship with one of the litigants in a case he was hearing, or a stockbroker's recommending his uncle's IPO. More than half of the guidelines examined in the JAMA study had not even established a formal process for declaring participants' relationships with drug companies.

The picture that emerges is so contrary to the faith that we doctors place in the process of how medical science gets translated into clinical practice that it may be hard for most doctors to believe. But it's true: the majority of participants in the formulation of clinical guidelines have active financial relationships with companies manufacturing the very drugs that are being decided upon.

CHAPTER 9

A SMOKING GUN

THE 2001 CHOLESTEROL GUIDELINES

In 2001, the Expert Panel on Detection, Evaluation, and Treatment of High Blood Cholesterol in Adults issued perhaps the most influential document in the history of modern American medicine. Written as part of the National Cholesterol Education Program, the updated guidelines incorporated the findings of the most recent clinical trials into concise recommendations designed to assist doctors in reducing their patients' risk of developing coronary heart disease (CHD). The recommendations are bold and offer the tantalizing hope that coronary heart disease in all but the very old will become a far less common occurrence. This goal can be reached, according to the guidelines, by increasing the number of Americans taking statin drugs, from 13 million to 36 million.

The new recommendations call for doctors to measure adult patients' cholesterol and triglyceride levels every five years. A two-step assessment of risk is then suggested: First, "major risk factors" are identi-fied, including cigarette smoking, high blood pressure, low HDL (good) cholesterol (less than 40 mg/dL), a strong family history of coronary heart disease, and older age—i.e., men who have reached the age of 45 and women who have reached the age of 55. For people with two or more major risk factors, the probability of developing coronary heart disease over the next 10 years is then calculated based upon a "risk score" developed from the findings of the Framingham Heart Study. If the risk of developing CHD over the next ten years is 10 percent or more, and the LDL cholesterol level remains 130 mg/dL or higher* after a trial of diet and exercise, the new guidelines call for treatment with a statin drug to head off coronary heart disease at the pass.

The excitement generated by these new guidelines was unprecedented. Dr. Claude Lenfant, the director of the National Heart, Lung, and Blood Institute, under whose auspices the NCEP does its work, told the *New York Times* that if the new guidelines were followed, coronary heart disease "would no longer be the number one killer [in the United States]." With even greater enthusiasm, the lead author of the guidelines, Dr. Scott M. Grundy, said, "These statins are amazing drugs. . . . When you say you can't put that many people on drugs, you've got to balance that against the tremendous devastation of coronary heart disease." This certainly seems like due cause for excitement.

The new guidelines were formulated by a panel of 14 experts and approved by representatives from 22 prestigious nonprofit medical societies, including the American College of Cardiology and the American Medical Association. The guidelines make specific recommendations for men, women, and people 65 and older who do not have coronary heart disease ("primary prevention"), and for those who already do ("secondary prevention"). An 11-page executive summary of the full report was published in the May 16, 2001, issue of JAMA. Virtually all cardiologists and primary care doctors who treat adults are familiar with these recommendations. But few have read the uninviting 284-page full-length version of the NCEP expert panel's report, available on the Internet. Most doctors probably figured it wasn't necessary. The summary assures its readers that the full document is "an evidence-based and extensively referenced report that provides the scientific rationale for the recommendations contained in the executive summary."

---

*More than half of adult Americans over the age of 35 have LDL cholesterol levels of 130 mg/dL or higher.

The updated guidelines rely heavily on the findings of five large clinical trials of CHD prevention with statins that had become available since the previous version of the guidelines were issued in 1993. The executive summary published in JAMA is clear about its primary approach to CHD prevention: after a brief discussion of the changes introduced in the new guidelines and the new method of individual risk assessment, the bulk of the recommendations address LDL cholesterol as "the primary target of therapy." Largely as a result of these guidelines, cholesterol control has become the main focus of preventive health care in the United States.

Doctors aren't required to follow these (or any) guidelines to the letter, but most do for several reasons: they want to practice the best medicine possible; they want their medical decisions to be consistent with community standards; and they know that if they do not follow current guidelines, they have a greater risk of getting sued should something go wrong. For these reasons, plus the enormous publicity that continues to surround the issue of cholesterol, the updated guidelines are playing a larger role than any guidelines that have come before in shaping both doctors' and patients' health care priorities.

But careful scrutiny of the full report of the NCEP—and of the key studies supporting its recommendations—reveals a picture strikingly different from what is presented in the executive summary. Rather than presenting a balanced interpretation of the scientific findings, the report seems intent upon building the case for greater use of statins, preferentially presenting data that support greater statin use and even misrepresenting findings reported in the original articles. And rather than promoting a balanced approach to coronary heart disease prevention and overall health promotion, the guidelines seem more intent upon getting doctors to focus on lowering LDL cholesterol.

THE CHOLESTEROL LINK

The link between elevated cholesterol and increased risk of heart disease was initially identified by researchers from the Framingham Heart Study. Beginning in 1948, this study enrolled 5000 residents of Framingham, Massachusetts, with the goal of identifying the factors that contribute to

coronary heart disease. In 1957 the study first reported that high cholesterol levels increased the risk of heart disease. The different effects of
HDL and LDL cholesterol were described in 1977. (Cholesterol is a waxy
fat that is attached to a protein for transport in the blood. The difference
between "good" cholesterol, HDL, and "bad" cholesterol, LDL, is the protein to which the cholesterol is attached.)

Coronary heart disease develops when one or more of the arteries
that supply blood to the heart muscle become blocked, depriving the
muscle cells of the oxygen and nutrients needed to function properly.
The process starts when LDL cholesterol particles circulating in the
blood pass into the walls of the coronary arteries. This sets off an inflammatory reaction that leads to the buildup of white blood cells and other
material, collectively called plaque, within the walls of the arteries. HDL
cholesterol, on the other hand, seems to pull cholesterol out of the arteries, like a scavenger, and transport it back to the liver.

The buildup of plaque on the inside of artery walls is a slow process,
taking many years. Usually there are no symptoms until the internal
diameter of a coronary artery becomes narrowed by at least 60 percent.
Then, like a garden hose that is being stepped on, the capacity of the partially blocked coronary artery to carry blood to the heart muscle becomes
compromised. When the blood supply to an area of the heart is inadequate to meet increased metabolic demand (during exercise or emotional stress, for example), patients often feel crampy, pressure-like pain
in the left side of the chest, known as angina. When a coronary artery
becomes completely blocked by plaque and there is no other blood supply to the downstream heart tissue, muscle cells die. This is known as a
heart attack.

Most heart attacks are not, however, caused by a gradual buildup of
plaque. The more frequent scenario is that a smaller area of plaque, for
unknown reasons, breaks open ("fractures") or becomes eroded on its
surface. This causes the tiny platelets circulating in the blood to become
sticky and form a small blood clot, or thrombus, on top of the plaque.
Without any warning, thrombus formation can quickly and completely
obstruct the flow of blood through a coronary artery, causing a heart
attack. (Aspirin decreases the risk of heart attack by decreasing the stick-
iness of platelets, thereby making thrombus formation less likely.)

Lowering total and LDL cholesterol with medication, the theory goes, lowers the risk of coronary heart disease by decreasing plaque formation. From the 1960s to the 1980s, drugs of the fibrate class were used to lower cholesterol (though exactly how they worked was not known) and decrease the risk of heart attack. This they did quite well for people who did not yet have heart disease. But after many years of use, as a study done by the World Health Organization found, clofibrate (brand name Atromid-S) *increased* the overall risk of death by 47 percent. (About half the excess deaths were due to cancer.) Similarly, a study done by the National Public Health Institute at the University of Helsinki, Finland, showed that the death rate among people taking the other popular fibrate, gemfibrozil (brand name Lopid), for 8.5 years was 21 percent *higher* than that for the people taking placebos.

The current era of treatment to lower total and LDL cholesterol began in 1987, with the introduction of the first statin drug. Most of the cholesterol in our bodies does not come from our diet but is manufactured in the liver. Statins were developed specifically to mimic one of the intermediate molecules produced in the process of cholesterol synthesis, and thereby trick the liver into slowing down cholesterol production. This decreases the amount of total and LDL cholesterol circulating in the bloodstream. The first statin, Mevacor, is now available as a generic called lovastatin, which costs less than half as much as the brand-name statins. The best-selling statins as of 2003 were Lipitor, Pravachol, and Zocor. The newest entry into the U.S. statin market, Crestor, was approved by the FDA in August 2003.

WHY DOES CHOLESTEROL GET SO MUCH ATTENTION?

It is important to keep in mind that cholesterol is not a health risk in and of itself. In fact, cholesterol is vital to many of the body's essential functions. For example, cholesterol is the most common organic molecule in the brain (this could explain why statins have a small but statistically significant negative effect on cognitive function). It is also an essential building block of many of the body's most important hormones, such as stress hormones, blood sugar–regulating hormones, and sex hormones. (One study that specifically looked for sexual problems associated with cholesterol-lowering therapy found that statins increase the frequency of sexual dysfunction by about 50 percent in men.) Cholesterol is also necessary for the transmission of signals from one nerve cell to the next, and is an integral component of the membrane that surrounds each cell.

The essential role that cholesterol plays in many of the body's biological functions is easily forgotten when one is reading and following the updated guidelines for cholesterol management, and getting caught up in the growing cholesterol-lowering frenzy. The real goal of medical care is, after all, to improve overall health—in this case to decrease the risk of coronary heart disease, serious illness of all kinds, and premature death from all causes—and not simply to lower blood levels of LDL cholesterol.

Even though much of what we know about the relationship between cholesterol and coronary heart disease comes from the Framingham Heart Study, the mother of all cholesterol studies, some of its most important findings will come as a surprise—especially to doctors. An article published in the *Archives of Internal Medicine* in 1993 analyzing data from the Framingham study showed that higher total cholesterol levels significantly correlate with an increased risk of death from coronary heart disease only through the age of 60. This correlation does *not* extend to age 70 or beyond. More important, the article showed that elevated total cholesterol levels correlate with an increased overall risk of death only through the age of 40, and not once the age of 50 is reached. An even more alarming finding from this study, given the current cholesterol-lowering craze, is that the risk of death from causes other than coronary heart disease *increases* significantly with *lower* total cholesterol levels for men and women after they reach the age of 50. (The authors specifically considered but rejected the hypothesis that people with lower cholesterol levels had higher noncardiac death rates because of undiagnosed underlying illness.) Other data from the Framingham Heart Study published in 1999 show that physical activity, unlike total cholesterol levels, is highly correlated with overall mortality rate: The most active third of the original 5000 men and women in the study had a 40 percent lower death rate than the least active third.

So why has our collective national attention become so narrowly focused on lowering LDL cholesterol as the single most important preventive health strategy when the evidence shows that it plays a relatively limited role in our overall health? Part of the answer has to do with the experts' intellectual commitment to the role of cholesterol in heart disease, having dedicated their careers to furthering the scientific understanding of this relationship. Another part of the answer may have to do with some of the authors' potential conflicts of interest: Five of the 14 experts who participated in writing the guidelines, including the chair of the panel, disclosed financial relationships with manufacturers of statin drugs. Four of these five, including the chair of the panel, had relationships with all three manufacturers of the best-selling statins.

And curiously, although the guidelines recommend reduced intake of saturated fat and cholesterol, the words "egg," "beef," and "dairy" do not appear anywhere in the executive summary. (Animal products such as egg yolks, red meat, and dairy fat are the primary dietary sources of saturated fat and cholesterol, and therefore reducing intake of these foods is an integral part of the "therapeutic lifestyle interventions" suggested in the guidelines.) Perhaps the omission has something to do with the fact that, according to the Center for Science in the Public Interest, several of the authors and expert reviewers of the guidelines have, or have had, financial ties to one of the following organizations: the American Egg Board, the National Cattlemen's Association, and the National Dairy Promotion and Research Board. In contrast, increasing fiber intake is mentioned five times in the executive summary. (One of the authors and two of the reviewers have done research on fiber funded by Procter and Gamble, the manufacturer of Metamucil.)

The drug companies have plenty to gain from the pro-drug orientation of the updated guidelines. If the guidelines are followed, sales of cholesterol-lowering statin drugs will increase by at least $20 billion to $30 billion per year. (The total cost will be even more because of the extra doctor visits and blood tests necessary to make sure that the drugs are not causing side effects such as inflammation of the liver or breakdown of muscle tissue.) Of course, experts' financial ties to corporations do not necessarily mean that the report itself is biased by corporate influence. A close comparison of the data and recommendations presented in the guidelines to the available scientific evidence speaks for itself.

PRIMARY PREVENTION OF HEART DISEASE IN MEN YOUNGER THAN 65

Two of the five major studies incorporated into the new guidelines tested the effectiveness of statin therapy in the primary prevention of coronary heart disease. One was the West of Scotland Coronary Prevention Study (WOSCOPS), published in the *New England Journal of Medicine* in 1995. Western Scotland has one of the highest rates of heart disease in the world, and the 6600 men included in the WOSCOPS study were at particularly high risk: their average LDL cholesterol level was 192 mg/dL; 44 percent of them smoked; and, though men with a history of heart attack were excluded from the study, one out of five had symptoms of blocked arteries, such as angina or leg pain with exertion. The men were randomly assigned to receive either a statin drug, Pravachol 40 mg per day, or a placebo.

After almost five years, the men who took Pravachol had 31 percent fewer heart attacks (statistically significant) and 22 percent fewer deaths (not quite statistically significant) than the men in the control group. More relevant than these large reductions in relative risk in determining the real benefit of treating these very high risk men with Pravachol is the actual number of heart attacks and deaths prevented. This turns out to be a much less impressive number: 100 men in the study had to take Pravachol for two full years in order to prevent a single heart attack.* The cost of treating 100 people for two years with Pravachol 40 mg per day was $336,000 (for the drugs alone). In order to prevent a single death, 100 men in the WOSCOPS study would have had to take Pravachol for five and a half years.

Of course, when I was in practice, I wanted to protect my very high risk patients from suffering a heart attack, and recommended they take a statin. At the same time, it is important to remember that even among the

---

*The men who took Pravachol had 1.1 heart attacks per 100 per year; the men in the control group had 1.6. The relative risk reduction is 31 percent because 1.1 heart attacks per 100 men per year is 31 percent lower than 1.6 heart attacks per 100 men per year.

highest-risk men without coronary heart disease, 99 out of every 100 would take Pravachol for two years without any benefit. The problem is that we can't know in advance who the hundredth man is going to be, and for that individual the protection conferred by the statin drug is very important.

In contrast to the very high risk men in the WOSCOPS study, the other major study of primary prevention, the Air Force/Texas Coronary Atherosclerosis Prevention Study (AFCAPS/TexCAPS), included people with only a moderately elevated risk of developing heart disease. Researchers randomly assigned 6600 healthy middle-aged and older people with mildly elevated LDL cholesterol and below-normal HDL cholesterol levels* to be treated with lovastatin (brand name Mevacor) or a placebo for five years. The study then compared the frequency of several health outcomes in the two groups: occurrence of coronary heart disease, any serious disease, death from coronary heart disease, and death from any cause. The guidelines summarize the results: "AFCAPS/TexCAPS is important because it showed that LDL-lowering therapy in persons with only borderline-high LDL cholesterol levels produces a large reduction in relative risk."

Well, sort of. The report neglected to specify the relative risk of what, exactly, the statin reduced. The relative risk of developing coronary heart disease was indeed significantly lower (37 percent) in the people who took the statin compared with those who took placebos. However, the guidelines failed to disclose an even more important measure of the impact of treatment with a statin, a finding that was reported in the original article published in JAMA in 1998. The risk of developing any serious disease (the kind of illness that requires hospitalization or that causes death) was identical in the people who took the statin and those who took the placebo. The new guidelines report that the effect of statin treatment on the overall risk of death in the AFCAPS/TexCAPS study was inconclusive. Not so. A definitive conclusion can be drawn: In a five-year study involving 6600 people with moderately elevated LDL cholesterol levels, treatment with a statin did not decrease overall mortality. In fact, a

---

*LDL cholesterol levels averaged 150 mg/dL. HDL cholesterol levels averaged 36 and 40 mg/dL, respectively, for men and women.

few more of the people who took the statin died (80) than those who took the placebo (77).

In other words, the net result of treating people with moderate risk of developing coronary artery disease with a statin was simply to trade coronary heart disease for other serious diseases, with no overall improvement in health.

Disregarding, for the moment, the fact that statins had no effect on the overall risk of serious illness or death, even the "large reduction in relative risk" of developing coronary heart disease touted in the guidelines translates into a much less impressive reduction in absolute risk. One hundred people in this study would have to be treated with a statin drug for two and a half years to prevent a single episode of heart disease—and the other 99 people would not have derived any benefit. In order to prevent one death from cardiovascular disease, 100 people in this study would have to have been treated with a statin drug for 25 years.* The updated guidelines relied heavily on AFCAPS/TexCAPS to develop the two-step risk-assessment process that doctors now use to determine which patients should take statins. A look at how those criteria actually apply to the men in this study, however, reveals a paradoxical result. At least 85 percent of the men are in the risk category for which the executive summary of the guidelines states, "Use of LDL-lowering drugs at this risk level reduces CHD risk and is cost-effective."

Notwithstanding the lack of overall health benefits in the people who received statin therapy in AFCAPS/TexCAPS, the guidelines later contradict their own recommendation, concluding that the "incremental cost per additional year of life gained would be >\$100,000 for the whole cohort of AFCAPS/TexCAPS," and that this is too expensive to justify statin treatment. In other words, if you do the arithmetic, the guidelines recommend statin therapy for everyone who has a health profile similar to 85 percent of the men in AFCAPS/TexCAPS. But the report then goes on to say that the cost would be prohibitive. And notwithstanding this internal contradiction, it is simply nonsensical (or perhaps a diversion)

---

*The cardiovascular death rate in the AFCAPS/TexCAPS study was 1.4 per 1000 people treated with a placebo each year compared with 1.0 per 1000 who were treated with a statin.

to even contemplate how much each year of life gained in AFCAPS/Tex-CAPS would cost, because the overall death rate was *higher*, not lower, in the people who took a statin drug.

The bottom line is that these two studies show that men who do not have CHD but do have very high cholesterol levels might benefit from taking a statin drug, though not nearly as much as all the talk of "miracle drugs" leads us to believe. The case for prescribing statins for men with only moderately elevated cholesterol levels is far less compelling.

PRIMARY PREVENTION FOR WOMEN BELOW THE AGE OF 65

The updated guidelines are definitive: "In recent trials, statin therapy reduced risk for CHD in . . . women, in those with or without heart disease." The NCEP's full report convincingly cites six references to back up this statement.

None of the six references cited, however, provides significant evidence to back up the claim that statin therapy reduces the risk of CHD in women without heart disease: three apply to people who already have heart disease; one is the WOSCOPS study, which included no women; one is AFCAPS/TexCAPS, in which there were only a total of 20 episodes of heart disease among the women in the study—not nearly enough to reach statistical significance; and one was a compilation of five other studies. A review article published in JAMA in 1995 concluded: "There is no evidence from primary prevention trials that cholesterol lowering affects total mortality in healthy women."

It is hard to believe that the only evidence from randomized controlled (gold standard) studies that addresses the primary prevention of heart disease in women with statins consists of these statistically inconclusive 20 episodes of coronary heart disease, which are being used to justify putting millions of healthy women on statins. This fact is not disputed in the guidelines, which later state under the heading "Special Considerations for Cholesterol Management in Women (Ages 45–75)": *"Clinical trials of LDL lowering generally are lacking for this risk category; rationale for therapy is based on extrapolation of benefit from men of similar risk"* (italics mine).

The cholesterol guidelines' cavalier extrapolation to women of the benefit of lowering cholesterol in men, especially after the recent surprise provided by the results of the "Heart and Estrogen/Progesterone Replacement Study" (HERS study),* demonstrates the medical industry's unrepentant opportunism in its attempt once again to impose scientifically unsubstantiated medical treatment on women. Such a sweeping recommendation, without unimpeachable evidence from the gold standard of at least one large randomized clinical trial, and optimally several such trials, makes a travesty of the claim that American medicine upholds its standards of excellence by adhering strictly to scientific evidence.

PRIMARY PREVENTION FOR PEOPLE WHO HAVE REACHED THE AGE OF 65

The guidelines are very enthusiastic about the prospects for reducing heart disease in people age 65 and older who have an increased risk of, but have not yet developed, coronary heart disease. Specifically for this group, the report states that recent trials have shown "aggressive LDL-lowering therapy [meaning with a statin drug] is effective in reducing CHD (see Table II.2-3)." The table cites nine references to support this strong claim.

Checking each reference produced the same results as checking the references that supposedly showed that women without heart disease benefit from statin therapy: only one of the nine references (AFCAPS/TexCAPS) is at all relevant to primary prevention of CHD in the elderly, and even in this study only one-fifth of the people involved had reached the age of 65, and the reduction in their risk of heart disease was not statistically significant.

What about the other studies? Six were of secondary prevention (people who are at much higher risk because they already have CHD); two were of primary prevention, but one of these did not include patients over the age of 64, and the other was published in 1978, long before

---

*Hormone replacement therapy was found to reduce LDL cholesterol significantly and increase HDL, but did not reduce the risk of heart attacks.

statins were available, and the average age was 51. So, the nine references notwithstanding, no significant evidence from randomized controlled trials has been presented to support this recommendation.

The guidelines also refer to population-based (epidemiological) data to justify the increased use of statins: "The relationship between serum cholesterol levels and lifetime risk for CHD has been evaluated in the Framingham Heart Study. . . . Even at age 70 the lifetime risk for CHD remains high." Though both halves of this statement are true independently, their juxtaposition could easily lead the reader to draw the wrong conclusion.

Of course the lifetime risk for CHD is high once the age of 70 is reached; eventually hearts give out in people lucky enough to reach a ripe old age and otherwise in good health. And it's true that the Framingham study examined the relationship between increased cholesterol levels and the risk of heart disease at different ages. But, as mentioned before, the data showed exactly the opposite of what the guidelines imply: total cholesterol is not significantly related to mortality from coronary heart disease beyond the age of 60. Indeed, the authors of the paper, based on data from the Framingham Heart Study, warned: "Physicians should be cautious about initiating cholesterol-lowering treatment in men and women above 65 to 70 years of age. Only randomized clinical trials in older people can settle the debate over the efficacy and cost-effectiveness of lipid-lowering interventions for reducing mortality and morbidity in this population." At the time the updated guidelines were published, no such studies had been reported. Furthermore, a study published in the *Archives of Internal Medicine* in 1999 and referenced by the guidelines showed that "None of the lipid measures (total, high-density lipoprotein, and low-density lipoprotein cholesterol or triglycerides) was associated with the risk of MI [myocardial infarction] in this population [of people aged 65 and older]." In other words, there is not even an increase in the risk of heart attack associated with higher cholesterol levels once the age of 65 is reached.

The guidelines then rely on two assumptions that make statins appear very effective in the primary prevention of CHD in people who have reached the age of 65. The first is that statin therapy reduces the risk of coronary heart disease in people between the ages of 65 and 80 "by approximately one-third." The only problem is that none of the nine ref-

erences cited to justify this assumption provides any significant evidence
of benefit from statin therapy after the age of 65 is reached.

The second assumption is that in the elderly, the risk of coronary
heart disease increases with increasing cholesterol levels. The article cited
to justify this assumption does indeed show that the risk of developing
coronary heart disease remains high in the elderly, but the article does
not examine the relationship between cholesterol levels and the risk of
developing CHD.

As we will see at the end of the chapter, when a randomized controlled study of the effect of statins in elderly patients without heart disease was published in 2002, the overreaching estimates of the benefits of
statin therapy for people in this age group were not borne out.

SHOULD MEN WITH CORONARY HEART DISEASE TAKE STATINS?

Most should. Clearly, the people with the highest risk of heart attack are
those who already have CHD. This is the situation in which statins are
most helpful (called secondary prevention). The results of three large
randomized controlled studies of statin drugs in secondary prevention
were incorporated into the 2001 guidelines: the 4S study of Zocor, and
the CARE and LIPID studies of Pravachol. The primary difference
among them is the average LDL cholesterol levels of the people in the
studies.

In the 4S and LIPID studies, LDL cholesterol levels averaged 188 and
150 mg/dL, respectively. In both of these studies, treatment with a statin
significantly reduced the risk of another heart attack, the risk of dying of
coronary heart disease, and the overall mortality rate. In the CARE study,
LDL cholesterol levels averaged 139 mg/dL—very close to the average for
people who develop coronary heart disease (140 mg/dL)—and the
results were not quite as impressive: there was a significant decrease in
the risk of heart disease but no significant reduction in the risk of death
from heart disease or the overall risk of death.

Just how many heart attacks are prevented by treating people who
already have heart disease with a statin drug? In the CARE and LIPID

studies, the reduction in fatal and nonfatal heart attacks in the people treated with Pravachol was 0.6 percent each year. This means that 166 people need to be treated for a full year to prevent one heart attack. If my patient is that 1 out of 166, I certainly want him or her to be taking a statin; yet given all the media hype about statin drugs, it is easy to be misled into believing that statins will help everybody or almost everybody who has already had a heart attack.

SHOULD WOMEN WITH CORONARY HEART DISEASE TAKE STATINS?

The guidelines refer to the three major clinical trials of secondary prevention to support the statement that statin therapy effectively reduces the risk of recurrent CHD in women. The 4S study shows that treatment with a statin does decrease the risk of recurrent CHD for women but does not decrease the risk of death from CHD. Furthermore, the overall death rate was actually 12 percent *higher* in the women who took the statins compared with the women who took the placebo (not statistically significant). The CARE study similarly showed that statins significantly reduce the risk of recurrent heart attack, but not the risk of death from coronary heart disease in women, and not the risk of death from all causes in the study population as a whole. The LIPID study failed to show a significant reduction in the risk of recurrent CHD in women and did not present mortality data for women. At best, these studies show that statins probably lower the risk of recurrent CHD in women with coronary heart disease, but do not appear to lower their overall mortality rate.

THE NEW GUIDELINES ARE TESTED (AND FAIL MISERABLY)

Wouldn't it be interesting to be able to test the recommendations of the 2001 cholesterol guidelines against the older standard of care to see how much benefit would actually result from tripling the number of Americans taking statins? Of course this would be completely impractical, requiring another large, costly, many-year clinical trial. Even more of an obstacle is the fact that such a study would be highly unethical—volunteers assigned to receive treatment according to the old standards would receive therapy that was less than the best medical care currently being recommended.

In a remarkable coincidence, the findings of almost exactly such a study were published in JAMA about a year and a half after the 2001 guidelines were released. The ALLHAT study had been designed in the early 1990s in a way that fortuitously turned out to be a good test of the expanded use of statin drugs recommended in the 2001 guidelines.

Starting in 1994, the ALLHAT study enrolled more than 10,000 patients at high risk of coronary heart disease—equal numbers of men and women age 55 and older whose risk factors for heart disease would have qualified about 90 percent of the men and 75 percent of the women for statin therapy according to the new guidelines. The patients were randomly assigned to take a statin drug (Pravachol) or simply to receive the usual care from their own doctors and let the chips fall where they may with regard to drug therapy. By the end of the study, 83 percent of the group assigned to take Pravachol were still taking a statin and 26 percent of the "usual care" group had been started on cholesterol-lowering therapy by their own doctors—a perfect test to see how much more heart disease could be prevented if the number of Americans being treated with statins were tripled.

The study found that tripling the number of people on statins neither prevented heart disease nor decreased the overall risk of death. There was no benefit to increasing the number of patients taking statins beyond the community norm of the mid-1990s: not for people age 55 to 64 or 65 and older, not for men or women, not for those with or without diabetes, not for those with or without heart disease, and not for those with LDL cholesterol higher or lower than 130 mg/dL. The only group that derived any significant benefit from more statins were African Americans who had fewer episodes of heart disease but no fewer deaths.

These findings should have been major news. Yet the *Wall Street Journal* was the only major newspaper that I could find that carried the story; otherwise there seemed to be a virtual press blackout. Within the medical journals, the study findings were largely rejected by experts on the basis that so many of the people in the usual-care group had been put on statins that the difference in cholesterol levels between the Pravachol and usual-care groups was not enough to show the benefit of statins. But that was *exactly* the point of the study. High-risk patients treated by their own doctors according to the prevailing standards of the mid-1990s were already getting the maximum benefit of statin therapy. Tripling the number of people taking statins—coincidentally, almost exactly in line with the recommendations of the new guidelines—provided no further benefit.

Dr. Richard C. Pasternak, the cardiologist who wrote the editorial that accompanied the publication of the ALLHAT study results in JAMA, concluded, "Physicians might be tempted to conclude that this large study demonstrates that statins do not work; however, it is well known that they do." So much for evidence-based medicine. From my perspective, Pasternak was wrong. The study did not tempt me to think that statins don't work—it just made me think that tripling the number of people on statins doesn't provide any additional benefit. Dr. Pasternak was one of the original 14 authors of the 2001 cholesterol guidelines. He declared financial relationships with nine drug companies in the "financial disclosures" that accompanied his editorial in JAMA.

Like the ALLHAT study, the PROSPER study (Pravastatin in Elderly Individuals at Risk of Vascular Disease), published in *The Lancet* in 2002 also got very little press coverage—no news of breakthroughs or paradigm shifts, though in a negative way it, too, should have contributed to both. The study tested the effect of statin therapy in high-risk elderly patients between the ages of 70 and 82. For those who did not already have heart disease, statin therapy did not reduce their risk of developing heart disease or stroke. It did, however, significantly increase their risk of developing cancer ($p = .02$). This risk increased each year these elderly patients took the statin, so that by the fourth year of the study there was more than 1 extra case of cancer for every 100 people taking a statin *each year*.

The 2001 cholesterol guidelines were reassuring about statins' not causing cancer: "There is no evidence that currently used cholesterol-lowering drugs promote development of cancer. . . . " However, a paper titled "Carcinogenicity of Lipid-Lowering Drugs," published in JAMA in 1996, was apparently overlooked. This paper pointed out that statins cause cancer in laboratory animals at blood levels only three to four

times those typically achieved in cholesterol-lowering therapy for people. The authors raised the possibility that increases in the risk of cancer caused by statins could take many years to be detected, and therefore
would not be evident in the large studies that had been done to date.
(The average duration of the studies is about five years, and the average
age of patients is less than 60.) We cannot know whether statins will turn
out to increase the risk of cancer when used long term, nor can we know
from one study whether older people might be particularly susceptible.
The one thing we can know is that the denials of the evidence of such a
relationship in the 2001 cholesterol guidelines and by the authors of the
PROSPER article (sponsored by Bristol-Myers Squibb) suggest that the
principle "First do no harm," which should be fresh in our minds from
the increased rate of breast cancer caused by HRT, seems, once again, to
have been forgotten.

Also published subsequent to the 2001 guidelines were two randomized controlled clinical trials that supported the guidelines' target of
reducing LDL cholesterol below 100 mg/dL in people who already have
heart disease (the Heart Protection Study and the Prove It study). This
leaves unanswered the question why some studies show no benefit to
cholesterol-lowering in heart patients whose LDL cholesterol level is less
than 125 mg/dL, while other studies support the lower target. The only
conclusion we can draw about the optimal level of LDL cholesterol in
people who already have heart disease is that it is still to be determined.

THE CHOLESTEROL CASH COW

The disparity between the recommendations of the 2001 guidelines and
the subsequent findings of the PROSPER and ALLHAT studies cannot be
dismissed as simply due to the normal zigs and zags of science. The findings of these two studies directly contradict the guidelines' recommendations, but they don't contradict the best scientific evidence that was
available at the time the guidelines were formulated. The guidelines'
interpretation of the scientific evidence stretches credulity beyond reasonable limits to recommend statin therapy for primary prevention of
heart disease in women, people over 65, and men with only moderately

elevated cholesterol levels. The experts must have believed that future studies would validate their assertions regarding statin therapy, but the results of the studies that came out the following year did just the opposite. Even when the contradictory results were published, the response of many recognized experts in the field seemed to focus more on damage control to protect statin sales than on unbiased evaluation of the scientific evidence.

Why do doctors accept such obvious distortions and commercial intrusions into what ought to be the inviolable standards of medical science and medical care? There are several reasons: Practicing doctors are far too busy to do this kind of research for themselves and, as we have seen, the drug companies play a large role in determining how doctors are "educated" about the new developments in medicine (including all the "good news" about the benefits of statins). Another reason is that significant conflicts of interest have become a normal part of American medicine today. Dr. Scott Grundy, the chair of the panel that created the latest cholesterol guidelines, told the *Wall Street Journal*, "You can have the experts involved, or you could have people who are purists and impartial judges, but you don't have the expertise." Unfortunately, in American medicine that expertise is now virtually inseparable from financial ties to industry. When asked why a more balanced approach to heart disease prevention gets pushed aside by these guidelines, Dr. Walter Willett, professor of epidemiology and nutrition at the Harvard School of Public Health, said, "Drug companies are extremely powerful. They put huge efforts into promoting the benefits of these drugs. It's easier for everyone to go in this direction. There's no huge industry promoting smoking cessation or healthy food."

The ultimate impact of the 2001 cholesterol guidelines is this: competent and caring physicians trying to provide the best possible care for their patients are being misled—and are misleading their patients. As shown in Chapter 13, inexpensive, easily accessible, and often more effective interventions to prevent heart disease and improve overall health are being abandoned in favor of expensive drugs. This issue highlights the question of whether our society ought to or needs to tolerate medical care that serves the interests of the drug companies and medical industry before it serves the health of the American people. The 2001 cholesterol guidelines provide one important example of just how far the pendulum has swung toward the interests of the drug companies.

The obvious question is this: Who will benefit from expanding the number of Americans on statins from 13 million to 36 million? The most honest answer (though admittedly taken out of context) probably comes from the Morgan Stanley Dean Witter newsletter: "Who will benefit most from an expanding [statin] market? We have identified three likely incremental winners in the 2006 statin market—AstraZeneca, Schering-Plough, and an undisclosed marketing partner for Crestor." The newsletter continues: "there are not likely to be any outright losers." No mention is made of the patients and the doctors who are more concerned about their own and others' health and well-being than about pharmaceutical company profits. We are the losers.

CHAPTER 10

DIRECT-TO-CONSUMER

ADVERTISING, PUBLIC RELATIONS, AND THE MEDICAL NEWS

And so it's come to this: The American public can no longer blindly trust that its vaunted medical journals and world-class medical experts put the interests of patients first. Naturally, this makes us want to take matters into our own hands. This is a healthy instinct. Becoming well informed and reclaiming personal responsibility are the best antidote to a fundamentally flawed system.

But there's a hitch. Most of the information available to you (and your doctor) about the diagnosis and treatment of common medical problems comes from the drug and other medical companies themselves. The medical industry has finely honed its ability to mold public knowledge about the best medical care—slanting our beliefs in favor of the most profitable medical therapies. Its most obvious technique involves the nearly ubiquitous drug ads that pepper our television shows, newspapers, and magazines. More insidious—and, for that reason, potentially more influential—are the public relations campaigns that translate into seemingly unbiased news stories and nonprofit public awareness campaigns.

These marketing efforts are specifically designed to appear to inform the public about important health issues, but their real purpose is to serve their sponsors' commercial interests. Health has little to do with the process, except that its singular importance, combined with recent advances in medical science and changes in medical insurance, has created what is probably the greatest marketing opportunity of all time. Whether the products actually improve our health is irrelevant. This may sound harsh, but just think back to hormone replacement therapy, or the pushing of Celebrex and Vioxx as safer arthritis remedies, or the exaggerations of the cholesterol guidelines.

Patients do indeed need to become medical consumers, but not just of drugs, doctors, and hospitals. We need to become critical consumers of medical knowledge itself. The first step is to understand where our medical information comes from.

LAUNCHING THE AD CAMPAIGNS

For years the pharmaceutical industry was allowed to market its drugs only to doctors. It did this through medical journals, continuing medical education, sponsored events, sales calls, and junk mail. Then, in 1981, the drug industry proposed that the FDA allow advertising directly to consumers, arguing that the public should not be denied access to the "knowledge" that would be provided by such marketing. Four years later, the pharmaceutical industry got its foot in the door when the FDA agreed to allow "direct-to-consumer" (DTC) advertising. But the rules were strict, and the content of the ads was, therefore, limited: Drugs could be mentioned by name, but advertisements that discussed the treatment of specific conditions were required to include a lengthy list of side effects and contraindications (situations in which the drug should not be used). As a result, the ads were vague and unfocused, primarily brand-awareness campaigns designed to smooth the way at the doctor's office.

Drug companies kept pressure on the FDA to loosen these restrictions. In 1997, the FDA changed its rules so that TV and radio ads could include the condition or conditions a drug was designed to treat without presenting all of the information previously required—only major side effects and contraindications had to appear in the ad itself (audiences could be directed to a magazine ad or website for more complete information). For example, in a recent TV ad, after Zoloft whisks away clouds of depression, the words "See our ad in *Shape* magazine" flash briefly on the screen. Few television viewers—least of all depressed ones—are likely to search newsstands for specific magazines to find out about the side effects of advertised antidepressants.

The 1997 change unleashed an unprecedented onslaught of commercials. By 1999, the average American was exposed to nine prescription drug advertisements on television every day. The number of television ads increased 40-fold between 1994 and 2000. Suddenly it became a normal part of our everyday experience to be confronted with the idea that we or a loved one might be suffering from ED (erectile dysfunction, for those not in the know), arthritis pain, high cholesterol, nasal congestion, osteoporosis, heartburn, or even the heartbreak of toenail fungus. In the "teachable moments" created by these skillfully raised concerns, consumers are "educated" about readily available drugs to solve the problem.

The explosion of drug ads in the 1990s was exquisitely coordinated with the transition of large numbers of Americans to health plans that covered the cost of prescription drugs. Drug companies could now "help" consumers realize that they had the power to request or demand expensive new brand-name drugs from their doctors (and their greedy insurance plans) for which they had to pay only a small fraction of the real cost. This became a nearly perfect system for maximizing demand, untempered by the usual discipline of cost in a well-functioning market.

As Christopher Lasch wrote in 1979, long before the advent of advertising prescription drugs to the public, "Advertising serves not so much to advertise products as to promote consumption as a way of life." Beyond promoting specific drugs, these expertly crafted commercial messages carry strong but unspoken themes that make prescription drug use seem like a routine part of life. First, the ads create the impression not only that can health and happiness be achieved by using the right drugs, but that drugs are *necessary* for health and happiness. Then the ads evoke a positive emotional connection to the drug, and finally challenge the viewer to take action. Viewers are encouraged to discuss the drug with their doctor (in the office, "discuss" usually morphs into "request" or "demand"), a suggestion that taps into every viewer's desire to take charge of his or her health. Meanwhile, this powerful commercial message, the alleged purpose of which is to help improve health and enjoyment of life, diverts attention from the healthy life habits that usually play a far greater role than advertised drugs in preventing illness and achieving happiness.

CLARITIN: THE FIRST DRUG BORN OF THE NEW ADVERTISING ERA

Claritin, a formerly prescription antihistamine used to control allergic symptoms, was far and away the most heavily advertised prescription drug in the two years following the FDA's 1997 rules change. And indeed, the unprecedented advertising blitz for Claritin was an unparalleled success. It certainly convinced many of my patients that they needed not just *any* allergy medicine, but Claritin and only Claritin. They resisted the idea that there were equally good and perhaps even better ways to relieve their allergy symptoms than a new (and therefore less well tested) drug. Moreover, they were unconcerned about Claritin's cost (more than $2.10 per day): most had prescription drug coverage as part of their health insurance. With an advertising budget greater than that of Budweiser beer or Coca-Cola, Claritin took off: sales grew from $1.4 billion in 1997 to $2.6 billion in 2000.

One question was not addressed in the advertising campaign: How well does Claritin relieve allergy symptoms?

In a well-researched article about Claritin in the *New York Times Magazine* in 2001, writer Stephen Hall reported that the FDA medical officer assigned to review the application for Claritin concluded that the dose approved by the FDA, 10 mg, was only "minimally effective versus placebo." The company's own tests had shown that Claritin relieved allergy symptoms only 11 percent better than the placebo (that is, 11 percent better than nothing). The FDA officer further noted that 40 mg was the "minimum effective dose" for Claritin and requested that Schering-Plough, the manufacturer, perform tests on a higher dose. According to a former FDA official, Schering-Plough resisted. Its reason? At the higher dose, Schering-Plough would risk losing the all-important right to claim that its drug was "nonsedating." Drowsiness can be an annoying side effect of the older and far less expensive allergy pills. With the primary focus of the marketing campaign for Claritin being that it did not cause drowsiness, marketing a more effective dose that could no longer be sold as "nonsedating" just wouldn't do.

It is hard to make the argument that the $2.6 billion spent on a minimally effective drug for what is usually a relatively minor affliction was the best use of the nation's health resources. In fact, while we were spending billions on Claritin, an experienced researcher could not get a relative pittance in funding to determine if a fraction of an $0.08 pill called chlorpheniramine (brand-name Chlor-Trimeton, sold without a prescription) would be as effective as, or more effective than, Claritin, without causing sedation. As the patent to Claritin expired, it was made available without prescription, and Schering-Plough's marketing support for the drug decreased precipitously. The first drug to come of age in the new era of drug advertising was the first to fade away—it no longer made business sense for its manufacturer to sustain the huge advertising budget.

Understanding how drug patents work can be difficult because the drug companies use so many legal ploys to extend their valuable exclusive rights to manufacture and sell drugs like Claritin. Drug patents are supposed to last for 20 years from the date the patent application is filed. As the drug companies reasonably argue, the patent clock is ticking while the drug is being studied and going through the FDA approval process. According to PhRMA, the effective life of patents after drugs come on the market is about 11 to 12 years. Schering-Plough was unsuccessful in its final attempt to extend its patent on Claritin. The manufacturer's argument went like this: it still owned the patent on the chemical into which Claritin is metabolized after being taken (sold as Clarinex). Therefore, Schering-Plough argued, its patent would be infringed if people were allowed to swallow a generic form of Claritin and metabolize it into a chemical on which Schering-Plough still held the patent. The U.S. Court of Appeals for the federal circuit did not agree.

The next drug to take center stage in direct-to-consumer advertising was Vioxx. Merck spent more than $160 million to advertise this new and supposedly "improved" arthritis drug to consumers in 2000—half again more than its closest rival and $20 million more than the previous record set by Claritin in 1999. Overcoming the lack of scientific evidence that Vioxx provides better relief or is safer for most patients than its less expensive competitors, sales of Vioxx grew more than any other drug in 2000, to $1.1 billion.

The real purpose of DTC advertising is revealed in the drugs that patients most frequently request. In 2001, these were Claritin, Viagra, Celebrex, Vioxx, and Allegra (another nonsedating prescription antihistamine)—not exactly the kind of drugs for which creating greater demand through advertising is going to improve health or head off disease at an early stage.

EDUCATION OR PROPAGANDA?

Nonetheless, the drug companies claim that their ads provide an important educational service. As explained by Alan Holmer, president of PhRMA, in a recent issue of JAMA, direct-to-consumer advertising "is an excellent way to meet the growing demand for medical information, empowering consumers by educating them about health conditions and possible treatments."

Studies show, however, that drug ads usually stay away from the facts that count. Researchers from Dartmouth Medical School found that only 13 percent of drug ads in magazines used data to describe drug benefits; the remaining 87 percent relied on vague statements. Not a single ad in the study mentioned the cost of the drug. Only 27 percent of ads presented the cause of or risk factors for the disease, and only 9 percent clarified myths and misconceptions about the disease. The positive effects of lifestyle change were mentioned in less than 25 percent of the ads and fewer than three out of 10 acknowledged that other treatments were available. Two out of five ads attempted to medicalize ordinary life issues. (Routine hair loss or a runny nose, for example, became a medical problem requiring treatment with expensive prescription drugs.)

Widespread public misconceptions about drug ads contribute to their effectiveness. An article in *Health Affairs* reported that half of all respondents in a survey conducted in Sacramento County, California, believed that the government approved each drug ad before it was shown to the public, and 43 percent believed that only "completely safe" drugs could be advertised. Neither belief is true. Moreover, Americans with less education find drug ads to be more credible than do those with more education. Perhaps most telling, the survey showed that the people who are most misinformed about drug ads are also the most supportive of direct-to-consumer drug advertising.

The drug companies capitalize on the public's naïveté about their marketing techniques. Two-thirds of drug ads create a positive emotional association with the drug they represent. Recall for a moment the image of the former Olympic champion Dorothy Hamill lacing up her skates—a beautiful aging athlete smiling and renewed. Who wouldn't want to feel like that? The ad indelibly links her moment of joy to the name Vioxx in every viewer's mind. As Ernestine McCarren, general manager of Ehrenthal & Associates, an advertising agency specializing in direct-to-consumer ads, explained in an interview for a trade magazine, "We want to identify the emotions we can tap into to get that customer to take the desired course of action. If you can't find that basic insight, you might as well forget everything else."

DISEMPOWERING THE DOCTOR-PATIENT RELATIONSHIP

Advertisers know that their challenge is to evoke emotional responses that are strong enough to override traditional doctor-patient relationships. Does it work? The facts speak for themselves: more often than not, doctors accede to patients' requests. As my patients' ideas about the best approach to their medical care became increasingly influenced by the drug ads, I would try to help them understand how this process serves the drug companies' interests, not their health. Often I was successful, but once it became clear that a patient was unwilling or unable to reconsider, I often gave in (unless there was a real danger, such as a patient with a history of heart disease requesting Vioxx).

Working within tight time constraints, doctors are reluctant to be drawn into these difficult discussions and usually go along with their patients' requests for advertised drugs. A study done by the FDA in 2002 showed that patients receive prescriptions for requested drugs 50 percent of the time. A study published in the *British Medical Journal* showed that doctors in Vancouver, British Columbia, and Sacramento, California, prescribed requested drugs about three-quarters of the time. (Canadian patients made these requests less than half as often as American patients. Direct-to-consumer advertising is not allowed in Canada, but some drug ads arrive in American magazines and over cable television.) A study done by *Prevention* magazine in 1999 showed that doctors prescribed requested prescription drugs 80 percent of the time.

The drug industry would probably argue that these successful requests are evidence of their excellent consumer education, and that better-informed patients get better medical care. Doctors, however, have a different opinion. Not surprisingly, most doctors do not agree with the drug industry's claims that advertising "can help to improve public health because a number of leading diseases are underdiagnosed and undertreated" or because it "enhances the patient-physician relationship." More than four out of five family doctors feel that direct-to-consumer advertising is not a good idea. Interestingly, although primary care doctors consistently express unfavorable opinions about the impact of DTC advertising on medical care, dermatologists have a positive view, perhaps reflecting the increase in visits generated by advertisements for skin products.

At its best, the trust between doctor and patient creates the opportunity for open discussion of symptoms, fears, models of disease, life circumstances, and expectations. Once all of these are on the table, an optimal approach can be developed to meet individual patient's needs. Often approaches and solutions to health problems emerge through these open encounters that had not been previously apparent to either the doctor or the patient. Rarely can the best solutions be achieved simply by prescribing a drug and being done with the issue.

From my perspective as a family doctor, I found the requests for specific drugs deleterious to both the process and content of good doctoring. Once a patient made a request for a specific drug, the success of the visit from the patient's point of view became defined by whether or not the drug was prescribed. At that point, it became hard to recoup the full potential of the encounter. I was less able to broaden discussion beyond the use (or not) of the latest drugs to more effective ways to control symptoms and preserve health—like avoiding allergens or adopting a more active lifestyle.

PROTECTING SPEECH OR PROTECTING PROFITS?

It seems obvious to Americans that drug companies should be allowed to advertise. DTC drug ads have become such a prominent part of our cultural landscape that they seem completely normal, appropriately protected by the First Amendment. But outside the United States, DTC advertising is anything but normal, allowed in only one other industrialized country in the world, New Zealand, with a population of only 4 million people. An editorial in the *Canadian Medical Association Journal* summed up the issue: "By being marketed in media traditionally used to flog cars, fast food and shampoo, prescription drugs have become name-brand commodities, enveloped in the kind of fantasy and desire that surrounds the purchase of lifestyle products."

The European Union voted in 2003 to continue its ban on DTC drug ads. In the debate, consumer groups argued that medical information should be disseminated by independent national sources, not drug companies. A spokesperson for the European Union went even further, saying that the ban on drug company ads was not sufficient to protect its citizens from commercially sponsored misinformation coming from the United States. "The problem is you now have all sorts of medical data and claims on American websites," he said, "and that issue is still not being addressed."

In the United States the rights of commercial speech are given far greater priority than in the other countries—a balance that is tipping ever more in favor of commercial activity. With the explosion of marketing for prescription drugs, for example, an expansion of oversight by the FDA would seem essential. (After all, it took only 11 days after the 1997 rule change for Schering-Plough to be cited for two advertising infractions about its marketing of Claritin.) Yet just the opposite has occurred. The number of letters citing drug companies for advertising violations declined from an average of 95 in 1999 and 2000 to only 27 in 2002 and 24 in 2003. Why the precipitous drop when the number of ads was increasing?

In August 2001, at a time when the FDA was without a commissioner, President George W. Bush chose an accomplished lawyer, Daniel Troy, to be the FDA's new chief counsel. Daniel Troy had extensive experience in First Amendment issues, with a particularly strong record in defending the right of commercial speech. He successfully represented the Brown & Williamson Tobacco Corporation before the Supreme Court in the company's bid to block the FDA from assuming regulatory authority over tobacco products. He was also part of a legal team that sued the FDA to allow drug companies to promote "off-label" (non–FDA-approved) use of prescription drugs, partially bypassing the FDA's review process. In short, one of the FDA's chief adversaries became its chief counsel.

Three months after Troy had assumed his new position, the Department of Health and Human Services instructed the FDA that all letters to drug companies concerning marketing violations must be reviewed by its Office of the Chief Counsel prior to being sent out. In a 2002 report, the U.S. General Accounting Office (GAO) noted that prior to this change, letters had been issued within several days of identifying a violation, but the additional legal review was taking so long, an average of 41 days and as many as 78, that "misleading advertisements may have completed their broadcast life cycle before FDA issued the letters."

In response to the concerns raised about increased public misinformation resulting from these delays, FDA commissioner Mark McClellan wrote a letter to Representative Henry A. Waxman (D-CA), saying that a goal of completing legal reviews of FDA notification letters within 15 days would be established. The result? A report issued by the Special Investigations Division of the U.S. House of Representatives' Committee on Government Reform—Minority Staff in January 2004 found that the average delay had increased from 41 days in 2002 to 177 days for many of the ads in 2003.

One thing about direct-to-consumer advertising is not in question: since the advertising began in earnest in 1991 it has been a financial boon for the drug industry. Since 1991, when spending on DTC advertising was a mere $55 million, expenditures on drugs have increased at about four times the rate of expenditures on hospital or physician services. Melody Petersen reported in the *New York Times* that in 1998 the largest drug companies generated $22.50 in sales for every dollar spent on advertising to consumers and primary care doctors. It should come as no surprise, then, that the biggest drug companies increased their marketing budgets by more than 32 percent each year for the next three years. For comparison, marketing expenditures in France and England, which don't allow DTC advertising, went down 4 percent annually during the same period. Between 1991 and 2003, spending on DTC ads in the United States increased 58-fold, reaching $3.2 billion per year.

During the same years, drug industry profit margins have skyrocketed from about 12 percent of revenues (net of all research and development expenses) in 1991 to 18 percent of revenues in 2001, while the rest of the Fortune 500 industries averaged 5 percent or less.

UNDER THE RADAR SCREEN: PUBLIC RELATIONS

Even more insidious than misleading advertising is the subtle influence of public relations campaigns. At least with advertising, the fundamentally commercial purpose of the message is clear. With public relations campaigns, news stories and supposed public service messages from nonprofit organizations about a particular drug or issue just seem to emerge spontaneously, usually with no obvious connection to a commercial source. Public relations firms earn their keep by skillfully blurring the line between independent news and commercially planted "information." With repetition in trusted sources television, newspapers, radio, and magazines—the messages carried in these so-called news stories gradually take hold. It is a very effective way to influence both public opinion and health policy.

The issue of counterfeit drugs provides a good example. In the past few years, many American senior citizens have been taking bus rides to Canada to buy prescription drugs to avoid prices in the United States that average up to 70 percent higher. Others are ordering drugs by mail and over the Internet from Canadian pharmacies. This end run around the high price of drugs in the United States is costing the drug companies significant profits—about $350 million to $650 million worth of drugs are purchased by Americans at the lower Canadian prices each year. PhRMA wanted to curb this trend, especially while Medicare prescription drug coverage was being debated on Capitol Hill.

As if out of nowhere, the safety of drugs purchased from other countries became a major issue in the United States. In July 2003, FDA Commissioner Mark McClellan announced a new initiative to protect Americans from counterfeit drugs that were purportedly being substituted for drugs that were "safe and effective." For example, an article in the September 22, 2003, *Wall Street Journal* was headlined "Fakes in the Medicine Chest." The article reported that the FDA had noted an alarming increase in counterfeit prescription drugs entering the United States. According to this report, state and federal regulators said that counterfeits may get into the United States through a "growing number of online vendors [who] promise cheaper Canadian or 'generic' drugs." The same story was all over the news. But there was something odd about the big concern over drugs imported from Canada. A spokeswoman for the Canadian drug authority told the *Wall Street Journal*: "We're not aware of any counterfeit activity at this time."

Appearing on the very same page of the *Wall Street Journal*, but with a much smaller headline, was an article that explained the real story behind the story. "Drug Companies Cry 'Danger' Over Imports," by Scott Hensley, reported that PhRMA had hired a public relations firm, Edelman, to help it develop an effective "communications campaign" to stop drug importation. The first step was to find the themes that would have the greatest impact. Focus groups of people without insurance coverage for drugs (like many senior citizens covered by Medicare alone) were convened. Edelman found that people were not fazed by the illegality of importing drugs. But Edelman was successful in finding an issue that did get people's attention: "fear and accountability 'move the needle' of consumer perceptions." Edelman's report, according to Hensley, suggested that PhRMA could create doubts about the wisdom of saving money by importing drugs if they focused on the "safety and effectiveness" of drugs bought from foreign sources.

The PR campaign to raise concern about the safety of imported drugs has succeeded in the short term: included in the Medicare prescription drug bill are provisions that make drug importation cumbersome and therefore unlikely. Ironically, as pointed out in a *New York Times* editorial, "While the drug industry has been railing against the dangers of foreign imports, it has increasingly transferred its own production to foreign factories to save on labor costs." So it turns out that the biggest importer of foreign drugs is the American pharmaceutical industry itself. Just how concerned is the drug industry about protecting the public from the danger of imported drugs? While 1300 people were being added to the division of the FDA that approves new drugs (to decrease new drug approval time), 1000 were being taken off other FDA surveillance duties, including inspection of drug manufacturing sites. And the real truth about counterfeit drugs from Canada? Jirina Vlk, spokesperson for Health Canada, the equivalent of the FDA, told me on January 28, 2004, that she was not aware of any counterfeit drug's *ever* having been sent from a registered Canadian pharmacy or pharmacist to the United States.

Public relations campaigns are also waged in support of specific drugs. This occurs both around the initial introduction of a new drug and to help a drug that is not living up to its anticipated market potential. For example, Eli Lilly thought it had a real winner in 2001 when the FDA approved Xigris. This breakthrough high-tech drug had been shown to improve the survival rate of people who were critically ill with septic shock—an extremely serious condition caused by bacterial infection in the bloodstream, which is responsible for 225,000 deaths in the United States each year. The *New England Journal of Medicine* published a report in 2001 showing that Xigris decreased the mortality rate from this dreaded condition by 6.1 percent, saving the life of 1 out of every 16 patients treated. Another article in the NEJM concluded that Xigris was "relatively cost-effective when targeted to patients with severe sepsis."

The future of Xigris (and Eli Lilly) seemed bright. According to *Business Week,* Xigris had "one of the higher profit margins in the business." But sales were soon lagging far below projections: up to $475 million in sales had been projected for 2002, but actual sales came in at less than a quarter of that. Sales for 2003 had been projected to be as high as $700 million, but Eli Lilly's data from the first two quarters of 2003 showed Xigris sales of only $72 million, less than one-ninth of projections. Why was Xigris such an underperformer?

It turns out that the study published in the *New England Journal of Medicine* didn't tell the whole story. Data provided to the FDA by Eli Lilly showed that of the six extra patients out of 100 who survived after being treated with Xigris, only one had been well enough to be discharged from the hospital 28 days later. The other five were still too sick to go home, and some of them were still in the ICU. The FDA reviewer who analyzed these data concluded that "without longer follow-up, the ultimate outcomes of the hospitalized patients cannot be determined."

Furthermore, Xigris is very expensive, costing about $6800 for each patient treated. Medicare and Medicaid agreed to Eli Lilly's request to cover half of the cost of Xigris as a new medical technology, but this still leaves hospitals paying about $3400 for each patient treated.

With sales lagging so far behind projections, Eli Lilly did the only reasonable thing: it fired the public relations firm that had been in charge of the Xigris account and looked for a new one that could do a better job. According to the *Wall Street Journal*, the winning proposal was titled "The Ethics, the Urgency, and the Potential." The new campaign would focus the public's attention not on the merits of the drug itself but on a word that evokes terror and anger in most Americans when it comes to health care: rationing.

In an article titled "To Sell Pricey Drug, Eli Lilly Fuels a Debate Over Rationing," the *Wall Street Journal* reported that Eli Lilly's new PR firm developed a strategy to convince the public that use of Xigris was being unethically withheld from critically ill patients. Eli Lilly then committed $1.8 million to fund, according to the *Boston Globe*, a task force charged with developing "national guidelines for the rationing of expensive intensive-care unit treatment—and to get doctors to openly admit they withhold care from patients who would benefit the least."

No doubt the critical care doctors on this task force are seeking a legitimate forum in which to develop guidelines to help health professionals with the often agonizing ethical dilemmas that routinely arise in the care of critically ill patients. And no doubt the task force's report will merit very careful attention for its suggestions about the most responsible and ethical ways to approach these problems. But Eli Lilly's largesse has another goal as well. The task force's report and guidelines are at high risk of falling prey to a public relations clamor about the rationing of medical care for critically ill patients, with underuse of Xigris woven seamlessly into the "debate." One could easily see the case for Xigris developing as an extension of the patients' rights issue—inappropriately withholding potentially lifesaving drugs from critically ill patients. Rational public debate about the use of Xigris will be at risk of getting drowned out by the public's emotional response to news reports about de facto rationing. If this happens, the public relations campaign will almost certainly have succeeded in its primary goal of increasing sales of Xigris. Besides, only 265 additional patients have to be treated with Xigris to cover the cost of the ethics task force.

Commercially sponsored public relations campaigns also use non-profit organizations very effectively to get their message out. Consider the story of social anxiety disorder, or SAD. An investigative article in *Mother Jones* by Brendan Koerner tells the story of how this "disease" was virtually created to sell the cure. According to the psychiatric diagnostic manual, SAD is (or, probably more accurately, was) an "extremely rare" condition. Nonetheless, SmithKline Beecham, the manufacturer of the antidepressant Paxil, hired a PR firm to coordinate a broadly targeted educational campaign about the "disease" through three nonprofit organizations: the American Psychiatric Association, the Anxiety Disorders Association of American, and Freedom From Fear. Within a month after the FDA's approval of Paxil for the treatment of SAD, articles about this "underdiagnosed illness" appeared in the *New York Times* and *Vogue* magazine. The PR campaign was deemed such a success that it earned recognition as the "Best P.R. Program of 1999" by the New York chapter of the Public Relations Society of America. Not surprisingly, Paxil sales increased by 25 percent between 1999 and 2000.

When for-profit money gets cycled through nonprofit organizations, especially trusted service and professional organizations, the commercial goals of the donors become nearly invisible.

THE GOOD NEWS NARRATIVE

Have you ever noticed how much good news about medical progress is on television and in newspapers? With this constant stream of breakthroughs, you would think that by now we would have cured all diseases known to humanity two or three times over.

The narrative is familiar: A medical problem is described; one or more patients suffering from the disease are introduced with whom the viewer or reader can readily identify; experts are interviewed to explain why the discovery or procedure is a breakthrough in terms readily understandable to the public; and the story concludes with a calculation of how many people can be helped by this latest discovery. Temporizing opinions are often included for balance, but the criticism is rarely enough to quash the excitement. Our underlying faith that medical science is progressing in its battle against suffering and death is confirmed. The medium that brought us the message has successfully captured our attention. And the interests of the advertisers are supported by this rosy narrative. All at the same time.

A good example was provided by the press coverage that followed the publication of a 2002 article in the *New England Journal of Medicine:* Researchers concluded that an inexpensive test that measures the level of inflammation in the body, C-reactive protein, or CRP, can predict a person's risk of developing cardiovascular disease (heart attack, ischemic stroke, coronary revascularization, or cardiovascular death) even better than cholesterol levels. The *New England Journal of Medicine* reported that among 28,000 women followed over eight years, the 20 percent with the highest CRP levels were 2.3 times more likely to develop cardiovascular disease than were the 20 percent with the lowest levels. The researchers also concluded that much of this risk would not have been identified by measuring cholesterol levels alone. Finally, according to the article's authors, identifying people with elevated CRP levels would allow "optimal targeting of statin therapy." In other words, people with high levels of CRP would be well advised to take statins to decrease their risk of cardiovascular disease.

According to my nonrandom sample, three major newspapers (the *Boston Globe,* the *New York Times,* and the *Washington Post*) and two newsmagazines (*Time* and *Newsweek*) each carried a story about the potential benefit of the new CRP test. Without exception, the stories were enthusiastic: "groundbreaking," "the most promising advance in a long time," "paradigm-shaking," "extremely important," and "a home run" were among the accolades. It is safe to assume that much of the reading public concluded that this was an important medical breakthrough and requested CRP tests from their doctors.

What's wrong with this story? The research was spun to make a very small diagnostic improvement look like an important medical "breakthrough" and in the process distract attention from the things that can be easily done to decrease the risk of cardiovascular disease.

The NEJM article reported that the women with the highest CRP levels had 2.3 times more risk of developing cardiovascular disease than the women with the lowest levels. That sounds like a lot. But this is the *relative* risk; comparison of the ratio of the low risk of disease in one group to the even lower risk of disease in another can make very small differences seem very big. The women in this study were quite healthy, and their average age was less than 55, so their underlying risk of suffering heart attacks, strokes, or blocked arteries was quite small. For example, among 1000 women with the highest CRP levels, there was only slightly more than one (1.3) additional episode of cardiovascular disease each year than among 1000 women with the lowest CRP levels. All five publications reported that women with elevated CRP levels had double the (relative) risk of cardiovascular disease, but only the *Washington Post* mentioned anything about absolute risk, reporting that the increase was "very small." With all the talk about "most promising advance in a long time" and "home runs," readers had few clues that the dramatic-sounding relative risk translated into a minimal absolute risk of about 1 in a 1000.

Nonetheless, concern about even this level of risk is not unreasonable. So how much would statin therapy help? An article by the same group of researchers published in JAMA in 2001 showed that a daily dose of 40 mg of Pravachol significantly reduced CRP levels. But remember: reduction of CRP is a surrogate end point (not clinically important in and of itself), and statins have never been shown in randomized clinical trials to significantly reduce the risk of cardiovascular disease in women without heart disease. Nonetheless, assuming (very generously, because no benefit has yet been proven) that taking Pravachol could decrease the risk of cardiovascular disease in women with higher CRP levels by 40 percent, less than one episode of cardiovascular disease per 1000 women would be prevented each year. Forty milligrams of Pravachol per day cost about $1650 per year. This works out to $2 million (in drugs alone, not counting the extra lab tests and doctor visits) to prevent a single episode of cardiovascular disease among healthy women with elevated CRP levels—if in fact Pravachol has any benefit at all. You don't have to be a doctor to understand that there might be better ways to spend that much money on 1000 women over the course of a year to improve their health and the quality of their lives.

What's the harm in all this excitement about something that may not be a real breakthrough? The hype creates false hope that moves us further away from real prevention, most of which has to do with a healthy lifestyle, and drains resources needlessly from far more effective health interventions.

Is the reporting of the CRP story typical? Unfortunately it is. A study of 207 medical news stories on television and in newspapers shows that fewer than one in 10 presented data on absolute risk reduction and only three out of 10 mentioned cost. Only four out of 10 disclosed the financial ties of "experts" to the products they were presenting or discussing. How many times have you ever heard a researcher who worked on a drug company–sponsored study express a negative or even ambivalent opinion in an interview? There is a reason why drug companies establish financial ties with experts. Interviews of these enthusiastic authorities are often better described as infomercials than dispassionate science reporting.

Why the tendency for the media to present medical research in such hyperbolic and uncritical terms? People like to read good news more than bad, and they like to hear about progress and hope. There is another reason, too, though it is an impolite subject. Gloria Steinem, founding editor of *Ms.* magazine, stated it quite succinctly: "You don't get product ads unless you praise the product."

With advertising of prescription drugs and other medical products having emerged as a major source of revenue for all media (especially television—the greatest source of people's health information), the pressure to have news content that supports or at least does not directly oppose advertisers' interests has grown. And therein lies the Achilles' heel of the media when it comes to medical reporting. Even if medical reporters had the scientific and statistical expertise to cut through commercial spin (an unfair expectation, given that it involves untangling the work of the medical industry's best and brightest), could they report the truth and stay in business? Unlikely.

The public needs access to independent expert opinion that can counterbalance the enormous influence that the medical industry wields over our beliefs about the best approach to health and medical care. Unfortunately, with rare exceptions (Center for Medical Consumers, the University of British Columbia Therapeutics Initiative, and Public Citizen's worstpills.org are examples of unbiased sources of information), we are left with medical reporting that is handicapped by a structural disadvantage: the public's interest gets overwhelmed by the financial resources, political influence, and marketing expertise of the drug industry. As a result, the public often gets commercially biased medical news, and is left more vulnerable than ever to the explicit appeals of advertisers and the subtle persuasion of public relations campaigns.

The successful mass marketing of drugs, tests, and procedures to American consumers—regardless of their true health value—explains a great deal about how the myth of excellence in American medicine is sustained. While there certainly have been many real breakthroughs in research and practice, it turns out that most of the medical news, especially the commercially advantageous news, is too good to be true. Americans, as patients, consumers, and taxpayers, are paying an enormous price for that deception.

CHAPTER 11

FOLLOW THE MONEY

SUPPLY-SIDE MEDICAL CARE

Mr. and Mrs. Wilkins had planned carefully for their retirement. Well into their eighties, they were spending their winters in Florida and the rest of the year in their home about a mile from my office. Besides Mr. Wilkins' prostate cancer, which was under control, they both enjoyed good health. But one winter, Mr. Wilkins suffered a heart attack.

While he was still in the hospital, his cardiologist recommended that he undergo cardiac catheterization. This is a diagnostic test commonly done after a heart attack to look for blockages in the coronary arteries. The test involves injecting dye into each of the coronary arteries through a small tube, or catheter, so that blood flow can be assessed on x-ray pictures. The test showed that two of Mr. Wilkins' coronary arteries were partially blocked, and the blockages were too far into the arteries and too diffuse to be opened by a balloon-tipped catheter (a procedure known as angioplasty). So Mr. Wilkins underwent coronary artery bypass surgery to decrease the risk of these arteries becoming completely blocked and causing another heart attack. The surgery involves taking a vein from the leg and attaching it to vessels that bring blood to the heart, providing a "bypass" around the obstructed areas.

Mr. Wilkins came through the surgery without a problem, but over the next few days, pain and redness developed in the area around the incision, and he started to run a low-grade fever. It soon became obvious that an infection had developed in his sternum, where the surgeon had cut through the bone on his way to repair the coronary arteries. The surgeon partially reopened the incision to let the infection drain out and put Mr. Wilkins on antibiotics.

Spring came, and Mr. and Mrs. Wilkins returned north about six weeks after his surgery. He needed to see me every two or three days to change the drain in his chest so that the infection would not close over and become an abscess again. This procedure caused some discomfort, though over time we worked out a method of partially numbing the sensitive area by washing it with a local anesthetic, before reinserting the gauze wick. Mr. Wilkins remained good-natured with me throughout his ordeal.

His relationship with his wife of over 60 years was another story. Mr. Wilkins' wife would usually come with him to his office visits. Virtually every time I walked into the exam room, I would find them arguing. They argued constantly. Previous to this, they had seemed a happy enough couple, and I had certainly never witnessed this kind of discord. Every time Mrs. Wilkins could talk to me out of her husband's earshot, she would register the same complaints: "He asks me the same thing over and over again" and "He just isn't himself anymore."

One day Mr. Wilkins came to his visit without his wife. As I was working on him, concentrating on being as gentle as possible while I reinserted the drain, Mr. Wilkins said to me, "You know, Doc, I finally figured out the secret to a happy marriage." With great interest, I stopped what I was doing and asked him what it was. "When we disagree," he explained, "I just let my wife think she's right." I was impressed and humbled by his newfound wisdom. Two days later Mr. Wilkins returned to the office, again unaccompanied by his wife. At about the same point in the visit he said, "Doc, remember what I said last time about a happy marriage?" I certainly did. He said, "Well, just forget it." I confess that I felt relieved.

The infection improved gradually over several months. Sadly, almost as soon as Mr. Wilkins' infection resolved, his prostate cancer began to spread to his bones, causing him increasing pain. Radiation therapy did not help. When it became clear that the spread of his cancer could not be stopped, I arranged for hospice to become involved in Mr. Wilkins' care, and he died peacefully without further hospitalization.

IS MORE CARE BETTER FOR HEART ATTACK PATIENTS?

Despite the postoperative infection, Mr. Wilkins and his wife remained confident that he had received the best possible care after his heart attack—immediate access to the latest diagnostic procedures and heart surgery to protect him from another heart attack. Given what I have subsequently learned, I am not so sure.

There is no doubt that Americans have the best access to the latest and most expensive medical treatments. For example, heart attack patients in the United States who have reached the age of 65 are five times more likely to have a diagnostic cardiac catheterization looking for blocked arteries than are similar patients in Canada. And senior citizens in the United States are seven and a half times more likely to undergo balloon angioplasty or coronary artery bypass surgery. Obviously, this kind of care is very expensive. Overall health care costs are 75 percent higher per person in the United States than in Canada and rose much more quickly during the 1980s and 1990s as these cardiac procedures were becoming standard therapy for heart attack patients in the United States. This is the price that Americans have to pay for unimpeded access to the most advanced medical care. But there is more to the story.

Despite the fact that we treat senior citizens with so many more heart procedures after heart attacks than are given in Canada, it turns out that one year after their heart attacks, patients treated in the United States are no more likely to be alive than those treated in Canada. Still, survival rates alone may not be a sensitive enough measure to detect more subtle clinical benefits. Perhaps the extra procedures done in the United States leave patients with better exercise capacity or an improved quality of life, medical outcomes that weren't measured in this study.

This is unlikely, as we learn from a study published in NEJM that capitalized on the "natural experiment" created by the difference in post–heart attack care between Texas and New York state. Medicare patients in Texas were 50 percent more likely than similar patients in New York to have a cardiac catheterization within 90 days after a heart attack. Surprisingly, patient outcomes in Texas were actually *worse* over the following two years: The death rate was significantly higher in Texas (15 percent). Also, the patients in Texas reported about 40 percent more angina (heart pain), and 62 percent more of the patients in Texas were unable to do tasks that required moderate exertion compared with the patients in New York. The authors concluded that there appeared to be no benefit to the greater number of post–heart attack cardiac procedures being done in Texas.

Post–heart attack care has changed dramatically since the early 1980s, when only about 10 percent of heart attack patients in the United States underwent diagnostic cardiac catheterization. By 1998, more than half of our heart attack patients were receiving this diagnostic test, with more than half of these going on to angioplasty or coronary artery bypass surgery. The increased number of procedures added about $10,000 (adjusted for inflation) to the care of each heart attack patient between 1984 and 1998. During this same time, the life expectancy of the average heart attack patient in the United States increased by about one year. An article in the health policy journal *Health Affairs* used these facts to argue that the increased number of procedures being done on heart attack patients in the United States was extremely cost-effective—$10,000 is a very small amount in terms of medical interventions for an additional year of life.

The story, however, gets a lot more complicated when we compare the situation regarding death rates due to heart disease and the cardiac care provided in the United States with that of the other industrialized countries. On a per-person basis for patients of all ages, the United States does three and a half times as many coronary angioplasties and coronary artery bypass surgeries as the other industrialized countries. One might conclude that this investment in the treatment of heart disease in the United States and increased longevity for heart attack victims is proof positive of the superiority of our treatment of heart disease, end of story.

Not so, according to data from the National Heart, Lung, and

Blood Institute of the National Institutes of Health. The United States has the third highest death rate from coronary artery disease among 10 wealthy industrialized countries. Despite the greater number of invasive cardiac procedures being performed and all the cholesterol-lowering statin drugs being taken, not only is the death toll from coronary heart disease higher in the United States, but the United States is losing ground to most of these wealthy industrialized countries as well. Even more disappointing, despite the increased use of invasive cardiac procedures after heart attacks, the in-hospital death rate for heart attack patients in the United States remained virtually unchanged between 1993 and 2000.

Doing too many cardiac procedures can waste more than money. A study published in NEJM in 2001, two years after Mr. Wilkins died, showed that more than half of the people who go through coronary artery bypass surgery experience a significant decrease in mental capacity postoperatively, and the risk is even higher for older patients. In retrospect Mrs. Wilkins' frustration with her husband ("he's not himself") was almost certainly a reaction to mental impairment he had suffered as a result of his surgery.

There is no way we can know whether Mr. Wilkins was the one American patient out of seven and a half who would really benefit from heart surgery. But given his age and prostate cancer, there is a pretty good chance that the coronary artery bypass surgery that looked like the best care for him at the time of his heart attack may not have been.

AN OVERSUPPLY OF SERVICES AT THE OTHER END OF THE LIFE CYCLE

Perhaps the use of invasive cardiac procedures for older patients in the United States is an isolated instance of providing more care than appears to be necessary or beneficial. Not so, as we see from medical care at the other end of the life cycle.

Neonatology is the highly specialized field of caring for sick newborns. My colleagues and I were pleased when a full-time neonatologist was added to the staff of our community hospital. Typically, community physicians request a consultation from the neonatologist when there is anything more than a minor concern about a newborn's health. The neonatologist then plays the key role in deciding whether to transfer the baby to the special care nursery.

In 2002, a study done by researchers from Dartmouth Medical School's Center for Evaluative Clinical Sciences, published in NEJM, showed that the concentration of intensive care neonatology services varies widely in different regions of the United States, by a factor of four or more. The researchers found that the distribution of these services was not, however, based on the number of low-birth-weight babies being born in an area. Nor was neonatal mortality further reduced after a basic level of intensive care was available for sick newborns. Much of the country, it turns out, has about twice as many of these services as necessary to achieve optimal survival rates.

The point is driven home by a study that compared neonatal care in the United States, Canada, Australia, and the United Kingdom. There are almost twice as many neonatologists and neonatal intensive care beds for each baby born in the United States as for babies born in the other countries. Nonetheless, survival rates for equivalent birth-weight babies are no better in the United States. And because of the greater frequency of low-birth-weight babies, the United States has the highest infant mortality rate of the four countries. Part of this problem is the consequence of social issues that go beyond the health care system (such as poverty and racial disparities). Still, part of the problem is that the United States commits far more resources to expensive hospital-based treatment after birth than the other countries, but it offers fewer public health services before conception and during pregnancy. As with post–heart attack cardiology procedures, the oversupply of neonatologists and neonatal intensive care facilities appears to be driven more by financial incentives than documented health needs—and even less by an effective strategy for achieving better health.

MARKET PRESSURES TRUMP SCIENTIFIC EVIDENCE

If American medicine is really guided by scientific evidence, how has our pattern of cardiac care evolved so that, on a per-person basis, the United

States is doing three and half times as many invasive cardiac procedures, but has one of the highest death rates from heart disease of 10 industrialized nations, and is losing ground to most of them? Similarly, how is it that we invest about twice as much as other countries in the care of sick newborns, yet our infant mortality rate ranks poorly and, like our cardiac death rate, is losing ground? Is it our science that is failing us?

Three editorials from the *New England Journal of Medicine* shed some light on this issue. In 1997, an editorial mused about why so many more cardiac surgeries were being done on American heart attack patients aged 65 and over compared with similar patients in Canada, when there was no evidence of better outcomes from the extra surgery. The author, Dr. Harlan Krumholz, suggested that at least part of the answer had to do with the prestige and the billions of dollars these procedures generate each year for "hospitals, physicians, and vendors of medical equipment." One year later, Drs. Richard Lange and L. David Hillis wrote an editorial addressing the same subject. A major study (VANQWISH) had shown, once again, that there was no advantage to performing cardiac catheterizations routinely on clinically stable post–heart attack patients with no warning signs of further heart problems. The editorial underscored the fact that this was the fourth such major study that had come to the same conclusion, noting that the previous studies had had little effect in slowing the growth in the number of post–heart attack cardiac procedures being done in the United States. Commenting on the widespread disregard for the scientific evidence, the editorial concluded, like the one a year before, that the reason for the greater number of cardiac procedures in the United States as compared with Canada and Europe was "monetary remuneration to the facilities and physicians."

It's no wonder that hospitals aggressively market their "state-of-the-art" procedures, trying to attract "customers." At first glance, this may seem like the health care market working well, with hospitals competing to provide the best service to sick patients. The reality is that financial incentives motivate the medical industry to expand the supply of profitable procedures, and then maximize demand for those services. The fees paid by Medicare for coronary artery bypass surgery, for instance, range from about $26,000 for nonteaching hospitals to between $30,000 and $40,000 for academic medical centers. According to an article in the

Boston Globe, the profit margin on these procedures is more than 40 percent. Despite the aura of medical progress and public service, this is business, pure and simple.

Finally, Dr. Kevin Grumbach wrote an editorial that accompanied the article documenting the oversupply of neonatologists and neonatal intensive care beds in many parts of the United States. Searching for an explanation of this apparently irrational use of health care resources, he concluded: "One important explanation is money. Neonatal intensive care units are profit-making centers for hospitals, commanding high payments from private and public insurance plans." The editorial reported that an investor-owned group of 600 neonatologists had earned more than $30 million in 2001.

Why don't the findings of studies like those documenting the overuse of costly cardiology procedures and neonatology services play more of a role in shaping the American health care system? The truth is that American medical practice today is based on scientific evidence as long as the evidence supports commercial interests; but all too often when the science conflicts with commercial interests, science gets nudged aside.

You would think that there would be a mechanism in place to ensure that our medical care was based upon a solid foundation of medical research. The United States was actually the first country to implement just such a program, known as health technology assessment, in 1975. Since then, most of the other industrialized nations have established formal mechanisms to determine the optimal use of new medical technologies and to protect their citizens from unproven or wasteful innovations. In accomplishing this public service, however, these programs may compromise the entrepreneurial potential of medical innovation, and therein lies the rub.

As the influence of technology assessment programs has grown abroad, the United States has virtually dismantled its own. A 1999 article in JAMA explains that this occurred, "despite the fact that strong arguments have been made for such an entity for more than 20 years, most recently by a federal commission in 1994." Why? The medical-device industry and several doctors' organizations opposed government control over the research and evaluation of new technologies. Specifically, the American Society of Cataract Surgery, the American Board of Ophthalmologists, and the North American Spine Society were not pleased with government-sponsored guidelines (issued by the Agency for Health Care Policy and Research, AHCPR) defining appropriate criteria for cataract and low-back-pain surgery. The final battle took place in 1995 over spinal fusion surgery. Spine surgeons took umbrage at the government's proposed limitation on treating herniated disks in the low back this way. The surgeons' protests resonated with the antigovernment environment in Congress at the time—not only were the guidelines discredited, but the entire AHCPR was almost zero-funded for the following year.

A December 2003 article in the *New York Times* explained the controversy about back surgery. This excellent piece of investigative medical journalism points out that although the spinal fusion procedure is more complex and more expensive, and the recovery time is longer, there has never been proof of its superiority over laminectomy. Why the push to do the more complex procedure before it has been proven to be superior to the simpler procedure? Part of the answer, according to the *Times* article, is that doctors are paid approximately $4000 per spinal fusion procedure versus $1000 per laminectomy, and hospitals are paid $16,000 versus $7000. There is another part of the answer as well: Since the AHCPR's guidelines were overturned, the number of spinal fusion operations being done in the United States has tripled, and the amount spent on materials for the procedure has increased fivefold, from $500 million to $2.5 billion each year. The *New York Times* reported that a former sales rep for Medtronic (the largest manufacturer of hardware for spinal fusion surgery) said in a lawsuit against his former employer that he had been told to do "whatever it takes" to sell more supplies for spinal fusion surgery. In his lawsuit, he charged that "whatever it takes" included "sham" consulting contracts and first-class trips to Hawaii. Medtronic settled the lawsuit and denied any wrongdoing. However, it did disclose, in September 2003, that it was being investigated by the Department of Justice for allegedly making illegal kickbacks, representing improper inducements under the Federal Antikickback Statute.

Two other former Medtronic employees told the *Times* that surgeons were routinely enticed to use Medtronic hardware with offers that included expensive trips, nights on the town that cost up to $1000, and sometimes even visits to the local strip club.

Is this how you would want the decision to be made about which operation your surgeon is recommending for you or a family member? (Perhaps when good data become available we will find that there is a role for spinal fusion sugery in the treatment of back pain. It is, however, quite telling that we still don't know—at this late date.)

SUPPLY-SENSITIVE MEDICAL SERVICES

The term "supply-sensitive care" is applied to the kinds of medical services that are most vulnerable to getting pushed into use by the providers' financial interests rather than pulled into service by the health needs of the surrounding community. Without a formal mechanism of health technology assessment, new medical services can be brought into use without strong scientific evidence of benefit. And without limits on spending, new services can be brought into use without evidence that they provide more health value than the services they would be replacing. The absence of both of these constraints on the growth of medical technology allows the U.S. health care system to be uniquely shaped by financial incentives.

Four features are shared by the medical services that are most vulnerable to overuse because of this supply-side push.

First, supply-sensitive services must be covered by insurance. When insurance coverage shields patients from the real cost of their care, they are unlikely to question whether the health value of a test or procedure justifies its cost. If, for example, heart attack patients had to pay the extra $10,000 that American-style invasive post–heart attack care now costs, many would demand access to the kind of information presented above. My guess is that most patients with uncomplicated heart attacks, when presented with the best available evidence, would conclude that the likelihood of benefit from invasive cardiac testing and procedures is not great enough to justify the increased risk and cost, and they would opt for more conservative care. I also suspect that if the technological razza-matazz were no longer such a distraction, the kinds of commonsense interventions that lead to better health outcomes for most people would then move into the foreground, where they belong.

Second, supply-sensitive services must appear on the surface to be beneficial, preempting the need for proof. How many women with advanced breast cancer, facing a poor prognosis, would turn down the opportunity to have a bone marrow transplant when the prevailing attitude is "It's your only chance"? How many heart attack patients would require de-tailed proof of the benefit when their cardiologist says, "We should do a cardiac catheterization to make sure that none of your coronary arteries is about to become completely blocked and cause more damage to your heart"? How many new mothers would say no if their baby's doctor recommended transfer to the intensive care nursery?

Third, the need for supply-sensitive services must be determined by the doctors who perform the service. Even though doctors almost universally believe that their decisions are scientifically based, financial ramifications have a way of exerting subtle influence over their interpretation of scientific evidence. We know, for example, that cardiologists who perform cardiac catheterization and angioplasty are more likely to recommend these procedures than are other cardiologists and primary care doctors—though all claim to be guided by the best evidence available. In my experience, doctors rarely recommend procedures simply to make more money, but like most people, they like to use their special skills to help others; this creates a predisposition to want to use the latest tests, drugs, and procedures (not to mention defend themselves against the ever-present risk of a malpractice suit). As the saying goes, "When you have a hammer, the whole world looks like a nail."

Fourth, supply-sensitive services must provide attractive enough financial opportunities to motivate hospitals and other facilities to invest in the capacity required to provide the service. The increased capacity to do cardiac procedures and the growth of neonatal intensive care units are examples of "good investments" for hospitals.

In a health care system lacking effective health technology assessment and limits on spending, paying doctors and hospitals more for doing more, and disconnecting patient costs from health care value, supply-sensitive services are sure to be overused.

MORE CARE DOESN'T NECESSARILY MEAN BETTER CARE

The most compelling data showing that more care is not necessarily better for health come from the ongoing studies performed by Dartmouth Medical School's Center for Evaluative Clinical Sciences, headed by Drs. John Wennberg and Elliott Fisher. Their research focuses on the impact of regional variations in the use of medical services on health outcomes and costs. Intuitively, we would expect Medicare patients who receive more care in the higher-spending regions of the country to get better care and be healthier. But studies funded by the Robert Wood Johnson Foundation and the National Institute on Aging show that this is not the case. For example, without any discernible benefit in health outcomes, more than twice as much is spent taking care of Medicare patients in Manhattan than is spent on similar patients in Portland, Oregon. Over the 18-year life span of the average Medicare patient after turning 65, this difference amounted to $100,000 per person in 2000, without even taking into account differences in spending on prescription drugs.

Fisher and colleagues specifically studied Medicare patients admitted to the hospital with a first diagnosis of heart attack, broken hip, or cancer of the colon. The cost of caring for the patients was 60 percent more in the highest-spending regions than in the lowest-spending regions. The patients in the highest-spending regions spent more days in the hospital and the ICU, and had more visits with specialists, more diagnostic tests, and more minor, but not major, surgical procedures. The extra services provided to patients in the higher-spending regions did not, however, translate into better outcomes. The patients in the lower-spending regions had *better* access to care, *higher-quality* care, and *less* chance of dying over the five years of the study. The bottom line appears to be that once an adequate amount of care is being provided, as in the lowest-spending regions of the country for

Medicare patients, more care is worse care. This seems to be particularly true for the kind of care that is pushed into service by supply-side pressure.

SCANS: DOCTORS' NUMBER-ONE RANKED INNOVATION

American medicine's predilection for high-tech tests and procedures often leads to overuse of useful new technologies. The new body scans are a good example. In just the years 1999–2001, the number of MRI scanners in the United States increased by about 50 percent. Where are the data showing that the tremendous increase in the number of MRIs and CT scans being done improves clinical outcomes? There aren't any to speak of. Though we don't know the health consequence of these additional scanners, we do know their economic consequence. We can also be quite confident that the key consideration in the decision to put the vast majority of these new scanners into service was the bottom line.

Consider the use of CT scans for patients with suspected appendicitis. CT scans of the abdomen are routinely used for patients who arrive at the hospital with the usual symptoms of appendicitis: abdominal tenderness, fever, and vomiting. The scan, doctors presume, helps to confirm or rule out the diagnosis of appendicitis. Yet a large study of patients in Washington state, published in JAMA in 2001, revealed that the use of CT scans, abdominal ultrasounds, and laparoscopic appendectomy did nothing of the sort: neither the rate of unnecessary appendectomies (removal of what turned out to be a normal appendix) nor the rate of perforated appendixes—the most serious complication of delay in diagnosis—decreased after these newer technologies became available.

The saga of back pain and high-tech scans tells a similar story. Back pain is one of the most common complaints seen by primary care physicians. The vast majority of healthy people who come in with acute back pain recover completely. Many recover without any therapy, or with physical therapy, or occasionally with manipulation. Yet one of the most overused technologies that I see as a family physician is the MRI for patients with back pain. Though the MRI is an elegant technology that produces beautiful anatomical pictures, these beautiful pictures don't necessarily translate into better clinical results.

A patient of mine, Mr. Oscar, was 69 years old when he developed low back pain that radiated into his left buttock. After four weeks of treatment with anti-inflammatory medication and back exercises, his orthopedic specialist ordered an MRI, which revealed a bulging disk between two of Mr. Oscar's lower vertebrae. Mr. Oscar wanted to know what to do next. The answer wasn't simple, because about 80 percent of people older than 50 without any back symptoms have at least one bulging disk in their lumbar spine on their MRIs, and two-thirds have more than one disk abnormality. So what was the chance that the abnormality seen on Mr. Oscar's MRI really represented the cause of his discomfort? There was no way to know. The only real benefit of the MRI was to rule out serious unsuspected problems like tumors or fractures, though these were extremely unlikely, given Mr. Oscar's history and the results of a physical exam. In short, the MRI wasn't much help. His pain improved slowly over the next few weeks with physical therapy and exercises—which could have been prescribed without the MRI.

Mr. Paul's back pain story is my favorite: An avid mountain biker in his mid-forties, Mr. Paul came to me because of moderate to severe back pain, radiating down one leg to his midcalf. His history and exam did not lead me to expect that his recovery would be unusually slow. I suggested that he rest his back (no biking), take an anti-inflammatory drug, and use ice on his back and heat for the muscle spasm in his leg. After three weeks, Mr. Paul's pain had not improved, so I recommended physical therapy and manipulation. Mr. Paul waited patiently, but after he had experienced two or three months of pain and an inability to go biking, I referred him to a thoughtful and conservative neurosurgeon at Lahey Clinic. An MRI revealed a herniated disk that corresponded to the location of his symptoms. Because of the persistent pain, Mr. Paul opted to have surgery to relieve the pressure on his sciatic nerve root— the presumed cause of his pain. Given the duration and degree of his pain, I supported his decision. (I also would have supported a decision to wait.)

On the day of surgery, Mr. Paul was lying on a stretcher, about to be brought into the operating room, when the neurosurgeon came by to ask him how he was feeling. Mr. Paul said that his pain had actually improved considerably in the previous few days. The neurosurgeon recommended that he get up off the stretcher and go home without surgery. He did. That was several years ago. When last I saw Mr. Paul he was almost completely pain free. The nonsurgery was a great success.

SUPPLY-SIDE TERMINAL CARE

The saddest aspect of our excess spending occurs with end-of-life care, when people are most vulnerable and excess care can cause the most suffering. Unfortunately, this may also be the time when people are also most vulnerable to having supply-side care foisted upon them. Most of the terminally ill patients in my practice were elderly and ready to pass on when their time came. (The two most common fears, being alone and suffering, could usually be allayed by supportive families and good hospice care.) Often, however, the children of elderly dying patients were far less able to accept the inevitability of death—looking at the situation, as they must, through their own eyes and from their own station in life. Yet when seniors are actually given the opportunity to express their end-of-life preferences, 71 percent say they would rather die at home than in a hospital, and 86 percent express the opinion that people with a terminal illness would prefer to be cared for at home.

Despite these clear preferences for less invasive and less hospital-based care, people's end-of-life wishes are usually ignored. Sadly, even those people who have expressed a clear preference not to die in a hospital are no less likely than others to die in a hospital after all. The primary variable determining where and how people die is not their expressed preferences but the availability of hospital beds in their area. One of the most disturbing findings from the Dartmouth study of variations in Medicare spending was that people in the high-spending regions were almost three times as likely to receive "invasive life support," meaning intensive care, emergency intubation, use of a ventilator, and feeding tubes, without any demonstrable benefit.

It behooves all of us to make our wishes known to our loved ones and especially to a person designated to speak on our behalf (a health care proxy) and to empower them to stand up, if necessary, to unwanted treatment at the end of our lives.

THE PROFIT MOTIVE TAKES OVER

The cost of the oversupply of medical services to our nation's pocketbook is staggering. Fisher and his colleagues estimate that 30 to 33 percent of Medicare expenditures could be saved nationally without compromising the quality of medical care. The goal of achieving these savings, they conclude, is "not unreasonable; after all, large metropolitan areas such as Minneapolis and Portland [Oregon] are getting along just fine with relatively modest Medicare expenditures."

The comparison of health care expenditures among the OECD countries presented in Chapter 4 comes to almost exactly the same conclusion. Whether we say we could spend 30 percent less on health care or we say we are spending 42 percent extra, the bottom line is that excess health care expenditures in the United States in 2004 will amount to about *$530 billion* (based on estimated total health care expenditures of $1.8 trillion).

The 2002 Annual Report of the White House's Council of Economic Advisers (among them, Dr. Mark McClellan, before being appointed commissioner of the FDA and then Administrator of the Centers for Medicare and Medicaid Services) articulated the council's general approach to health care: "Markets respond more rapidly than bureaucracies to the changing technology and new innovations in products and services that characterize the American Health Care System." Markets do indeed respond quickly to changes in health care technology, but these responses do not necessarily lead to better health. Using the field of neonatology as an example, it's easy to see that market-based solutions provide about twice the level of costly intensive care hospital services as other comparable countries—with no discernible health benefit. An article in *Health Affairs*, "Hooked on Neonatology," suggests a different solution to improving the health of newborns: "Data from here and abroad suggest that some combination of comprehensive social support, preventive health care for women, comprehensive prenatal care, and easy access to family planning services may be far more cost-effective than neonatal intensive care." Though the preventive approach is more likely to lead to healthier newborns, the market—left to its own devices—will not direct health care in that direction. Preventive medicine does not bring in the big bucks.

It is easy to understand why those profiting from this monumentally lucrative system want us to believe that market-driven health care is the best of all possible health care worlds. It is much harder to understand why doctors who have been trained to base their decisions on the best available evidence go along so willingly with health care American-style. That is the subject of the next chapter.

PART III

TAKING BACK OUR HEALTH

CHAPTER 12

THE KNEE IN ROOM 8

BEYOND THE LIMITS OF BIOMEDICINE

Even acknowledging the medical industry's exquisitely honed ability to shape our medical knowledge, it is still hard to understand why doctors—who are almost universally committed to providing the best care possible for their patients—are such willing participants in this overly commercialized dysfunctional system. Why don't doctors just say no to providing medical care that is not supported by evidence that meets the highest standards of medical science?

Part of the problem is that professionals on the front lines of medicine have no reliable way to differentiate between care that is necessary and beneficial and care that has been pushed into use by financial incentives and will not stand the test of time. Much more important, however, is the template of "good medicine" that is permanently imprinted on doctors during their long years of training. Ever since Louis Pasteur discovered that bacteria cause disease, doctors have been committed to the biomedical approach to medicine: the idea that the cause and cure of every symptom and every disease can, with enough research, be understood and successfully treated at its most basic biological level. Modern scientists and doctors find this idea enormously appealing—identify the biological process that has gone awry, and fix it.

NO KNEE IS AN ISLAND

Consider the case of Mrs. Martin, a woman in her late fifties who had been my patient for many years. She always arrived for her appointments with her hair and makeup carefully attended to, and her greeting was always friendly and respectful—if a bit overly enthusiastic. At the beginning of one typical appointment, I walked into exam room 8 and found her sitting on the examination table with her feet, clad in the usual sneakers, swinging back and forth nervously.

When I asked how she was doing, she wasted no time getting right to the point. She said that her right knee had been hurting for about two weeks and had been swollen for several days. Tylenol hadn't helped at all. She couldn't remember any injury, hadn't had a fever or a tick bite that would raise suspicion about infection (Lyme disease is common north of Boston), and no other joints were bothering her to suggest a systemic problem. She said she was particularly frustrated because her knee pain was interrupting her walking routine. Mrs. Martin had always been proud about keeping up her exercise—walking three to five miles at least five days each week.

As I finished my questions and was getting up off the stool to examine her knee, she made her expectations clear. She asked if I thought she needed an x-ray or MRI, and if one of the new drugs for arthritis might help. I said that those might be helpful, but asked if we could postpone a decision until I had a chance to examine her knee; then we could figure it out together. She agreed. I was relieved that the visit could proceed without becoming a contest of wills at the outset.

I started the exam by asking her to take a few steps across the room. She was favoring her right leg. On exam, her right knee was slightly warmer than the left, indicating the presence of inflammation. There was no redness that would have meant more intense inflammation or possibly even infection. With firm pressure I slid my hand down toward the upper part of her kneecap, and I could feel fluid inside her knee joint being pushed toward my other hand, which was cupped around the bottom of her kneecap. Full bending of her knee was restricted because the fluid inside the joint was acting like a water balloon, with the pressure increasing the more the knee was bent. On the positive side, there was no unusual looseness in the joint, ruling out a ligament injury. And there was no "catch" in the knee, which is sometimes, but not always, detectable when the meniscal cartilage is torn or frayed.

Mrs. Martin's knee pain and swelling were almost certainly due to an acute flare-up of osteoarthritis, a weakening and erosion of the tough "articular cartilage" that covers the ends of the bones in our joints. When functioning normally, cartilage allows the joint to function with remarkably little friction—even with weight on the knee, there is only one-fifteenth the amount of friction between healthy cartilage-covered bones as there is when two smooth ice cubes are rubbed together. In osteoarthritis, however, the small fibers of the cartilage break down, disrupting the smooth surfaces and making the ends of the bones look moth-eaten. This is by far the most common kind of arthritis.

The fundamental cause of osteoarthritis is still not entirely clear. It appears that excess wear and tear somehow leads cells within the tough cartilage to release enzymes that destroy the fibers that make healthy cartilage so resilient. Unfortunately, there are no medications available that inhibit the intracellular process that is responsible for osteoarthritis; yet modern medicine does offer several remedies, mostly to relieve the pain. The first line of defense is weight loss, exercise, and, occasionally, physical therapy. Tylenol (acetaminophen) is the initial drug recommended for pain relief. If this doesn't work, the American College of Rheumatology's guidelines for the treatment of osteoarthritis recommend a "COX-2-specific inhibitor," meaning Celebrex or Vioxx, to decrease the local inflammatory response (the biochemistry of which is quite well understood).

This is what doctors are trained to do: learn about the underlying biochemical and microscopic pathology that produces a problem such as osteoarthritis of the knee. Then we keep up to date with the best ways to intervene in this pathological process to help the tissues return to normal or at least control the symptoms—which, in this case, involved suggesting that Mrs. Martin cut back on her walking, lose a few pounds, and take expensive, long-term drug therapy.

Understand, diagnose, and treat, if possible, the local body part that is causing symptoms. This is the essence of the biomedical model.

But no knee is an island. Even if the biological process of cartilage destruction were completely understood, the biomedical explanation of osteoarthritis would still provide a grossly inadequate understanding of the inflammation in Mrs. Martin's knee and would, by itself, still lead to minimally effective medical care. Mrs. Martin's problem cannot be reduced to a description, even a perfect description, of the pathology in her knee. Of course there is pathology within these cells and the surrounding tissues, but it is impossible to understand the knee problem separated from the rest of her body and the rest of her life.

As her primary care doctor for many years, I knew that Mrs. Martin needed more than what the clinical guidelines advised. The cells in Mrs. Martin's knee were malfunctioning because her walking was causing more wear and tear than Mother Nature had designed her knee to withstand. But I understood Mrs. Martin well enough to know that simply suggesting that she reduce her walking, as common sense would dictate, would have been very bad advice for her.

I first met Mrs. Martin about 15 years before this visit, when I was taking care of her husband, who was dying of lung cancer. Through the sadness and stress of her husband's illness, I got to know her quite well. She is what you would call a worrier. Over the years, she had come to me seeking relief from panic attacks and insomnia. I referred her for psychotherapy, but it didn't help, and she had no interest in trying counseling again. I prescribed several different medications, trying to ease her symptoms, but none provided enough relief to make the side effects worth putting up with. No doubt a combination of her genetic makeup, her formative childhood experiences, and her current life situation contributed to the chronic anxiety that plagued her. My job was to help her maintain her psychological equilibrium in ways that were not harmful to her health or, better yet, promoted it.

Mrs. Martin had learned over the years that the best medicine to keep the anxiety at bay was exercise, and her exercise of choice was walking. She knew all too well that the unpleasant fight-or-flight sensation would come roaring back as soon as she slacked off. Walking was a positive coping mechanism, especially compared with self-destructive alternatives such as smoking or alcohol abuse, but her knees weren't designed to withstand the amount of walking required to control her anxiety. In fact, one could argue that the primary cause of Mrs. Martin's osteoarthritis was her anxiety. And therein lies the problem with the biomedical approach. When we focus exclusively on the local cellular and biochemical pathology as the cause of disease, we often overlook other important sources of the problem and forgo opportunities to provide cure and relief.

Through the downs and ups of her life over the past 15 years, Mrs. Martin had come to trust that I understood that her walking was essential to keeping her anxiety and panic attacks under control. Walking meant the difference between a tortured life and a fulfilling life. Because she knew that I knew this, she was able to consider my suggestions. That is where we started our discussion.

Instead of ordering an x-ray or MRI and starting her on Celebrex or Vioxx, we decided on a more practical approach: swimming as her only exercise until her knee started to improve; taking a low dose of an over-the-counter anti-inflammatory drug that would provide maximum or very near maximum pain relief and be much less likely to upset her stomach than a full dose; taking glucosamine and chondroitin sulfate daily, which would not start to help for a month or two but had a good chance of providing relief from the pain and making her knee somewhat more resilient to the trauma of exercise. I advised her to call me in one week if her knee pain and swelling were not improving. At that point she might benefit from my withdrawing the fluid and injecting some steroid into her knee joint to quiet down this acute episode more quickly (though this still would not allow her to resume her walking where she left off).

I told Mrs. Martin that I thought the fundamental problem with her knee was that she was asking it do too much. She was proud of and committed to her walking, but as soon as the knee problem was framed as a consequence of her commitment to her health and sense of well-being, she was willing to search for other ways to achieve the same goal. Swimming, though not her favorite activity, would allow her to keep up her exercise even while her knee was acutely inflamed. Once the swelling and pain resolved, she could begin a routine of cross-training. Activities such as bicycling and using an elliptical trainer machine would allow her to get just as much exercise without the repetitive trauma to her knees caused by walking.

The temptation to order an x-ray or MRI and prescribe the latest arthritis medicine for a patient like Mrs. Martin is great. She would believe that she was getting the best care, and I (or any doctor) would believe that I had done my job well. End of story, next patient. But the truth is that pictures of Mrs. Martin's knee were very unlikely to help it get better any sooner, and no amount of Celebrex or Vioxx was going to allow Mrs. Martin to resume walking enough to control her anxiety. There was plenty of time for other diagnostic tests if her symptoms did not respond to these simple measures.

THE ROOTS OF THE BIOMEDICAL MODEL

In the second half of the nineteenth century, medical science took a giant leap forward. Microbiology, the study of infectious microorganisms, or germs, began shortly after Louis Pasteur accepted a position as chair of the department of chemistry at the University of Lille, in the north of France. The local industry relied upon the precise harnessing of fermentation in the production of beer and wine, and the making of alcohol from beet juice. Pasteur's work on the industrial problems associated with fermentation led to the discovery that fermentation was caused by live organisms. Pasteur also discovered the difference between yeast, which appeared round when viewed through a microscope and turned out to be essential for fermentation, and bacteria, which appeared rod-shaped under the microscope and turned out to be responsible for "souring" the beer. In 1865 he turned his attention to the epidemic that was devastating the silkworm industry in France, and discovered that a bacterial infection was responsible for the silkworms' failure to spin silk cocoons or reproduce.

In 1877 Pasteur showed that a germ, anthrax, was the cause of a disease that was killing cattle. He went on to develop an anthrax vaccine, made from a weakened strain of the disease that caused only a mild illness, but then protected vaccinated sheep and cattle from getting the full-blown disease. A few years later, a 9-year-old boy, Joseph Meister, was brought to Pasteur, not yet sick but doomed to die within four to eight weeks after having been bitten many times by a rabid dog. At the time, Pasteur was working on a rabies vaccine made from infected spinal cord tissue taken from rabid rabbits. The specific infectious agent had not yet been identified because it was a virus—too small to see through a microscope and not amenable to being grown by the same techniques that Pasteur had used successfully to grow bacteria. Nonetheless, Pasteur was able to produce weakened "germs" by air-drying the infected tissue for two weeks, then incorporating this dried tissue into an injectable vaccination. In theory, injection of the weakened germs would evoke enough of an immune response to prevent the real rabies infection, which is universally fatal, from taking hold. Immunization with inactivated "germs" had never before been tried on a human, but this boy was sure to die without treatment. So, despite Pasteur's self-described "acute and harrowing anxiety," he gave the boy a series of 12 injections of the experimental vaccination. Joseph Meister never became ill.

Over the following 15 months, Pasteur went on to treat 2490 people who had been bitten by rabid animals. Only one person died. The dramatic success of the rabies vaccine led to the creation of the Pasteur Institute, still one of the world's great institutions of medical research. Joseph Meister went on to become a gatekeeper there. (Tragically, in 1940, 55 years after receiving his lifesaving treatment, Joseph Meister took his own life rather than accede to an order issued by invading German soldiers to open Pasteur's burial crypt.)

While Pasteur was making so much progress in France, Robert Koch, a German physician, was putting the finishing touches on the germ theory of disease. In 1882, he reported that the cause of tuberculosis, the tubercle bacillus, could be identified by looking at infected tissue under the microscope. And further, he found that the organisms that cause tuberculosis could be grown in culture, produce disease when injected into laboratory animals, be extracted from these infected animals, and be grown again in culture. These four steps, known as "Koch's postulates," became accepted as proof that a specific organism was the cause of a specific disease. Using these postulates, Koch went on to identify the microorganisms that cause cholera, typhoid, and diphtheria. Another German physician, Paul Ehrlich, who had worked as Koch's assistant, identified the organisms that cause malaria and sleeping sickness. It was Ehrlich who coined the term "magic bullet" in the search for drugs that would block microorganisms from causing disease but not injure healthy tissue. In 1909 he discovered a treatment for syphilis, Salvarsan (an arsenic-based compound), which was soon used worldwide and represented a giant step forward for the German pharmaceutical industry.

Meanwhile in the United States, Johns Hopkins University started a

medical school in 1893 that would set a new standard of medical education, according to Paul Starr's extensive historical account, *The Social
Transformation of American Medicine*. This was the first medical school
with a four-year curriculum, and students were required to have completed four years of college before enrolling. Starr explains that the divide
soon widened between universities such as Johns Hopkins and Harvard,
which were incorporating the scientific basis of medicine into their medical school curricula, and schools with far lower standards that were basically run for the financial gain of the faculty. A study done by the
American Medical Association in 1906 showed that too many poorly
trained doctors were being turned out by substandard medical schools
(and providing a bit too much competition for established doctors, as
well). The AMA was unable to take any action against the inferior
schools, however, because its professional code of ethics prevented doctors from criticizing others in the profession publicly.

To avoid this problem, the Carnegie Foundation funded a study of
medical education in the United States, which was conducted by Abra-
ham Flexner, a graduate of Johns Hopkins with a degree in education,
not medicine. The doors of all 131 American medical schools were
opened widely for inspection by Flexner and the AMA representative
who accompanied him. The schools assumed that Flexner brought with
him the possibility of financial support from the Carnegie Foundation.
When the Flexner Report was completed in 1910, most of the schools
found that his mission had been quite different. Flexner's report concluded that the low quality of medical education in the majority of medical schools was depriving society of the great progress that was being
made in medical science. The report recommended that all but 31 of the
medical schools in the United States be closed because they were providing substandard medical education. In the end, about half the schools
survived, cutting the number of graduating doctors by more than half.

The Flexner Report marked the beginning of the modern era of
scientific medical education. One of the most important changes was
that medical schools were taken over by full-time scientists, medical
researchers, and academic specialists, diminishing what Starr calls American medicine's "practical" orientation. Subsequent to the report, the
Rockefeller and Carnegie Foundations became the primary sources of

funding for university-based research. The majority of Rockefeller's General Education Board grants went to seven of the top medical schools, ensuring that an orientation toward research was a key element in the prestige of a medical school, and setting the stage for what evolved into the growing synergy between universities and the pharmaceutical and other medical industries.

Support for the reforms suggested by Flexner was not unanimous, however. Sir William Osler, recognized as the greatest clinician of his time, had grave reservations. (Osler had been the first professor of medicine at Johns Hopkins, but left in 1905 to accept a professorship in Oxford, England.) After learning of the content of the Flexner report, Osler wrote a letter to the president of Johns Hopkins expressing his concerns:

> *I am opposed to the plan as likely to spell ruin to the type of school I have always felt the [Johns Hopkins] hospital should be. . . . The ideals would change, and I fear lest the broad open spirit which has characterized the school should narrow, as a teacher and a student chased each other down the fascinating road of research, forgetful of those wider interests to which a great hospital must minister.*

According to Starr, Flexner himself eventually became disappointed by the inflexible scientific orientation of medical education that followed his report, which, he came to realize, stifled students' creativity. Flexner's good intentions had laid the groundwork for the specialty- and research-dominated system of medical education that still stands—the more prestigious the school, the greater the emphasis on biomedical research and the less the emphasis on pragmatic medical care.

WHERE DO DOCTORS COME FROM?

Almost 100 years later, the scientific principles outlined in Flexner's report still dominate the training of American doctors. Before they've even entered medical school, medical students' understanding of the tasks of medicine is already well established. They have studied and excelled in biology, biochemistry, and physics; and they understand that the forefront of medical science lies in the discoveries that are based in these disciplines. This is the stuff of real medicine. The tools of healing that they want to learn about are blood tests, electrocardiograms, x-rays, MRIs, drugs, surgeries, and scopes of all kinds.

Doctors in training work in the teams that are frequently seen making rounds in teaching hospitals. These teams are made up of students and doctors at all levels of training, the most senior member being the attending physician, usually a faculty member of the medical school. Each team represents a microcosm of medicine's hierarchy of knowledge, experience, and authority. Over the course of seven or more years of medical training, doctors progress from team novice to one of the senior members, with increasing responsibility for the medical care provided.

One or more team members are on call each night, usually one first-year resident (formerly called an intern) and a third- or fourth-year medical student, if there is one on the team. They admit new patients and are available to respond to the medical needs of the patients being cared for by the other members of the team who are not on call. This can involve anything from getting called for a routine order for a laxative to evaluating a fever or chest pain to becoming involved in a true life-and-death emergency with all the tension and drama depicted so well on the TV show *ER*. Often the students and residents on call get little or no sleep, as their hours are filled with "working up" patients: recording medical histories, doing exams, getting blood work, looking at electrocardiograms and x-rays, doing urgent procedures, talking to family members and more senior doctors, and whatever else needs to be done. As a first-year resident, I remember feeling fortunate if I had enough time to brush my teeth before morning rounds began and was truly grateful if I had enough time for a shower.

During morning rounds, the students and residents who were on call the night before present the new admissions and unexpected developments on the patients they were covering to the rest of the team. These formal public presentations are among the defining moments of medical training. Exhausted from being up all night and having done their best to take good care of their patients, trainees describe their patients' medical problems, the tests that were ordered, the results that are available, and the decisions that were made about therapies, consults, and procedures. All of this has to be backed up by the best scientific evidence available, often including reference to or actual copies of the latest articles from the medical journals.

Presenters are vulnerable to criticism of their medical care by more senior team members, vulnerable to getting grilled on their medical knowledge (the medical students call this "getting pimped"), and at risk of public humiliation. Rarely does this happen, but just knowing that it can is both highly motivating and highly intimidating. This system is elegantly designed to allow young physicians to be given progressively more responsibility while ensuring that proper standards of medical care are maintained. I know that I learned the most about being a doctor during the wee hours of the night when, tired and working alone, I had to decide for myself whether I was really sure about the medical care that I was about to render or whether I should wake up my senior resident to double-check my plan (and—truth be told—learn from my mistakes). The reaction to my night's work on morning rounds was the public measure of my competence as a doctor, which at that stage of training, life, and fatigue, was also the measure of my self-esteem.

Third- and fourth-year medical students, residents, and fellows (doctors receiving specialty training) spend almost all of their time in teaching hospitals, learning how to take care of the sickest patients. The intensity and the technological orientation of care are exactly what most of their patients need, and doctors-in-training learn that this is "real medicine." It turns out, however, that only about one out of every 200 patients seen by community-based doctors requires the intensity of care they learned to provide during their years of arduous training. Within the culture of university medical centers, taking care of the other 199 patients is looked down upon disparagingly as "medicine lite." This leaves community-based doctors often feeling inadequately challenged to use their hard-earned skills on a day-to-day basis, more typically being called upon to listen to patients' mundane complaints and treat routine illnesses. Like racehorses too tightly reined in, most doctors want to practice "real medicine": diagnosing complex illnesses by ordering tests to confirm or rule out hypotheses and implementing the latest therapies, which are aimed ever more precisely at specific biological causes of disease.

Through our years of intense training we learn that there is not, nor could there be, a more rational way to practice medicine. The unspoken underlying narrative of biomedicine shared by most doctors today can be summed up by four principles:

1. The origin of disease is best sought at the smallest level of function, usually molecular, genetic, and cellular. In the case of coronary heart disease, for instance, illness is caused by the migration of LDL cholesterol particles into the walls of the coronary arteries.

2. Dysfunction at the molecular level causes dysfunction at progressively higher levels of function. With CHD, the inflammatory reaction caused by oxidized LDL cholesterol particles attracts white blood cells and causes overgrowth of smooth muscle cells. These byproducts of the inflammatory reaction build up as plaque on the inside of the coronary arteries and can lead to a heart attack.

3. The most effective medical care is focused on individual patients. In this case, testing cholesterol levels and treating individual patients according to their level of risk is the best way to prevent coronary heart disease.

4. The challenges of medicine are adequately and completely addressed by the objective methods of science. Continuing with the same example, optimal risk assessment, prevention, and treatment of coronary disease are fully achieved by medical care based on relevant scientific evidence.

Medical anthropologist and psychiatrist Dr. Arthur Kleinman of Harvard describes the process by which medical students internalize these principles as learning "a hierarchical order of biological reality." It turns out, however, that this reductionist biomedical approach doesn't always lead to the most effective medical care.

BIOMEDICINE OR FOLK MEDICINE?

The temptation to believe that pure science—the four principles of bio-medicine—will protect us from being felled by coronary heart disease (or other diseases) before we have had the opportunity to live a complete life seems irresistible. But there are flaws in this model. While statins may seem like Ehrlich's "magic bullet," there are more effective ways to decrease the risk of heart disease. Indeed, plenty of evidence suggests that persuading people to live healthier lives can lower the risk of heart disease even more than statin drugs. A study of primary prevention of heart disease in high-risk men from Oslo, Norway, looked at the effect of lifestyle changes on the risk of heart disease and death. More than 1200 men with cholesterol levels above 300 mg/dL, four-fifths of whom also smoked, were randomized so that half received counseling about diet (decrease saturated fats by more than half and increase polyunsaturated fats) and smoking cessation. Over the subsequent 10 years, there were 44 percent fewer cases of heart disease and 39 percent fewer deaths among the men who had been counseled about diet and smoking than among the men in the control group (about two deaths were prevented for each 100 men who received counseling). For these high-risk men in Oslo, lifestyle counseling was half again *more effective* at preventing heart disease and premature death than was treatment with a statin drug in the high-risk men included in the West of Scotland Coronary Prevention Study (WOSCOPS).

For secondary prevention of heart disease, the situation in which the statins have the greatest benefit, studies also show that nondrug approaches can be more effective than treatment with statin drugs. The Lyon Diet Heart Study randomized people who had a heart attack between 1988 and 1992 either to be counseled on eating a Mediterranean-type diet or to receive routine post–heart attack dietary advice (reduced intake of total and saturated fat) from their doctors. Over almost four years of follow-up, the people on the Mediterranean diet experienced 70 percent less heart disease than the people in the control group (4 percent versus 12 percent), about three times the reduction in the risk of further heart disease achieved with statin drugs. The overall risk of death was 45 percent lower for those on the Mediterranean diet (6 percent versus 12 percent), about twice the reduction achieved by statins. Interestingly, in this study the Mediterranean diet had no significant effect on total or LDL cholesterol, showing that cholesterol is not the only culprit that increases the risk of heart disease.

In fact, results from the Nurses Health Study, published in 2000 in the NEJM, show that women who exercise regularly, eat a healthy diet, don't smoke, maintain a proper body weight, and drink moderately have only 17 percent as much risk of developing heart disease as women who don't follow these guidelines. This study also found that about five out of every six cases of heart disease that developed among the nurses could be attributed to an unhealthy lifestyle. So why, if we already know how to prevent the vast majority of heart disease, do we continue to place so much more emphasis on measuring cholesterol and C-reactive protein levels? And why does the decision to start a cholesterol-lowering statin drug dominate our preventive medicine strategy when healthy lifestyle changes have been shown to be so much more effective?

Could it be that, although we define our era by the tremendous scientific and technological progress that is being made (particularly in medicine), our desire to believe in this narrative of biomedical progress predisposes us to uncritical belief in its real merits? In other words, might the shared belief in the potential of medical science be, in large part, our cultural mythology?

We tend to look upon myths with romantic condescension as the stories of primitive societies that provide shared meaning and hope and ease the prospect of suffering and death—stories that are made of "facts" that we (scientifically sophisticated as we are) know are not really true. Our belief that we are too scientifically grounded to succumb to such nonrational beliefs may, in fact, *be* our myth. How else can we explain the widespread agreement that statins or the new antidepressants or the COX-2 inhibitors are genuine breakthroughs that will preserve and restore our health in ways never before possible? These are our myths, merging science and hope into our shared belief.

It is exactly myths such as these that Thomas Kuhn was referring to in his groundbreaking book *The Structure of Scientific Revolutions,* published in 1962. Kuhn coined the term "paradigm" to describe the unspoken professional values, beliefs, and techniques shared by a community of scientists or professionals. The shared paradigm then defines the range of problems that are legitimate to investigate, the range of legitimate solutions, and the criteria that justify belief that the findings are true. Particularly during all the years of intense medical training, the unspoken principles of biomedicine are communicated and enforced by the well-defined and ever-present structure of authority.

Kuhn's most important contribution was to show that what appears from the outside to be the unrestricted pursuit of scientific discovery is really the result of scientific inquiry within a tightly restricted field. Facts that don't fit the current paradigm, like the greater reduction of the risk of heart disease by lifestyle changes than by statin therapy, are discounted and ignored: "not real medicine," and "not what real doctors do."

For example, when I mentioned to a colleague that Vioxx causes 21 percent more serious complications overall than naproxen, he immediately fired back, "I don't believe it." I told him that the data from the manufacturer's own study showed this, and I could show him how to get the information on the FDA's website. He reiterated, "I still don't believe it." This exchange reminded me of the Richard Pryor comedy routine in which his wife walks into their bedroom and finds him with another woman. As she stands there aghast, trying to make sense of what she is seeing, Pryor says to her, "Who are you going to believe, me or your lying eyes?"

The evidence that Vioxx causes significantly more serious medical problems than naproxen, and that the ALLHAT study shows that there is no benefit to tripling the number of Americans taking statin drugs are as clear as any scientific evidence can be. But for practicing doctors even to consider the possibility that the experts and the most respected medical journals might be leading them astray represents a broader challenge to the integrity of what we think of as medical knowledge. Even more important, it's a challenge to the integrity of the process by which we come to believe that new medical information is true. For doctors, this is the ultimate Pandora's box. Once a doctor starts questioning accepted medical knowledge, he or she immediately risks becoming an outsider, a boat-rocker, losing the respect and legitimacy earned during those long years of training. It wasn't the facts about Vioxx that my colleague couldn't believe; it was the need to trust the system that produced and sanctioned his professional knowledge. Without this, he would have become paralyzed with doubt by each of the myriad decisions that he had to make every day. He couldn't let himself believe that his trusted sources of information had so misled him that three years after the publication of the VIGOR study in the NEJM, he was still unaware of the serious risks posed by treating patients with Vioxx.

In what has become a classic paper, "The Need for a New Medical Model: A Challenge for Biomedicine," published in the journal *Science* in 1977, Dr. George Engel wrote, "The historical fact we have to face is that in modern Western society biomedicine not only has provided a basis for the scientific study of disease, it has also become our own culturally specific perspective about disease, that is, our folk model." "Folk model" takes some of the shine off the great progress that has been made in biomedicine, but it is the only way to describe the intensity of our commitment to providing and receiving so much suboptimal medical care.

EXPANDING THE BIOMEDICAL PARADIGM

Of course, the biomedical model works exquisitely for some problems, from emergency surgery and successful organ transplantation to the treatment of strep throats and life-threatening infections. The problem is not the biomedical model itself; but like any good tool, it must be used in the right circumstances. The problem is the illusion that the biomedical approach is the *only* valid approach to all of our health problems.

An article published in JAMA in 2004, written by researchers from the U.S. Centers for Disease Control and Prevention, showed that "half of all deaths that occurred in the United States in 2000 could be attributed to . . . largely preventable behaviors and exposures." Heading the list were 435,000 deaths due to tobacco and 400,000 deaths due to obesity and physical inactivity. Researchers from the Robert Wood Johnson Foundation noted that another 6 percent of deaths (144,000) were attributable to poverty. The Institute of Medicine (part of the prestigious National Academy of Sciences) reports that "there is strong evidence that behavior and environment are responsible for over 70 percent of avoidable mortality." In comparison, researchers estimate that inadequate medical care is responsible for between 10 and 15 percent of deaths. Yet almost all (95 percent) of our health care spending is directed at biomedically oriented medical care. Assuming that the primary goal of our health care system is to improve our health, this allocation of our resources is simply not rational.

It is not a lack of scientific evidence that keeps us locked into the narrow paradigm of biomedicine. Few diseases can be reduced to a single biochemical, genetic, or cellular etiology. Certainly one factor contributing to coronary heart disease is LDL cholesterol particles entering the coronary artery walls and setting off an inflammatory cascade. But it is by no means the *only* cause. Untreated high blood pressure or diabetes can also contribute to coronary heart disease. Unhealthy behaviors (not exercising, poor diet, smoking, and obesity) play an even larger role, especially before the age of 70. To single out any of these as the only, the most primary, or the most scientifically valid cause of heart disease is simply to show an a priori commitment to a particular biological perspective.

Behavioral change is a complex process. Rarely do people change lifelong patterns of behavior simply in response to a recommendation from a health professional, though it does happen occasionally and is certainly worth a try. More typically, people's behaviors are anchored in their personal histories, social relationships, and cultural and economic circumstances: in what might be called a personal paradigm. Significant and lasting change in behavior often requires changing the deep assumptions that sustain this paradigm of self. If one of the goals of medical care is to prevent disease, then don't doctors have a professional responsibility to address the unique health needs, habits, and risks of each individual patient? Unfortunately, the training and culture of medicine leave many doctors feeling that this is too mundane, not worthy of their skills or time. In fact, a study done by researchers from the Rand Corporation, published in the NEJM in December 2003, shows that doctors provide appropriate counseling to their patients only 18 percent of the time.

If our model of heart disease prevention is dominated by reducing the number of LDL cholesterol particles migrating through arterial walls, then certainly the proper focus of care is the individual patient. But health is not just an individual phenomenon. There is a large ecological component that includes family, community, and cultural and social factors, as well as the physical environment. Just as individuals are made up of multiple levels of function, they are also embedded in these larger contexts that play an important role in their sense of identity, personal beliefs, and sources of meaning—all of which plays a large role in determining their health behaviors. As Richard Lewontin, professor of biology at Harvard University, says in *The Triple Helix,* "taken together, the relations of genes, organisms, and environments are reciprocal relations in which all three elements are both causes and effects."

THE DIFFERENCE BETWEEN A PATIENT AND A PERSON

Besides the enormous volume of basic medical science to be learned in the first two years of medical school, one of the most important tasks is to learn the difference between a "patient" and a "person." We all know that a person is someone who has "I-ness," with consciousness and subjective experience, a sense of values and purpose, like ourselves. A patient, on the other hand, is a body in which the experiences of pain and disease are understood as objective phenomena, observable and verifiable by the tools of science.

A first-year medical student who had recently started to dissect her cadaver in anatomy class told me, "I don't want to donate my body. I had gory dreams about desecration. It wasn't right that I was learning so much from a process that I did not want my body to be subjected to after I die. I don't think I could, knowing what goes on in the anatomy lab." What goes on is a kind of black humor that only partially mitigates the discomfort students inevitably feel as they learn to relate to the human body as a thing devoid of personhood. Dissecting a cadaver in the anatomy lab is an important medical school initiation rite, the beginning of what Byron Good, a medical anthropologist at Harvard Medical School, calls learning the "clinical gaze." The students' way of seeing the human body, at least their patients' bodies, is forever transformed.

As the students dissect their cadavers, they learn with a double-edged scalpel: at the same time that their knowledge about the physical body is expanding, their ability to relate to their future patients as people—with all of the feelings, fears, and yearning for meaning that they know in themselves—is shrinking. Professor Good observes, "This means of interpreting reality is both powerful, illuminating many disease phenomena and providing the basis for therapeutics, and at the same time profoundly ideological and often misleading." The misleading aspect of the interpretation is what makes so many of us cringe when we find ourselves in the dehumanized role of patient. There is no place in the biomedical model for patients to have personhood.

According to philosopher John Searle, subjective experience and consciousness are not the kinds of things that can be studied directly by the tools of science—they can only be experienced. Sure, medical researchers observe with increasing sophistication the physical correlates of subjective experience, relying upon galvanic skin response (the lie detector test), electroencephalogram (EEG or brain wave) recordings, and functional MRIs of the brain. These objective observations can help us understand what kind of physical changes take place during different experiences, but they get us not a whit closer to understanding what it feels like to be that person whose brain we are observing, nor to understanding the meaning of the experience for that person. This is why the extrascientific qualities that define personhood (and contribute so much to the personal decisions that are usually the most important determinants of our health) tend to get discounted or diminished in the world of biomedicine.

And this is the rebuttal to the last principle of the biomedical model, the tacit assumption that all valid knowledge is amenable to investigation by the tools of science. We all know that we are not "things" like the cadaver in the anatomy lab, that we possess "I-ness," and that our core of meaning and values is related to our sense of self and not to the kinds of knowledge that science reveals. Strict allegiance to the paradigm of biomedicine demands a hierarchical ordering of metaphysics with the facts that can be known by the methods of science alone at the top. A less constraining paradigm would value different metaphysical perspectives equally: One perspective is the body as a thing, that can be known by science. Another is the person, whose essence can be known directly only by first-person experience. And there is also a mysterious and dynamic relationship between the two that will, at least for the foreseeable future (and

I suspect forever), keep the "art" of medical care from being rendered obsolete by progress in medical science.

The challenge to doctors is to learn as much as possible about the scientific-technological skills of medicine, while maintaining the wisdom to integrate these skills into what are fundamentally moral and interpersonal relationships with their patients. It is only then that patients' beliefs and values become legitimate concerns in their medical care, and only then that the doctor-patient relationship reaches its healing potential.

The greatest distinguishing characteristic of primary care medicine—family medicine, general pediatrics, and general internal medicine—is that the subject of care is the person, not a particular disease, not a specific body part, and not just a physical body. Though metaphysics is not a frequent topic of conversation in primary care training programs, all good primary care doctors know that their first responsibility is the ongoing care of the person.

This distinction keeps primary care permanently at the bottom of the status hierarchy within academic medical centers. In the arena of modern biomedicine, attempts to integrate the interpersonal aspect of healing into patient care are looked upon, at best, as an extracurricular activity, and not uncommonly with haughty derision—a petty distraction from "real doctors' " concerns with "real medicine." This is the legacy of the Flexner Report: good medicine defined exclusively in the terms of biomedicine. If only Sir William Osler could return to help modern doctors understand once again that "It is much more important to know what sort of patient has a disease than what sort of disease a patient has."

CHAPTER 13

FROM OSTEOPOROSIS TO HEART DISEASE

WHAT THE RESEARCH REALLY SHOWS ABOUT STAYING HEALTHY

Pretending to care about our health is often just part of the drug and other medical industries' overall strategy to increase their sales. They dominate the medical journals, airwaves, newspapers, and magazines with "information" designed to convince doctors and patients that their products are essential for good health. They focus attention on the health problems and solutions that are the most commercially advantageous rather than most beneficial for our health. They even pathologize normal human experiences such as menopause and aging, reframing the transitions of a healthy life into medical problems that require diagnoses and drugs—and in the process alienating us from the meaning inherent in the landmarks of a healthy life.

The truth, as we have seen, is that the benefits of medical care are real but limited, and more is by no means always better, and is often worse. These awkward facts get shoved into the background of our common wisdom by the bright lights of advertising and medical news that shine incessantly on the "breakthroughs" in medical progress and the drugs that you should "talk to your doctor about." By saturating our sources of information, the medical industry has convinced most Americans that the answer to almost every health problem can be found in a brand-name pill or high-priced medical procedure.

That's the bad news. And it's very bad, costing Americans hundreds of billions of dollars a year and, even worse, compromising our health and quality of life. But there is good news, too—and it's enormously good: the evidence from study after study, including gold-standard randomized clinical trials, shows that we can usually do a great deal more to maintain our own health than the medical industry, particularly the drug industry, promises it can do for us.

The goal in this chapter is not to reject medical care, but to use the best available scientific evidence to place it in the proper perspective. Exposing the distortions of commercially driven medicine is an essential part of this process, but still it is important to remember that about two-thirds of our medical care is beneficial and even lifesaving. The challenge in determining optimal medical care is to identify the boundary between the effective care that truly improves health and the commercially driven care that at best misdirects our efforts to stay healthy and at worst is actually harmful (like routine hormone replacement therapy). These research findings may surprise you—and will probably surprise your doctor even more.

OSTEOPOROSIS

Most postmenopausal women worry about their bones becoming fragile. The National Osteoporosis Foundation states the problem succinctly: "Osteoporosis is often called the 'silent disease' because bone loss occurs without symptoms. People may not know that they have osteoporosis until their bones become so weak that a sudden strain, bump, or fall causes a fracture or a vertebra to collapse." Twenty percent of all women over the age of 50 have osteoporosis and another 40 percent have osteopenia, thinning of the bones that puts the women at risk of developing osteoporosis.

What causes osteoporosis? Healthy bones undergo constant remodeling to repair minor injuries, maintain strength in response to stress, and provide the body with a reservoir of calcium. The bone remodeling process is accomplished by a balance between the activity of cells that absorb the calcium out of existing bone, called osteoclasts, and cells that lay down new bone, called osteoblasts. In women, this balance changes somewhere between the ages of 30 and 45, so that more bone is absorbed than is replaced, leading to the net loss of calcium. As women (and men to a lesser degree) age, the mineral density of their bones naturally decreases, which can lead to osteoporosis.

Hip fractures are by far the most feared consequence. Data from the National Osteoporosis Foundation show that 24 percent of people who suffer a fractured hip die within one year; a quarter of those who had been living independently require long-term care; and only 15 percent are able to walk across a room unaided six months later. A bone mineral density (BMD) test can quickly determine the degree of bone loss in a woman's skeleton and whether or not she has osteoporosis or osteopenia.

If you are a woman who has reached the age of 50 and has not yet had a bone density test, you are probably thinking about calling your doctor to schedule one as soon as possible. And you are probably comforted to know that there are a number of new medications on the market that can reverse age-related bone loss for women who have osteoporosis or who are at high risk of developing it. But you may want to read on before making the call.

Most women were not even aware of the risk of osteoporosis before the early 1980s. As discussed in Chapter 5, this changed largely as a result of an educational campaign initiated in 1982. Researchers from the British Columbia Office of Health Technology Assessment point out that the campaign succeeded by addressing women's growing interest in preventive health care and their fear of aging. But it wasn't until 1993, when a study group hosted by the World Health Organization established clear-cut definitions of osteoporosis and osteopenia, that doctors were provided with straightforward criteria to make these diagnoses and upon which to base their treatment recommendations. According to the WHO study group, a woman has osteoporosis when her bone mineral density (BMD), as measured by a simple x-ray test, is 2.5 or more standard deviations below the average peak bone mass of healthy young adult women. This is defined as a T score of -2.5 or less. Osteopenia is diagnosed when a woman's T score is between -1.0 and -2.5.

So far this may sound compelling, but a closer look presents a very different picture: The definitions developed by the WHO Study Group are based on the assumption that the young adult skeleton is healthy and that as people age, their bones become progressively more "diseased." The study group's criteria, however, ignore the fact that loss of bone mass is a perfectly normal part of aging, especially in postmenopausal women. Simply on a statistical basis, according to the WHO study group's definition, about half of all women at age 52 who have BMD tests will be diagnosed as having osteopenia, and this percentage goes up quickly with age. Similarly, according to the WHO study group's definition of osteoporosis, about half of all American women will have the "disease" by the age of 72.

WHO's definitions transform the majority of healthy postmenopausal women whose bones are aging normally into "patients" having or being at risk of having a frightening bone "disease." A decrease in T score is usually no more a measure of disease than is the greater amount of time it takes an elderly jogger to run a mile than it did when she was at her peak performance. This reframing of normal aging into a pathological process is reminiscent of Dr. Robert Wilson's successful campaign to convince women and their doctors that menopause was not a natural event but a hormone-deficiency disease. We fell for that, hook, line, and sinker, with great harm to many women, and only later discovered that Dr. Wilson had been funded by the drug companies. In this case, however, the source of information is the trusted World Health Organization, on which public health officials in every country rely for health information and policy recommendations. Can't we trust that its recommendations are free of commercial influence and in the best interests of women around the world? Unfortunately, we cannot.

At the time that the WHO study group did its work, there were several new drugs for osteoporosis in the pipeline. The drug companies stood to benefit greatly if definitions of osteoporosis and osteopenia included large numbers of postmenopausal women and if bone mineral density testing was adopted into their routine medical care. It turns out that the WHO study group that developed the criteria for diagnosing osteoporosis and osteopenia was funded by three drug companies: the Rorer Foundation, Sandoz, and SmithKline Beecham. Of course, commercial funding does not necessarily impugn the conclusions of the study group, but its conclusions did happen to be in the drug companies' interest.

In a 1994 paper published in the journal *Osteoporosis International,* the WHO study group recommended that "an appropriate time to consider screening and intervention is at the menopause." If BMD became part of routine care for postmenopausal women—based on the statistical definitions developed by the study group—the drug companies would be assured that millions of women would be seeking billions of dollars' worth of their drugs, hoping to prevent and treat osteoporosis.

It may be hard to believe, especially with the debacle of routine HRT so fresh in our minds, but there has never been a randomized controlled study done to determine whether there is a benefit to screening women for osteoporosis with BMD tests. There simply is no gold-standard evidence showing that ordering all these tests and prescribing all those drugs is leading to better health for women. Nonetheless, the current recommendations call for women to have a BMD test at age 65 or earlier if there are risk factors for osteoporosis.

In 1995, Fosamax, the brand name for alendronate, was the first of the new generation of drugs approved by the FDA for the treatment of osteoporosis. Fosamax works by attaching itself to the surface of bone, interposed between the osteoclasts and the bone the osteoclasts are trying to absorb. Randomized clinical trials of Fosamax published in medical journals show dramatic reductions in the relative risk of hip fracture for women with osteoporosis. In a study published in JAMA in 1998, for example, women with an average age of 68 and a T score of -2.5 or less who took Fosamax for four years were 56 percent less likely to suffer a hip fracture than women in the control group.

This sounds like very good news for women with osteoporosis, but how many hip fractures were really prevented? With no drug therapy at all, women with osteoporosis had a 99.5 percent chance of making it through each year without a hip fracture—pretty good odds. With drug therapy, their odds improved to 99.8 percent. In other words, taking the drugs decreased their risk of hip fracture from 0.5 percent per year to 0.2 percent per year. This tiny decrease in absolute risk translates into the study's reported 56 percent reduction in relative risk. The bottom line is that 81 women with osteoporosis have to take Fosamax for 4.2 years, at a cost of more than $300,000, to prevent one hip fracture. (This benefit does not include a reduction of less serious fractures, including wrist and vertebral fractures. Most vertebral fractures cause no symptoms.)

A study published in the NEJM in 2001 showed that even women with severe osteoporosis* derived only small benefit from these drugs. The study randomized women between the ages of 70 and 79 to receive Actonel (the brand name of risedronate, a cousin of Fosamax) or a placebo for three years. Hip fractures were significantly reduced only in the women who already had a spine fracture when the study began (40 percent of the women in the study). One hundred such women would have to take Actonel for about one year to prevent one hip fracture. For the other 60 percent of women in the study without a preexisting spine fracture, Actonel did not significantly reduce the risk of hip fracture. Moreover, the drug appeared to have no beneficial effect on their overall health. There was no difference in the number of serious illnesses (causing death or hospitalization), including fractures, that occurred in the women who took Actonel compared with those who took the placebo. The same result was found in younger women, with an average age of 69, who had been diagnosed with osteoporosis and at least one spinal fracture: fewer fractures but no reduction in the occurrence of serious illness in the women who took Actonel. The net effect of drug treatment on the risk of serious illness in the highest risk women? Nothing—except the cost of the drug.

A study conducted in the Netherlands helps to put these lackluster results into perspective. It turns out that bone mineral density tests identify only a small part of the risk of hip fracture. The study found that for women between the ages of 60 and 80, only one-sixth of their risk of fracturing a hip is identified by BMD testing. Other factors were just as important as T score: increased frailty, muscle weakness, the side effects of other drugs, declining vision, and cigarette smoking. As a result of the WHO study group's definition of osteoporosis, however, women and their doctors mistakenly latch on to the results of BMD testing as the sole

---

*T scores of lower than - 4, or lower than - 3 with a major risk factor for hip fracture.

or primary predictor of fracture risk. Routine BMD testing may not be the best way to help women prevent hip fractures, but it is an excellent way to sell more drugs.

While nearly every postmenopausal woman fears osteoporosis, the reality is that two out of three hip fractures occur in women who have reached the age of 80. With 90 percent of hip fractures resulting from falls, it makes sense that the oldest and frailest women would be at the greatest risk. It also makes sense that a broken hip in these frail elderly women often marks the transition to no longer being able to live independently or walk safely without assistance.

Do the osteoporosis drugs protect these women from hip fractures? They don't appear to. The study of Actonel published in NEJM in 2001 included 3880 women over the age of 80 who had been diagnosed with osteoporosis or who had at least one major risk factor for falls (approximately 80 percent of the women in the study had osteoporosis). Treatment of these women with Actonel was reported in the article to have "no effect on the incidence of hip fracture." So it looks as though the women who have by far the greatest risk of hip fracture, and for whom the consequences of hip fracture are the most devastating, do not benefit from the drugs that are sold to help women with osteoporosis.

What about using these drugs to prevent osteoporosis? Fosamax and Actonel were approved by the FDA to treat women with osteopenia based on studies that showed that they significantly increase the bone density of these women. It is important to remember, however, that bone density is only a surrogate end point; the real reason for taking these drugs is to reduce fractures, and hip fractures in particular. The study of Fosamax published in JAMA in 1998 (mentioned earlier) also included women with osteopenia. Did Fosamax reduce their risk of fracture? The results show that the risk of hip fractures actually *went up* 84 percent with Fosamax treatment.* The risk of wrist fractures increased by about 50 percent (that figure may be statistically significant—but this can't be determined from the data as presented in the article).

---

*Even though this is a large increase in risk, the number of hip fractures was low, so the difference did not reach statistical significance.

How can it be that drugs approved for the prevention and treatment of osteoporosis succeed in increasing bone density but have such limited impact on reducing hip fractures? The answer can only inspire awe at Mother Nature's elegance. There are two types of bone. Eighty percent of the body's bone is made up of the hard and dense outer layer called cortical bone. In some areas of the body, bones also have an internal structure of trabecular bone, which works like an organic three-dimensional geodesic dome, providing additional strength in the areas of the skeleton most vulnerable to fracture, such as the hips, wrists, and spine.

The lacelike structure of trabecular bone creates a much greater surface area than the densely packed cortical bone and therefore allows the former to be more metabolically active when the body needs calcium. Its greater metabolic activity also makes trabecular bone more vulnerable than cortical bone to the changed balance between osteoclast and osteoblast activity. As a result, when bone mass starts to decline in women, trabecular bone is lost more quickly than is cortical bone. Once the architecture of these internal struts is lost, there is no structure left onto which calcium can be added. (See Figure 13-1.) The new bone, formed as a result of taking the osteoporosis drugs, is then formed primarily on the outer part of the bone, the cortical bone. This increases the

---

FIGURE 13-1. NORMAL BONE (*LEFT*) AND OSTEOPOROTIC BONE (*RIGHT*). REPRODUCED FROM *THE JOURNAL OF BONE AND MINERAL RESEARCH* 1 (1986): 15–21, WITH PERMISSION OF THE AMERICAN SOCIETY FOR BONE MINERAL RESEARCH.

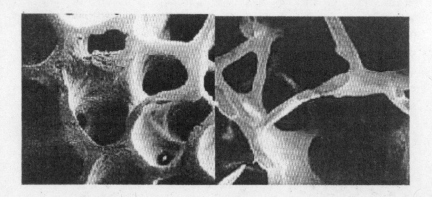

score on the bone density test but does not necessarily contribute proportionately to fracture resistance.

More drugs are now available to "help" women with osteoporosis. Evista (raloxifene) is in a new class of drugs called selective estrogen-receptor modulators, or SERMs. These drugs are designed to protect bones the same way that natural estrogen does, but without the risk of hormone therapy. Sounds great, but research shows that in women with osteoporosis, Evista reduces only vertebral fractures, not fractures of the hip or wrist. Nonetheless, Eli Lilly's advertising for Evista, according to an FDA letter to the company dated September 2000, "misleadingly suggests" that it does just that. The letter requested that Eli Lilly "immediately discontinue the broadcast of this violative advertisement" along with other marketing material that contained "the same or similar violative claims or representations."

Two other hormone-like drugs that regulate calcium metabolism are offered to treat osteoporosis; both were tested in women with osteoporosis and preexisting vertebral fractures. Miacalcin, administered by a nasal spray, has an inconsistent effect on hip fractures and vertebral fractures depending on the dose. Forteo, administered by daily self-injection, reduces fractures overall but has not been shown to significantly reduce hip fractures.

Even if loss of bone mass is a naturally occurring part of aging, hip fractures in old age are still a serious threat. So how can older women reduce their risk of hip fractures? As we've just seen, there are no magic pills. But there are ways to significantly strengthen bones and reduce the risk of fracture at any age.

Proper exercise and good nutrition are important through all stages of life to build and maintain strong bones. Reaching young adulthood with bones strengthened by routine exercise and a diet with adequate calcium makes future problems far less likely. There is good evidence that exercise builds up trabecular bone, which can then provide the internal support to vulnerable areas of the skeleton later in life.

The Study of Osteoporotic Fractures, sponsored by the NIH, included almost 10,000 independently living women aged 65 and older. Over seven years, women who exercised moderately had 36 percent fewer hip fractures (statistically significant) than the least active women. In absolute terms, the reduction in hip fractures in the women who exercised most compared with those who exercised least was 6 per 1000 per year—twice the reduction achieved with Fosamax. At least two hours of moderate-to-vigorous exercise each week is best.

In a study in Sweden, nursing home residents averaging 83 years of age, one-third of whom had dementia, were randomized to participate in a fall-prevention program (including exercise, medication reviews, hip protectors, and conferences among the staff after falls to minimize the risk of a repeat fall). During the course of the eight-month program, only 1.6 percent of the people in the fall-prevention program suffered a hip fracture compared with 6.1 percent in the control group—a dramatic reduction with no osteoporosis drugs involved (remember, Actonel did not reduce hip fractures in women of similar age).

Because nine out of 10 hip fractures result from falls, engaging in activities that increase strength and balance helps decrease the risk. Strength training is one of the best ways to increase bone density in the spine naturally and prevent falls. Tai chi, a form of exercise often used by elderly Chinese that is becoming popular throughout the world, improves balance and cuts the risk of falls in half for people 70 years of age and older.

Adequate calcium and vitamin D intake is also essential: the daily goal should be 1200–1500 mg of calcium (usually no more than 1000 mg from supplements are needed), and 400 to 800 IU of vitamin D. The cost of generic calcium and vitamin D is about $3.60 per month. Studies also suggest that diets with a higher ratio of animal to vegetable proteins increase the rate of bone loss in women 65 and older. In an observational study, women whose diets contained the highest proportion of animal protein were almost four times more likely to suffer a fractured hip than women whose primary source of protein was vegetables.

This is just a sampling of some of the research that doesn't get pushed out into the public's awareness by commercial sponsors. Where might you find additional information about bone health to guide your decisions? Almost half of Americans turn to the Internet for health information. If you go to the website sponsored by Merck, the manufacturer of Fosamax, you will be advised to "know your T score" and told that "If your T score is less than -1.0, talk to your doctor about treatment options." (Remember, on a statistical basis, half of women in their early fifties have a T score of -1.0 or less, but treating these women with drugs does not decrease, and may actually increase, their risk of fractures.) The information you find on the National Osteoporosis Society website won't be free of commercial influence, either. This tax-exempt nonprofit institution receives a large amount of drug company support, as indicated in its annual report.

Popular search engines quickly bring up numerous sites with information about BMD testing, many with no apparent ties to the drug industry. A 2004 article published in the *International Journal of Technology Assessment in Health Care* shows just how difficult it is to get unbiased information from the Internet. Researchers from the British Columbia Office of Health Technology Assessment identified the consumer health websites most frequently selected by widely used search engines. They then compared the information about bone mineral density testing presented on those sites with the information presented on the websites of noncommercially funded health technology assessment organizations.

The difference in the "information" could not have been greater. Consumer health sites, primarily commercially sponsored, present a consistent message: BMD is a simple, painless test that predicts the risk of fracture from osteoporosis—sounds like apple pie and motherhood. The message on the health technology assessment organizations' websites was equally consistent: BMD measurements are not good predictors of fracture risk.

One website with good information about osteoporosis (and many other medical issues as well) is offered by the Center for Medical Consumers. *Our Bodies, Ourselves* is an excellent reference book on women's health issues.

In the final analysis, the "disease" of age-related osteoporosis is not a disease at all, but the quintessential example of successful "disease mongering." The drug industry has succeeded in planting the fear that bones will suddenly and without warning "snap" in women who had naively believed they were healthy. This is very far from the reality of osteoporotic fractures, and in the end it harms women's health by diverting attention away from the constructive, evidence-based, inexpensive, do-it-yourself ways to prevent fractures and maintain overall health. All postmenopausal women should be exercising routinely, eating a healthy diet, taking calcium and vitamin D supplements, and decreasing their risk of falls. Bone density tests are hardly needed to make these recommendations.

If a fraction of the resources spent on the exaggerated risk of osteoporosis were invested in these other ways to improve women's health, hip fractures could be greatly reduced and overall health greatly improved. Unfortunately, the mainstream women's health movement seems to have been hijacked by commercial interests, acting more like a wolf in sheep's clothing or, more specifically, the biomedical-commercial model of health dressed in a healer's garb, and quite convincingly pretending to care.

CORONARY HEART DISEASE

The first thing most middle-aged and older people conjure up when they think about the greatest risk to their health is the "number one killer": heart disease. And the next thing they think about is their cholesterol level. Everyone knows that high cholesterol is the greatest risk factor for coronary heart disease, right? The National Cholesterol Education Program has been remarkably successful in achieving its goal of raising "awareness and understanding about high blood cholesterol as a risk factor for CHD [coronary heart disease] and the benefits of lowering cholesterol levels as a means of preventing CHD." So successful, in fact, that about twice as many people discuss cholesterol with their doctors during physical exams (67 percent) as are counseled about the importance of routine exercise (34 percent) or as are advised (if smokers) to quit smoking (37 percent). Even the most obvious counseling, advising obese people to lose weight, occurs at only 42 percent of obese people's yearly checkups.

Heart disease is the number one killer only because eventually, if nothing else kills us, our hearts will give out. Of much greater importance is what robs us of the prime years of our lives. On that score, cancer is far worse; it deprives Americans of twice as many years below the age of 75 as heart disease does. Nonetheless, CHD is still a major health problem that deserves major attention.

The good news is that the death rate from coronary heart disease has dropped quite dramatically since its peak in 1968. Several factors have contributed to this improvement: After the first Surgeon General's report on the dangers of smoking was issued in 1964, the percentage of adult smokers in the United States declined steadily, from 42 percent in 1965 to 25 percent in 1990. (Smoking is responsible for as much as 30 percent of all deaths from coronary heart disease in the United States each year.) Beginning in 1970, Americans' per capita consumption of beef, eggs, and whole milk began to decline, leading to a decrease in the percentage of calories derived from saturated fats and cholesterol. And good progress was made during the 1970s and 1980s in reducing the number of Americans with uncontrolled high blood pressure. Largely as a result of these lifestyle changes and improved blood pressure control, the death rate from heart disease in the United States went down by half between 1970 and 1990.

In the second half of the 1980s, the "revolution" in prevention and treatment of heart disease began with the introduction of clot-busting drugs and angioplasty to open up blocked arteries in people who were having heart attacks. The number of angioplasty procedures in the United States tripled in the 1990s, accelerated by the introduction in 1995 of wire mesh stents to keep narrowed coronary arteries from becoming completely blocked. Despite the advent of stents, the number of coronary artery bypass surgeries increased by about a third during the 1990s. In 1987 the FDA approved the first cholesterol-lowering statin drug, Mevacor. Sales of statins climbed steadily, so that in 2002 they took over as the best-selling class of drug in the United States.

What effect did all of these breakthroughs have on the death rate from coronary heart disease? Instead of a dramatic improvement, the rate of decline in the death rate actually slowed during the 1990s (from an average decline of 3.1 percent per year between 1970 and 1990 to 2.8 percent per year between 1990 and 2000). Why didn't the death rate decline at an even faster rate after all these great breakthroughs in prevention and treatment?

The advances, it appears, diverted attention from the lifestyle changes that had been working so well over the previous two decades. The declining percentage of Americans who smoked abruptly leveled off in 1990, with no further decline through 2002. The decline in per capita beef and egg consumption stalled in the 1990s and actually went up slightly in 2000. The decline in whole milk consumption leveled off, while the increase in the consumption of lower-fat milk peaked in 1990. There was little improvement in the number of Americans engaging in regular exercise. The percentage of obese Americans nearly doubled between 1990 and 2002 (11.6 percent versus 22.1 percent). The number of Americans with type 2 diabetes, which significantly increases the risk of heart disease, increased proportionately. Likewise, the progress made in reducing the number of people with uncontrolled high blood pressure in the 1970s and 1980s stalled in the early 1990s—the total number of people with high blood pressure actually increased, probably as a result of the increasing prevalence of obesity combined with inadequate exercise.

The problem is that all the current medical recommendations, public education campaigns, drug advertisements, and news of breakthroughs in the prevention of heart disease give the benefits of a healthy lifestyle just enough lip service to preempt criticism that these issues are being ignored. The end result is that doctors and patients are being distracted from what the research really shows: physical fitness, smoking cessation, and a healthy diet trump nearly every medical intervention as the best way to keep coronary heart disease at bay.

An article published in JAMA in 1999, for example, shows how much more of a health risk poor fitness is than elevated cholesterol levels. The study collected data on 25,000 executive and professional men at the time they underwent "executive physical exams." Ten years later, the findings of the exams were correlated with the deaths that occurred from cardiovascular disease (heart attack, stroke, and blood clots) and from all causes to determine which factors contributed the most. It turns out that being among the 20 percent least physically fit (as determined by the results of a treadmill test) is a far greater health risk than is an elevated total cholesterol level (above 240 mg/dL). For the normal-weight men, low fitness accounted for three times as many deaths from cardiovascular disease as did elevated cholesterol. For the overweight and obese men, low fitness accounted for one and a half times as many cardiovascular deaths as did elevated cholesterol. Even more important was the overall risk of death: The normal-weight men with elevated cholesterol levels had no additional risk, but the unfit men had a 60 percent higher risk of death. For the overweight men, elevated cholesterol levels increased the rate of death from all causes by 30 percent, but low fitness increased the death rate by more than twice as much, 70 percent. In absolute terms, poor physical fitness was associated with seven extra deaths per thousand normal and overweight men each year. For comparison, among the very high-risk men in the WOSCOPS study (LDL cholesterol averaged more than 190 mg/dL), not taking a statin was associated with only two extra deaths per thousand men each year.

Don't despair if you have let yourself get out of shape. The evidence shows that it's not too late to change your sedentary ways. A study published in JAMA followed almost 10,000 men who underwent exercise testing to establish a baseline level of fitness. They were retested five years later to see if their level of fitness had changed, and then followed for another five years after that. The men who had been among the least fit on the first test but who then improved on the second test cut their risk of dying of cardiovascular disease over the subsequent five years in half, compared with the men who remained among the least fit at both exams. In absolute terms, there were five fewer deaths each year for each 1000 men who became fit.

There is also good evidence showing that physical fitness plays a major role in protecting women from heart disease. In the early 1970s, 3000 women underwent physical exams, blood tests, and exercise testing on a treadmill. The findings were somewhat of a surprise. The typical reason for performing stress tests is to see if the EKG pattern changes in ways that suggest that the heart is not getting enough blood during maximum exercise. It turned out, however, that these changes did not predict an increased risk of premature death. The women who were among the least fit, on the other hand, had far more risk of dying of CHD and more than twice the overall risk of death during 20 years of follow-up than did the most fit women.

Does exercise help people who already have heart disease? Post–heart attack patients randomized to participate in an exercise program had a statistically significant (27 percent) lower death rate than those in the control group. (Most of the randomized studies of statin treatment in post–heart attack patients do not show this much benefit.) It is likely that for secondary prevention of heart disease, statins and exercise together result in lower mortality rates than either alone, but such a study has not yet been done. It would be a risky proposition for a drug company when sales were going so well, especially when the current evidence suggested that the benefits of exercise would outshine the benefits of taking a statin drug.

Exercise isn't everything when it comes to reducing the risk of coronary heart disease. Diet and other lifestyle changes can also make a big difference, as shown by the randomized studies of primary and secondary prevention of heart disease done in Oslo and Lyon reviewed in the last chapter.

The American Heart Association was so impressed with the findings of the Lyon Diet Heart Study that it issued an "AHA Science Advisory" in July 2000, calling the results an "unprecedented reduction in coronary recurrence rates," and noting that, "it clearly points to other important risk factor modifications [besides cholesterol levels] as major influences in the development of coronary heart disease." The American Heart Association's Advisory concluded with the statement that "it would be short-sighted to not recognize the enormous public health benefit that this diet could confer."

The expert panel of the National Cholesterol Education Project, on the other hand, was not even impressed enough to mention the American Heart Association's Advisory in its 2001 cholesterol guidelines. The guidelines were strikingly understated with regard to the spectacular results of the Lyon Diet Heart Study, saying simply "compared to the control group, subjects consuming the Mediterranean diet had fewer coronary events." There was no mention that the patients in the Lyon Diet Heart Study derived more than two and a half times more benefit from eating a Mediterranean diet than did similar patients taking cholesterol-lowering statin drugs.

Why the cold shoulder? Not only did the Lyon Diet Heart Study show that the Mediterranean diet was much more effective at reducing the risk of recurrent heart disease than the statins, but the decrease in risk came without lowering cholesterol levels. Giving the Lyon Diet Heart Study its due would have called into question the NCEP's very mission of bringing LDL cholesterol to the public's attention as the single most important culprit in heart disease. Given the amount of resources committed to educating people about lowering cholesterol compared with helping people eat a healthy diet, one might correctly surmise that drug companies have much more money to spend promoting the "scientific evidence" that supports lowering LDL cholesterol with statins than do the flaxseed, canola, olive, soybean, walnut, and vegetable farmers who would benefit from the widespread promotion of the Mediterranean diet.

The only reasonable conclusion from the best scientific evidence available is that taking a statin while ignoring routine exercise, a healthy diet, and the dangers of smoking may be good for drug company profits but is not good for your health. It's not uncommon to hear doctors say that we should "just put statins in the water." Wherever that phrase came from, it is certainly not from unbiased research. The narrow focus on cholesterol levels, statins, and cardiac tests and procedures has succeeded in drawing attention away from far more effective lifestyle changes that cost little more than a shift toward vegetables, whole grains, and unprocessed foods at the supermarket; and a pair of sneakers for a walk or jog around the park or a workout at the gym.

STROKE

Stroke is the third leading cause of death in the United States. Between 1970 and 1990 the death rate from stroke declined even more quickly than the death rate from coronary heart disease. But then progress in stroke mortality stalled even more abruptly than it did with coronary heart disease.

Why? The risk factors for stroke are similar to the risk factors for heart disease, and the lack of progress after 1990 had an even greater effect. In October 2003, at the Centers for Disease Control and Prevention's Third Annual Primary Care and Prevention Conference, Dr. Wayne H. Giles (an epidemiologist with the CDC) reported that compared with participating in regular exercise, a sedentary lifestyle increases the risk of stroke eightfold. Smoking increases the risk sixfold. High blood pressure increases the risk of stroke by two to four times. And diabetes doubles the risk of stroke.

It's the same basic story: attention diverted from prevention to lucrative, but less effective, intervention. For example, you may have noticed that strokes today are sometimes called "brain attacks." The name is actually quite fitting as a description of the problem. Eighty percent of strokes are caused by blockage of an artery that cuts off the supply of oxygen and nutrients to an area of the brain, causing the death of brain cells in much the same way that blockage of coronary arteries causes heart attacks. These are called "ischemic strokes." (The other 20 percent of strokes, called "hemorrhagic strokes," are caused by bleeding either within or just outside the brain.) The analogy also holds for the consequences of stroke, which can be as devastating as a severe heart attack. But the analogy does not hold quite so well for the benefit of emergency treatment, which is really what is behind the proposed name change.

The term "brain attack" was introduced into the lexicon by a marketing campaign sponsored by the biotech company Genentech. Genentech makes an expensive clot-busting drug, Activase (generic name, alteplase), that has been used, and perhaps overused, in the United States to treat heart attacks. It is now being pushed as a breakthrough in the treatment of ischemic strokes, at the cost of $2700 per patient treated. The term "brain attack" is designed to focus public attention on the urgency of getting stroke victims to the hospital as quickly as possible so that appropriate treatment (the term "lifesaving" was deleted because it wasn't true) can be administered.

The results of a manufacturer-sponsored study show that when Activase is administered to 100 properly selected patients within three hours of the onset of stroke symptoms, 12 more patients have minimal or no disability three months later. In order to make sure that a stroke patient is more likely to be helped than harmed by Activase, within those three hours patients must have blood tests, a review of their medical history, a medical examination, and a CT scan to make sure that the symptoms are not being caused by a hemorrhagic stroke, in which case the clot-busting properties of Activase would make the stroke worse. In a paper published in the *British Medical Journal* in 1999, Danish researchers calculated that if all stroke victims got to the hospital in time (an admittedly unrealistic goal), only one out of 25 would derive any benefit from being given Activase. The Danish researchers concluded that ". . . treatment with alteplase [Activase] may benefit single patients but will have no impact on the general prognosis of stroke. . . . Before it is decided to offer this expensive, potentially harmful, and possibly only marginally effective treatment we suggest that another, much larger, European trial is needed to test the results of the U.S. trial."

Nonetheless, the 2000 American Heart Association guidelines for the treatment of acute stroke, published in its journal *Circulation*, upgraded the recommendation for the use of Activase in ischemic strokes from "optional" to "recommended." Dr. Rose Marie Robertson, president of the AHA, described the nine experts who formulated these guidelines as "independent." Each of the panelists had been required to file conflict-of-interest statements with the AHA, but no conflicts were reported in the American Heart Association's guidelines published in *Circulation*. In a 2002 article published in the *British Medical Journal*, investigative journalist Jeanne Lenzer reported that the American Heart Association "will not release the conflict of interest statements for public inspection and verification." However, a subsequent independent investigation reported that six out of the eight experts who supported the upgrade in the recommendations had financial ties to Genentech. In addition, contributions from Genentech to the AHA totaled $11 million between 1991 and 2001, including $2.5 million to help build the AHA's new headquarters in Dallas.

This investigative work provides a rare look into the financial relationships among the American Heart Association, a drug manufacturer, and respected medical experts. Although there is no evidence of impropriety, one would expect that in the face of a decision as important and potentially controversial as its recommendation on the use of Activase for strokes, the American Heart Association would have gone out of its way to avoid even the hint of financial influence. The end result is that Activase, a very expensive therapy that can help fewer than 1 out of 25 stroke victims, is getting the majority of our medical attention regarding strokes, while exercise, not smoking, control of blood pressure, and prevention of diabetes are all far more effective ways to decrease the terrible toll of strokes and improve overall health at the same time.

Activase hasn't been getting all of the attention. "Worried about having a stroke?" read the ads in widely circulated magazines and newspapers. They continue, "Pravachol is the only cholesterol lowering drug proven to help protect . . . against stroke." The problem with these ads is that Pravachol has never been shown to prevent strokes in people who don't already have heart disease. The manufacturer just publicly repeated the little slip it had made in the original misleadingly titled NEJM article "Pravastin and the Risk of Stroke," which may have led busy readers to draw the same incorrect conclusion. But in this case the FDA was paying attention. These "false and misleading" ads earned Bristol-Myers Squibb one of only five Warning Letters sent to drug makers for advertising violations in 2003. The FDA seemed particularly irked because, the letter said, it had sent two less severe letters to Bristol-Myers Squibb for similar "overstated" and "unsubstantiated" claims in 2001.

If stroke prevention is the goal, lowering cholesterol with a statin drug is hardly the first strategy we should turn to. According to the data presented by Giles at the CDC conference, an elevated cholesterol level increases the risk of stroke one-eighth as much as diabetes, one-eighth to one-sixteenth as much as elevated blood pressure, and less than a thirtieth as much as a sedentary lifestyle.

With expensive therapies getting all the attention, the very effective and inexpensive basics of stroke prevention have been pushed aside. Engaging in routine exercise, not smoking, eating fish at least once a week, and controlling blood pressure (often with diuretics that cost less than $0.15 a day) would go a long way toward decreasing the amount of harm done by strokes in the United States.

TYPE 2 DIABETES

The United States is in the midst of an epidemic of type 2 diabetes. In the past 12 years, the number of people with this disease increased by 78 percent, to more than 16 million, and the number is going up by 1.3 million each year.

There are two forms of diabetes. Type 1 starts abruptly, typically in childhood or adolescence. Its cause is unknown, but it is thought to involve an immune reaction against the cells in the pancreas that make the hormone insulin, perhaps triggered by a viral infection. The vast majority of Americans with diabetes (90 to 95 percent) have type 2. This has a more gradual onset, and is caused by slowly decreasing insulin production in the pancreas combined with decreasing sensitivity to the insulin that is produced. The risk factors for type 2 diabetes are excess body weight, lack of physical exercise, advancing age, and a family history of diabetes.

In the United States, deaths caused directly by high and low blood sugar are rare, but the complications of diabetes are responsible for more than 200,000 deaths and many other serious health problems each year. Almost half of the new cases of kidney failure in the United States are caused by diabetes. More than 80,000 diabetics undergo amputation of a foot or lower leg each year. Diabetes is the most common cause of blindness in American adults. Diabetics have twice the risk of stroke and two to four times the risk of developing heart disease. In 2002, the total cost of diabetes was $132 billion; $92 billion in direct medical costs and $40 billion in disability, work loss, and premature death.

Given the enormous toll of type 2 diabetes in terms of both human suffering and health care resources, one would expect that controlling this epidemic would be a top health priority. But most of what doctors and the public are hearing about diabetes recently has more to do with statin drugs. In April 2004, the American College of Physicians issued clinical guidelines recommending that all diabetics age 55 and older take a statin to protect against cardiovascular disease. One of the important studies upon which these guidelines are based is the widely publicized Heart Protection Study, which showed that treatment of diabetics with a statin drug decreases their relative risk of developing cardiovascular disease by 22 percent and the overall death rate by 13 percent. These sound like important reductions in risk and are the basis of the television advertisements recommending that diabetic viewers "talk to their doctor" about taking a statin. As with so many other studies, translating the relative risk reduction into the absolute risk reduction produces a different picture. More than 100 people with diabetes must be treated with a statin for a year to prevent a single cardiovascular complication.

Though drug therapy for diabetes is getting most of the attention, a number of recent studies show that changes in lifestyle offer much greater potential to control the number of new cases of diabetes and to decrease the health risks for people who already have diabetes. Data from the Nurses' Health Study, published in NEJM in 2001, for example, show that 91 percent of the risk of developing type 2 diabetes can be attributed to lifestyle factors such as being overweight, getting insufficient exercise, having a poor diet, and smoking. The study found that overweight women had 7.5 times the risk of developing diabetes as normal-weight women, and obese women had 20 times the risk. As a result of the childhood obesity epidemic, even young children in the United States are beginning to develop type 2 diabetes, a disease that until recently was seen only in adults.

Perhaps doctors don't put much effort into encouraging patients to exercise and lose weight because they don't believe their efforts will produce positive results. This conventional wisdom is not borne out by the scientific evidence. Two randomized studies, for example, tested the effectiveness of counseling for people at high risk of developing diabetes and came up with exactly the same results. Both studies found that overweight men and women at high risk of developing diabetes randomly assigned to receive exercise and weight loss counseling were 58 percent less likely to develop diabetes than the people randomized to receive no counseling. Among those who received counseling, six fewer people out of 100 developed diabetes each year.

Why is there so little public awareness about the effectiveness of simple measures to prevent diabetes and its complications? A big clue is provided on the nonprofit American Diabetes Association's website, in an announcement for a program called "Make the Link! Diabetes, Heart Disease and Stroke," an initiative of the American Diabetes Association and the American College of Cardiology. The home page informs the reader that diabetes management involves more than just blood sugar control: "People with diabetes must also manage blood pressure and cholesterol and talk to their health provider to learn about other ways to reduce their chance for heart attacks and stroke." There is no mention of the benefit of exercise or diet; for this you must access other web pages. However, the site does mention that the two nonprofit organizations participating in this educational initiative have a number of "corporate partners," namely AstraZeneca, Aventis, Bristol-Myers Squibb, Eli Lilly, GlaxoSmithKline, Merck, Merck/Schering-Plough, Monarch, Novartis, Pfizer, and Wyeth.

When corporate partners fund the flow of information, the message is likely to accentuate treatment strategies that are in their interest and downplay those that are not. For example, fewer than one-third of the diabetics in the United States get adequate exercise. Simply by walking two or more hours each week, diabetics can lower their death rate by 39 percent. How does this compare with the highly touted benefit of cholesterol-lowering statin therapy? Treating 250 diabetic patients in the Heart Protection Study with a statin drug for one year prevented one death. In contrast, inactive diabetics can get four times more benefit simply by walking for at least two hours weekly, preventing four deaths among 250 formerly inactive diabetics each year.

Similarly, the 13 percent reduction in death rate among those treated with a statin in the Heart Protection Study is greatly overshadowed by the benefit of moderate weight loss. A study done in Sweden treated overweight and sedentary diabetic and prediabetic men with a diet and exercise program for five years. The men in the program who sustained at least a 5 lb. weight loss over the five years of the study had an 83 percent lower death rate than the men who did not lose weight—almost five times more benefit than treatment with a statin. Given the clarity of research about the impact of lifestyle on diabetes, one would expect a special effort by doctors to counsel their diabetic patients about the benefits of exercise and diet. However, according to an article published in the *Journal of the American Medical Association*, only half of diabetic patients were counseled about exercise at their last physical exam.

Another study showed that a 12-week intensive weight-loss program for diabetics decreased their expenditures on prescription drugs and diabetic supplies by two-thirds; and at one year the expenditures were still only half of what they had been at the beginning of the study. In a more effective and efficient health care system, these savings could be reinvested in health promotion campaigns that help people adopt healthier lifestyles, improve the quality of their lives, stem the diabetes epidemic, and at the same time reduce deaths from heart disease, stroke, and cancer. This is the kind of strategy that most Americans probably expect from major nonprofit institutions ostensibly dedicated to improving Americans' health. But when drug companies are funding the "educational" effort, nonprofit organizations can be used to direct doctors and patients toward their drugs.

The bottom line is that type 2 diabetes is primarily a disease of lifestyle. When doctors and the public are encouraged to pursue drug therapies over changes in health habits, patients miss the opportunity to benefit from the most effective interventions—exercise, diet, and not smoking. Ideal care combines both approaches, with the emphasis proportional to the potential benefit.

DEPRESSION AND SOCIAL ANXIETY DISORDER

Social anxiety disorder used to be a rare disease—that is, before public relations firms went into action representing the makers of the new antidepressants. Today, according to an advertisement for Zoloft, this "medical condition affects over 16 million Americans." "Sufferers" feel anxious about meeting new people, talking to their bosses, speaking before large crowds, or drawing attention to themselves. (Most of us can think of times when we have experienced these unpleasant feelings.) Pfizer's website for Zoloft promises that these symptoms can be treated with drug therapy. According to the Pfizer website, depression is an even more common disorder, affecting 20 million Americans each year. Published studies show that treatment with the new SSRI (selective seratonin reuptake inhibitor) antidepressants provides significant benefit to people suffering from both of these conditions.

An exquisitely designed study (sponsored—to give credit where credit is due—by Pfizer, the manufacturer of Zoloft) randomized people suffering from social anxiety disorder into four groups: two of the groups were treated with Zoloft for 24 weeks and two with a placebo. In turn, one of the groups treated with Zoloft received "exposure therapy" consisting of eight 15-minute sessions with a primary care doctor to talk about their symptoms. These patients also received "homework" to do between sessions to help them learn how to identify and break through their social habits and fears. Similarly, one of the groups treated with the placebo received exposure therapy, and the other group no counseling. The patients' symptoms were then monitored for 52 weeks—the first 24 weeks while undergoing therapy, and then for 28 weeks after the therapy had been completed.

During the first 24 weeks of the study, the patients in all four groups showed significant improvement, but an unexpected finding emerged when the drug was no longer being taken. The patients who had received "exposure" training without Zoloft continued to improve significantly, while the people who had received Zoloft (with or without counseling) showed slight worsening of their symptoms after the drug was stopped. The most likely explanation is that the people whose symptoms were relieved by drug treatment were less motivated to learn how to change the dysfunctional patterns of reaction and interaction that had given rise to their symptoms in the first place. On the other hand, the patients not given medication were probably more motivated to learn how to make these changes, and proved that it could be done successfully. The discomfort of social anxiety is real, but approaching these symptoms as a fundamentally biomedical disorder and treating dysfunctional social skills or habits with a drug makes about as much sense (for all but the most severe cases) as "treating" a splinter with a narcotic painkiller instead of removing it.

A similar picture emerges in the treatment of depression. In a study published in the journal *Psychosomatic Medicine,* patients suffering from major depression were randomly assigned to one of three groups: a group to receive Zoloft, a group to receive three exercise sessions a week, and a group to receive both Zoloft and exercise for four months. Depression in all three groups was significantly improved after four months of treatment. Six months after the completion of treatment, however, the results were quite different. Depression had recurred in only 8 percent of the people in the exercise-only group. In contrast to this lasting benefit, relapse occurred in 38 percent of the people treated with Zoloft alone and 31 percent of the people treated with both Zoloft and exercise.

This pattern mirrors the study of social anxiety: short-term treatment with an antidepressant medication relieves symptoms but appears to decrease the likelihood of patients making the positive life changes necessary to prevent symptoms from recurring. These randomized controlled studies suggest that at least some depression could be called an "exercise-deficiency disease," and some social anxiety disorder could be thought of not as a medical disease but as the consequence of dysfunctional patterns of social interaction shown to be amenable to significant improvement by eight 15-minute sessions of counseling with a family doctor.

To see these "diseases" through this evidence-based lens would turn American medicine on its head. The drug companies have a great deal at stake in persuading doctors and the public to limit their view of social anxiety disorder and depression to the biomedical model of disease. They provide persuasive "scientific" explanations for mental health symptoms, while deflecting consideration of the evidence that, in many cases, lifestyle changes and short-term counseling offer more enduring benefit. Not coincidentally, their approach is also the best way to sell more drugs. Though successful in the short term, these biomedical interventions undermine the natural motivation provided by patients' symptoms to make the real and lasting changes that would lead to sustained improvement in the quality of their lives.

CANCER

While medical science works toward finding cures for cancer with occasional but all too limited success, we already know a lot about how to prevent cancer. We know, for example, that from 1965 to 1998, lung cancer quadrupled in women, overtaking breast cancer as the number one cancer killer in women in 1986. Smoking not only is responsible for 87 percent of lung cancers but also increases the risk of cancer of the mouth, throat, esophagus, and bladder.

A review of all the studies that looked at the relationship between cancer and exercise showed that the risk of developing some of the most common cancers is significantly reduced by exercise. For example, routine exercise is associated with a 40 to 50 percent reduction in the risk of developing cancer of the colon and with a 30 to 40 percent reduction in the risk of breast cancer. It is also possible that exercise reduces the risk of prostate cancer.

Diet plays a role in about 30 percent of the cancers that occur in developed countries, according to a review of international cancer rates published in *The Lancet* in 2002. Age-adjusted rates of the four most common cancers (lung, breast, prostate, and colon) are all much higher in the developed countries, and increase when diets change or people move from less to more developed countries.

Another study compared the diet of 2000 people who developed colon cancer with a control group of the same number. Eating a "Western diet"—associated with a higher body mass index and a greater intake of calories and dietary cholesterol—was twice as common among those diagnosed with colon cancer, and the association was strongest among people diagnosed at a younger age.

Consistent with these findings, the patients in the Lyon Diet Heart Study who developed less heart disease on a Mediterranean diet (high in vegetables and fruits, whole grains, and vegetable oil, and low in red meat) also developed 61 percent fewer new cancers compared with the people who ate the "prudent Western-style heart diet" (meaning lower in total and saturated fats than the normal diet).

A study conducted in Canada found that being obese (compared with having a normal body weight) increased the overall risk of developing cancer by 34 percent, with much larger risks for certain cancers: 95 percent for cancer of the ovary, 93 percent for cancer of the colon, 66 percent for breast cancer in postmenopausal women, and 61 percent for leukemia. The researchers calculated that obesity was responsible for 7.7 percent of all cancers in Canada. Given that twice as many Americans are obese as Canadians (31 percent versus 15 percent, in 2003), obesity may be responsible for about 15 percent of cancer in the United States.

Finding medical cures for this terrible disease is desperately important, but we can't forget that the very best cure is prevention. (The U.S. Preventive Services Task Force recommendations for cancer screening are widely recognized as the best available resource. These can be accessed through the Agency for Healthcare Research and Quality.)

OBESITY: A SOCIAL DISEASE

The biomedical-commercial approach to health fragments medical care into seemingly separate and unrelated diseases—each with its own cause and its own cure. This distracts people (including health professionals) from the fact that many diseases share the same cause, and that cause is often rooted in lifestyle choices such as poor diet, smoking, and lack of

exercise; environmental factors; or economic status. The telling characteristic of the biomedical-commercial approach to health is that regardless of the primary source of disease, the biomedical-commercial
approach offers ("pushes" is perhaps a better word) commercially advantageous solutions.

The obesity epidemic in the United States is a perfect example. As
awareness of this serious problem grows, attention is becoming focused
not on its cause, but on medical treatments to mitigate its consequences.
These interventions include preventing heart disease (with statin drugs),
mitigating the complications of diabetes (with drugs to control blood
sugar, statins to protect the heart, and ACE inhibitors to protect the kidneys), treating strokes after they occur (with an expensive new treatment
that actually helps fewer than one out of 25 stroke victims), and relieving
the pain of osteoarthritis (with expensive new arthritis drugs). There are
also medical treatments for obesity itself: surgery (now even in children)
and new medications in the pipeline that are sure to be instant blockbusters.

The real cause of obesity is embarrassingly simple: Americans consume more calories than they need to maintain a healthy body weight.
According to the U.S. Department of Agriculture, the average American
consumed 500 calories more per day in 2000 than in 1970. Much of this
increase is explained by the doubling in the amount of food eaten outside
the home from the mid-1970s to the mid-1990s, by which time restau-
rant and takeout food accounted for one-third of total energy consumption. Restaurants offer high-calorie foods and increased portion sizes to
attract customers. Marketing of fast food and high-calorie snacks to children continues to become ever more sophisticated, creating an unhealthy
appetite for calorie-rich foods.

Americans' increase in sugar consumption tells an interesting story.
The USDA recommends that the average diet include no more than
10 teaspoons of sugar each day. In the 1950s, Americans' average daily
intake of sugar and other sweeteners was 23 teaspoons. By 2000 this had
increased to 32 teaspoons of sweeteners per day, providing an additional
135 calories. (Just one 20-ounce bottle of soda, for example, contains
about 16 teaspoons of sugar.) Without any other changes in diet or exercise, a person taking in an extra 135 calories per day gains more than

1 pound each month (3500 extra calories lead to 1 pound of weight gain). The result is perfectly predictable: the percentage of obese adults doubled between the early 1970s and 2000, and during the same period, the percentage of obese children and adolescents increased by a factor of almost four.

Dr. Julie L. Gerberding, director of the Centers for Disease Control and Prevention, told the *Washington Post* in March 2004 that by 2005 the number of deaths in the United States caused by obesity and physical inactivity was projected to reach 500,000—more deaths than are caused by smoking, and almost the same number of deaths caused by cancer. Genetic predisposition and just plain bad luck play a role in most diseases, including those contributed to by obesity, but the greatest determinants of health are the habits, choices, demands, and environment of daily life. Obesity is primarily a social disease—the result of aggressive marketing of high-calorie foods and our physically inactive culture—in much the same way that tuberculosis was largely a social disease of the nineteenth century, the result of overcrowding and the uncontrolled ravages of the industrial revolution. Clearly, the outlook for Americans' health is not good when one of the key risk factors for most chronic diseases is increasing at an epidemic pace and little is being done to get at the heart of the problem.

PUTTING THE EVIDENCE TOGETHER: FINDING THE BASIC CONSTELLATION OF HEALTH

What does the research show that we can do to increase our chances of staying healthy? On an individual basis, the answers are remarkably simple. In 2002 the medical journal of the American Heart Association,* *Circulation,* published an article that reviewed the important studies on coronary heart disease prevention through diet and lifestyle interventions. The article concluded that by following the recommendations that emerge from the scientific evidence, "coronary heart disease can be elim-

---

*Though I have been critical of the connection of the AHA and many other organizations to the medical industry, they still may offer important information and advice (free of bias).

inated to a large extent" among people less than 70 years of age. From the studies presented in this chapter, we see that these same recommendations also apply to the prevention of type 2 diabetes, osteoporosis, and stroke, and help prevent cancer and depression as well. With slight modifications and the inclusion of safety recommendations, here is the list:

1. Avoid tobacco.

2. Exercise moderately for at least 30 minutes or more on most days, engaging in activities such as brisk walking, biking, or gardening.

3. Consume alcohol in moderation, if at all.

4. Eat a healthy diet:

   • Cut down on red meat in favor of chicken, fish (including fatty fish at least once a week)*, and vegetable proteins.
   • Eat at least a pound of vegetables and fruits every day.
   • Limit salt to less than a teaspoon a day.
   • Cut down on sugar.
   • For cooking, use vegetable oils such as canola and olive oil.
   • Minimize intake of saturated fats and cholesterol.
   • Consume less than 2 percent of calories in trans fat (the "partially hydrogenated oil" found in many margarines and many baked goods, cookies, crackers, candy bars, and breakfast cereals; check ingredient labels). The optimal daily intake of trans fat: none.

5. Keep your body mass index (BMI) from going over 25 (meaning, don't be overweight for your height). The good news is that if you do the other things on this list, your weight will be much easier to keep in check.

6. Use seat belts and bike helmets. Most important, don't drink

---

*As an unfortunate sign of the times, pregnant women and children must be cautious about mercury and PCB content of oily fish.

and drive; and do work within your community to help create a social climate that discourages those most at risk—
young adults between the ages of 16 and 25—from drinking
and driving.

7. Don't engage in unsafe sex.

This may sound quite formidable at first, but two studies show just
how simple and effective healthy habits can be. A study published in the
New England Journal of Medicine followed the activity level and health of
retired, nonsmoking men in Honolulu between the ages of 61 and 81.
During the 12 years of the study, almost twice as many of the men who
walked less than 1 mile each day died (41 percent) as the men who walked
more than 2 miles per day (24 percent).

Another study, published in the *Journal of the American Medical
Association* in 2003, followed the health of 9700 independently living
women, age 65 and older, for up to 12 years. (This study was originally
designed to determine risk factors for fractures in older women.) Among
the women who were walking 2 miles or less each week at the beginning
of the study, those who increased their walking to at least 1 mile per day
cut their death rate in half compared with those who remained sedentary.
(Both of these studies are observational and could be biased by underlying differences that led to healthier people walking more, though the
researchers took all possible measures to exclude this possibility.)

Just knowing these recommendations, however, is not enough: Making positive changes is often complicated by personal inertia and social,
economic, and environmental factors beyond the control of individuals
and even whole communities. This is where ongoing relationships with
primary care doctors and other medical professionals can help to bridge
the gap between the science that informs preventive health care and the
personal resistance that can make change so difficult. Still, the obesity
and diabetes epidemics show that the focus of medicine cannot be limited to the health of individuals. The cultural environment in which our
lives unfold also plays a major role in determining our health. Pediatri-
cians and family doctors, for example, cannot possibly stem the tide of
childhood obesity by themselves when advertisements for fast food and
snack foods and vending machines containing high-calorie snacks satu-

rate children's environment, presenting a far more compelling message.

Hopefully, in the years to come we will look back and see how ridiculous we were to have believed that biomedicine alone—without considering the health consequences of how we live our lives—could possibly provide optimal health. The measure of America's recovery from this era of commercially distorted medicine will be the extent to which real and effective encouragement of healthy ways of living is reintegrated into the best medical care available—not replacing, but supported by, the appropriate clinical application of biomedical science.

HEALING OUR AILING HEALTH CARE SYSTEM, OR HOW TO SAVE $500 BILLION A YEAR WHILE IMPROVING AMERICANS' HEALTH

There was a time not so long ago when breakthroughs in medical science were driven more by health needs than by the search for corporate profits. Perhaps the best example is the research that produced the polio vaccine, one of the truly great breakthroughs of modern medicine. In 1955, amid the great fanfare that accompanied the initial release of the vaccine, Dr. Jonas Salk was asked who owned the patent. He replied, "Well, the people, I would say. Could you patent the sun?"

American medicine has changed a lot since then, especially in the last 10 or 15 years. Many of these changes come not from medical science itself, but from the changed purpose for which medical knowledge is created and disseminated. Most of us take for granted that the well-established rules of science ensure the validity of medical research, regardless of the purpose for which the research is undertaken or the context in which it is performed. Nothing could be further from the truth.

The privatization of the majority of clinical research, the diminished role of universities as impartial overseers of medical knowledge, and the drug and medical-device industry's growing influence on government have all contributed to the changed role of medical knowledge in our society. The goal of performing rigorous medical studies is often replaced by the goal of creating the perception that rigorous medical studies call for increased use of the sponsors' products.

In this climate, the editors of the most respected medical journals have warned that they cannot protect their readers from the pro-industry bias seeping into many of the scientific articles they publish. Nonetheless, publication in respected medical journals still anoints research findings as the scientific evidence upon which good doctors confidently base their clinical decisions. It is not simply due to the "play of chance" that the odds are five times greater that new products will be supported by commercially sponsored studies than by studies with noncommercial sponsorship. The bias is, at best, difficult and often impossible for even the most careful readers to spot, let alone unravel. And simply knowing that it exists is not enough to protect readers from being misled.

If we are to begin to solve the crises in American medicine, we first need to stop pretending that the current organization of the production and dissemination of medical knowledge is serving the public's interest. The ideal of "well-ordered science" (a phrase coined by philosopher Philip Kitcher in his book *Science, Truth, and Democracy*) is often replaced in commercially sponsored medical research by the ideal of profit-maximizing science. Dr. Andrew Bodnar, a senior vice president at Bristol-Myers Squibb, summarized this issue when he told the *New York Times*, "In a science-driven organization, the notion of marketing versus science is really a false dichotomy." Disciplined science performed by impartial researchers and openly shared with professional colleagues and the public is often replaced with games of cat and mouse in which corporate sponsors do their best to hide both the ways that their scientific results have been spun, and the results that can't be spun. But medical research is not a game, and, as Kitcher points out, the more important the consequences, the higher the scientific standards should be.

This is the mother of all sleights of hand: the transformation of medical science from a public good whose purpose is to improve health into a commodity whose primary function is to maximize financial returns. As a result of this sleight of hand, the gap is widening between the scientific evidence that impartial experts (not paid or threatened by the medical industry, not biased by other personal concerns, and granted unrestricted access to all of the evidence) would agree upon and the perceptions that actually drive American health care. This growing gap is at the core of the crisis in American medicine. And why are we surprised? The drug companies have no more responsibility to oversee the public's health than the fast-food industry has to oversee the public's diet.

The substitution of narrow corporate interests for medical progress has produced some dramatic excesses. When the manufacturer of Paxil performs nine clinical studies on the treatment of adolescents for depression and finds that Paxil is no more effective than placebos and, in fact, significantly increases the frequency of "emotional lability" (including suicidal thoughts and attempts), it's no problem. The company publishes one study that shows a benefit, fails to publish the other eight, and markets away. When British drug authorities spill the beans? No problem. A task force of the American College of Neuropsychopharmacolgy is convened, and concludes that the new antidepressants are safe for adolescents after all. Too bad the task force didn't have access to some of the information that was available to the British drug authorities. But perhaps that didn't seem like so much of a problem, because, according to the *New York Times,* "Critics of the medicines noted that 9 of the 10 task force members had significant financial ties to the pharmaceutical industry. . . ." (However, the task force insisted that no industry money financed their report.) What to do when the FDA epidemiologist in charge of analyzing all the antidepressant studies involving children concludes, just like the British drug authorities, that twice as many children treated with the new drugs (except Prozac, which is available as an inexpensive generic) became suicidal, and that the FDA should therefore discourage doctors from treating children with these drugs? Just bar the expert from testifying at the FDA's public hearing. Then don't make him available for an interview with the *New York Times,* which reported the story on April 16, 2004.

You don't like the way the study of an expensive drug for blood pressure is going? A nonissue—just stop the study before the results reach statistical significance.

Endovascular Technologies (a wholly owned subsidiary of Guidant, the company that manufactures implantable defibrillators) manufactured a $10,000 device to repair aortic aneurysms that dangerously malfunctioned in a third of the 7600 patients in whom it had been used. Did this frequency of malfunction stop Endovascular Technologies? No. The company reported 7 percent of these events to the FDA and sold on. According to a plea agreement entered into with the United States government in 2003, the company belatedly disclosed another 2628 serious malfunctions and 12 deaths. No problem. It agreed to pay $92 million to cover criminal and civil penalties and then picked up with business as usual on other products.

Your drug company just received an official warning letter from the FDA for the "false and misleading" marketing of Celebrex, Vioxx, Pravachol, or OxyContin? No problem. The FDA's corrective action is unlikely to displace the false information already firmly planted in the public's mind.

And the list goes on. Controlling medical costs in this near free-for-all commercial grab is not just impossible, it is a contradiction in terms. Does it make sense to talk about reducing national expenditures for cars or clothes or beer? Medical care, by far the largest consumer commodity in the United States, is now no different.

THE ILLUSION OF ACCESS: THE MEDICARE RX BILL

Like any well-functioning consumer market, the medical industry does its best to stimulate ever-greater demand. In this context, being assured of ongoing access to "the best" medical care is as much a contradiction as controlling medical costs. The Medicare prescription drug bill is a perfect example.* This bill was supposedly designed to improve senior citizens' access to the prescription drugs they need. For those with the lowest incomes, it will make prescription drugs more accessible—with the drug companies receiving full price from a segment of the market that would not otherwise have been able to afford these drugs. However, according to the Consumers Union and 19 labor union and public interest groups, after the new prescription drug "benefit" takes effect, the average Medicare patient, who spent $2318 out of pocket for prescription drugs in 2003, will spend $2911 out of pocket in 2007. Ostensibly designed to

---

*The actual name of this legislation, signed into law by President George W. Bush on December 8, 2003, is the Medicare Prescription Drug Improvement and Modernization Act of 2003.

decrease the financial burden of prescription drugs for senior citizens, the legislation will do just the opposite.

How can this happen? Expenditures for prescription drugs have been increasing seven times faster than the rate of inflation, but the 2003 legislation *specifically prohibits* the federal government from using its purchasing power to negotiate prices with drug makers, as is done successfully by the Veterans Health Administration and Defense Department (and by Canada and the European countries—which is why their drug prices are so much lower than those in the United States). The U.S. government will pay the full price as set by the drug companies, while the need for the drugs will be determined largely by industry-sponsored research, industry-sponsored guidelines, industry-sponsored continuing education and marketing for doctors, and industry-sponsored advertising and public relations campaigns. At the same time, importation of drugs from countries with lower prices has been effectively blocked.

But even this does not capture the depth of the problem. PhRMA was successful in helping to defeat an amendment to the Medicare prescription drug bill that would have funded research to determine the comparative effectiveness and value of the drugs senior citizens are struggling to afford. A quick look at the 15 most frequently prescribed drugs for seniors in 2003 shows that, before coming up with a very expensive plan to provide access to these drugs, it would be wise to determine which drugs actually provide effective and efficient treatment for senior citizens.

Celebrex 200 mg was the sixth most frequently prescribed drug for American seniors in 2003. As we saw in Chapter 3, when the results from the second half of the manufacturer-sponsored study (not included in the article published in JAMA) are taken into account, as FDA reviewers deemed appropriate, Celebrex offers no significant advantage over much less expensive anti-inflammatory drugs, and may actually cause more GI problems when taken for longer than six months.

The second and tenth most frequently prescribed drugs for seniors are Norvasc 5 mg and 10 mg for blood pressure control, costing $549 and $749 per year, respectively. Evidence shows, however, that, for most people, neither is as effective at preventing the complications of high blood pressure as a diuretic that costs only $29 per year, hydrochlorothiazide— the forty-second most frequently prescribed drug.

Three of the top fifteen drugs for seniors are cholesterol-lowering statins. We don't know how many of those are being prescribed to prevent recurring heart attacks, the situation in which statins are most effective. We do know, however, from the PROSPER study that high-risk elderly patients with no previous history of heart disease have no fewer heart attacks when they are treated with a statin for three years. But they do develop significantly more cancer. Furthermore, the first statin introduced to the market, Mevacor, is now available as a generic drug, lovastatin, which costs less than half as much as the brand-name drugs and has never been shown to be any less effective at preventing heart attacks in people over the age of 65. (In the Prove It study, the people over the age of 65 derived no greater benefit from Lipitor than from Pravachol, one of the earlier statins.) Lovastatin, however, did not make the top 50 list.

Vioxx made the top 15 as well, despite a little-known fact buried in data from the manufacturer's own study: treating 100 patients over the age of 65 with Vioxx instead of naproxen will lead to 2.5 additional serious cardiovascular complications each year. To put the risk of Vioxx in perspective, treating patients over the age of 65 with Vioxx instead of naproxen is about four times more likely to *cause* a cardiovascular complication than a statin is likely to prevent one, even in patients who have already had a heart attack.

Two of the top 15 drugs are stomach acid–blocking drugs costing about $4.60 a day. One of these, Prilosec, is now available without a prescription for about $0.62 a day—and even this price will soon come down with generic competition. I found that most patients with symptoms of heartburn could be started on the more powerful acid-blocking drugs, then switched to less strong medication, such as ranitidine (brand name Zantac) once their symptoms were under control. If symptoms recurred, patients could easily be switched back to one of the more powerful drugs.

The third most frequently prescribed drug for seniors is Fosamax for osteoporosis. One wonders how many of the women taking this drug actually benefit, since, as we have seen, it does not reduce fractures when used to prevent osteoporosis. And for women over 70—even those with severe osteoporosis—Fosamax's cousin, Actonel, significantly reduces the risk of hip fractures only in women who have already had spine fractures. Meanwhile, how many women taking these drugs are aware of the research showing the significant benefits of exercise in preventing fractures and, more important, improving overall health and longevity?

Those are 10 of the 15 best-selling drugs for seniors. If the government's real goal were to increase senior citizens' access to the most effective medications, its first step would have been to determine the best care based on the best scientific evidence available, helping patients and doctors to make informed decisions. Instead, the Medicare prescription drug bill simply opens the public coffers to pay full price for expensive brand-name drugs. One might conclude that the purpose of this drug bill was to transfer wealth from the taxpayers to the drug companies rather than to ensure senior citizens access to the most effective drugs at the lowest possible cost to themselves and to the federal government. As an unnamed drug lobbyist told the *New York Times* when this legislation was being debated, "Having both houses of Congress Republican-controlled was great. Like in Monopoly, when you get to add hotels."

As if that weren't bad enough, Congress was not even allowed to see Medicare's own estimate of the real cost of the prescription drug bill before it voted (this estimate was $100–$200 billion higher than the projected cost that the Bush administration was presenting to Congress). Medicare's chief actuary, Richard S. Foster, told the *New York Times* that he had been ordered not to provide this information to Congress and ordered not to respond directly to Congressional requests for data. Foster said that his understanding was that Medicare officials "would try and fire me" for doing so. The *Times* reported that the director of Medicare, Thomas A. Scully, denied having threatened to fire Foster, but did acknowledge having instructed Foster to "withhold certain information from Congress."

Just six weeks after the president signed the bill, the price tag was publicly acknowledged to be fully one-third higher than the $400 billion Congress had been promised. How did this happen? Thomas Scully had received an ethics waiver in May of 2003 that allowed him to continue to work on the drug bill while he was seeking employment in the private sector. One month after receiving the waiver, he changed the long-standing practice of allowing Medicare actuaries to report requested information directly to Congress. Under the new rules, actuarial information had to go through Mr. Scully (reminiscent of the change at the FDA that required all letters to drug companies about marketing violations to be reviewed by the office of the chief counsel). At least some of Medicare's estimates of the cost of the drug bill were sent to the White House; but they weren't sent to Congress. According to the *Wall Street Journal*, within weeks of the final vote on the bill, Scully told Foster, "We can't let that [estimate] get out." In March 2004, Foster told the *New York Times*, "There was a pattern of withholding information for what I perceived to be political purposes, which I thought was inappropriate."

One month after the Medicare prescription drug bill was passed, Mr. Scully announced that he had accepted a position with a law firm that, according to the *Times*, represents many companies in the health care industry affected by the new prescription drug bill, and is a registered lobbyist for Johnson and Johnson and the National Association for Home Care.

An article published in *Health Affairs* in February 2004 shows that once coverage for prescription drugs for Medicare patients becomes effective, prescription drug costs are likely to increase even more than predicted. The study found that use of Celebrex and Vioxx more than doubles when senior citizens have insurance that covers at least 75 percent of the cost of prescription drugs. (The Medicare prescription drug bill will provide 75 percent coverage.) The authors conclude that health policymakers should "be concerned with potential overuse of drug therapy by Medicare beneficiaries once the benefit is implemented." Surely the use of expensive drugs by senior citizens will skyrocket—regardless of their proven value—unless measures are taken to base prescription drug use on the real scientific evidence.

If the crisis in American medicine were simply due to the rising cost of ever more effective care, there would be no choice but to cobble together the least noxious combination of increased spending and rationing. But the bad news about American medicine—and, paradoxically, the good news as well—is that the primary problem is not the escalating cost but the low quality of medical care that results when those with health insurance receive too much of the wrong kind of care and those without health insurance receive too little of the care that is necessary. Dr. Donald Berwick, one of the nation's leading crusaders for improving quality in medicine and an author of the Institute of Medi-

cine's report "Crossing the Quality Chasm," states the problem succinctly: "Hundreds of billions of dollars are being flushed away because
care isn't related closely to need."

Commercial interests are so successful in appearing to represent the
public's interest that doctors, health policy experts, and the public are
unable to discern the commercial distortions of the medical knowledge
upon which they rely. "Quality of care" is now defined largely in ways that
best serve the financial interests of drug and other medical industries
rather than the health needs of the American people.

In this context, the most urgent challenge facing American medicine
is not how to guarantee adequate access, but first to determine "access to
what?" Nor is it even how to ensure quality of care, because this presumes
that the available scientific evidence is adequate to make that determina-
tion. The most important health care issue in the United States today is
whether our current method of creating medical knowledge realizes the
full potential of medical science to improve our health, and whether this
knowledge is then best applied to clinical practice and communicated
effectively to the public. By these standards, American medicine is clearly
failing to fulfill its promise.

RESTORING THE INTEGRITY AND PURPOSE OF CLINICAL RESEARCH

The first step in reorienting American medicine toward the effectiveness
the American people have a right to expect and are more than paying for
would be to relieve the foxes of their responsibility for guarding the hen-
house. How absurd to have more than half the budget of the FDA division that approves new drugs (the Center for Drug Evaluation and
Research, CDER) paid directly by the drug companies' user fees because
the federal government is unwilling to provide adequate funding. Completely invisible to the public, officials at the National Institutes of
Health are allowed to participate in lucrative consulting contracts with
the drug companies. Experts with financial ties to the drug companies
dominate the FDA's Advisory Committees and the panels that write the
clinical guidelines that define the standards of care for practicing doc-

tors. The medical industry even funds the majority of doctors' continuing education.

The production and implementation of medical knowledge in the United States is by now so riddled with conflict of interest at virtually every level and every stage that nothing less than a new independent national public body is needed to protect the public's interest in medical science. Such a body must have the independence and expertise of the Institute of Medicine (part of the National Academies of Science), which would be well suited to accept responsibility for evaluating the scientific evidence. Lessons from the past show that this public body would require maximum insulation from political and commercial influence, on the model of the Federal Reserve Board—long and staggered terms, no financial ties to industry, and secure funding from Congress—to avoid evisceration when its findings were not to the liking of powerful interest groups. Surely the health of the American people and almost $2 trillion in annual expenditures are important enough to warrant such rigorous oversight.

This new independent board would have a threefold mission. First, it would ensure that medical research was designed, conducted, analyzed, and disseminated with the primary purpose of improving health and in accordance with accepted scientific standards. Second, it would provide oversight in developing clinical guidelines for the prevention, diagnosis, and treatment of specific medical problems and overall health through independent analysis of all the available scientific evidence.* Third, it would identify, fund, and oversee research when important scientific evidence was lacking. For example, the absence of evidence from randomized controlled trials precludes informed recommendations about whether routine bone mineral density testing for postmenopausal women has any clinical benefit, or whether drug therapy, lifestyle modification, or both will best prevent hip fractures in women with osteo-

---

*The United Kingdom developed an agency to perform this function in 1999, the National Institute for Clinical Excellence (NICE). Its role is defined as providing "patients, health professionals and the public with authoritative, robust, and reliable guidance on current 'best practice.'" It does this with a budget of less than $30 million per year.

porosis. Although clinical trials to study these two issues might not be advantageous to the companies that make bone density testing equipment or drugs for osteoporosis (and therefore would be unlikely to be funded by them), such trials would certainly be beneficial to American women.

To accomplish this threefold mission, the new body would need authority to require that all clinical trials were registered at the outset, with a clearly identified research design ("protocol"), including the duration of the study, the outcomes, and adverse effects to be measured. This would put an end to the current "Heads, I win. Tails, you lose" situation in which studies that support their sponsors' interests are published quickly while unfavorable results are published slowly or not at all and therefore never become part of our medical knowledge. Although registration of all clinical studies may seem like a simple and obvious way to improve the benefit that society derives from medical research, the drug companies, through their trade organization PhRMA, have stated: "Sponsors [of clinical research] do not commit to publish the results of every exploratory study performed, or to make the designs of clinical trial protocols available publicly at inception, as in a clinical trial registry."

The new body would also have the power to require that studies include people of similar age, gender, and medical condition to those to whom the results would be applied. Comparison with proven therapies (not just placebos)—including lower-cost treatments, generic drugs, and lifestyle interventions—would be required before a new drug could be considered the "best therapy." The body would also have the authority to require that studies be continued long enough to determine the benefits and side effects of the various treatments and strictly forbid interrupting a study for "commercial reasons."

The body would have the authority to require that clinical research measure the most important clinical outcomes, such as serious illnesses, overall mortality, and the quality of life—not merely intermediate end points such as bone mineral density, blood pressure, cholesterol level, and the amount of plaque in arteries.

Probably the single most important change that the fully empowered regulatory body could implement would be requiring transparency in medical research—making all research data available for external audit and public scrutiny. Nontransparency is now the norm for commercially sponsored medical research in much the same way that it had become the norm in accounting and business practices in companies such as Enron and Worldcom, and with much the same results—though the magnitude of the cost in dollars and health still remains a well-kept secret. Medical researchers must have access to all the results of their studies, perform their own analyses of the data, write up their own conclusions, and submit the report for publication to peer-reviewed medical journals. Research data must also be made available to peer reviewers for medical journals and to the new oversight body for independent evaluation.

How would these standards be enforced? Only studies that met these standards would be certified by the new body—thus establishing an effective performance threshold for validation of clinical research. This certification would become part of the peer-review process for medical journals—publication could be restricted to certified research or articles' certification status could be clearly identified for readers. Certification would also be identified in all the scientific evidence presented to doctors in marketing material and continuing education. The public would be similarly informed about the certification status of research referred to in advertising and presented in the media. If drug companies threatened to withdraw advertising, the cost of public funding for the journals would be a pittance compared with the savings to the public that would result from basing medical care on unbiased scientific evidence.

Of course, the medical industry would do everything in its enormous power to prevent having to relinquish its control over medical knowledge. But what purpose is served by the current situation, in which the public's interest in effective and efficient health care is subjugated to the commercial goals of the medical industry?

Would this oversight of the relevance and integrity of clinical research bring commercial funding to a halt? The drug and medical-device industries might use such a scare tactic to quash the growing public demand to rein in their excesses. Such a threat, if not simply posturing, would reveal industry's need to bias research in order to make the undertaking worthwhile from a business perspective. If this were true, then all the more reason to return responsibility for producing medical knowledge back to the government, shielded from commercial distortion. Yes, it would be expensive in the short run to lose industry's enormous financial contribution to medical research, but the net result would save Americans hundreds of billions of dollars each year as medical care became redirected away from commercial goals and back to the goal of producing the best health with the greatest efficiency.

PROVIDING QUALITY HEALTH CARE
TO ALL AMERICANS

In January 2004 the Institute of Medicine reported that 18,000 Americans die unnecessarily each year as a result of not having health insurance. This death toll is six times greater than the one we experienced on September 11, 2001—and it's happening every year. Have you ever wondered why the United States, the country with the highest per capita gross domestic product (except for tiny Luxembourg), is alone among industrialized nations in not providing health care coverage to all of its citizens? Our lack of universal coverage becomes even more puzzling when we realize that, according to an ABCNews/*Washington Post* poll conducted in the fall of 2003, four out of five Americans support universal health care and are willing to sacrifice their tax cuts to pay for it.

The key to understanding this paradox is that the medical industries maximize profits by providing the most care possible to those who pay full or almost full price. As long as the definitions of "quality of care" and the price structure of drugs, devices, and procedures are determined largely by commercial interests, universal health care will continue to appear unrealistic and in some vague way "un-American." Yet the additional cost of covering all Americans is estimated to be $34–$60 billion annually—a trivial sum compared with the extra $500 billion spent each year on medical care "informed" by the findings of commercially biased science.

The prospect of extending health care coverage to the uninsured would jeopardize the medical industry's excess profits and almost certainly trigger a demand for accountability: Americans of all political stripes would demand evidence of the real value that they (and the uninsured) were receiving for their tax dollars. Ideally, the independent federal oversight body I've described would determine the benefits to be included in universal coverage, based upon all of the scientific evidence (meaning that commercial sponsors of research would not be allowed to keep their data hidden). The cost of this care, according to the best evidence currently available, would be about one-third less than the current cost of commercial insurance or Medicare. The privileged profiteering of the drug, medical device, medical equipment, and hospital industry would be sharply curtailed.

However, the most serious threat posed to these industries under such a system would be the public realization that people covered by the universal health plan were receiving higher-quality care and better health outcomes than the people with regular insurance. When that happened, many Americans would demand similarly high value, low cost health insurance, effectively extending to all Americans coverage for medical services, drugs, tests, procedures, and therapies based upon certification by the independent federal body. All Americans would then be winners— the currently uninsured and the insured alike—as the quality of their health care improved and their costs declined as the result of objective standards of medical excellence replacing our current commercially based standards of care.

MARKET FAILURE OR MARKET SUCCESS?

As the leaders of the Commonwealth Foundation wrote in *Health Affairs* at the end of 2003, "The inability of the health care industry to improve care sufficiently on its own and to increase the value that Americans receive for their dollars is an indication of private market failure."

The failure of the market to serve Americans' medical needs is certainly demonstrated by the combination of our poor health status compared with that of other industrialized countries, the low quality of our medical care (barely half of the standards for basic medical care are being met, according to a study done by the Rand Corporation and published in the NEJM in December 2003), and the singularly high cost of our medical care. But these are just symptoms of a more fundamental problem, which is not market failure, but market success. The medical industries have thrived as health care spending in the United States increased more than fivefold and the percentage of our GDP devoted to health care rose from 8.8 to 15.5 between 1980 and 2004.

How could the market have allowed the medical industries to thrive while serving Americans' health needs so poorly and inefficiently? The problem is not with the market itself, but with the inadequate information and flawed incentives that currently shape our health care market. Drug companies earn higher profits when more people use expensive drugs, not when more people achieve better health. Doctors and hospitals are paid more for doing more, largely without regard for evidence of improved health outcomes (examples are the rapid increase in the number of MRI machines, excess capacity for neonatology and invasive cardiac procedures that lead to excess use, and the approximately 12,000 deaths that occur each year as the result of unnecessary surgery). Health care providers that deliver high quality, efficient care are financially penalized for not delivering a higher volume of more intensive services, beneficial or not (referred to as the "perverse incentive").

Four fundamental changes are necessary to redirect American medicine toward what most agree is its rightful mission: to best improve the health of all Americans most efficiently.

First, accurate and transparent information is essential to support wise decision-making at all levels. Whether individuals are deciding about the best approach to their own health, or patient and doctor are deciding together about the best therapy, or purchasers of health care and government agencies are trying to improve the quality and control the costs of care, everyone needs much better information than is currently available. The federal board described earlier would go a long way toward making good information available to all.

Second, the mix of physicians needs to be rebalanced. The research of Dr. Barbara Starfield and her colleagues at Johns Hopkins, as well as the research of Dr. Elliott Fisher and his colleagues at Dartmouth, shows that, despite our faith in the latest high-tech medical care, the areas of the country that have higher concentrations of specialist physicians have both higher health care costs and worse health care outcomes; the areas that have more primary care physicians have lower health care costs and better health outcomes. However, because of the financial, lifestyle, and intellectual incentives that are brought so heavily to bear on medical students and practicing doctors, interest in careers in primary care is plummeting. The percentage of graduates of American medical schools entering family practice residencies declined by almost half between 1997 and 2004 (from 17.3 to 8.8 percent). What ought to be the basic unit of good health care, the primary care doctor-patient relationship, is at risk of soon becoming an endangered species.

Third, policy makers and payers should focus their attention on health care systems (groups of doctors, hospitals, and other medical services)—especially on figuring out how to reward them for providing the right care in the right amount, for achieving high levels of patient satisfaction, and, most important, for improving the health of the people they serve.

And, finally, the government cannot simply stand by as a paid-off sugar daddy to the medical (and especially the drug) industry. Well-functioning markets require active government oversight to make sure that the public's interests are being served. The medical watchdogs need to be revived, and the industry money that has become a staple of their otherwise meager diet needs to be withdrawn and replaced with adequate, stable funding from noncommercial sources. The FDA and NIH should be independent of, instead of seamlessly interwoven with, the drug and medical device industries. Drug company lobbying can no longer be allowed to stand in the way of legislation that clearly serves the health interests of the American people, such as setting aside less than $0.02 per prescription in the Medicare prescription bill to determine the best drugs and therapies for seniors, or simply allowing the market to function so the government can negotiate the best price from drug makers to obtain the best value for American senior citizens.

RECLAIMING RESPONSIBILITY FOR YOUR HEALTH

Don't forget the good news. You can take charge of many of your biggest health risks. The recommendations about a healthy lifestyle may at first seem too simplistic, but the research repeatedly shows that this is the best way to stay healthy. The challenge comes not in knowing what to do to optimize your health, but in integrating these simple recommendations into daily habits. Genuine change requires the exercise of real autonomy. This means a willingness to accept responsibility for maintaining your own health, with a realistic view of economic conditions and environmental factors, setting goals, honestly confronting resistance, and getting help when necessary to overcome that resistance. It also means a willingness to let go of old habits to make room for growth.

Though it may seem antiquated in our era of high-tech medicine, the foundation of good medical care is an ongoing relationship with a primary care physician with whom you feel comfortable (sometimes in conjunction with a nurse practitioner or physician's assistant). The two essential components of such a relationship are that the patient trust the provider and have confidence in his or her competence, and that the provider have a sense of who the patient is and be willing and able to understand the patient's concerns. Perhaps a third essential component is the patient's being able to share his or her concerns about the commercial distortion of health care, and the ability for patient and doctor to decide together how to proceed in the context of this uncertainty.

How can you become a better health care consumer? The next time you hear about a medical "breakthrough," try to determine who sponsored the study and whether the experts interviewed disclosed any financial ties to the products being discussed. Go a step further: see if the results are presented as relative risk (people who took the new drug were x percent less likely to develop a disease than the people who didn't take the new drug) or as absolute risk reduction (taking the new drug protects x number of people out of 100 from developing the disease). The second approach provides much more information about the real benefit of the drug or therapy. Notice whether lifestyle and other interventions are discussed in addition to expensive drugs as a part of the solution. Most of all, immunize yourself from the drug companies efforts to convince you that you desperately need their advertised products. If you really needed the product, it is unlikely that the drug companies would be spending money on advertising. Remember, there aren't many ads for insulin on TV.

Since leaving medical practice to research and write about these issues, I have found problems far more profound than I ever suspected—

and I have found far more opportunity for Americans to improve their health as well. I am still a physician and want to do my best to help people achieve better health and a sense of well-being. So what can we do?

Ultimately, the issue is not the quality of our medical science, but the political context in which American medicine unfolds. The overwhelming power that the drug and other medical industries now wield over American politics, science, and health care has created an imbalance between corporate goals and public interest that is no longer self-correcting. In fact, it has become resistant to correction. If democracy is to be more than a ritual dance choreographed by powerful corporations in this postindustrial "information age," government must actively protect the integrity of the information on which we rely to guide our personal and political choices. As individuals we have the opportunity to reclaim responsibility for much of our health through intelligent lifestyle decisions and informed use of medical care. As citizens we must demand that our government restore the balance between public health and corporate profits, so that the drug, medical-device, and other medical industries can only achieve their goals by effectively and efficiently maximizing Americans' health. Needless to say, these industries, as well as many doctors whose high-priced specialty services would not be needed in such high volume in a more efficient health care system, will do everything possible to prevent reform, as they have so successfully done in the past.

Courageous leadership is urgently needed to redirect American health care—not unlike the leadership provided by President Teddy Roosevelt a century ago when the enormously concentrated power of the railroad, steel, and oil "combines" similarly threatened the public's interests. Government needs to be re-empowered, and a good place to start might be public hearings that investigate the commercial distortion of our medical knowledge. The first "case" might be an investigation of the process by which Celebrex and Vioxx, two drugs of very limited clinical value, have become blockbusters in the United States but not in the rest of the world (nearly 80 percent of all sales occur in the United States). Such hearings could publicly review the unprocessed data from the manufacturers' own studies that have been submitted to the FDA; expose the discrepancies between these data and the articles that reported the "scientific evidence" about the two drugs, published in our two most respected medical journals; inform the public about the financial ties between each of the four authors of the clinical practice guidelines issued by the American College of Rheumatology in 2000, which recommended the use of these drugs, and at least one of the manufacturers of Celebrex and Vioxx; show that in 2001 (when these drugs were becoming established as the standard of care) they were the two most heavily advertised to the public and two of the most heavily marketed to doctors; show how drug company–funded continuing education has persuaded doctors to prescribe these drugs; show how the FDA has known this whole story since February 2001 and, despite issuing Warning Letters to the manufacturers of both Celebrex and Vioxx about false and misleading marketing, has not effectively corrected doctors' and the public's erroneous beliefs about the true clinical value of these drugs; and, finally, show how all these tactics were masterfully orchestrated to produce $5.3 billion of COX-2 inhibitor sales in the United States in 2003.

Public hearings investigating the commercial bias in the 2001 update of the cholesterol guidelines would be similarly revealing. The public has the right to know that the recommendations that guide their medical care are not nearly as "evidence based" as they claim to be; that many of the references cited to support key recommendations do not provide that support; that the directions of the estimations and extrapolations presented in the guidelines tend to justify the use of more statin drugs; and that these guidelines are driving up sales of cholesterol-lowering statin drugs while diverting doctors' and the public's attention away from far more effective and far less expensive ways to prevent heart disease.

This brings me to the end of my story. I hope that I have answered Mrs. Francis's question about why I chose to leave my practice to write this book, and that I have helped to improve the health of more people than I might have otherwise. I also hope that in sharing what I have learned about the distortion of our medical knowledge with hardworking colleagues I will have inspired some to become more critical consumers of scientific evidence and the recommendations of "thought leaders" on the payroll of the drug and other medical industries.

I will have succeeded in my task if I have motivated some readers to be more regular about exercise, adopt a healthier diet, stop smoking, and think more critically about the relationship between their own needs and goals and those that are externally imposed by the push of the market. My greatest hope is that this book will inspire readers to consider the responsibility of citizenship in this time of excessive medical profiteering and corporate influence, and to take up one of the most important challenges of our time: high-quality health care for all based on the translation of well-ordered science into accurate, unbiased medical information.

We have come to a critical juncture, and our future depends on our willingness to act on our country's highest ideals. In this sense, the health we seek for ourselves, for our families, and for all Americans is a metaphor for something greater even than physical well-being: wholeness and connectedness that extend beyond the narrow confines of the biomedical-commercial paradigm of medicine.

NOTES

PREFACE TO THE PAPERBACK EDITION

xiii **British drug authorities had mandated a similar warning:** Alan Cowell, "Second Thoughts on Restricting Drugs To Treat Depression in Adolescents," *New York Times*, September 21, 2004.

xiii **nine studies showing just the opposite:** Gardiner Harris, "Expert Kept From Speaking At Antidepressant Hearing," New Warnings Sought on Antidepressants," *New York Times*, April 16, 2004.

xiii **outside experts agreed with its own:** Gardiner Harris, "Antidepressant Study Seen to Back Expert," *New York Times*, August 20, 2004.

xiii **FDA belatedly mandated the highest level of caution:** Gardiner Harris, "FDA Toughens Warning on Antidepressant Drugs," *New York Times*, October 16, 2004.

INTRODUCTION

xvii **securities analysts were receiving bonuses:** Speech given by Lori Richard, director of the Office of Compliance Inspections and Examinations, U.S. Securities and Exchange Commission, to the Financial Women's Association, May 8, 2002. Viewed at http://www.sec.gov/news/speech/spch559.htm. Accessed January 30, 2004.

xvii **three times the average:** Henry J. Kaiser Family Foundation, "Prescription Drug Trends: A Chartbook Update," November 2001. Viewed at http://www.kff.org/rxdrugs/loader.cfm?url=/commonspot/security/getfile.cfm&PageID=1 4267. Accessed January 31, 2004.

xvii **increased by more than $1000:** Milt Freudenheim, "Workers Feel Pinch of Rising Health Costs," *New York Times*, October 22, 2003.

xvii **$469 for the average American family:** Paul Krugman, "The Tax-Cut Con," *New York Times*, September 14, 2003.

xvii **an additional $469 per year:** Freudenheim, op. cit.

xvii **half of all personal bankruptcies:** "Harper's Index," *Harper's Magazine*, August 2002.

CHAPTER 1
MEDICINE IN TRANSITION:
CARING FOR PATIENTS AT THE CROSSROADS

4 **Celebrex:** L. S. Simon, A. L. Weaver, D. Y. Graham, et al., "Anti-Inflammatory and Upper Gastrointestinal Effects of Celecoxib in Rheumatoid Arthritis: A Randomized Controlled Trial." *Journal of the American Medical Association* 282:1921–1928, 1999.

4 **Vioxx:** M. J. Langman, D. M. Jensen, D. J. Watson, et al., "Adverse Upper Gastrointestinal Effects of Rofecoxib Compared with NSAIDs," *Journal of the American Medical Association* 282:1929–1933, 1999.

5 **accompanying editorial:** W. L. Peterson and B. Cryer B., "COX-1-Sparing NSAIDS: Is the Enthusiasm Justified?" *Journal of the American Medical Association* 282:1961–1963, 1999.

5 **two of the four drugs:** "Prescription Drug Expenditures in 2000: The Upward Trend Continues," a report by the National Institute for Health Care Management Research and Educational Foundation, May 2001. Viewed at http://nihcm.org/spending2000.pdf. Accessed August 3, 2003.

7 **doctor and patient working together:** H. Benson, M.D., and M. Stark, *Timeless Healing: The Power and Biology of Belief,* New York: Scribner, 1996, p. 32.

10 **the four medications:** I started Sister Marguerite on an angiotensin-converting enzyme (ACE) inhibitor to decrease her chance of going into congestive heart failure again, but she couldn't tolerate even a low dose because of her already low blood pressure.

CHAPTER 2
SPINNING THE EVIDENCE: EVEN THE MOST RESPECTED
MEDICAL JOURNALS ARE NOT IMMUNE

13 **"Pravastatin Therapy and the Risk of Stroke":** H. D. White, R. J. Simes, N. E., et al., "Pravastatin Therapy and the Risk of Stroke," *New England Journal of Medicine* 343:317–326, 2000.

15 **there would be about one less stroke:** There was also a benefit in reduction of the risk of recurrent heart disease in the patients being treated with Pravachol, but those results had been published two years earlier and were not news. The point of this paper was to inform doctors about the additional benefit of stroke reduction.

16 **age at which most strokes:** R. D. Brown Jr., J. P. Whisnant, J. D. Sicks, et al., "Stroke Incidence, Prevalence, and Survival: Secular Trends in Rochester, Minnesota, Through 1989," *Stroke* 27(3):373–380, 1996.

16 **three out of five stroke victims in the general population are women:** Ibid.

16 **do not take aspirin routinely:** Lawrence Goldkind, M.D., "Medical Officer's

Gastroenterology Advisory Committee Briefing Document. Celebrex (celecoxib)," February 7, 2001. p. 51. Viewed at http://www.fda.gov/ohrms/dockets/ac/01/briefing/3677b1_05_gi.doc.P. 10. Accessed September 26, 2001.

16 **her risk of stroke would have been increased:** To be fair, none of the individual factors associated with an increased risk of stroke in the people treated with Pravachol reached statistical significance, but had these characteristics been grouped together into a typical stroke patient, the increased risk of stroke associated with taking Pravachol might well have reached statistical significance. And we cannot be sure that the same pattern of increased risk of stroke in these groups would occur in people who had not had a heart attack.

17 **simply eating fish once a week:** H. Iso, K. M. Rexrode, M. J. Stampfer, et al., "Intake of Fish and Omega-3 Fatty Acids and Risk of Stroke in Women," *Journal of the American Medical Association* 285:304–312, 2001.

17 **Controlling high blood pressure:** S. E. Straus, S. R. Majumdar, F. A. McAlister, "New Evidence for Stroke Prevention: Scientific Review," *Journal of the American Medical Association* 288:1388–1395, 2002.

17 **moderate exercise for less than two hours:** R. L. Sacco, R. Gan, B. Boden-Albala, et al., "Leisure-Time Physician Activity and Ischemic Stroke Risk: The Northern Manhattan Stroke Study," *Stroke* 29(2):380–387, 1998.

18 **a study about stroke prevention:** L. Sacco, R. Benson, D. Kargman, et al., "High-Density Lipoprotein Cholesterol and Ischemic Stroke in the Elderly," *Journal of the American Medical Association* 285:2729–2735, 2001.

19 **follow-up letter to the editor:** K. Sheikh, "High-Density Lipoprotein Cholesterol and Risk of Stroke [Letters]," *Journal of the American Medical Association* 286:1573–1574, 2001.

20 **Statins raise HDL-cholesterol:** P. R. Hebert, J. M. Gaziano, K. S. Chan, and C. H. Hennekens, "Cholesterol Lowering with Statin Drugs, Risk of Stroke, and Total Mortality: An Overview of Randomized Trials," *Journal of the American Medical Association* 278:313–321, 1997.

20 **far more than enough to significantly raise the risk of stroke:** Statins raise HDL cholesterol an average of 7 percent, or 2.8 mg/dL, and lower total cholesterol by 22 percent, or 42 mg/dL.

20 **used data from the same case-control study:** R. L. Sacco, R. Gan, B. Boden-Albala, et al., op. cit.

20 **earlier NEJM article about Pravachol:** H. D. White, R. J. Simes, N. E. Anderson, et al., "Pravastatin Therapy and the Risk of Stroke," *New England Journal of Medicine* 343:317–326, 2000.

21 **life expectancy of a black man in Harlem:** Michael Marmot, "Inequalities in Health [Editorial]," *New England Journal of Medicine* 345:134–136, 2001.

21 **Pfizer had a new "HDL elevator" drug:** Jami Rubin and Andrew Baum. "Our Survey of the Statin Market Projects Strong Growth: Morgan Stanley Dean Witter," *U.S. Investment Perspectives,* March 16, 2001, pp. 65–66.

CHAPTER 3
FALSE AND MISLEADING: THE MISREPRESENTATION
OF CELEBREX AND VIOXX

23 **editorial about Celebrex and Vioxx:** W. L. Peterson and B. Cryer, COX-1-Sparing NSAIDS: Is the Enthusiasm Justified?" *Journal of the American Medical Association* 282:1961–1963, 1999.

24 **over $3 billion in sales:** The National Institute for Health Care Management Research and Educational Foundation, "Prescription Drug Expenditures in 2000," op. cit.

24 **one-third of all arthritis drug sales:** "Prescription Drug Expenditures in 2001: Another Year of Escalating Costs," a report by the National Institute for Health Care Management Research and Educational Foundation." Revised May 6, 2002. Viewed at http://nihcm.org/spending2001.pdf p.15. Accessed February 20, 2004.

25 **"The Coxibs, Selective Inhibitors of Cyclooxygenase-2":** G. A. FitzGerald and C. Patrono, "The Coxibs, Selective Inhibitors of Cyclooxygenase-2," *New England Journal of Medicine* 345:433–442, 2001.

26 **prohibited by the *New England Journal of Medicine*:** M. Angel, R. D. Utiger, A. J. J. Wood, "Disclosure of Authors' Conflicts of Interest: A Follow-Up," *New England Journal of Medicine* 342:586–587, 2000.

26 **NEJM loosened its editorial policy:** J. M. Drazen and G. D. Curfman, "Financial Associations of Authors," *New England Journal of Medicine* 346:1901–1902, 2002.

27 **results of the VIGOR study from the fall of 2000:** C. Bombardier, L. Laine, A. Reicin, et al., op. cit.

27 **keep the results of their studies secret:** T. Bodenheimer, Uneasy Alliance: Clinical Investigators and the Pharmaceutical Industry," *New England Journal of Medicine* 342:1539–1544, 2000.

28 **Arthritis Advisory Committee meeting of February 7–8:** FDA Arthritis Advisory Committee, "Briefing Information. Celebrex (celecoxib)," February 7, 2001. Viewed at http://www.fda.gov/ohrms/dockets/ac/01/briefing/3677b1.htm. Accessed September 16, 2001. FDA Arthritis Advisory Committee, "Briefing Information. Vioxx (rofecoxib)," February 8, 2001. Viewed at http://www.fda.gov/ohrms/dockets/ac/01/briefing/3677b2.htm. Accessed September 16, 2001.

28 **consider the manufacturers' request:** Carol Eustice, "FDA Advised on Celebrex and Vioxx," *What You Need to Know About Arthritis*. Viewed at http://arthritis.about.com/cs/cox/a/celebvioxxlabel.htm.

29 **results of the CLASS study:** Silverstein, Faich, Goldstein, et al., op. cit.

29 **The accompanying editorial:** D. R. Lichenstein and M. M. Wolfe, "COX-2-Selective NSAIDs: New and Improved?" *Journal of the American Medical Association* 284(10):1297–1299, 2000.

29 manufacturer's original research plan: Goldkind, op. cit.

30 "the sponsor's presentations of 6-month data . . . are not statistically valid or supportable": Ibid.

30 FDA's gastroenterology reviewer concluded: The FDA's gastroenerology reviewer commented: "There appears to be a higher risk of late CSUGIEs [clinically significant upper gastrointestinal events] with C [Celebrex] compared to *both* ibuprofen and diclofenac." Ibid, p. 52

30 story that had been published in the *Washington Post*: S. Okie, "Missing Data on Celebrex Full Study Altered Picture of Drug," *Washington Post*, August 5, 2001, p. A11. Viewed at http://www.washingtonpost.com. Accessed October 24, 2001.

31 "The primary objective of this study: Goldkind, op. cit., p. 70.

31 "be categorized and analyzed separately": Ibid., p. 80.

31 "major strength of the current study": Ibid., p. 8.

32 experienced 11 percent more serious complications: Ibid., p. 63.

32 The letter cites repeated unsubstantiated marketing claims: FDA warning letter, February 1, 2001. Viewed at http://www.fda.gov/cder/warn/2001/DD8432.pdf. Accessed February 25, 2004.

34 "cardiovascular thrombotic or embolic": Lawrence Goldkind, M.D., Medical Officer's Advisory Committee GI Briefing Document. Review of Vioxx Gastrointestinal Outcomes, February 8, 2001. Viewed at http://www.fda.gov/ohrms/dockets/ac/01/briefing/3677b2_05_gi.doc P. 54. Accessed October 17, 2001.

34 27 *more* serious cardiovascular complications: Shari L. Targum, M.D., "Review of Cardiovascular Safety Data Base: Rofecoxib (Vioxx)," February 1, 2001, p. 17. Viewed at http://www.fda.gov/ohrms/dockets/ac/01/briefing/3677b2_06_cardio.pdf. Accessed October 17, 2001.

34 increased risk of heart attacks, strokes, and sudden death: The NEJM review article did not include the cardiovascular complications of unstable angina, serious blood clots, or transient ischemic attacks that had been submitted by the manufacturer to the FDA. See Targum, op. cit., p. 18.

35 statistical significance of this finding (p = .0016): Qian, Li, "Statistical Reviewer Briefing Document for the Advisory Committee," February 8, 2001. Viewed at http://www.fda.gov/ohrms/dockets/ac/01/briefing/3677b2_04_stats.doc p. 12. Accessed October 17, 2001.

35 one additional serious cardiovascular complication: Targum, op. cit., p. 15.

35 1.9 times the risk, p = .041: Qian, op. cit., p. 13.

35 would be the preferred drug: Targum, op. cit., p. 13

35 between 7 and 11 additional serious cardiovascular complications each year: Ibid., p. 21. The VIGOR study included people who might have had fewer cardiovascular complications if they had been taking low-dose aspirin, which was not permitted by the study design. For people with a pre-

vious history of cardiovascular disease, it is not known whether taking low-dose aspirin along with Vioxx would counteract the increased cardio-vascular risk of taking Vioxx instead of naproxen. Nonetheless, although the magnitude of the risk of taking Vioxx instead of naproxen for people with a history of cardiovascular disease was not included in the NEJM review article, it did recommend that such people take low-dose aspirin along with their Vioxx. See www.fda.gov/ohrms/dockets/ac/01/briefing/367762_06_cardio.pdf, pp. 20–21.

36 had 21 percent more "serious adverse events": Qian, op. cit., p. 11.

36 Vioxx costs $127.99 a month: Viewed at http://www.cvs.com. Accessed February 25, 2004.

36 Warning Letter to Merck: Viewed at http://www.fda.gov/cder/warn/2001/9456.pdf. Accessed February 20, 2004.

38 57 percent of all the money spent on prescription arthritis medication: "Prescription Drug Expenditures in 2001," op. cit.

CHAPTER 4
THE MYTH OF EXCELLENCE

42 one out of every 100 Americans: M. Beddow Bayly, "The Story of the Salk Anti-Poliomyelitis Vaccine," 1956. Published in WHALE, November 2000. Viewed at http://www.whale.to/vaccine/bayly.html. Accessed October 01, 2003.

43 cardiopulmonary bypass was done in Sweden in 1953: " 'Internal' Workings of the Cardiopulmonary Bypass Machine, The Chemical Engineers Resource Page." Viewed at http://www.cheresources.com/cardiopul.shtml. Accessed February 24, 2004.

43 Dialysis, to filter the blood: William B. Schwartz, Life Without Disease, Berkeley, Calif.: University of California Press, 1998, pp. 9–13.

43 Gleevac is a true miracle: Arnold S. Relman and Marcia Angell, "America's Other Drug Problem: How the Drug industry Distorts Medicine and Politics," The New Republic, December 16, 2002, pp. 27–41.

44 rated . . . as the most important development: V. R. Fuchs and H. C. Sox, "Physicians' Views of the Relative Importance of Thirty Medical Innovations," Health Affairs 20:30–34, 2001.

45 "the U.S. population does not have anywhere near the best health in the world.": B. Starfield, "Is U.S. Health Care Really the Best in the World?" Journal of the American Medical Association 284(4):483–485, 2000.

45 comparison of 13 industrialized nations: The rankings on health outcomes in the world's industrialized nations, were, from best to worst: Japan, Sweden, Canada, France, Australia, Spain, Finland, the Netherlands, the United Kingdom, Denmark, Belgium, the United States, and Germany.

45 United States again ranked poorly: "Health at a Glance." Organization for

Economic Co-Operation and Development, 2001, p. 13.

45 **United States ranks a lowly 24 among all the OECD countries on infant mortality:** Ibid., p. 17.

45 **United States' position improves only from 24 to 20:** "International Health Statistics, Chapter 4: Infant Mortality." Woodrow Wilson School of Public and International Affairs, p. 46. Viewed at http://www.wws.princeton.edu/cgi-in/byteserv.prl/~ota/disk1/1994/9418/941806.PDF. Accessed February 24, 2004.

45 **"healthy life expectancy":** "World Health Report 2003—Shaping the Future" World Health Organization, 2003, pp. 156–159. Viewed at http://www.who.int/whr/2003/annex_4_en.xls. Accessed May 11, 2004.

46 **measures of health system performance:** "World Health Report 2000: Statistics." Viewed at http://www.who.int/whr2001/2001/archives/2000/en/statistics.htm. Accessed February 24, 2004. By 1998, Americans were losing more years of life; see G. Anderson and P. S. Hussey, "Comparing Health System Performance in OECD Countries," *Health Affairs* 20:219–232, 2001.

46 **health expenditures in the United States are projected to exceed $6100:** S. Heffler, S. Smith, S. Keehan, et al., "Health Spending Projections Through 2013," *Health Affairs.* Viewed at http://content.healthaffairs.org/cgi/reprint/hlthaff.w4.79v1.pdf. Accessed February 26, 2004.

46 **United States spends 42 percent more on health care:** U. E. Reinhardt, P. S. Hussey, and G. F. Anderson, "U.S. Health Care Spending in an International Context: Why Is U.S. Spending So High, and Can We Afford It? *Health Affairs* 23:10–25, 2004.

47 **Sources of data for Figure 4-1:** "The World Health Report 2003—Shaping the Future," the World Health Organization, www.who.int/whr/2003/annex_4_en.xls (Access 3/21/04). "Health at a Glance, OECD Indicators 2003," Organisation for Economic Co-Operation and Development. 2003, Paris, France.

47 **U.S. relative performance declined:** "World Health Report 2000: Statistics," op. cit.

47 **health of the citizens in the other OECD countries is improving more quickly:** "Health at a Glance," op. cit., pp. 94–95.

48 **prescription drugs cost about 70 percent more in the United States:** Patented Medicine Price Review Board of Canada, *Annual Report,* 2001, p. 21. Viewed at http://www.pmprb-cepmb.gc.ca/english/pdf/ar2001/ar2001-e.pdf. Accessed February 26, 2003.

48 **pharmaceutical companies in the United States:** "Why the Pharmaceutical Industry's 'R&D Scare Card' Does Not Justify High and Rapidly Increasing U.S. Drug Prices," *Public Citizen,* January 26, 2000. p. 19.

48 **of the 569 new drugs approved:** National Institute for Health Care Management Research and Educational Foundation, "Changing Patterns of Pharmaceutical Innovation, May 2002. p. 9. www.nichm.org/innovations.pdf. Accessed February 27, 2003.

48 **patients in the United States:** "World Health Report 2000: Statistics," op. cit.

48 "Since 1900, the average lifespan: "Ten Great Public Health Achievements—United States, 1900–1999," *CDC MMWR Weekly* 48:241–243, 1999.

49 preventive care as recommended: J. P. Bunker, H. S. Frazier, and F. Mosteller, "Improving Health: Measuring Effects of Medical Care," *Milbank Quarterly* 72:225–258, 1994.

49 tuberculosis was the leading cause of death: National Center for Health Statistics, "Age-Adjusted Death Rates for Selected Causes, Death Registration States, 1900–1932, and United States, 1933–98." Viewed at http://www.cdc.gov/nchs/datawh/statab/unpubd/mortabs/hist293.htm. Accessed February 8, 2003.

49 first effective *medical* therapies for tuberculosis: J. B. McKinlay and S. M. McKinley, "The Questionable Contribution of Medical Measures to the Decline of Mortality in the United States in the Twentieth Century," *Millbank Memorial Fund,* Summer 405–428, 1977.

50 inexpensive cotton undergarments: René Dubos, *Mirage of Health: Utopias, Progress, and Biological Change,* New York: Harper & Row, 1959, p. 268.

50 death rate for cancer in the United States: National Center for Health Statistics, "Age-Adjusted Death Rates," op. cit.

50 it had become the number one killer: National Center for Health Statistics, U.S. Centers for Disease Control and Prevention. Viewed at http://www.cdc.gov/nchs/data/hus/tables/2003, 2003hus030.pdf. Accessed January 14, 2004.

50 President Nixon boasted: Jerome Groopman, "The Thirty Years' War," *The New Yorker,* June 4, 2001, p. 32.

50 Cancer death rates were going up: Quoted ibid.

50 a few tremendous successes in this war: J. C. Bailar and H. L. Gornik, "Cancer Undefeated," *New England Journal of Medicine* 336:1569–1574, 1997.

50 overall death rate from cancer was exactly the same: National Center for Health Statistics, U.S. Centers for Disease Control and Prevention. Viewed at http://www.cdc.gov/nchs/datawh/statab/unpubd/mortabs/hist293.htm. Accessed January 30, 2003. And H. K. Weir, M. J. Thun, B. F. Hankey, et al., "Annual Report to the Nation on the Status of Cancer, 1975–2000, Featuring the Uses of Surveillance Data for Cancer Prevention and Control," *Journal of the National Cancer Institute* 95:1276–1299, 2003.

50 proper goal of a nation's health care system: D. M. Berwick, "A User's Manual for the IOM's 'Quality Chasm' Report," *Health Affairs* 21(3):80–90, 2002.

51 $80,000 to $200,000 per procedure: Gina Kolata and Kurt Eichenwald, "Hope for Sale: A Special Report: Business Thrives on Unproven Care, Leaving Science Behind. *New York Times,* October 3, 1999.

52 found that his data were fraudulent: Denise Grady, "More Deception Is Suspected in Cancer Study," *New York Times,* March 10, 2000.

52 The researcher's article was retracted: Eric Nagourney, "National briefing: Cancer Study Retracted," *New York Times,* April 27, 2001.

52 **failed to show any benefit:** Stadtmauer E. A., O'Neill A., Goldstein L. J., et al., "Conventional-Dose Chemotherapy Compared with High-Dose Chemotherapy Plus Autologous Hematopoietic Stem-Cell Transplantation for Metastatic Breast Cancer," *New England Journal of* Medicine, 342(15): 1069–1076, 2000.

52 **"this form of treatment for women:** Lippman M. E., "High-Dose Chemotherapy Plus Autologous Bone Marrow Transplantation for Metastatic Breast Cancer," *New England Journal of Medicine,* 342:1119–1120, 2000.

53 **"One thing is for certain:** George W. Bush, "President Bush's Vision for More Health Care Choices," speech before the Illinois State Medical Society, June 11, 2003. Viewed at http://www.georgewbush.com/HealthCare/Read.aspx?ID= 1874. Accessed February 26, 2004.

CHAPTER 5
A CASE IN POINT: THE SAGA OF HORMONE REPLACEMENT THERAPY

57 **risk of breast cancer increases by 8 percent:** C. Schairer, J. Lubin, R. Troisi, et al., "Menopausal Estrogen and Estrogen-Progestin Replacement Therapy and Breast Cancer Risk," *Journal of the American Medical Association* 283(4): 485–491, 2000.

58 **"The hormonal dance doesn't end:** Susan M. Love, M.D., with Karen Lindsey, *Dr. Susan Love's Hormone Book: Making Informed Choices About Menopause,* New York: Three Rivers Press, 1997, p. 7.

59 **Dr. Christiane Northrup:** Christiane Northrup, M.D. *The Wisdom of Menopause: Creating Physical and Emotional Health and Healing During the Change,* New York: Bantam Books, 2001.

59 **Premarin (brand name for estrogen) was approved by the FDA in 1942:** See Amanda Spake with Susan Headden, Katy Kelly, the U.S. News library staff, and Nancy Cohen, "Making Sense of Menopause," *U.S. News and World Report,* 2003.

59 **each mare produces enough estrogen:** National Women's Health Network, *The Truth About Hormone Replacement Therapy: How to Break Free from the Medical Myths of Menopause,* Roseville, Calif.: Prima Publishing, 2002, p. 24.

60 **In a 1962 article published in** *JAMA:* Cited by Amanda Spake, in "Making Sense of Menopause," op. cit.

60 **hormone pills "are prophylactic:** Ibid.

60 **best-selling book,** *Feminine Forever:* Robert Wilson, M.D., *Feminine Forever,* New York: M. Evans & Co., 1968, p. 97. Love, *Dr. Susan Love's Hormone Book,* op. cit., p. 26.

60 **contributions from drug companies:** Ibid.

60 **Wilson's foundation:** Ibid.

61 **The Wilsons likened female aging to a disease:** R. A. Wilson and T. A. Wilson, "The Basic Philosophy of Estrogen Maintenance," *Journal of the American Geriatrics Society* 20(11):521–523, 1972.

61 **transform his own personal trauma:** Interview with Ron Wilson by Judy Carmen. Copyright Judy Carmen and Ron Wilson, 2002. Sent via e-mail from Ron Wilson to the author, 2003.

62 **most frequently prescribed brand-name drug:** The Hormone Foundation, "The Evolution of Estrogen Timeline." Viewed at http://www.hormone.org/publications/estrogen_timeline/et3.html. Time line covering the period from the 1920s through 2002 is supported by an unrestricted educational grant from Wyeth Pharmaceuticals.

62 **one of the five most frequently prescribed drugs:** National Women's Health Network, op. cit., p. 24.

62 **estrogen therapy increased the risk of cancer:** D. C. Smith, R. Prentice, D. J. Thompson, and W. L. Herrmann, "Association of Exogenous Estrogen and Endometrial Carcinoma. Abstract," *New England Journal of Medicine* 293(23):1164–1167, 1975.

62 **(endometrial cancer), up to 14-fold:** H. K. Ziel and W. D. Finkle, "Increased Risk of Endometrial Carcinoma Among Users of Conjugated Estrogens. Abstract," *New England Journal of Medicine* 293(23):1167–1170, 1975.

62 **adding another hormone, progestin:** M. H. Thom, P. J. White, R. M. Williams, et al., "Prevention and Treatment of Endometrial Disease in Climacteric Women Receiving Estrogen Therapy," *The Lancet* 2(8140):455–457, 1979.

62 **studies soon confirmed that progestin protected women:** See Spake, op. cit.

62 **HRT had been linked with cancer:** In 1977 the American College of Obstetricians and Gynecologists participated in an unsuccessful lawsuit against the FDA, attempting to block package inserts for estrogen products from including a warning about the increased risk of cancer of the uterus. See National Women's Health Network, op. cit., p. 25.

62 **"Marketing a disease:** Love, *Dr. Susan Love's Hormone Book,* op. cit., p. 28.

62 **To educate the doctors:** Ibid.

63 **public relations firm:** See Spake, op. cit.

63 **The campaign was successful:** Ibid.

63 **The National Osteoporosis Foundation:** The National Osteoporosis Foundation's 2001 *Annual Report* lists a number of pharmaceutical companies among its major donors: Aventis Pharmaceuticals; Eli Lilly; GlaxoSmithKline; Merck; Novartis Pharmaceuticals; Pfizer, Procter & Gamble Pharmaceuticals; Solvay Pharmaceuticals; Wyeth Pharmaceuticals; and Wyeth (formerly American Home Products).

63 **a 1985 report in NEJM:** M. J. Stampfer, W. C. Willett, G. A. Colditz, et al., "A Prospective Study of Postmenopausal Estrogen Therapy and Coronary Heart Disease," *New England Journal of* Medicine 313(17):1044–1049, 1985.

63 **Framingham Heart Study:** P. W. Wilson, R. J. Garrison, and W. P. Castelli, "Postmenopausal Estrogen Use, Cigarette Smoking, and Cardiovascular Morbidity in Women over 50," *New England Journal of Medicine* 313(17): 1038–1043, 1985.

63 **Premarin sales:** Spake, op. cit.

63 **American College of Physicians issued guidelines:** American College of Physicians, "Guidelines for Counseling Postmenopausal Women About Preventive Hormone Therapy," *Annals of Internal Medicine* 117:1038–1041, 1992.

63 **American College of Obstetrics and Gynecology:** Dr. Susan S. Love, "Sometimes Mother Nature Knows Best," *New York Times,* op-ed, March 27, 1997.

63 **Premarin use increased another 40 percent:** Spake, op. cit.

64 **most frequently prescribed brand-name drug:** Love, op. cit.

64 **in a 1997 article:** F. Grodstein, M. J. Stampfer, G. A. Colditz, et al., "Postmenopausal Hormone Therapy and Mortality," *New England Journal of Medicine* 336(25):1769–1775, 1997.

66 **lower mortality rate among women taking HRT:** Grodstein, op. cit.

67 **wealthier and better educated, were twice as likely to be white:** D. Friedman-Koss, C. J. Crespo, M. F. Bellantoni, and R. E. Anderson, "The Relationship of Race/Ethnicity and Social Class to Hormone Replacement Therapy: Results from the Third National Health and Nutrition Examination Survey 1988–1994," *Menopause* 9(4):264–272, 2002

67 **received more preventative health care:** E. Barrett-Connor, "Postmenopausal Estrogen and Prevention Bias," *Ann Intern Med* 115:455–456, 1991

67 **Dr. Elizabeth Barrett-Connor:** Spake in "Making Sense of Menopause," op. cit.

67 **first randomized controlled clinical trial of HRT:** S. Hulley, D. Grady, T. Bush, et al., "Randomization Trial of Estrogen plus Progestin for Secondary Prevention of Coronary Heart Disease in Postmenopausal Women," *Journal of the American Medical Association* 280:605–613, 1998.

68 **Wyeth-Ayerst had requested that the FDA approve:** National Women's Health Network, "The Truth About Hormone Replacement Therapy," Roseville, CA: Prima publishing, 2002, p.180.

68 **Even aspirin:** Gina Kolata and Melody Petersen, "Hormone Replacement Study a Shock to the Medical System," *New York Times,* July 10, 2002, p. 1.

68 **The FDA ruled that a randomized controlled trial was necessary:** Ibid.

68 **did not prevent heart disease:** Hulley, Grady, Bush, et al., op. cit.

68 **8 percent per year increase in the risk of breast cancer in women:**

68 **still the third most frequently prescribed drug:** *Family Practice News,* June 1, 2002.

69 **government-sponsored Women's Health Initiative study:** Writing Group for the Women's Health Initiative, op. cit.

69 **HRT not only did not prevent Alzheimer's disease:** K. Yaffe, "Hormone Ther-

apy and the Brain: Déjà Vu All Over Again?" *Journal of the American Medical Association* 289(20):2717–2719, 2003.

69 **Million Women Study:** Million Women Study Collaborators, op. cit.

70 **women in the United States were about four times more likely:** Love, *Dr. Susan Love's Hormone Book,* op. cit., p. 23.

70 **women taking estrogen:** The Women's Health Initiative Steering Committee, "Effects of Conjugated Equine Estrogen in Postmenopausal Women with Hysterectomy: The Women's Health Initiative Randomized Controlled Trial," *Journal of the American Medical Association* 291:1701–1712, 2004.

CHAPTER 6
AMERICAN MEDICINE'S PERFECT STORM: A BRIEF HISTORY

76 **Per-person health care expenditures:** K. Levit, C. Smith, C. Cowan, et al., "Trends in U.S. Health Care Spending, 2001," *Health Affairs* 22(1):154–164, 2002.

76 **premiums rose a whopping 43 percent:** Kaiser Family Foundation and Health Research and Educational Trust, "Employer Health Benefits: 2003 Summary of Findings."

76 **Health care costs now account:** Heffler, Smith, Keehan, et al., op. cit.

77 **HMOs, on the other hand, offered:** Initially, prepaid groups of health care providers were employed by the HMO and worked together in a central location or locations. These are called "staff" or "closed-model" HMOs. A variation of this arrangement, the "open-panel" HMO, evolved in which community-based doctors contracted to take care of HMO patients in their own offices, again with a prepaid arrangement to control costs. The open-panel plans were attractive to patients who wanted the broader coverage and cost savings of an HMO but did not want to leave their current doctor. Open-panel HMOs also have the advantage of avoiding the cost of establishing a central facility and are more practical in less densely populated areas.

77 **Managed care plans differ from HMOs:** Within these broad categories of HMO and managed care plans there are an almost infinite number of variations: the plans can be for profit or not for profit; doctors can be prepaid a certain amount per patient per month or get paid on a fee-for-service basis out of a collective pot; fee-for-service payment can be at 100 percent of the fee schedule or a lesser percentage with a "withhold," later returned based on individual and/or group financial performance, sometimes with an additional payment for higher quality of care; patients can be restricted to plan doctors or have greater choice for which they have to pay more; the co-pay for drugs can vary between generic and brand-name drugs, and between necessary and more optional drugs—like hair regrowth drugs or expensive drugs when less expensive alternatives are available. See R. A. Dudley and H. S. Luft, "Managed Care in Transition," *New England Journal of Medicine* 344:1087–1092, 2001.

77 **increasing between 10 percent and 18 percent per year:** Kaiser Family Foun-

dation and Health Research and Educational Trust, op. cit.

78 **In the late 1970s, almost all:** J. Oberlander, "The U.S. Health Care System: On a Road to Nowhere?" *Canadian Medical Association Journal* 167:163–168, 2002.

78 **By the end of the 1990s:** Dudley and Luft, op. cit.

78 **In 1990, stories about the new types:** M. Brodie, L. E. Brady, and Altman, "Media Coverage of Managed Care: Is There a Negative Bias?" *Health Affairs* 17(1):9–25, 1998.

78 **less than 2 percent by 1996:** Kaiser Family Foundation and Health Research and Educational Trust, op. cit.

79 **93 percent of the cost:** E. R. Berndt, "The U.S. Pharmaceutical Industry: Why Major Growth in Times of Cost Containment," *Health Affairs* 20(2):100–114, 2001.

79 **Between 1990 and 1997:** J. R. Gabel, P. B. Ginsburg, Pickreign, J. D. Reschovsky, "Trends in Out-of-Pocket Spending by Insured American Workers, 1990–1997," *Health Affairs* 20(2):47–57, 2001.

79 **half again as many Americans as Europeans:** K. Minah, R. J. Blendon, and J. M. Benson, "How Interested Are Americans in New Medical Technologies? A Multicountry Comparison," *Health Affairs* 20(5):194–201, 2001.

79 **more rather than less money:** Blendon and Benson, op. cit.

79 **80 percent of the Internet sites that address back pain:** L. Li, E. Irvin, J. Guzman, and C. Bombardier, "Surfing for Back Pain Patients: The Nature and Quality of Back Pain Information on the Internet. Abstract," *Spine* 26:545–557, 2001.

80 **In 1991 the drug companies spent:** "Direct-to-Consumer Ads—The Numbers," *American Medical News,* February 10, 1997. Viewed at http://www.ama-assn.org/sci-pibs/amnews/pick_97?add0210.htm. Accessed March 2, 2001.

80 **over $3 billion in 2003:** Scott Hensley, "As Drug Ad Spending Rises: A Look at Four Campaigns," *Wall Street Journal,* February 9, 2004.

80 **"The market sells dreams and hopes:** Daniel Callahan, *False Hopes,* New York: Simon & Schuster, 1998, pp. 40–41.

80 **News stories about HMOs unreasonably withholding care:** M. Brodie, et. al., op. cit.

80 **The public's esteem for managed care companies:** R. J. Blendon and J. M. Benson, "Americans' Views on Health Policy: A Fifty-Year Historical Perspective," *Health Affairs* 20(2):33–46, 2001.

81 **quality of care neither improved nor deteriorated:** Dudley and Luft, op. cit. See also J. Oberlander, "The U.S. Health Care System: On a Road to Nowhere?" *Canadian Medical Association Journal* 167(2)163–168, 2002.

81 **frequency with which people saw their doctors:** D. Mechanic, D. D. McAlpine, and M. Rosenthal, "Are Patient Visits with Physicians Getting Shorter?" *New England Journal of Medicine* 344:198–204, 2001.

81 **fewer than one in 100 requests for referrals:** Dudley and Luft, op. cit.

81 **"Regardless of the evidence:** Oberlander, op. cit.

82 **In one survey in which 59 percent:** "Doctors, Media Seen Fueling Hostility to Managed Care," *Physicians' Financial News,* April 30, 2001, p S2.

82 **Yearly increases in health insurance premiums:** Kaiser Family Foundation and Health Research and Educational Trust, op. cit.

82 **access to comprehensive, family-oriented primary care:** B. Starfield and L. Shi, "Policy Relevant Determinants of Health: An International Perspective," *Health Policy* 60:201–218, 2002. See also L. Shi, "Primary Care, Specialty Care, and Life Chances," *International Journal of Health Services* 24(3):431–458, 1994.

83 **In 1965 there were as many:** K. Grumbach, "Fighting Hand to Hand over Physician Workforce Policy," *Health Affairs* 21(5):13–27, 2002.

83 **health policy experts recommend that between 42 percent and 50 percent:** "Summary of Eighth Report, Patient Care Physician Supply and Require-ments: Testing COGME Recommendations," November 1996. Viewed at http://www.cogme.gov/rpt8.htm. Accessed April 7, 2003.

83 **Only 36 percent of U.S. medical students:** D. A. Newton and M. S. Grayson, "Trends in Career Choice by U.S. Medical School Graduates," *Journal of the American Medical Association* 290:1179–1182, 2003.

83 **only three out of 1000 thought that good students:** S. D. Block, N. Clark-Chiarelli, A. S. Peters, and J. D. Singer, "Academia's Chilly Climate for Primary Care," *Journal of the American Medical Association* 276:677–682, 1996.

83 **average debt of over $100,000:** Braden J. Hexom (legislative affairs director, American Medical Student Association), "Letter to House Education and Workforce Committee," August 12, 2003. Viewed at http://www.amsa.org/meded/studentdebtltr.cfm. Accessed September 29, 2003.

83 **boundary between professional responsibilities and personal time:** E. R. Dorsey, D. Jarjoura, and G. W. Retecki, "Influence of Controllable Lifestyle on Recent Trends in Specialty Choice by U.S. Medical Students," *Journal of the American Medical Association* 290:1173–1178, 2003.

84 **who do commit malpractice are not sued:** Philip K. Howard., "The Best Course of Treatment," *New York Times,* July 21, 2003.

84 **Three-fifths of doctors in the United States admit:** R. J. Blendon, K. Donelan. R. Leitman, et al., "Health Reform Lessons Learned from Physicians in Three Nations," *Health Affairs* 12(4):193–204, 1993

84 **set off a cascade effect:** R. A. Deyo, "Cascade Effects of Medical Technology," *Annual Review of Public Health* 23:23–44, 2002.

85 **"a servant of industry":** R. Horton, "Lotronex and the FDA: A Fatal Erosion of Integrity," *The Lancet* 357:1544–1545, 2001.

85 **AIDS activists drew attention:** David Willman, "How a New Policy Led to Seven Deadly Drugs," *Los Angeles Times,* December 20, 2000.

85 **2002 GAO report:** United States General Accounting Office, "Food and Drug

Administration: Effect of User Fees on Drug Approval Times, Withdrawals, and Other Agency Activities," September 2002.

85 **increase the staff at the Center for Drug Evaluation and Research, or CDER, from 1300 to 2300:** U.S. General Accounting Office, "Food and Drug Administration: Effect of User Fees on Drug Approval Times, Withdrawals, and Other Agency Activities," September 2002, p. 8, 10.

86 **Public Citizen in 1998:** Peter Lurie and Sidney M. Wolfe, "FDA Medical Officers Report Lower Standards Permit Dangerous Drug Approvals," Public Citizen Health Research Group. Viewed at http://www.citizen.org/publications/release.cfm?ID=7104. Accessed September 22, 2002.

86 **the inspector general of the U.S. Department of Health and Human Services:** Department of Health and Human Services, Office of Inspector General, "FDA's Review Process for New Drug Applications," March 2003.

86 **creating "a sweatshop environment:** Larry Thompson, "User Fees for Faster Drug Reviews: Are They Helping or Hurting Public Health," *FDA Consumer Magazine,* September–October 2000. Viewed at http://www.fda.gov/fdac/features/2000/500_pdufa.html. Accessed April 1, 2003.

86 **drugs approved by the FDA but later withdrawn:** U.S. General Accounting Office, op. cit., pp. 3–4.

86 **causing more than 1000 deaths:** Willman, op. cit.

86 **Rezulin is one of the drugs:** David Willman, "Diabetes Drug Rezulin Pulled Off the Market," *Los Angeles Times,* March 22, 2000.

86 **Pulitzer Prize–winning series of investigative reports:** The series of articles make a great read if you want to get the inside scoop on a deadly failure of the FDA and NIH, available on the Pulitzer Prize website: Viewed at http://www.pulitzer.org/year/2001/investigative-reporting/. Accessed September 25, 2003.

87 **Dr. Richard Eastman was the director of the NIH division:** David Willman, "FDA's Approval and Delay in Withdrawing Rezulin Probed," *Los Angeles Times,* August 16, 2000. Viewed at http://www.pulitzer.org/year/2001/investigative-reporting/works/willman6.html. Accessed September 25, 2003.

87 **Dr. Eastman announced that Rezulin:** David Willman, "Waxman Queries NIH on Researcher's Ties," *Los Angeles Times,* December 9, 1998. Viewed at http://www.house.gov/waxman/news_files/news_letters_rezulin_press_NIH_sci_ties_12_9_98.htm. Accessed September 27, 2003.

87 **Warner-Lambert submitted Rezulin to the FDA:** David Willman, " 'Fast Track' Drug to Treat Diabetes Tied to 33 Deaths," *Los Angeles Times,* December 6, 1998. Viewed at http://www.house.gov/waxman/news_files/news_letters_rezulin_press_FDA_fast_track_12_6_98.htm. Accessed February 26, 2004.

87 **"complained about Gueriguian:** Philip J. Hilts, *Protecting America's Health: The FDA, Business, and One Hundred Years of Regulation,* New York: Knopf, 2003, p. 133.

87 **reports of fatal liver toxicity due to Rezulin:** David Willman, "FDA's Approval . . . ," op. cit.

87 **Audrey LaRue Jones:** David Willman, "Fears Grow Over Delay in Removing Rezulin," *Los Angeles Times,* March 10, 2000.

87 **$1.8 billion worth of the drug:** David Willman, "Diabetes Drug Rezulin Pulled Off the Market," *Los Angeles Times,* March 22, 2000. Viewed at http://www.pulitzer.org/year/2001/investigative-reporting/works/willman5b.html. Accessed September 29, 2003.

87 **Dr. Gueriguian told the *Los Angeles Times:*** David Willman, "How a New Policy Led to Seven Deadly Drugs," *Los Angeles Times,* December 20, 2000. Viewed at http://www.pulitzer.org/year/2001/investigative-reporting/works/willman1.html. Accessed September 28, 2003.

88 **former supporter of Rezulin:** David Willman, "Physician Who Opposes Rezulin Is Threatened by FDA with Dismissal," *Los Angeles Times,* March 17, 2000.

88 **Dr. Janet B. McGill, an endocrinologist:** David Willman, "Fears Grow Over Delay in Removing Rezulin," *Los Angeles Times,* March 10, 2000. Viewed at http://www.pulitzer.org/year/2001/investigative-reporting/works/willman4.html. Accessed September 25, 2003.

88 **Dr. Eastman, while in charge of diabetes research:** David Willman, "Researcher's Fees Point to Other Potential Conflicts at NIH," *Los Angeles Times,* January 28, 1999. Viewed at http://www.house.gov/waxman/news_files/news_letters_rezulin_press_NIH_conflict_1_28_99.htm. Accessed September 30, 2003.

88 **no fewer than 12 of the 22:** David Willman, "Scientist Who Judged Pill Safety Received Fees; Grants: Records Show Varied Financial Ties Between Researchers and Maker of Diabetes Drug Linked to Deaths," *Los Angeles Times,* October 29, 1999.

88 **multiple examples of NIH officials receiving payments:** David Willman, "Stealth Merger: Drug Companies and Government Medical Research," *Los Angeles Times,* December 7, 2003.

89 **54 percent of the experts:** Dennis Cauchon, "FDA Advisers Tied to Industry," *U.S.A. Today,* September 25, 2000.

90 **spent $177 million on lobbying in 1999 and 2000:** Leslie Wayne and Melody Petersen, "A Muscular Lobby Rolls Up Its Sleeves," *New York Times,* November 11, 2001.

90 **$65 million for so-called issue ads:** "The Other Drug War: Big Pharm's 625 Washington Lobbyists," Public Citizen Congress Watch, July 2001.

90 **tipping progressively more toward the Republicans:** Ibid.

90 **made public:** Letter from Jim Nicholson, chairman of the Republican National Committee, to Charles A. Heimbold Jr., chairman and CEO of Bristol-Myers Squibb Company, April 9, 1999. Viewed at http://www.publici.org/

dtaweb/downloads/story_01_062403_BCRA7.pdf. Accessed September 15, 2003.

CHAPTER 7
THE COMMERCIAL TAKEOVER OF MEDICAL KNOWLEDGE

94 **Prior to 1970, medical researchers:** T. E. Andreoli, "The Undermining of Academic Medicine," *Academe* 6:32–37, 1999. Viewed at http://www.aaup.org/publications/Academe/1999/99nd/ND99Andr.htm. Accessed January 15, 2004.

94 **thumbing "their academic noses:** Quoted from Sheldon Krimsky, *Science in the Private Interest,* Lanham Md.: Rowman & Littlefield, 2003, p. 79.

94 **medical industry was more than willing:** Derek Bok, *Universities in the Marketplace,* Princeton, N.J.: Princeton University Press, 2003, p. 174.

94 **by 1990 almost two-thirds of requests:** Andreoli, op. cit.

94 **drug company expenditures on research and development:** Chapter 2: Dramatic Growth of Research and Development, Pharmaceutical Research and Manufacturers of America (PhRMA), *Pharmaceutical Industry Profile 2003.* Washington, D.C.: PhRMA, 2003. Viewed at http://www.phrma.org/publications/publications/profile02/2003%20CHAPTER%202.pdf. Accessed February 14, 2003.

94 **In 1991, four out of five:** T. Bodenheimer, "Uneasy Alliance: Clinical Investigators and the Pharmaceutical Industry," *New England Journal of Medicine* 342:1539–1544, 2000.

95 **reaching 80 percent:** "Clinical Trial Spending in the U.S. Forecast to Cross $26.5 Billion by 2007," *Business Communications Company, Inc.,* April 17, 2003. Accessed on May 12, 2004 at http://www.bccresearch.com/editors/RB-171.html.

95 **By 2000, only one-third:** Melody Petersen, "Madison Ave. Has Growing Role in the Business of Drug Research," *New York Times,* November 22, 2002.

95 **"They are seduced by industry:** Quoted in Richard A. Knox, "Science and Secrecy: A New Rift Proprietary Interests Found to Intrude on Research Disclosure," *Boston Globe,* March 30, 1999.

96 **September 2001, an unprecedented alarm:** F. Davidoff, C. D. DeAngelis, J. M. Drazen, et al., "Sponsorship, Authorship, and Accountability," *Journal of the American Medical Association* 286:1232–1234, 2001.

97 **published in JAMA:** J. E. Bekelman, Y. Li, and C. P. Gross, "Scope and Impact of Financial Conflicts of Interest in Biomedical Research: A Systematic Review," *Journal of the American Medical Association* 289:454–465, 2003.

97 *British Medical Journal:* J. Lexchin, L. A. Bero, B. Djulbegovic, and O. Clark, "Pharmaceutical Industry Sponsorship and Research Outcome and Quality: A Systematic Review," *British Medical Journal* 326:1167–1170, 2003.

97 **the highest-quality clinical trials:** B. Als-Nielsen, W. Chen, C. Cluud, and L. L. Kjaergard, "Association of Funding and Conclusions in Randomized Drug Trials," *Journal of the American Medical Association* 290:921–928, 2003.

97 **The techniques used:** This article provides many examples of the techniques that can be and are used to influence the outcome of medical research. L. A. Bero and D. Rennie, "Influences on the Quality of Published Drug Studies," *International Journal of Technology Assessment in Health Care* 12:209–237, 1996.

98 **The risk:** K.-H. Kuck, R. Cappato, J. Siebels, et al., "Randomized Comparison of Antiarrhythmic Drug Therapy with Implantable Defibrillators in Patients Resuscitated from Cardiac Arrest, *Circulation* 748–754, 2000.

98 **cost of the defibrillator:** Melody Petersen, "Heart Device to Get More U.S. Support," *New York Times,* June 7, 2003.

99 **turned its attention to the 400,000 Americans:** A. J. Moss, Z. Wojciech, J. Hall, et al., "Prophylactic Implantation of a Defibrillator in Patients with Myocardial Infarction and Reduced Ejection Fraction," *New England Journal of Medicine* 346:877–883, 2002.

100 **a group of Italian researchers:** R. Belardinelli, D. Georgiou, G. Cianci, and A. Purcaro, "Randomized, Controlled Trial of Long-Term Moderate Exercise Training in Chronic Heart Failure: Effects on Functional Capacity, Quality of Life, and Clinical Outcome," *Circulation.* 99:1173–1182, 1999.

100 **not exactly the same as in the defibrillator study:** The patients in the exercise study had more severe heart failure, were younger (55 versus 64 years old), and did not all have heart disease caused by inadequate blood supply through the coronary arteries (85 percent versus 100 percent).

101 **smoking cessation after heart attack:** Average reduction in the absolute risk of death among the 12 studies reviewed is 11.1 percent, and the relative risk reduction in smokers is 46 percent compared with those who continued to smoke. The patients in these studies all had heart attacks, but ejection fraction or the incidence of congestive heart failure is not reported, precluding direct comparison with the defibrillator study. K. Wilson, N. Gibson, A. Willan, and D. Cook, "Effect of Smoking Cessation on Mortality After Myocardial Infarction: Meta-Analysis of Cohort Studies," *Archives of Internal Medicine* 160:939–944, 2000.

101 **the acid-blocking drug Prilosec:** Organic molecules of identical chemical composition can occur in two forms that are mirror images of each other. Prilosec is a mix of both forms. Nexium is composed of only one form.

102 **"head-to-head" studies between Prilosec and Nexium:** J. E. Richter, P. J. Kahrilas, J. Johanson, et al., "Efficacy and Safety of Esomeprazole Compared to Omeprazole in GERD Patients with Erosive Esophagitis: A Randomized Controlled Trial," *American Journal of Gastroenterology* 96:656–665, 2001.

102 **Would 40 mg of Prilosec daily:** See http://www.nexium-us.com/science/cva05c.asp. Accessed November 29, 2003.

102 **sufficient for the FDA:** M. Angell, "The Pharmaceutical Industry—To Whom Is It Accountable?" *New England Journal of Medicine,* 342:1902–1904, 2000.

102 **OxyContin's ability to provide relief:** A. Cheville, A. Chen, G. Oster, et al., "A Randomized Trial of Controlled-Release Oxycodone During Inpatient Rehabilitation Following Unilateral Total Knee Arthroplasty," *Journal of Bone and Joint Surgery* 83-A(4):572–576-12, 2001.

103 **editorial in the *Canadian Medical Association Journal*:** P. A. Rochon, P. B. Berger, and M. Gordon, "The Evolution of Clinical Trials: Inclusion and Representation," *Canadian Medical Association Journal* 159:1373–1374, 1998.

104 **Studies of cancer drugs:** M. Mitka, "Too Few Older Patients in Cancer Trials: Experts Say Disparity Affects Research Results and Care," *Journal of the American Medical Association* 290:27–28, 2003.

104 **a study sponsored by Pharmacia, ironically titled CONVINCE:** B. M. Psaty and D. Rennie, "Stopping Medical Research to Save Money: A Broken Pact with Researchers and Patients," *Journal of the American Medical Association* 289:2128–2131, 2003.

105 **sponsor's drug, costing about $1.50 per day:** Viewed at http://www.drugstore.com. Accessed January 15, 2004.

105 **Dr. Thomas Bodenheimer brought many of these issues to light:** T. Bodenheimer, op. cit.

106 **A follow-up study:** K. A. Schulman, D. M. Seils, J. W. Timble, et al., "A National Survey of Provisions in Clinical-Trial Agreements Between Medical Schools and Industry Sponsors," *New England Journal of Medicine* 347: 1335–1341, 2002.

107 **Melody Petersen in the *New York Times*:** Melody Petersen, "Madison Ave. Has Growing Role in the Business of Drug Research," *New York Times,* November 22, 2002.

107 **11 percent of the articles published:** A. Flanagin, L. A. Carey, P. B. Fontanarosa, et al., "Prevalence of Articles with Honorary Authors and Ghost Authors in Peer-Reviewed Medical Journals," *Journal of the American Medical Association* 280:222–224, 1998.

107 **The Antihypertensive and Lipid-lowering Treatment to Prevent Heart Attacks Trial study:** The ALLHAT Officers and Coordinators for the ALLHAT Collaborative Research Group, "Major Cardiovascular Events in Hypertensive Patients Randomized to Doxazosin vs Chlorthalidone: The Antihypertensive and Lipid-Lowering Treatment to Prevent Heart Attack (ALLHAT)," *Journal of the American Medical Association* 283:1967–1975, 2000.

107 **stopped prematurely:** The ALLHAT Officers and Coordinators for the ALLHAT Collaborative Research Group, op. cit.

107 **$800 million worth of Cardura:** Lenzer, op. cit.

108 **a report in the *British Medical Journal*:** Lenzer, op. cit.

108 **marketing consultant for the pharmaceutical industry:** Ibid.

109 **Not long before a dramatic meeting:** Douglas M. Birch and Gary Cohn, "Standing Up to Industry," *Baltimore Sun,* June 26, 2001.

109 **explaining the reason for their departure:** W. B. Applegate, C. D. Furberg, R. P. Byington, and R. Grimm Jr., "The Multicenter Isradipine Diuretic Atherosclerosis Study (MIDAS)," *Journal of the American Medical Association* 277:297–299, 1997.

109 **three largest advertising agencies:** Petersen, op. cit.

110 **Drs. Bruce Psaty and Drummond Rennie:** B. M. Psaty and D. Rennie, "Stopping Medical Research to Save Money: A Broken Pact with Researchers and Patients," *Journal of the American Medical Association* 289:2128–2131, 2003.

CHAPTER 8
THE SNAKE AND THE STAFF: DUPING THE DOCTORS

111 **doctors are responsible for about 80 percent:** About 20 percent of health care expenditures goes to doctors' salaries, and doctors control an additional 60 percent of all expenditures. See Robert A. Hahn, *Sickness and Healing: An Anthropological Perspective,* New London, Conn.: Yale University Press, 1995, p. 162.

112 **editor of the** *British Medical Journal*: R. Smith, "Medical Journals and Pharmaceutical Companies: Uneasy Bedfellows," *British Medical Journal,* 326:1202–1205, 2003.

113 **Dr. Marcia Angell:** Interview by the author, March 26, 2003.

113 **Dr. Robert Fletcher:** R. H. Fletcher, "Adverts in Medical Journals: Caveat Lector," *The Lancet* 361:10–11, 2003.

114 **a 2003 article in JAMA:** K. Dickersin and D. Rennie, "Registering Clinical Trials," *Journal of the American Medical Association* 290:516–523, 2003.

114 **ranked the new antidepressants:** V. R. Fuchs and H. C. Sox, "Physicians' Views of the Relative Importance of Thirty Medical Innovations," *Health Affairs* 20:30–41, 2001.

115 **application was made to the Swedish Drug Authority:** H. Melander, H. Ahlqvist-Rastard, G. Meijer, and B. Beermann. "Evidence B(i)ased Medicine: Selective Reporting from Studies Sponsored by Pharmaceutical Industry: Review of Studies in New Drug Applications," *British Medical Journal,* 326:1171, 2003.

115 **all of the studies . . . that the FDA had reviewed:** A. Khan, H. A. Warner, and W. A. Brown, "Symptom Reduction and Suicide Risk in Patients Treated with Placebo in Antidepressant Clinical Trials: An Analysis of the Food and Drug Administration Database," *Archives of General Psychiatry* 57:311–317, 2000.

116 **for people with less severe depression:** "Less severe" defined as initial Hamilton Rating Scale for Depression (HAM-D) score of 24 or less. A. Khan, R. M. Leventhal, S. R. Khan, and W. A. Brown, "Severity of Depression and Response to Antidepressants and Placebos: An Analysis of the Food and Drug Administration Database," *Journal of Clinical Psychopharmacology* 22:40–45, 2002.

116 **4.6 more committed suicide:** Statistical significance was not reported for comparison of suicide rates between the new antidepressant and the placebo. For the three groups—new and old antidepressants and placebo—the differences in suicide rates were not statistically significant.

117 **depressed adolescents were significantly more likely:** M. D. Keller, N. D. Ryan, M. Strober, et al., "Efficacy of Paroxetine in the Treatment of Adolescent Major Depression: A Randomized Controlled Trial (Abstract)," *Journal of the American Academy of Child and Adolescent Psychiatry* 40:762–772, 2001.

117 **British drug authorities reviewed all nine studies:** "SSRIs: Suicide Risk and Withdrawal (Editorial)," *The Lancet* 361:1999, 2003.

117 **antidepressants (almost exclusively the newer ones):** "Prescription Drug Expenditures in 2000," op. cit. See also "Prescription Drug Expenditures in 2001: Another Year of Escalating Costs," a report by the National Institute for Health Care Management Research and Educational Foundation, May 6, 2002, p. 11. Viewed at http://nihcm.org/spending2001.pdf. Accessed August 3, 2003.

117 **ranked number three behind:** "IMS Reports 11.8 Percent Dollar Growth in 2002 U.S. Prescription Sales," IMS Health, February 21, 2003. Viewed at http://www.imshealth.com/ims/portal/front/arti-cleC/0,2777,1763_3665_41276589,00.html. Accessed October 13, 2003.

118 **doctors' continuing education meetings:** Arnold S. Relman and Marcia Angell, "America's Other Drug Problem," *The New Republic*, December 16, 2002.

118 **funded more than three-fifths:** Doctors' CME received a total of $729 million in commercial support in 2001. See Scott Hensley, "When Doctors Go to Class, Industry Often Foots the Bill," *Wall Street Journal*, December 4, 2002.

118 **increased by another 30 percent:** A. S. Relman, "Industry Sponsorship of Continuing Medical Education," *Journal of the American Medical Association* 290:1150, 2003.

119 **cultivate relationships with these experts:** Sheryl Gay Stolberg and Jeff Gerth, "Drug Makers Design Studies with Eye to Competitive Edge," *New York Times*, December 23, 2000.

119 **"food, flattery, and friendship:** D. Katz, A. L. Caplan, and J. F. Merz, "All Gifts Large and Small: Toward an Understanding of the Ethics of Pharmaceutical Industry Gift-Giving," *American Journal of Bioethics* 3:39–46, 2003.

120 **prescribing habits of 20 doctors:** J. Dana and G. Loewenstein, "A Social Science Perspective on Gifts to Physicians from Industry," *Journal of the American Medical Association* 290:252, 2003.

121 **Nearly half of the members of the task force:** A. S. Relman, "Separating Continuing Medical Education from Pharmaceutical Marketing," *Journal of the American Medical Association* 285(15):2009–2012, 2001.

121 **own their own educational subsidiaries:** Scott Hensley, "Drug Firms Shown the Classroom Door: Continuing-Ed Programs for Doctors Aim to Reduce Influence of Big Companies," *Wall Street Journal*, January 14, 2003.

121 **the whole new industry that has emerged:** Joseph S. Ross, Peter Lurie, and Sidney M. Wolfe, "Medical Education Services Suppliers: A Threat to Physician Education," Health Research Group Report, Public Citizen, July 19, 2000.

121 **$3 million to the prestigious Massachusetts General Hospital:** Raja Mishra, "Deal May Tie MGH to Furor on Pain Pill," *Boston Globe,* March 14, 2002.

121 **George Annas, commented:** Quoted ibid.

122 **Permissible offerings:** D. Grande and K. Volpp, "Cost and Quality of Industry-Sponsored Meals for Medical Residents," *Journal of the American Medical Association* 290:1150–1151, 2003.

122. **Alan Holmer, claims that the drug industry:** A. F. Holmer, "Industry Strongly Supports Continuing Medical Education," *Journal of the American Medical Association* 285:2012–2014, 2001.

123 **review article published in JAMA:** A. Wazna, op. cit.

123 **gifts and meals start in medical school:** "Drug-Company Influence on Medical Education in U.S.A. (Editorial)," *The Lancet* 356:781, 2000.

123 **Eight out of 10 medical residents:** M. A. Steinman, M. G. Shilpak, and S. J. McPhee. "Of Principles and Pens: Attitudes and Practices of Medicine Housestaff Toward Pharmaceutical Industry Promotions," *Journal of the American Medical Association* 110:551–557, 2001.

124 **"Twisted together like the snake:** R. Moynihan, "Who Pays for the Pizza? Redefining the Relationships Between Doctors and Drug Companies—1: Entanglement," *British Medical Journal* 326:1189–1192, 2003.

124 **number of reps making sales pitches:** Scott Hensley, "As Drug-Sales Teams Multiply, Doctors Start to Tune Them Out," *Wall Street Journal,* June 13, 2003.

125 **80 to 95 percent of doctors:** Moynihan, op. cit.

125 **42 percent of the material given to doctors:** D. Stryer and L. A. Bero, "Characteristics of Materials Distributed by Drug Companies: An Evaluation of Appropriateness," *Journal of General Lateral Medicine* 11:575–583, 1996.

125 **mostly negative effect:** A. Wazna, op. cit.

126 **having drug samples on hand:** "U.S. Physicians Responsive to Patient Requests for Brand-Name Drugs," IMS Health, April 1, 2002. Viewed at http://www.imshealth.com/ims/portal/front/articleC/0,2777,6599_3665_1003811,00.html. Accessed January 16, 2004.

126 **Doctors who interact with drug companies:** M.-M. Chren and C. S. Landefeld, "Physicians' Behavior and Their Interactions with Drug Companies: A Controlled Study of Physicians Who Requested Additions to a Hospital Drug Formulary," *Journal of the American Medical Association* 27:684–689, 1994.

126 **Nine out of 10 doctors:** Earl Lane, "Doctors Still Know Little About Drug Costs," *Newsday,* February 4, 2003.

127 **evaluating the quality of the guidelines:** T. M. Shaneyfelt, M. F. Mayo-Smith, and J. Rothwangl, "Are Guidelines Following Guidelines? The Methodological

Quality of Clinical Practice Guidelines in the Peer-Reviewed Medical Literature," *Journal of the American Medical Association* 281:1900–1905, 1999.

127 **only one out of the 20 clinical guidelines:** R. Grilli, N. Magrini, A. Penna, et al., "Practice Guidelines Developed by Specialty Societies: The Need for a Critical Appraisal," *The Lancet* 355:103–106, 2000.

127 **four out of five of these guidelines:** I. Savoie, A. Kazanjian, and K. Bassett, "Do Clinical Practice Guidelines Reflect Research Evidence? (Abstract)," *Journal of Health Services Research Policy* 5:76–82, 2000.

127 **the most damning study of all:** N. K. Choudry, H. T. Stelfox, and A. S. Detsky, "Relationships Between Authors of Clinical Practice Guidelines and the Pharmaceutical Industry," *Journal of the American Medical Association* 287: 612–617, 2002.

CHAPTER 9
A SMOKING GUN: THE 2001 CHOLESTEROL GUIDELINES

131 **even misrepresenting findings reported:** The full report erroneously indicates that the reduction in total mortality in the WOSCOPS study of primary prevention reached statistical significance (Table II.7-1), Similarly, the reduction in coronary mortality in the CARE study of secondary prevention is erroneously reported as statistically significant (Table II.8-2).

134 **statins increased the frequency of sexual dysfunction:** E. Bruckert, P. Giral, H. M. Heshmati, and G. Turpin, "Men Treated with Hypolipidaemic Drugs Complain More Frequently of Erectile Dysfunction," *Journal of Clinical Pharmacology and Therapeutics* 21:89–94, 1996.

135 **Five of 14 experts:** From the extensive summary in JAMA: "Financial Disclosure: Dr. Grundy has received honoraria from Merck, Pfizer, Sankyo, Bayer, and Bristol-Myers Squibb. Dr. Hunninghake has current grants from Merck, Pfizer, Kos Pharmaceuticals, Schering-Plough, Wyeth-Ayerst, Sankyo, Bayer, AstraZeneca, Bristol-Myers Squibb, and G. D. Searle; he has also received consulting honoraria from Merck, Pfizer, Kos Pharmaceuticals, Sankyo, AstraZeneca, and Bayer. Dr. McBride has received grants and/or research support from Pfizer, Merck, Parke-Davis, and AstraZeneca; has served as a consultant for Kos Pharmaceuticals, Abbott, and Merck; and has received honoraria from Abbott, Bristol-Myers Squibb, Novartis, Merck, Kos Pharmaceuticals, Parke-Davis, Pfizer, and DuPont. Dr. Pasternak has served as a consultant for and received honoraria from Merck, Pfizer, and Kos Pharmaceuticals, and has received grants from Merck and Pfizer. Dr. Stone has served as a consultant and/or received honoraria for lectures from Abbott, Bayer, Bristol-Myers Squibb, Kos Pharmaceuticals, Merck, Novartis, Parke-Davis/Pfizer, and Sankyo."

137 **Air Force/Texas Coronary Atherosclerosis Prevention Study:** J. R. Downs, M.

Clearfield, S. Weis, et al., "Primary Prevention of Acute Coronary Events with Lovastatin in Men and Women with Average Cholesterol Levels: Results of AFCAPS/TexCAPS," *Journal of the American Medical Association* 279:1615–1622, 1998.

138 **At least 85 percent of the men in this study:** The first step: at least 85 percent of the men in the study had at least two major risk factors (all were over 45 years of age and 85 percent had an HDL cholesterol level of less than 40 mg/dL). The second step: the men in the study had an average age of 57, average total cholesterol of 221 mg/dL, average HDL cholesterol of 36 mg/dL, average systolic blood pressure of 138 mmHg. According to the Framingham Risk Score, these men had, on the average, a 16 percent risk of developing coronary heart disease over the next 10 years. Finally, all of the people in the study had LDL cholesterol levels of at least 130 mg/dL. The guidelines call for statin therapy in people with two or more major risk factors, a Framingham Risk Score of 10 percent or greater, and an LDL cholesterol of 130 mg/dL or higher (if the LDL cholesterol level does not respond to diet and exercise within three months).

138 **"incremental cost per additional year:** NCEP Full Report, p. II-59.

139 **statin therapy reduced risk for CHD in . . . women:** NCEP Full Report, p. II-3.

139 **NCEP full report convincingly cites six references:** NCEP Full Report, p. II-5.

139 **"There is no evidence from primary prevention trials:** J. M. E. Walsh and D. Grady, "Treatment of Hyperlipidemia in Women." *Journal of the American Medical Association* 274:1152–1158, 1995.

139 **"Special Considerations for Cholesterol Management in Women (Ages 45–75)":** NCEP Full Report, p. VIII-3.

140 **"aggressive LDL-lowering therapy:** NCEP Full Report, p. II-32.

140 **The table mentioned cites nine references:** NCEP Full Report, p. II-5.

141 **average age was 51:** The Upjohn study was the only one that was difficult to find, having been completed in 1978, nine years before the first statin came on the market. S. B. Manuck, A. B. Mendelsohn, J. R. Kaplan, and S. H. Belle, "Cholesterol Reduction and Non-Illness Mortality: Meta-Analysis of Randomized Clinical Trials," *British Medical Journal* 322:11–15, 2001.

141 **"The relationship between serum cholesterol:** NCEP Full Report, p. II-34.

141 **total cholesterol is not significantly related to mortality:** Framingham Heart Study reported in 1993. See Kronmal, Cain, Ye, and Omenn, op. cit.

141 **not even an increase in the risk of heart attack:** B. M. Psaty, C. D. Furberg, L. H. Kuller, et al., "Traditional Risk Factors and Subclinical Disease Measures as Predictors of First Myocardial Infarction in Older Adults: The Cardiovascular Health Study," *Archives of Internal Medicine* 159:1339–1347, 1999.

142 **remains high in the elderly:** D. M. Lloyd-Jones, M. G. Larson, A. Beiser, and

D. Levy, "Lifetime Risk of Developing Coronary Heart Disease," *The Lancet* 353:89–92, 1999.

142 **average LDL cholesterol levels:** NCEP Full Report, p. II-39.

142 **4S:** Scandinavian Simvastatin Survival Study Group, "Randomized Trial of Cholesterol Lowering in 444 Patients with Coronary Heart Disease: The Scandinavian Simvastatin Survival Study (4S)," *The Lancet* 344(8934): 1383–1389, 1994.

142 **LIPID:** Long-Term Intervention with Pravastatin in Ischemic Disease (LIPID) Study Group, "Prevention of Cardiovascular Events and Death with Pravastatin in Patients with Coronary Heart Disease and a Broad Range of Initial Cholesterol Levels," *New England Journal of Medicine* 339:1349–1357, 1998.

142 **CARE:** F. M. Sacks, M. A. Pfeffer, L. A. Moye, et al., "The Effect of Pravastatin on Coronary Events After Myocardial Infarction in Patients with Average Cholesterol Levels," *New England Journal of Medicine* 335(14):1001–1009, 1996.

143 **4S:** Scandinavian Simvastatin Survival Study Group, op. cit.

143 **CARE:** F. K. Welty, "Cardiovascular Disease and Dyslipidemia in Women," *Archives of Internal Medicine* 161(4):514–522, 2001.

143 **LIPID:** Long-Term Intervention with Pravastatin in Ischemic Disease (LIPID) Study Group, op. cit.

144 **The ALLHAT study:** The ALLHAT Officers and Coordinators for the ALLHAT Collaborative Research Group, "Major Outcomes in Moderately Hypercholesterolemic, Hypertensive Patients Randomized to Pravastatin vs Usual Care," *Journal of the American Medical Association* 288:2998–3007, 2002.

144 **10,000 patients at high risk:** The study included people age 55 and older, with LDL cholesterol between 120 and 189 mg/dL, triglycerides lower than 350 mg/dL, who had hypertension and at least one other risk factor for coronary heart disease.

144 *Wall Street Journal:* Ron Winslow and Scott Hensley, "Statin Study Yields Contrary Data," *Wall Street Journal,* December 18, 2002. Many newspapers picked up the findings of the other part of the ALLHAT study, which showed that treatment of high blood pressure with inexpensive diuretics was as good as or better than treatment with much more expensive, newer drugs.

145 **"Physicians might be tempted:** R. C. Pasternak, "The ALLHAT Lipid Lowering Trial: Less Is Less," *Journal of the American Medical Association* 288:3042–3044, 2002.

145 **"financial disclosures":** Dr Pasternak has served as a speaker for or on the speakers bureau for Merck, Merck/Schering-Plough, Kos, Pfizer, and Bristol-Myers Squibb/Sanofi; has served as a consultant to or on the advisory board for Merck, Pfizer Health Solutions, AstraZeneca, Kos, Johnson & Johnson–Merck, and Bristol-Myers Squibb/Sanofi; and has received a research grant from Merck-Medco."

145 **the PROSPER study:** J. Shepherd, G. J. Blauw, M. B. Murphy, et al., "Pravastatin in Elderly Individual at Risk of Vascular Disease (PROSPER): A Randomized Controlled Trial," *The Lancet* 360:1623–1630, 2002.

145 **"There is no evidence:** NCEP Full Report p. I–44.

145 **"Carcinogenicity of Lipid-Lowering Drugs":** Newman T. B., Hulley S. B., "Carcinogenicity of Lipid-Lowering Drugs," *Journal of the American Medical Association,* 275:55-60, 1996.

146 **could take many years:** Bjerre L.M., LeLorier J., "Do Statins Cause Cancer? A Meta-Analysis of Large Randomized Clinical Trials," *American Journal of Medicine,*: 110:716–723, 2001.

147 **Dr. Scott Grundy:** Quoted in Thomas M. Burton and Chris Adams, "New Government Cholesterol Standards Would Triple Number of Prescriptions," *Wall Street Journal,* May 16, 2001.

147 **Dr. Walter Willett:** Naomi Aoki, "Drug Makers Influence Pondered Eye on U.S. Advice to Cut Cholesterol," *Boston Globe,* May 31, 2001.

148 **Morgan Stanley Dean Witter newsletter:** Jami Rubin and Andrew Baum, "Our Survey of the Statin Market Projects Strong Growth," *Morgan Stanly Dean Witter U.S. Investment Perspectives,* March 21, 2001.

CHAPTER 10
DIRECT-TO-CONSUMER: ADVERTISING, PUBLIC RELATIONS, AND THE MEDICAL NEWS

150 **in 1981, the drug industry proposed:** M. S. Wilkes, R. A. Bell, and R. L. Kravitz, "Direct-to-Consumer Prescription Drug Advertising: Trends, Impact, and Implications," *Health Affairs* 19(2):110–128, 2000.

150 **the FDA changed its rules:** U.S. General Accounting Office, "Prescription Drugs: FDA Oversight of Direct-to-Consumer Advertising Has Limitations," October, 2002. p. 8.

151 **nine prescription drug advertisements:** "Too Much Medicine?" *Post & Script,* Greater Glasgow Area Drug Percent Therapeutics Committee, Issue 20, July 2003.

151 **increased 40-fold:** Richard Frank, Ernst R. Berndt, Julie Donohue, Arnold Epstein, and Meredith Rosenthal, "Trends in Direct-to-Consumer Advertising of Prescription Drugs," Henry J. Kaiser Family Foundation, February 2002.

151 **Christopher Lasch wrote in 1979:** Christoher Lasch, *The Culture of Narcissism: American Life in An Age of Diminishing Expectations,* New York: Warner Books, 1979, p. 137.

152 **most heavily advertised prescription drug in the two years:** Frank, Berndt, Donohue, Epstein, and Rosenthal, op. cit.

152 **advertising budget greater than that of Budweiser or Coca-Cola:** Jean K.

Haddad, "The Pharmaceutical Industry's Influence on Physician Behavior and Health Care Costs," *San Francisco Medicine.* Viewed at http://www.sfms.org/sfm/sfm602a.htm. Accessed September 20, 2003.

152 *New York Times Magazine* in 2001: Stephen S. Hall, "Claritin and Schering-Plough: A Perfect Prescription for Profit," *New York Times,* March 11, 2001.

153 **Understanding how drug patents work:** For a complete discussion of drug patents and legal ploys, see Robin J. Strongin, "Hatch-Waxman, Generics, and Patents: Balancing Prescription Drug Innovation, Competition, and Affordibility," *National Health Policy Forum,* June 21, 2002.

153 **Schering-Plough was unsuccessful:** Reuters, "Schering-Plough Loses Claritin Patent Appeal," *Forbes.com,* August 1, 2003.

153 **take center stage in direct-to-consumer advertising was Vioxx:** Frank, Berndt, Donohue, Epstein, and Rosenthal, op. cit.

154 **drugs that patients most frequently request:** "IMS Study: U.S. Physicians Responsive to Patient Requests for Brand-Name Drugs," *IMSHealth.* Viewed at http://www.imshealth.com/ims/portal/front/articleC/0,2777,6599_3665_1003811,00.html. Accessed October 24, 2003.

154 **ads provide an important educational service:** A. F. Holmer, "Direct-to-Consumer Prescription Advertising Builds Bridges Between Patients and Physicians," *Journal of the American Medical Association* 281:380–382, 1999.

154 **only 13 percent of drug ads:** S. Woloshin, L. M. Schwartz, J. Tremmel, and H. G. Welch, "Direct-to-Consumer Advertisements for Prescription Drugs: What Are Americans Being Sold?" *The Lancet* 358:1141–1146, 2001.

154 **positive effects of lifestyle change:** M. S. Wilkes, R. A. Bell, and R. L. Kravitz, "Direct-to-Consumer Prescriptioni Drug Advertising: Trends, Impact, and Implications," *Health Affairs* 19(2):110–128, 2000.

154 **Widespread public misconceptions:** Ibid.

155 **drug companies capitalize on the public's naïveté:** Woloshin, op. cit.

155 **"We want to identify the emotions:** Quoted in Warren Ross, "Why Rubin-Ehrenthal Sticks Exclusively to DTC Accounts," *Medical Marketing & Media,* 1999. Viewed at http://www.cpsnet.com/reprints/1999/09/McCarren.pdf. Accessed October 14, 2003.

156 **receive prescriptions for requested drugs 50 percent:** U.S. Food and Drug Administration, Center for Drug Evaluation and Research, "Attitudes and Behaviors Associated with Direct-to-Consumer Promotion of Prescription Drugs, Main Survey Results," 1999. Viewed at http://www.fda.gov/cder/ddmac/dtctitle.htm. Accessed February 24, 2004.

156 **prescribed requested drugs about three-quarters of the time:** B. Mintzes, M. L. Barer, R. L. Kravitz, et al., "Influence of Direct to Consumer Pharmaceutical Advertising and Patients' Requests on Prescribing Decisions: Two-Site Cross-Sectional Survey," *British Medical Journal* 324:278–279, 2002.

156 **prescribed requested drugs 80 percent of the time:** Phyllis Maguire, "How

Direct-to-Consumer Advertising Is Putting the Squeeze on Physicians," *ACP-ASIM Observer*, March 1999.

156 **drug industry claims:** Holmer, op. cit.

156 **four out of five family doctors:** M. S. Lipsky and C. A. Taylor, "The Opinions and Experiences of Family Physicians Regarding Direct-to-Consumer Advertising (Abstract)," *Journal of Family Practice* 45:485, 1997.

157 **media traditionally used to flog cars:** "Ads and Prescription Pads (Editorial)," *Canadian Medical Journal Association* 169(5): 2003.

157 **European Union voted in 2003:** R. Watson, "EU Health Ministers Reject Proposal for Limited Direct to Consumer Advertising," *British Medical Journal* 326:1284, 2003.

157 **11 days after the 1997 rule change:** FDA Letter to Schering Corporation, August 19, 1997. Viewed at http://www.fda.gov/cder/warn/aug97/5738.pdf. Accessed February 26, 2004.

157 **number of letters citing drug companies:** "Comments of Public Citizen," Docket No. 02N-0209, October 28, 2002. Viewed at http://citizen.org/publications/release.cfm?ID=7214. Accessed February 28, 2004. And FDA, "Center for Drug Evaluation and Research, Warning Letters and Untitled Letters to Pharmaceutical Companies, 2003." Viewed at http://www.fda.gov/cder/warn/warn2003.htm. Accessed February 2, 2004.

158 **Daniel Troy, to be the FDA's new chief counsel:** Michael, Kranish, "FDA Counsels Rise Embodies U.S. Shift," *Boston Globe*, December 22, 2002.

158 **the U.S. General Accounting Office (GAO):** U.S. General Accounting Office, "Prescription Drugs: FDA Oversight of Direct-to-Consumer Advertising Has Limitations," October 2002. Viewed at http://www.gao.gov/new.items/d03177.pdf. Accessed January 7, 2003.

158 **Special Investigations Division:** United States House of Representatives Committee on Government Reform—Minority Staff Special Investigations Division, January 2004. Accessed May 10, 2004, at http://www.house.gov/reform/min/pdfs_108_2/pdfs_inves/pdf_prescrip_drug_ad_enforcement_jan_29_rep.pdf.

159 **Melody Petersen reported in the *New York Times*:** Melody Petersen, "Less Return in Marketing of Medicines, A Study Says," *New York Times*, December 12, 2002.

159 **reaching $3.2 billion:** Scott Hensky, "As Drug Ad Spending Rises: A Look at Four Campaigns," *Wall Street Journal*, February 9, 2004.

159 **drug industry profit margins have skyrocketed:** "Pharmaceutical Industry Ranks as Most Profitable Industry—Again," *Public Citizen*, April 18, 2002.

159 **American senior citizens have been taking bus rides:** David Gross, "Prescription Drug Prices in Canada: What Are the Lessons for the United States?" AARP, 2003. Viewed at http://www.aarp.org/international/Articles/a2003-07-11-ia-perspectives.html. Accessed October 7, 2003.

160 **$350 million to $650 million worth of drugs:** Scott Hensley, "Drug Companies Cry 'Danger' over Imports," *Wall Street Journal*, September 22, 2003.

160 **FDA Commissioner Mark McLellan announced a new initiative:** "FDA Announces Initiative to Heighten Battle Against Counterfeit Drugs," *FDA News,* July 16, 2003.

160 **"Fakes in the Medicine Chest":** Leila Abboud, Anne Wilde Matthews, and Heather Won Tesoriero, "Fakes in the Medicine Chest," *Wall Street Journal,* September 22, 2003.

160 **"Drug Companies Cry 'Danger' Over Imports":** Hensley, op. cit.

161 *New York Times* **editorial:** "The Safety of Imported Drugs (Editorial)," *New York Times,* September 20, 2003.

161 **The *New England Journal of Medicine* published a report in 2001:** G. R. Bernard, J.-L. Vincent, P.-F. Laterre, et al., "Efficacy and Safety of Recombinant Human Activated Protein C for Severe Sepsis," *New England Journal of Medicine* 344:699–709, 2001.

161 **Xigris was "relatively cost-effective:** B. J. Braden, H. Lee, C. J. Doig, D. John son, C. Donaldson, "An Economic Evaluation of Activated Protein C Treatment for Severe Sepsis," *New England Journal of Medicine* 347:993–1000, 2001.

161 **future of Xigris (and Eli Lilly) seemed bright:** David Shook, "A Shock to Lilly's System?" *BusinessWeek online,* March 7, 2002.

161 **less than a quarter of that:** Eli Lilly and Company Second Quarter Financial Review, July 24, 2003.

162 **only one had been well enough:** "FDA Clinical Review, Drotrecogin Alfa (Activated), Xigris Approved: November 21, 2001." Viewed at http://www.fda.gov/cder/biologics/review/droteli112101r1p2.pdf. Accessed on February 26, 2004.

162 **the ultimate outcomes of the hospitalized patients:** Ibid.

162 **PR firm developed a strategy:** Antonio Regaldo, "To Sell Pricey Drug, Eli Lilly Fuels a Debate Over Rationing," *Wall Street Journal,* September 18, 2003.

162 **charged with developing "national guidelines:** Liz Kowalczyk, "Rationing of Medical Care Under Study: Doctors Seeking Plan as Costs Soar," *Boston Globe,* September 14, 2003.

163 **manufacturer of the antidepressant Paxil, hired a PR firm:** Brendan I. Koerner, "Disorders Made to Order," *Mother Jones,* July–August 2002. Viewed at http://www.motherjones.com/magazine/JA02/disorders.html. Accessed October 7, 2003.

164 **CRP, can predict . . . a person's risk of developing cardiovascular disease:** P. M. Ridker, R. Nader, L. Rose, et al., "Comparison of C-Reactive Protein and Low-Density Lipoprotein Cholesterol Levels in the Prediction of First Cardiovascular Events," *New England Journal of Medicine* 347:1557–1565, 2002.

164 **the *Boston Globe*:** Anne Barnard, "Boston Researchers Call Protein Test Best Gauge of Heart-Disease Risk," *Boston Globe,* November 14, 2002.

164 **the *New York Times*:** Denise Grady, "Study Says a Protein May Be Better Than Cholesterol in Predicting Heart Disease Risk," *New York Times,* November 14, 2002.

164 **the *Washington Post*:** David Brown, "New Test for Risk of Heart Disease Study Shifts Focus from Cholesterol," *Washington Post,* November 14, 2002.

164 ***Time*:** Alice Park, "Beyond Cholesterol: Inflammation Is Emerging as a Major Risk Factor—and Not Just in Heart Disease," *Time,* November 25, 2002.

164 ***Newsweek*:** Anne Underwood, "In the News: A New Affair of the Heart," *Newsweek,* November 25, 2002.

165 **only slightly more than one (1.3) additional episode:** For a complete discussion of this issue see an article that I wrote about medical reporting for journalists: John Abramson, "Medical Reporting in a Highly Commercialized Environment," *Nieman Reports,* Summer 2003. Viewed at http://www. nieman.harvard.edu/reports, 2003–2NRsummer/54-57V57N2.pdf. Accessed February 27, 2004. In the NEJM article's absence of age- and risk factor–adjusted event-free survival rates, a reasonable approximation of the risk of the women with the highest 20 percent of CRP levels can be reconstructed from one of the graphs: The absolute risk of a cardiovascular event was 7 per 1000 for 20 percent of the women with the lowest CRP levels over the eight years of the study. Multiplying this by the adjusted relative risk of 2.3 for the 20 percent of women with highest CRP levels gives an approximate absolute risk of 16.1 per 1000 over eight years. The difference in absolute risk of developing cardiovascular disease between the women with the highest and lowest CRP levels is 16.1 minus 7, or about 9.1 per 1000 over an eight-year period.

165 **less than one episode of cardiovascular disease:** The women with the highest CRP levels have about 2.3 cardiovascular events per 1000 each year, so a 40 percent reduction would mean 0.8 per 1000 fewer events per year.

166 **207 medical news stories on television:** R. Moynihan, L. Bero, Ross-D. Degnan, et al., "Coverage by the News Media of the Benefits and Risks of Medications," *New England Journal of Medicine* 342:1645–1650, 2000.

166 **Gloria Steinem:** Quoted in Barbara Seaman, "The Media and the Menopause Industry," Fair.org, March–April 1997. Viewed at http://www.fair.org/extra/ 9703/hormone.html. Accessed November 24, 2003.

CHAPTER 11
FOLLOW THE MONEY: SUPPLY-SIDE MEDICAL CARE

170 **change the drain in his chest:** When the infection was not improving, I discussed Mr. Wilkins's situation with a chest surgeon from one of the Boston teaching hospitals, an expert in the care of this kind of infection, wondering if there was perhaps a better treatment than our mutually tiresome modus operandi. The surgeon said that he could cut out the infected bone, but the risks would be significant and the recovery would be long. The discussion left me confident that we were doing the best that could be done. Conservative advice from a good surgeon, recommending less rather than more aggressive treatment, is almost always good advice.

171 **five times more likely:** J. V. Tu, C. L. Pashos, C. D. Naylor, et al., "Use of Cardiac Procedures and Outcomes in Elderly Patients with Myocardial Infarction in the United States and Canada," *New England Medical Journal* 336(21):1500–1505, 1997.

171 **75 percent higher per person:** "Health at a Glance," op. cit. p. 59.

171 **between Texas and New York state:** E. Guadagnoli, P. J. Hauptman, J. Z. Ayanian, et al., "Variation in the Use of Cardiac Procedures After Acute Myocardial Infarction," *New England Medical Journal* 333:573–578, 1995.

172 **1998, more than half of our heart attack patients:** D. M. Cutler and M. McClellan, "Is Technological Change in Medicine Worth It?" *Health Affairs* 20(5):11–29, 2001.

172 **United States does three and a half times as many coronary angioplasties and coronary artery bypass surgeries:** "Health at a Glance," op. cit.

172 **United States has the third-highest death rate from coronary heart disease:** National Institutes of Health, "Morbidity and Mortality: 2002 Chartbook on Cardiovascular, Lung, and Blood Diseases," p. 36. Viewed at http://www.nhlbi. nih.gov/resources/docs/02_chtbk.pdf.

173 **in-hospital death rate for heart attacks:** Ibid, p. 31.

173 **experience a significant decrease in mental capacity:** M. F. Newman, J. L. Kirchner, Phillips- B. Bute, et al., "Longitudinal Assessment of Neurocognitive Function After Coronary Artery Bypass Surgery," *New England Medical Journal* 344(6):395–402, 2001. Possibly there will be less cognitive impairment with cardiac surgery done without cardiopulmonary bypass ("off-pump"), but initial studies show the problem to be about the same both ways.

174 **neonatology services varies widely:** D. C. Goodman, E. S. Fisher, G. A. Little, et al., "The Relation Between the Availability of Neonatal Intensive Care and Neonatal Mortality," *New England Medical Journal* 346:1538–1544, 2002.

174 **almost twice as many neonatologists and neonatal intensive care beds:** The United States has twice as many neonatal intensive care and intermediate care beds as Canada, yet the neonatal mortality rate (death within the first 28 days of life) is 27 percent higher in the United States than Canada (4.7 versus 3.7 deaths per 1000 live births). The comparability of infant mortality statistics between countries has been questioned because of variations in the recording of very premature babies as not live births or as live births and neonatal deaths. Health statistics from Canada and the United States show the same number of infant deaths occurring in the first day of life, suggesting similar patterns of resuscitation of extremely premature babies, and therefore that the infant mortality rates of the two countries are measuring the same way.

174 **United States has the highest infant mortality:** "Health at a Glance: OECD Indicators 200s, Organisation for Economic Co-Operation and Development, 2003." International comparisons of infant mortality are unreliable because some countries are more likely to attempt to resuscitate very low birth-weight babies (thus counting them as infant deaths instead of fetal deaths). Canada and the United States have similar patterns of resuscitation, yet the U.S. infant

mortality rate is 30 percent higher (6.9 versus 5.3 deaths per 1000 births).

175 **the billions of dollars these procedures generated:** H. M. Krumholz, "Cardiac Procedures, Outcomes, and Accountability," *New England Medical Journal* 336:1521–1523, 1997.

175 **A major study (VANQWISH):** R. A. Lange and L. D. Hillis, "Use and Overuse of Angiography and Revascularization for Acute Coronary Syndromes," *New England Journal of Medicine* 388: 1838–1839, 1998.

175 **fees paid by Medicare:** Liz Kowalczyk, "Heart Stent's New Promise May Be Costly for Hospitals," *Boston Globe,* February 2, 2003.

176 **"One important explanation is money:** K. Grumbach, "Specialists, Technology and Newborns—Too Much of a Good Thing," *New England Medical Journal* 346(20):1574–1575, 2002.

176 **country to implement just such a program:** S. Perry and M. Thamer, "Medical Innovation and the Critical Role of Health Technology Assessment," *Journal of the American Medical Association* 282:1869–1872, 1999.

176 **most recently by a federal commission in 1994:** Ibid.

177 **not pleased with government-sponsored guidelines:** B. H. Gray, M. K. Gusmano, and S. R. Collins, "AHCPR and the Changing Politics of Health Services Research," *Health Affairs Web Exclusive,* June 25, 2003.

177 **explained the controversy about back surgery:** Reed Abelson and Melody Petersen, "An Operation to Ease Back Pain Bolsters the Bottom Line, Too," *New York Times,* December 31, 2003. In a laminectomy, bone is removed from the vertebrae above and below the compressed nerve, to make room for it to traverse through the spinal column. In a spinal fusion, bone is similarly removed, then metal rods are fixed to the vertebrae by metal screws to help "fuse" the two vertebrae together to add stability.

177 **allegedly making illegal kickbacks:** Reuters, "Company News: Inquiry into Possible Kickbacks at Medtronic Unit, *New York Times,* September 9, 2003.

178 **"supply-sensitive care":** J. E. Wennberg, E. S. Fisher, and J. S. Skinner, "Geography and the Debate over Medicare Reform," *Health Affairs—Web Exclusive.* February 13, 2002.

179 **cardiologists who perform cardiac catheterization:** R. A. Lange, "Use and Overuse of Angiography and Revascularization for Acute Coronary Syndromes." *New England Medical Journal* 338:1838–1839, 1998.

179 **spins completely out of control in for-profit hospitals:** In 2003, Tenet Health Care Corporation agreed to pay a record $54 million to settle charges by the Department of Justice that cardiologists and cardiac surgeons at its Redding, California, hospital had performed hundreds of unnecessary cardiac procedures. Hospital administrators were being pushed to beat projections, and a cardiologist and cardiac surgeon were all too willing to perform the unnecessary procedures. According to the settlement "fact sheet" Tenet agreed to pay the U.S. Department of Justice a record $54 million for the performance "of

alleged unnecessary cardiac procedures." Redding Medical Center/Tenet Set-
tlement Fact Sheet. Viewed at http://www.heartlaw.info/heartlaw/news/
RmcFactSheetMah.pdf. Accessed September 22, 2003.

180 **more than twice as much:** Elliott S. Fisher, "Medical Care—Is More Always
Better?" *New England Journal of Medicine* 349:1665–1667, 2003.

180 **was 60 percent more in the highest-spending regions:** E. S. Fisher, D. E.
Wennberg, T. Stukel, et al., "The Implications of Regional Variations in
Medicare. Part 1: The Content, Quality, and Accessibility of Care," *Annals of
Internal Medicine* 273–287.

181 **the most important medical innovation:** V. R. Fuchs and H. C. Sox Jr., "Physicians' Views of the Relative Importance of Thirty Medical Innovations,"
Health Affairs 20(3):30–42, 2001.

181 **number of MRI scanners in the United States:** L. Baker, H. Birnbaum, J. Gep-
pert, et al., "The Relationship Between Technology Availability and Health
Care Spending," *Health Affairs* Web Exclusive, November 5, 2003.

181 **patients in Washington state:** D. R. Flum, A. Morris, T. Kooepsell, et al., "Has
Misdiagnosis of Appendicitis Decreased Over Time? A Population-Based
Analysis," *Journal of the American Medical Association* 286:1748–1753, 2001.

182 **80 percent of people older than 50:** M. C. Jensen, M. N. Brant-Zawadzki, N.
Obuchowski, et al., "Magnetic Resonance Imaging of the Lumbar Spine in
People Without Back Pain," *New England Medical Journal* 331:69–73, 1994.

183 **71 percent say they would rather die at home than in a hospital:** "Means to a
Better End: A Report on Dying in America Today," *Last Acts,* November 2002,
p.92. Viewed at www.lastacts.org. Accessed November 12, 2003.

183 **people's end-of-life wishes are usually ignored:** R. S. Pritchard, E. S. Fisher,
J. M. Teno, et al., "Influence of Patient Preferences and Local Health System
Characteristics on the Place of Death," *Journal of The American Geriatrics
Society* 46: 1242–1250, 1998.

184 **expenditures of $1.8 trillion:** S. Heffler, S. Smith, S. Keehan, et al., "Health Spend-
ing Projections Through 2013." *Health Affairs* Web Exclusive, February 11, 2004.

184 **Markets respond more rapidly:** Economic Report of the President, Transmit-
ted to the Congress 2002, p. 148.

184 **combination of comprehensive social support:** J. D. Lants, "Hooked on
Neonatology: A Pediatrician Wonders About NICU's Hidden Cost of Success," *Health Affairs* 20(5):233–240, 2001.

CHAPTER 12
THE KNEE IN ROOM 8: BEYOND THE LIMITS OF BIOMEDICINE

191 **one-fifteenth the amount of friction:** "Osteoarthritis," *Harrison's On-line,*
chapter 321. Accessed August 4, 2002.

191 **release enzymes that destroy the fibers:** Ibid.

191 **American College of Rheumatology's:** American College of Rheumatology Subcommittee on Osteoarthritis Guidelines, "Recommendations for the Medical Management of Osteoarthritis of the Hip and Knee," *Arthritis and Rheumatism* 43:1905–1915, 2000.

194 **Louis Pasteur accepted a position:** René Dubos, *Pasteur and Modern Science.* Garden City, N.Y.: Anchor Books, 1960, p. 40.

194 **bacteria, which appeared rod-shaped:** Louis Pasteur (1822–1895), *Zephyrus.* Viewed at http://www.zephyrus.co.uk/louispasteur.html. Accessed December 16, 2003.

194 **devastating the silkworm industry:** Dubos, op. cit., p. 101.

194 **working on a rabies vaccine:** Ibid, pp. 122–123.

195 **"acute and harrowing anxiety":** "Historical Perspectives: A Centennial Celebration: Pasteur and the Modern Era of Immunization," *MMWR Weekly* 34:389–390, 1985.

195 **Pasteur went on to treat 2490 people:** Dubos, op. cit., 122–123.

195 **Robert Koch:** Ibid, p. 106.

195 **"magic bullet":** Paul Starr, *The Social Transformation of Medicine,* New York: Basic Books, 1982, p. 135.

195 **Johns Hopkins University:** Ibid., p. 115.

196 **American Medical Association in 1906:** Ibid., p. 118.

196 **Flexner Report:** Ibid., pp 119–122.

197 **Osler wrote a letter:** Harvey Cushing, *The Life of Sir William Osler,* vol. 2, London: Oxford University Press, 1925, pp. 292–293.

197 **Flexner himself eventually became disappointed:** Starr, op. cit., p. 123.

199 **one out of every 200 patients:** L. A. Green, B. P. Yawn, D. Lanier, et al., "The Ecology of Medical Care Revisited," *New England Journal of Medicine* 344:2021–2025, 2001.

200 *The challenges of medicine:* Ken Wilber, *The Marriage of Sense and Soul,* New York: Random House, 1998, p. 56.

200 **Dr. Arthur Kleinman of Harvard:** Arthur Kleinman, *Writing at the Margin: Discourse Between Anthropology and Medicine,* Berkeley: University of California Press, 1995, pp. 243–244.

201 **high-risk men from Oslo, Norway:** I. Hjermann, Velve K. Byre, I. Holme, and P. Leren, "Effect of Diet and Smoking Intervention on the Incidence of Coronary Heart Disease, Report from the Oslo Study Group of a Randomised Trial in Healthy Men (Abstract)," *The Lancet* 2(8259):1303–1310, 1981.

201 **The Lyon Diet Heart Study:** F. M. Sacks and Katan Martijn, "Randomized Clinical Trials on the Effects of Dietary Fat and Carbohydrate on Plasma Lipoproteins and Cardiovascular Disease," *American Journal of Medicine* 113(9/supp. 2):13–24, 2002.

202 **twice the reduction achieved by statins:** In the LIPID study, post–heart attack

patients were randomized to receive a statin or placebo. After 6.1 years, 11 percent of the treatment group had died compared with 14.1 percent of the control group, for a relative risk reduction of 22 percent. See Long-Term Intervention with Pravastatin in Ischemic Disease (LIPID) Study Group, op. cit.

202 **Nurses Health Study:** M. J. Stampfer, F. B. Hu, J. E. Manson, et al., "Primary Prevention of Coronary Heart Disease in Women through Diet and Lifestyle," *New England Journal of Medicine* 343:16–22, 2000.

202 **unspoken professional values, beliefs, and techniques:** Kuhn used the phrase "tacit knowledge" to describe the unspoken presuppositions that are shared by scientists that define what they do. Michael Polyani developed the idea: "When we accept a certain set of presuppositions and use them as our interpretative framework, we may be said to dwell in them as we do in our own body. . . . As they are themselves our ultimate framework, they are essentially inarticulable." Quoted in Jan Golinski, *Making Natural Knowledge: Constructivism and the History of Science,* Cambridge, England: Cambridge University Press, 1998, p. 17.

203 **shared paradigm defines the range:** Thomas Kuhn, *The Structure of Scientific Revolutions,* Chicago: University of Chicago Press, 1962, pp. 64–65.

203 **criteria that justify belief:** Susan Haack, *Evidence and Inquiry: Towards Reconstruction in Epistemology,* Oxford: Blackwell Publishers, 1993, p. 206.

204 **"The Need for a New Medical Model:** G. L. Engel, "The Need for a New Medical Model: A Challenge for Biomedicine," *Science* 196:129–136, 1977.

204 **"half of all deaths:** A. H. Mokdad, J. S. Marks, D. F. Stroup, and J. L. Gerberding, "Actual Causes of Death in the United States, 2000," *Journal of the American Medical Association* 291:1238–1245, 2004.

204 **6 percent of deaths:** J. M. McGinnis, P Williams-Russo, and J. R. Knickman, "The Case for More Active Policy Attention to Health Promotion," *Health Affairs* 21:78-93, 2002.

204 **Institute of Medicine:** "The Future of the Public's Health in the 21st Century," *Institute of Medicine,* November 2002.

205 **almost all (95 percent) of our health care spending:** McGinnis, op. cit.

205 **chronic anxiety, and anger:** L. D. Kubzansky and I. Kawachi, "Going to the Heart of the Matter: Do Negative Emotions Cause Coronary Heart Disease?" *Journal of Psychomatic Research* 48:323–337, 2000.

205 **appropriate counseling:** E. A. McGlynn, S. M. Asch, J. Adams, et al., "The Quality of Health Care Delivered to Adults in the United States," *New England Journal of Medicine* 348:2635–2645, 2003.

206 **individuals are made up of multiple levels:** Wilber, op. cit., pp. 67–68.

206 **Richard Lewontin:** Richard Lewontin, *The Triple Helix,* Cambridge, Mass.: Harvard University Press, 2000, p. 100.

207 **"clinical gaze":** Byron J. Good, *Medicine, Rationality, and Experience: An Anthropological Perspective,* Cambridge: Cambridge University Press, 1994, p. 180.

207 "This means of interpreting reality: Ibid., p. 76.

207 subjective experience and consciousness: John R. Searle, *Mind, Language, and Society: Philosophy in the Real World*, New York: Basic Books, 1998, p. 57.

208 value different metaphysical perspectives equally: Arthur Kleinman, *Writing at the Margin: Discourse Between Anthropology and Medicine*, Berkeley, Calif.: University of California Press, 1995, pp. 243–244.

208 mysterious and dynamic relationship: Colin McGinn, *The Mysterious Flame: Conscious Minds in a Material World*, New York: Basic Books, 1999, p. 167.

208 keeps primary care permanently at the bottom: S. D. Block, N. Clark-Chiarelli, A. S. Peters, and J. D. Singer, "Academia's Chilly Climate for Primary Care," *Journal of the American Medical Association* 276:677–682, 1996.

208 Sir William Osler: Quoted in René Dubos. *Mirage of Health: Utopias, Progress, and Biological Change*, New York: Harper & Row, 1959, p. 143.

CHAPTER 13
FROM OSTEOPOROSIS TO HEART DISEASE

210 so weak that a sudden strain, bump, or fall: National Osteoporosis Foundation. Viewed at http://www.nof.org/osteoporosis/stats.htm. Accessed October 24, 2002 and April 22, 2004.

210 Twenty percent of all women over the age of 50: E. Siris, P. Miller, E. Barrett-Connor, et al., "Design of NORA, the National Osteoporosis Risk Assessment Program: A Longitudinal U.S. Registry of Postemenopausal Women," *Osteoporosis International.* Supp. 1:S62–S69, 1998.

211 In women, this balance changes: Robert Lindsay and Felicia Cosman, chapter 342: Osteoporosis. Viewed at www.harrisonsonline.com October 23, 2002.

211 educational campaign initiated in 1982: C. J. Green, K. Bassett, V. Foerster, and A. Kazanjian, "Bone Mineral Testing: Does the Evidence Support Its Selective Use in Well Women?" Center for Health Services and Policy Research, British Columbia Office of Health Technology Assessment, December 1997.

211 bone mineral density (BMD): "Standard deviation" is a statistical measure: 2.5 standard deviations is equivalent to a bone density lower than all but 1 or 2 out of 100 women in their late twenties.

212 funded by three drug companies: Green, op. cit.

213 the WHO study group recommended: J. A. Kanis, "Assessment of Fracture Risk and Its Application to Screening for Postmenopausal Osteoporosis: Synopsis of a WHO Report," WHO Study Group, *Osteoporosis International* (6):368–381, 1994.

213 never been a randomized controlled study: C. Green, A. Kazanjian, and D. Herlmer, "Informing, Advising, or Persuading? An Assessment of Bone Mineral Density Testing Information from Consumer Health Web Sites," *International Journal of Technology Assessment in Health Care* 20:1–11, 2004.

213 **an average age of 68 and a T score of −2.5 or less:** S. R. Cummings, D. M. Black, D. E. Thompson, et al., "Effect of Alendronate on Risk of Fracture in Women with Low Bone Density but Without Vertebral Fractures: Results from the Fracture Intervention Trial," *Journal of the American Medical Association* 280(24):2077–2082, 1998.

214 **women between the ages of 70 and 79:** M. R. McClung, P. Geusens, P. D. Miller, et al., "Effect of Residronate on the Risk of Hip Fracture in Elderly Women," *New England Journal of Medicine* 344(5):333–340, 2001.

214 **The same result was found in younger women:** S. T. Harris, N. B. Watts, H. K. Genant, et al., "Effects of Risedronate Treatment on Vertebral and Nonvertebral Fractures in Women with Postmenopausal Osteoporosis: A Randomized Controlled Trial," *Journal of the American Medical Association* 282:1344–1352, 1999.

214 **A study conducted in the Netherlands:** C. E. D. H. DeLaiet, B. A. Hout, H. Burger, A. Hofman, and H. A. Pols, "Bone Density and Risk of Hip Fracture in Men and Women: Cross Sectional Analysis," *British Medical Journal* 315:221–225, 1997.

215 **two out of three hip fractures:** C. J. Green, K. Bassett, V. Foerster, and A. Kazanjian, "Bone Mineral Testing: Does the Evidence Support Its Selective Use in Well Women?" Center for Health Services and Policy Research, British Columbia Office of Health Technology Assessment, December 1997.

215 **90 percent of hip fractures resulting from falls:** X. Deprez, P. Fardellone, "Nonpharmacological Prevention of Osteoporotic Fractures," *Joint Bone Spine* 70:448–457, 2003.

215 **"no effect on the incidence of hip fracture":** McClung, op. cit.

215 **the risk of hip fractures actually *went up*:** The increase in clinical fractures in the women with osteopenia (T-score = −2.5 to −1.6) might well have reached statistical significance, but it was calculated only for the women with osteopenia divided into two separate groups, neither of which was large enough alone for the increase in fractures to reach clinical significance. One can only surmise why the statistics were presented in this way. See Cummings, Black, Thompson, et al., op. cit.

216 **lacelike structure of trabecular bone:** Review of Medical Physiology Medical Physiology, 20th ed. (2001), chapter 21. STAT!ref.Electronic Medical Library. Accessed October 23, 2002.

217 **Evista reduces only vertebral fractures:** B. Ettinger, D. M. Black, B. H. Mitlak, et al., "Reduction of Vertebral Fracture Risk in Postmenopausal Women with Osteoporosis Treated with Raloxifene: Results from A Three-Year Randomized Clinical Trial," *Journal of the American Medical Association* 282(7):637–645, 1999.

217 **an FDA letter to the company:** Letter from Margaret M. Kober, Division of Drug Marketing, Advertising, and Communications, FDA, to Gregory G. Enas, Director, U.S. Regulatory Affairs, Eli Lilly and Company, RE: Evista (ralixifene HCl) Tablets, September 14, 2000.

217 **Miacalcin, administered by a nasal spray:** C. H. Chestnut, S. Silverman, K. Andriano, et al., "A Randomized Trial of Nasal Spray Salmon Calcitonin in Postmenopausal Women with Established Osteoporosis: The Prevent Recurrence of Osteoporotic Fractures Study," *American Journal of Medicine* 109:267–276, 2000.

217 **Forteo, administered by daily self-injection:** R. M. Neer, C. D. Arnaud, J. R. Zanchetta, et al., "Effect of Parathyroid Hormone (1-34) on Fractures and Bone Mineral Density in Postmenopausal Women with Osteoporosis," *New England Journal of Medicine* 344:1434–1441, 2001.

217 **exercise builds up trabecular bone:** C. Rubin, A. S. Turner, R. Muller, et al., "Quantity and Quality of Trabecular Bone in the Femur Are Enhanced by a Strongly Anabolic, Noninvasive Mechanical Intervention," *Journal of Bone and Mineral Research* 17:349–357, 2002.

217 **The Study of Osteoporotic Fractures:** E. W. Gregg, J. A. Cauley, D. G. Seeley, et al., "Physical Activity and Osteoporotic Fracture Risk in Older Women," *Annals of Internal Medicine* 129:81–88, 1998.

218 **In a study in Sweden, nursing home residents:** J. Jensen, L. Lundin-Olsson, L. Nyberg, Y. Gustafson, "Fall and Injury Prevention in Older People Living in Residential Care Facilities: A Cluster Randomized Trial," *Annals of Internal Medicine* 136:733–741, 2002.

218 **Strength training:** M. E. Nelson, M. A. Fiatarone, C. M. Morganti, et al., "Effects of High-Intensity Strength Training on Multiple Risk Factors for Osteoporotic Fractures. A Randomized Controlled Trial (Abstract)," *Journal of the American Medical Association* 272:1909–1914, 1994.

218 **Tai chi:** S. L. Wolf, H. X. Barnhart, N. G. Kutner, et al., "Reducing Frailty and Falls in Older Persons: An Investigation of Tai Chi and Computerized Balance Training," *Journal of the American Geriatrics Society* 51:1794–1803, 2003.

218 **Adequate calcium and vitamin D are also essential:** M. C. Chapuy, M. E. Arlot, F. Duboeuf, et al., "Vitamin D3 and Calcium to Prevent Hip Fractures in the Elderly Women (Abstract)," *New England Journal of Medicine* 327:1637–1642, 1992.

218 **higher ratio of animal to vegetable proteins:** D. E. Sellmeyer, K. L. Stone, A. Sebastian, et al., "A High Ratio of Dietary Animal to Vegetable Protein Increases the Rate of Bone Loss and the Risk of Fracture in Postmenopausal Women," *American Journal of Clinical Nutrition.* 73:118–122, 2001.

218 **website sponsored by Merck:** The website was viewed at http://www.bonedensitytest.com/osteoporosis/thin_bones/learn_about_your_t_score/index.jsp. (No longer available.)

219 **National Osteoporosis Society:** National Osteoporosis Foundation 2001 Annual Report.

219 **A 2004 article published in the** *International Journal of Health Technology Assessment:* C. Green, A. Kazanjian, and D. Helmer, op. cit.

219 **Center for Medical Consumers:** Go to http://www.medicalconsumers.org.

219 *Our Bodies, Ourselves:* The Boston Women's Health Collective, *Our Bodies, Ourselves,* New York: Simon & Schuster, 1998.

220 **The National Cholesterol Education Program:** Viewed at http://www. nhlbi.nih.gov/about/ncep/. Accessed January 4, 2004.

220 **discuss cholesterol with their doctors:** I. S. Nash, L. Mosca, R. S. Blumenthal, et al., "Contemporary Awareness and Understanding of Cholesterol as a Risk Factor," *Archives of Internal Medicine* 163:1597–1600, 2003.

220 **importance of routine exercise:** C. C. Wee, E. P. McCarthy, R. B. Davis, and R. S. Phillips, "Physician Counseling about Exercise," *Journal of the American Medical Association* 282:1583–1588, 1999.

220 **are advised (if smokers) to quit smoking:** A. N. Thorndike, N. A. Rigotti, R. S. Stafford, D. E. Singer, "National Patterns in the Treatment of Smokers by Physicians," *Journal of the American Medical Association* 279:604–608, 1998.

220 **advising obese people to lose weight:** D. A. Galuska, J. C. Will, M. K. Serdula, and E. S. Ford, "Are Health Care Professionals Advising Obese Patients to Lose Weight?" *Journal of the American Medical Association* 282:1576–1578, 1999.

220 **cancer is far worse:** Viewed at http://www.cdc.gov/nchs/data/hus/tables/2003, 2003hus030.pdf. Accessed January 26, 2004.

221 **percentage of adult smokers in the United States declined:** Epidemiology and Statistics Unit, American Lung Association, "Trends in Tobacco Use," February 2001. Viewed at http://www.lungusa.org/data/smoke/SMK1.pdf. Accessed December 4, 2003.

221 **Smoking is responsible for as much as 30 percent:** I. S. Ockene and N. H. Miller, "Cigarette Smoking, Cardiovascular Disease, and Stroke," *Circulation* 96:3243–3247, 1997.

221 **Americans' per capita consumption:** "Profiling Food Consumption in America," *Agriculture Fact Book 2001–2002,* U.S. Department of Agriculture. Viewed at http://www.usda.gov/factbook/chapter2.htm.

221 **And good progress was made:** R. C. Cooper, J. Cutler, P. Desvigne-Nickern, et al., "Trends and Disparities in Coronary Heart Disease, Stroke, and Other Cardiovascular Diseases in the United States," *Circulation* 102:3137–3147, 2000.

221 **Largely as a result of these lifestyle changes:** /articles/cdc morbidity and mortality chart book, p. 32, one half figure reconstructed from chart 3-23.

221 **"revolution" in prevention and treatment of heart disease:** "Health at a Glance," OECD 2003, op. cit., p. 55.

221 **number of coronary artery bypass surgeries:** "Health at a Glance," OECD 2003, op. cit., p. 55.

221 **FDA approved the first cholesterol-lowering statin drug:** Susan Warner, "Hard Times in Star Part of the State Economy," *New York Times,* December 28, 2003.

221 rate of decline in the death rate actually slowed during the 1990s: *Morbidity & Mortality: 2002 Chart Book on Cardiovascular, Lung, and Blood Disease,* Bethesda, Md.: National Institutes of Health. 2002, p. 33.

221 Americans who smoked: "Current Smokers, Trends Data Nationwide, Behavioral Risk Factor Surveillance System," U.S. Centers for Disease Control and Prevention. Viewed at http://apps.nccd.cdc.gov/brfss/Trends/trendchart.asp?qkey=10000&state=US. Accessed January 27, 2004.

221 decline in per capita beef and egg consumption stalled: "Profiling Food Consumption in America," op. cit., http://www.usda.gov/factbook/tables/ch2table21.jpg.

221 decline in whole milk consumption leveled off: See http://www.ers.usda.gov/Amberwaves/June03/DataFeature/.

222 obese Americans nearly doubled: "Obesity: By Body Mass Index, Trends Data Nationwide, Behavioral Risk Factor Surveillance System," U.S. Centers for Disease Control and Prevention. Viewed at http://apps.nccd.cdc.gov/brfss/Trends/trendchart.asp?qkey=10010&state=U.S.

222 high blood pressure: H. Wayne and M. S. Giles, "Update on Risk Factors for Stroke Profiling Your Patient's Risk, Centers for Disease Control and Prevention," October 30, 2003. Viewed at http://www.i3m.org/main/pcpc/ppoint/ws1_giles.pdf. The total number of people with high blood pressure increased from 21.7 percent to 25.6 percent, even though the percentage of hypertensives whose blood pressure was controlled increased from 29 percent to 34 percent between 1990 and 2000. Viewed at http://www.cdc.gov/nchs/data/hus/tables/2003, 2003hus066.pdf.

222 The study collected data on 25,000 executive and professional men: M. Wei, J. B. Kampert, C. E. Barlow, et al., "Relationship Between Low Cardiopulmonary Fitness and Mortality in Normal-Weight, Overweight, and Obese Men," *Journal of the American Medical Association* 282:1547–1553, 1999.

223 almost 10,000 men who underwent exercise testing: S. N. Blair, H. W. Kohl, C. E. Barlow, et al., "Changes in Physical Fitness and All-Cause Mortality: A Prospective Study of Healthy and Unhealthy Men," *Journal of the American Medical Association* 273:1093–1098, 1995.

223 physical fitness plays a major role in protecting women: Fitness was measured by being above average on both exercise capacity and the rate of return of pulse toward normal in the two minutes following exercise compared with the women who were below average on both measures. S. Mora, R. F. Redberg, Y. Cui, et al., "Ability of Exercise Testing to Predict Cardiovascular and All-Cause Death in Asymptomatic Women," *Journal of the American Medical Association* 290:1600–1607, 2003.

223 Post–heart attack patients: J. A. Jilliffee, K. Rees, R. S. Taylor, et al., "Exercise-Based Rehabilitation for Coronary Heart Disease," *Cochrane Database Systematic Review* 1:CD001800, 2001 (abstract).

223 **randomized studies of statin treatment:** NCEP Full Report, p. II-39

224 **Lyon Diet Heart Study:** P. Kris-Etherton, R. H. Eckel, B. V. Howard, et al., "Lyon Diet Heart Study: Benefits of a Mediterranean-Style National Cholesterol Education Program/American Heart Association Step 1 Dietary Pattern on Cardiovascular Disease," *Circulation* 102:1823, 2001.

224 **National Cholesterol Education Project:** NCEP Full Report, p. V–15.

225 **progress in stroke mortality stalled:** *Morbidity & Mortality,* op. cit. p. 45.

225 **Dr. Wayne H. Giles:** H. Wayne and M. S. Giles, "Update on Risk Factors for Stroke Profiling Your Patient's Risk, Centers for Disease Control and Prevention," October 30, 2003. Viewed at http://www.i3m.org/main/pcpc/ppoint/ws1_giles.pdf.

226 **Activase:** D. L. Vance, "Treating Acute Ischemic Stroke with Intravenous Alteplase," *Critical Care Nurse* 21:25–32, 2001.

226 **only one out of 25 would derive any benefit:** Patients are excluded from receiving alteplase (Activase) if treatment cannot begin within three hours of symptom onset, stroke symptoms are mild, blood pressure is elevated, the stroke is hemorrhagic, blood clotting is too slow, seizure has occurred, the patient had a stroke within the past three months, blood sugar is abnormal, or symptoms abated before therapy was begun. H. S. Jorgensen, H. Nakayarna, L. P. Kammersgaard, et al., "Predicted Impact of Intravenous Thrombolysis on Prognosis of General Population of Stroke Patients: Simulation Model," *British Medical Journal* 319:288–289, 1999.

226 **2000 American Heart Association guidelines:** American Heart Association in Collaboration with the International Liaison Committee on Resuscitation, "Guidelines 2000 for Cardiopulmonary Resuscitation and Emergency Cardiovascular Care. Part 7: The Era of Reperfusion: Section 2: Acute Stroke," *Circulation* 102(8 suppl I.):1204–1216, 2000.

227 **Dr. Rose Marie Robertson:** J. Lenzer, "Alteplase for Stroke: Money and Optimistic Claims Buttress the 'Brain Attack' Campaign," *British Medical Journal* 324:723–726, 2002.

227 **six out of the eight experts:** Financial ties to Genentech or its marketing partner, Boehringer Ingelheim, included receiving fees for lecturing and consulting, or received research grants. Ibid.

227 **misleadingly titled NEJM article:** H. D. White, R. J. Simes, N. E. Anderson, et al., "Pravastatin Therapy and the Risk of Stroke," *New England Journal of Medicine* 343:317–326, 2000.

227 **earned Bristol-Myers Squibb one of only five warning letters:** Thomas W. Abrams, RPh, MBA, Director Division of Drug Marketing, Advertising, and Communications, FDA, Warning Letter to Peter R. Dolan, Chairman and Chief Executive Officer, Bristol-Myers Squibb Company, RE: Pravachol (pravastatin socium) Tablets, August 7, 2003. Viewed at http://www.fda.gov/cder/warn/2003/pravachol-wl.pdf on February 12, 2004.

228 **eating fish at least once a week:** K. He, E. B. Rimm, A. Merchang, et al., "Fish

Consumption and Risk of Stroke in Men," *Journal of the American Medical Association* 288:3130–136, 2002. See also H. Iso, K. Rexrode, M. J. Stampfer, et al., "Intake of Fish and Omega-3, Fatty Acids and Risk of Stroke in Women." *Journal of the American Medical Association* 285:304–312, 2001.

228 **epidemic of type 2 diabetes:** A. H. Mokdad, B. A. Bowman, E. S. Ford, et al., "The Continuing Epidemics of Obesity and Diabetes in the United States," *Journal of the American Medical Association* 286:1195–1200, 2001. See also "National Estimates on Diabetes," National Diabetes Fact Sheet, Centers for Disease Control and Prevention. Viewed at http://www.cdc.gov/diabetes/pubs/estimates.htm#incidence on January 12, 2004.

228 **complications of diabetes:** "Diabetes: Disabling, Deadly, and on the Rise, At a Glance 2003," Centers for Disease Control and Prevention.

229 **American College of Physicians issued clinical guidelines:** V. Snow, M. D. Aronson, R. Hornbake, et al., "Lipid Control in the Management of Type 2 Diabetes Mellitus: A Clinical Practice Guideline from the American College of Physicians," *Annals of Internal Medicine* 140:644–649, 2004.

229 **Heart Protection Study:** Heart Protection Study Collaborative Group. "MRC/BHF Heart Protection Study of Cholesterol-Lowering with Simvastatin in 5693 People with Diabetes: A Randomised Placebo-Controlled Trial," *The Lancet* 361:2005–2016, 2003.

229 **91 percent of the risk of developing type 2 diabetes:** F. B. Hu, J. E. Manson, M. J. Stampfer, et al., "Diet, Lifestyle, and the Risk of Type 2 Diabetes Mellitus in Women," *New England Journal of Medicine* 345:790–797, 2001.

230 **tested the effectiveness of counseling:** J. Tuomilehto, J. Lindstrom, J. G. Erisson, et al., "Prevention of Type 2 Diabetes Mellitus by Changes in Lifestyle Among Subjects with Impaired Glucose Tolerance," *Journal of the American Medical Association* 344:1343–1350, 2001.

230 **six fewer people out of 100:** Diabetes Prevention Program Research Group, "Reduction in the Incidence of Type 2 Diabetes with Lifestyle Intervention or Metformin," *Journal of the American Medical Association* 346:393–403, 2002.

230 **"Make the Link! Diabetes, Heart Disease and Stroke":** Viewed at http://www.diabetes.org/type-1-diabetes/well-being/heart-disease-and-stroke.jsp. Accessed January 27, 2004.

230 **a number of "corporate partners,":** Viewed at http://www.diabetes.org/info/link.jsp. Accessed January 8, 2004.

230 **fewer than one-third of the diabetics:** K. M. Nelson, G. Reiber, and Boyko, "Diet and Exercise Among Adults with Type 2 Diabetes: Findings from the Third National Health and Nutrition Examination Survey (NHAMESIII)," *Diabetes Care* 25:1722–1728, 2002.

230 **walking two or more hours each week:** E. W. Gregg, R. B. Gerzoff, C. J. Caspersen, et al., "Relationship of Walking to Mortality Among U.S. Adults

with Diabetes," *Archives of Internal Medicine* 163:1440–1447, 2003.

231 **overweight and sedentary diabetic and prediabetic men:** C. A. Maggio and F. X. Pi-Sunyer, "The Prevention and Treatment of Obesity: Application to Type 2 Diabetes," *Diabetes Care*. 20:1744–1766, 1997.

231 **only half of diabetic patients were counseled:** C. C. Wee, E. P. McCarthy, R. B. Davis, and S. Russell, "Physician Counseling about Exercise," *Journal of the American Medical Association* 282:1583–1588, 1999.

231 **weight-loss program for diabetics:** C. A. Maggio and F. X. Pi-Sunyer, op. cit.

232 **advertisement for Zoloft:** Viewed at http://www.zoloft.com/index.asp?pageid=52. Accessed February 1, 2004.

232 **Pfizer website:** Viewed at http://www.zoloft.com/index.asp?pageid=2. Accessed February 1, 2004.

232 **randomized people suffering from social anxiety:** T. T. Haug, S. Blomhoff, K. Hellstrom, et al., "Exposure Therapy and Sertraline in Social Phobia: 1-Year Follow-up of a Randomised Controlled Trial," *British Journal of Psychiatry* 182:312–318, 2003.

233 **patients suffering from major depression:** M. Babyak, J. A. Blumenthal, S. Herman, et al., "Exercise Treatment for Major Depression: Maintenance of Therapeutic Benefit at 10 Months," *Psychosomatic Medicine* 62:633–638, 2000.

234 **87 percent of lung cancers:** "Cancer Facts and Figures 2001," American Cancer Society, p. 29.

234 **routine exercise:** C. M. Friedenreich, "Physical Activity and Cancer Prevention: from Observational to Intervention Research," *Cancer Epidemiology, Biomarkers & Prevention* 10:287–301, 2001.

234 **Diet plays a role:** T. J. Key, N. E. Allen, E. A. Spencer, and R. C. Travis, "The Effect of Diet on Risk of Cancer," *The Lancet* 360: 861–868, 2002

234 **"Western diet":** M. L. Slattery, K. M. Boucher, B. J. Caan, et al., "Eating Patterns and Risk of Colon Cancer," *American Journal of Epidemiology* 148: 4–16, 1998.

234 **Lyon Diet Heart Study:** M. DeLorgeril, P. Salen, J.-L. Martin, et al., "Mediterranean Dietary Pattern in a Randomized Trial: Prolonged Survival and Possible Reduced Cancer Rate," *Archives of Internal Medicine* 158:1181–1187, 1998.

235 **A study conducted in Canada found that being obese:** S. Y. Pan, A.-M. Ugnat, S. W. Wen, et al., "Association of Obesity and Cancer Risk in Canada," *American Journal of Epidemiology* 159:259–268, 2004.

235 **twice as many Americans are obese as Canadians:** "Health at a Glance," OECD 2003, op. cit., p. 72.

235 **Agency for Healthcare Research and Quality:** These can be viewed at http://www.ahrq.gov.

236 **Americans' average daily intake of sugar:** "Profiling Food Consumption in America," op. cit.

236 **obese children and adolescents increased by a factor of almost four:** See

National Center for Health Statistics, Centers for Disease Control and Prevention. Viewed at http://www.cdc.gov/nchs/data/hus/tables/2003, 2003hus068.pdf. Accessed January 28, 2004.

236 **deaths in the United States caused by obesity and physical inactivity:** Rob Stein, "Obesity Passing Smoking as Top Avoidable Cause of Death," *Washington Post,* March 10, 2004.

237 **recommendations that emerge from the scientific evidence:** D. Kromhout, A. Menotti, H. Kesteloot, S. Sans, "Prevention of Coronary Heart Diseaes by Diet and Lifestyle: Evidence from Prospecti Cross-Cultural, Cohort and Intervention Studies," *Circulation* 105:893–898, 2002.

238 **retired, nonsmoking men in Honolulu:** A. A. Hakim, H. Petrovitch, C. M. Burchfiel, et al., "Effects of Walking on Mortality Among Nonsmoking Retired Men," *New England Journal of Medicine* 338:94–99, 1998.

239 **9700 independently living women:** E. W. Gregg, J. A. Cauley, K. Stone, et al., "Relationship of Changes in Physical Activity and Mortality Among Older Women," *Journal of the American Medical Association* 289:2379–2386, 2003.

CHAPTER 14
HEALING OUR AILING HEALTH CARE SYSTEM, OR HOW TO SAVE $500 BILLION A YEAR WHILE IMPROVING AMERICANS' HEALTH

241 **Dr. Jonas Salk:** Viewed at http://www.teachspace.org/lauren/polio/salk3.html. Accessed February 18, 2004.

241 **diminished role of universities:** Derek Bok, *Universities in the Marketplace: The Commercialization of Higher Education,* Princeton, N.J.: Princeton University Press, 2003, p. 117.

242 **"well-ordered science":** Defined as "what inquiry is to aim at if it is to serve the collective good." Philip Kitcher, *Science, Truth, and Democracy,* Oxford: Oxford University Press, 2001, p. xii.

242 **"In a science-driven organization:** Sheryl Gay Stolberg and Jeff Girth, "Drug Makers Design Studies with Eye to Competitive Edge," *New York Times,* December 23, 2000.

242 **the more important the consequences:** Kitcher, op. cit., p. 96.

243 **nine clinical studies:** "SSRIs: Suicide Risk and Withdrawal (Editorial)," *The Lancet* 361:1999, 2003. See also Gardiner Harris, "Debate Resumes on the Safety of Depression's Wonder Drugs," *New York Times,* August 7, 2003.

243 **task force of the American College of Neuropsychopharmacology:** Gardiner Harris, "Panel Says Zoloft and Cousins Don't Increase Suicide Risk," *New York Times.* January 22, 2004.

243 **FDA epidemiologist:** Gardiner Harris, "Expert Kept from Speaking at Antidepressant Hearing," *New York Times,* April 16, 2004.

243 **study of an expensive drug:** B. M. Psaty and D. Rennie, "Stopping Medical

Research to Save Money: A Broken Pact with Researchers and Patients," *Journal of the American Medical Association* 289:2128–2131, 2003.

243 **a $10,000 device to repair aortic aneurysms:** United States District Court, Northern District of California, San Francisco Division, No. CR 02-0179 SI, Plea Agreement. Viewed at http://www.findlaw.com. Accessed January 20, 2003.

244 **Consumers Union:** Consumers Union is the nonprofit publisher of *Consumer Reports.* Viewed at http://www.yuricareport.com/Medicare/21orgSignLettertoCongress.html. Accessed February 1, 2004.

245 **Canada and the European countries:** A. Maynard and K. Bloor, "Dilemmas in Regulation of the Market for Pharmaceuticals," *Health Affairs* 22(3):31–41, 2003.

245 **PhRMA was successful:** Sheryl Gay Stolberg and Gardiner Harris, "Industry Fights to Put Imprint on Drug Bill," *New York Times,* September 5, 2003.

245 **may actually cause more GI problems:** Lawrence Goldkind, M.D., "Medical Officer's Gastroenterology Advisory Committee Briefing Document. Celebrex (celecoxib)," February 7, 2001, p. 51 Viewed at http://www.fda.gov/ohrms/dockets/ac/01/briefing/3677b1_05_gi.doc.P. 51. Accessed September 26, 2001.

245 **Norvasc 5 mg and 10 mg:** "Out of Bounds: Rising Prescription Drug Prices for Seniors," *Families U.S.A.,* July 2003.

245 **diuretic that costs only $29 per year:** B. M. Psaty, T. Lumley, C. D. Furberg, et al., "Health Outcomes Associated with Various Antihypertensive Therapies Used as First-Line Agents: A Network Meta-Analysis," *Journal of the American Medical Association* 289:2534–2544, 2003.

246 **PROSPER study:** J. Shepherd, G. J. Blauw, M. B. Murphy, et al., "Pravastatin in Elderly Individuals at Risk of Vascular Disease (PROSPER): A Randomised Controlled Trial," *The Lancet* 360:1623–1630, 2002.

246 **patients over the age of 65:** Heart attacks, unstable angina, strokes, transient ischemic attacks, and blood clots. See Shari L. Targum, "Review of Cardiovascular Safety Data Base. Rofecoxib (Vioxx)," February 1, 2001, p. 20. Viewed at http://www.fda.gov/ohrms/dockets/ac/01/briefing/3677b2_06_cardio.pdf. Accessed October 17, 2001.

246 **four times more likely to** *cause* **a cardiovascular complication:** Post-heart attack patients in the LIPID study treated with a statin had 0.6 per *fewer* heart attacks and deaths due to heart disease per 100 patients each year (the rate of overall cardiovascular complications was not presented), compared with 2.5 *more* cardiovascular complications for every 100 patients over the age of 65 treated with Vioxx instead of naproxen each year.

246 **stomach acid–blocking drugs:** "Out of Bounds," op. cit.

246 **used to prevent osteoporosis:** M. R. McClung, P. Geusens, P. D. Miller, et al., "Effect of Residronate on the Risk of Hip Fracture in Elderly Women," *New England Journal of Medicine* 344(5):333–340, 2001.

247 "when you get to add hotels": Sheryl Gay Stolberg and Gardner Harris, "Industry Fights to Imprint on Drug Bill," *New York Times,* September 5, 2003.

247 Congress was not even allowed to see: Robert Pear, "Democrats Demand Inquiry into Charge by Medicare Officer," *New York Times,* March 14, 2004.

247 Thomas Scully had received an ethics waiver: Robert Pear, "Medicare Chief Joins Firm with Health Clients," *New York Times,* December 19, 2003.

248 "We can't let that [estimate] get out": David Rogers, "White House Suppressed Costs for Medicare Bill, Official Says, *Wall Street Journal,* March 15, 2004.

248 likely to increase even more than predicted: J. A. Doshi, N. Brandt, and B. Stuart, "The Impact of Drug Coverage on COX-2 Inhibitor Use in Medicare," *Health Affairs* Web Exclusive; February 18, 2004. W 4-94 to 105. Viewed at http://content.healthaffairs.org/cgi/reprint/hlthaff.w4.94v1.pdf.

248 Dr. Donald Berwick: Quoted in B. Sibbald, "U.S. Health System Needs Major Overhaul: Academy," *Canadian Medical Association Journal* 164:1197, 2001.

248 more than half the budget: U.S. General Accounting Office, "Food and Drug Administration: Effect of User Fees on Drug Approval Times, Withdrawals, and Other Agency Activities," September 2002.

250 independent national public body: Sheldon Krimsky, *Science in the Private Interest,* Lanham, Md: Rowman & Littlefield, 2003, p. 229. See also S. C. Schoenbaum, A.-M. J. Audet, and K. Davis, "Obtaining Greater Value from Health Care: The Role of the U.S. Government," *Health Affairs* 22(6):183–190, 2003.

250 National Institute for Clinical Excellence (NICE): Viewed at http://www.nice.org.uk/cat.asp?c= 137. Accessed February 19, 2004.

251 Sponsors [of clinical research]: K. Dickersin and D. Rennie, "Registering Clinical Trials," *Journal of the American Medical Association* 290:516–523, 2003.

253 18,000 Americans die unnecessarily each year: "Insuring America's Health: Principles and Recommendations," Institute of Medicine, January 2004.

253 ABCNews/*Washington Post* poll: This poll was conducted October 9–13, 2003.

253 cost of covering all Americans: J. Hadley and J. Holahan, "Covering the Uninsured: How Much Would It Cost?" *Health Affairs* Web Exclusive. June 4, 2003.

253 $500 billion: See Chapter 11.

254 barely half of the standards: E. A. McGlynn, S. M. Asch, J. Adams, et al., "The Quality of Health Care Delivered to Adults in the United States," *New England Journal of Medicine* 348:2635–45, 2003.

255 increased more than fivefold: K. Levit, C. Smith, C. Cowan, et al., "Health Spending Continues in 2002," *Health Affairs* 23:147–159, 2004.

255 approximately 12,000 deaths: B. Starfield, "Is U.S. Health Really the Best in the World?" *Journal of the American Medical Association* 284:483–485, 2000.

255 Health care providers that deliver high quality: Reed Abelson, "Hospitals Say They're Penalized by Medicare for Improving Care," *New York Times,* December 5, 2003.

258 **President Teddy Roosevelt:** Edmund Morris, *Theodore Rex,* New York: Random House, 2001.

258 **but not in the rest of the world:** Worldwide sales of COX-2 inhibitors totaled $6.7 billion in 2003. David L. Shedlarz, Executive Vice President and Chief Financial Officer, Pfizer, "Pfizer Themes: Performance, Opportunities, Differentiation," November 12, 2003.

258 **two most heavily advertised:** Kathy Blankenhorn and David Lipson, "Business Watch: 2001 in Review," *IMS Health,* May 2002. Viewed at http:// www.imshealth.com/vgn/images/portal/cit_759/2006112572bus2.pdf   on October 24, 2003.

259 **$5.3 billion of COX-2 inhibitor sales:** "IMS Reports 11.5 Percent Dollar Growth in 2003 U.S. Prescription Sales," *IMS Health,* February 17, 2004. Viewed at http://biz.yahoo.com/bw/040217/175915_1.html on March 11, 2004.

BIBLIOGRAPHY

Aronowitz, Robert A., *Making Sense of Illness: Science, Society, and Disease.* Cambridge, U.K.: Cambridge University Press, 1998.

Barkow, Jerome H., Leda Cosmonides, and John Tooby. *The Adapted Mind: Evolutionary Psychology and the Generation of Culture.* New York and Oxford: Oxford University Press, 1992.

Benson, Herbert, M.D., with Marg Stark. *Timeless Healing: The Power and Biology of Belief.* New York: Scribner, 1996.

Berger, Peter L., and Thomas Luckman. *The Social Construction of Reality: A Treatise in the Sociology of Knowledge.* New York: Anchor Books, Doubleday, 1967.

Bok, Derek. *Universities in the Marketplace: The Commercialization of Higher Education.* Princeton and Oxford: The Princeton University Press, 2003.

Brown, James Robert. *Who Rules in Science: An Opinionated Guide to the Wars.* Cambridge and London: Harvard University Press, 2001.

Callahan, Daniel. *False Hopes: Why America's Quest for Perfect Health Is a Recipe for Failure.* New York: Simon & Schuster, 1998.

Capra, Fritjof. *The Turning Point: Science, Society and the Rising Culture.* New York: Simon & Schuster, 1982.

Collins, Chuck, Betsy Leondar-Wright, and Holly Sklar. *Shifting Fortunes: The Perils of the Growing American Wealth Gap.* Boston: United for a Fair Economy, 1992.

Dacher, Elliot S., M.D. *Whole Healing: A Step-By-Step Program to Reclaim your Power to Heal.* New York: A Dutton Book, Penguin, 1996.

Dubos, René. *Mirage of Health: Utopias, Progress, and Biological Change.* New York: Harper and Brothers, 1959; reissued, New Brunswick and London: Rutgers University Press, 1987.

———— *Pasteur and Modern Science.* New York: Anchor Books, Doubleday & Company, 1960.

Fabrega, Horacio, Jr. *Evolution of Sickness and Healing.* Berkeley and Los Angeles: University of California Press, 1997.

Farmer, Paul. *Infections and Inequalities: The Modern Plagues.* Berkeley, Los Angeles, London: University of California Press, 1999.

Fukayama, Francis. *Our Posthuman Future: Consequences of the Biotechnology Revolution.* New York: Farrar, Straus and Giroux, 2002.

Garrett, Laurie. *Betrayal of Trust: The Collapse of Global Public Health.* New York: Hyperion, 2000.

Golinski, Jan. *Making Natural Knowledge: Constructivism and the History of Science.* Cambridge and New York: Cambridge University Press, 1998.

Good, Byron J. *Medicine, Rationality and Experience: An Anthropological Perspective.* The Lewis Henry Morgan Lectures: 1990. Cambridge, U.K.: Cambridge University Press, 1994.

Greenberg, Daniel S. *Science, Money and Politics: Political Triumph and Ethical Erosion.* Chicago and London: The University of Chicago Press, 2001.

Hack, Susan, *Evidence and Inquiry: Toward Reconstruction in Epistemology.* Oxford and Medford, Mass.: Blackwell Publishers Ltd., 1993.

Hacking, Ian. *The Social Construction of What?* Cambridge and London: Harvard University Press, 1999.

Hahn, Robert A. *Sickness and Healing: An Anthropological Perspective.* New Haven and London: Yale University Press, 1995.

Hilts, Philip J. *Protecting America's Health: The FDA, Business and One Hundred Years of Regulation.* New York: Alfred A. Knopf, 2003.

Health & Health Care 2010: The Forecast, the Challenge. Roy Amara et al., Institute for the Future for the Robert Wood Johnson Foundation. San Francisco: Jossey-Bass Publishers, 2000.

Kass, Leon R., M.D. *Life, Liberty and the Defense of Dignity: The Challenge of Bioethics.* San Francisco: Encounter Books, 2002.

Kitcher, Philip. *Science, Truth and Democracy.* New York: Oxford University Press, 2001.

Kleinman, Arthur, M.D. *The Illness Narratives: Suffering, Healing and the Human Condition.* New York: Basic Books, 1988.

———— *Writing at the Margin: Discourse Between Anthropology and Medicine.* Berkeley and Los Angeles: University of California Press, 1995.

Kuhn, Thomas S. *The Structure of Scientific Revolutions.* Chicago and London: The University of Chicago Press, 1962.

Krause, Elliot A. *Death of the Guilds: Professions, States and the Advances of Capitalism, 1930 to the Present.* New Haven and London: Yale University Press, 1996.

Krimsky, Sheldon. *Science in the Public Interest: Has the Lure of Profits Corrupted Biomedical Research?* Lanham, Md.: Rowman & Littlefield Publishers, Inc., 2003.

Lasch, Christopher. *The Culture of Narcissism.* New York: Warner Books, W. W. Norton & Company, 1979.

Leach, William. *Land of Desire: Merchants, Power and the Rise of a New American Culture.* New York: Vintage Books, Random House, 1993.

Lewontin, Richard. *The Triple Helix: Gene, Organism and Environment.* Cambridge and London: Harvard University Press, 2000.

Love, Susan M., M.D., with Karen Lindsey. *Dr. Susan Love's Hormone Book: Making Informed Choices about Menopause.* New York: Three Rivers Press, 1997.

McGinn, Colin. *The Mysterious Flame: Conscious Minds in a Material Field.* New York: Basic Books, 1999.

Miller, Matthew. *The 2% Solution: Fixing America's Problems in Ways Liberals and Conservatives Can Love.* New York: Public Affairs, Perseus Books Group, 2003.

Northrup, Christiane, M.D. *The Wisdom of Menopause: Creating Physical and Emotional Health and Healing During the Change.* New York: Bantom Books, 2001.

Our Bodies, Ourselves, for the New Century: A Book by and for Women. The Boston Women's Health Book Collective. Update. New York: A Touchstone Book, Simon & Schuster, 1998.

Panadian, Jacob. *Culture, Religion, and the Self: A Critical Introduction to the Anthropological Study of Religion.* Englewood Cliffs, N.J.: Prentice-Hall, Inc., Simon & Schuster, 1991.

Pearson, Cynthia, et al., The National Women's Health Network. *The Truth About Hormone Replacement Therapy: How to Break Free from the Medical Myths of Menopause.* Roseville, Calif.: Prima Publishing, Random House, 2002.

Pickstone, John V. *Ways of Knowing: A New History of Science, Technology and Medicine.* Manchester: Manchester University Press; Chicago: The University of Chicago Press, 2001.

Rampton, Sheldon, and John Stauber. *Trust Us, We're Experts: How Industry Manipulates Science and Gambles with Your Future.* New York: Penguin Putnam, 2001.

Schlosser, Eric. *Fast Food Nation: The Dark Side of the All-American Meal.* New York: Houghton Mifflin Company, 2001.

Searle, John R. *Mind, Language and Society: Philosophy in the Real World.* New York: Basic Books, 1998.

Sen, Amartya. *Development as Freedom.* New York: Anchor Books and Random House, 1999.

Sheridan, Alan. *Michel Foucault: The Will to Truth.* London: Tavistock Publications Ltd., 1980, Routledge, 1990.

Slaughter, Sheila, and Larry L. Leslie. *Academic Capitalism: Politics, Policies and the Entrepreneurial University.* Baltimore and London: The Johns Hopkins University Press, 1997.

Starfield, Barbara. *Primary Care: Balancing Health Needs, Services and Technology.* New York and Oxford: Oxford University Press, 1998.

Starr, Paul. *The Social Transformation of American Medicine: The Rise of a Sovereign Profession and the Making of a Vast Industry.* New York: Basic Books, 1982.

Stevens, Rosemary. *American Medicine and the Public Interest: A History of Specialization.* Updated edition. Berkeley, Los Angeles, London: University of California Press, 1998.

Tauber, Alfred I. *Confessions of a Medicine Man: An Essay of Popular Philosophy.* Cambridge and London: A Bradford Book, MIT Press, 1999.

Varela, Francisco J., Evan Thompson, Eleanor Rosch. *The Embodied Mind: Cognitive Science and Human Experience.* Cambridge and London: The MIT Press, 1991.

Waitzkin, Howard. *The Second Sickness: Contradictions of Capitalist Health Care.* Lanham, Md: Rowman & Littlefield Publishers, 2000.

Welch, H. Gilbert. *Should I Be Tested for Cancer? Maybe Not and Here's Why.* Berkeley, University of California Press, 2004.

Wilber, Ken. *The Marriage of Sense and Soul: Integrating Science and Religion.* New York and Toronto, Random House, 1998.

ACKNOWLEDGMENTS

First and last I thank Charlotte Kahn, who has been my inspiration, facilitator, and most fearless critic. She gave me the courage to explore the big issues and helped me focus my investigation, but most of all provided me with unfailing encouragement about the importance of this project.

Gail Winston, at HarperCollins, disproved almost everything I had been led to expect from a publisher. She coached me patiently throughout the process: from organizing themes to structuring chapters to crafting the language to preparing the final manuscript. Even more important, she was always enthusiastic and always believed in the value of telling this story fairly and completely. I quickly learned to trust Gail's wise advice. Christine Walsh, also at HarperCollins, provided support and adroitly focused my attention on necessary details.

Kris Dahl, my agent, understood the importance of these issues immediately—even though this must have sounded like a wild story when we first met in March 2002—and has provided guidance since.

Delia Marshall skillfully, tirelessly, and compassionately labored with me to help organize the argument and improve the language. Her attention to detail and commitment to bringing forth the important points are greatly appreciated.

Besides showing me that well-researched, unflinching investigative writing can make a difference, Eric Schlosser provided friendly writer's advice. He reassured me that the personal havoc that builds toward the end of a project is "normal." And he suggested that I work with Ellis Levine, who would provide excellent legal advice and help me produce a better book. Ellis certainly did both. His attention to detail helped to ensure that I was telling this at times far-fetched-sounding tale fairly and accurately, and his literary sense helped me to tell the story better.

Bruce Spitz first introduced me to the pleasures and challenges of health policy research in 1981. We have been colleagues (intermittently) and friends (consistently) since, and I greatly appreciate the advice and guidance that he has provided over more than 20 years.

Many people have offered expert suggestions, and I am grateful for their efforts: Barbara Starfield, M.D., MPH; Elliott Fisher, M.D., MPH; Susan Love, M.D.; James Wright, M.D., Ph.D.; Marcia Angell, M.D.; Joe Vitale, M.D.; Arminee Kazanjian, Dr. Soc.; Richard Yospin; William Taylor, M.D.; Marty Farnsworth Richie; Paul Spirn, M.D.; Eve Leeman, M.D.; Stanley Sagov, M.D.; George Mann, Sc.D., M.D.; Larry Sasich, Pharm.D.; Richard Einhorn, M.D.; Professor Richard Lewontin; and Michael Klein, M.D. Herbert Benson, M.D., has provided sage advice and made many suggestions as these ideas have developed over the past five years. The inaccuracies that remain are my own.

Mike Curtis at the *Atlantic Monthly* read an early version of the chapter on Celebrex and Vioxx and confirmed its importance while at the same time gently suggesting that I be kinder to my readers. Melissa Ludke, from *Nieman Reports,* encouraged me to write about the press coverage of C-reactive protein.

Other friends have discussed these issues at length and contributed views from outside the world of medicine: Wolf Kahn and Emily Mason (who also suggested the second best title, "Pandora's Pillbox"), Anne Spirn, Lynn and Joel Altschul, Thelma Dionne, Chester Wolfe, Bonnie and Peter Rollins, Nate Spiller, Rev. Edward Simms, Stephen Walker, Ron Fox, Elliot Lobel, Paula and Michael Nathanson, Carol Curry, Tom Jarvis, Ruth Kahn, Jean Abramson, Julie Nagazina, and Jay Altschul.

In the various stages of this project, Becky Shafir suggested that it was time for me to write a book; Jane Lawrence gave me the courage to put unrefined and disorganized ideas on paper as a first step; Jeannette Hopkins did her best to show me what I didn't know about writing and how themes are organized into a book; and Virginia LaPlante skillfully coached me in the preparation of the book proposal.

Thanks to the dedicated people who worked with me in the office (especially Holly Bouchard, the office manager), contributing so much to the care of our patients. Great thanks to my former patients for their trust and for the lessons that they taught me. (Except for Sister Marguerite Kiley, I have changed the names and characteristics of patients in order to protect their privacy.)

I want to remember David Schmidt, M.D., who guided me through the early stages of my career—respecting me enough to let me accept his mature advice. I also want to remember Sister Marguerite, whose spirit still shines as a beacon in my family.

Special thanks to my children, Rebecca and Seth. They have put up with my career as a family doctor and with the demands of this project. And they have given me the greatest gift a parent can receive—they have become adults guided by their own sense of compassion and integrity.

INDEX

health insurance and, 75–82,
253–54
ischemic stroke drug, 226
marketing and, 10, 154, 159, 166
Medicare prescription drug bill
and, 247–48
randomized controlled trials
(RCTs), 66
reducing, xvii–xviii, 249–56
statin drugs, 15, 135, 136, 138–39
supply-side medical care and,
184–85
surgical procedures, 174–78
unnecessary medical services,
xix–xx, 52–53, 84, 178–81
Xigris, 162
counseling, 11, 232–33
counterfeit Canadian drugs,
159–61
Covera, 104–5
COX-2 inhibitors. See Celebrex and
Vioxx
C-reactive protein (CRP) test,
164–66
Crestor, 133, 148
CT scans, 44, 181–83

damage control, 26, 107–9
data
FDA, 28, 37
manipulation (see commercial
research bias)
omission, 29–31
transparency, 27–28, 94, 105–6,
251–52
death rates. See mortality rates
defibrillators, 44, 98–101
dementia, 58, 69, 104

depression, 10–11, 114–17, 163,
232–34
design, changed research, 31
detailing drugs, 124–26
diabetes
hormone replacement therapy
and, 67
Rezulin drug, 86–88
strokes and, 225, 227
diagnostic tests, xix–xx, 84, 164–66,
169, 171–72, 211–20
dialysis, 43
diclofenac (Voltaren), 25, 29–30
diet. See also lifestyle health
factors
basic health and, 45, 238
cancer and, 234–35
cholesterol guidelines and, 135
coronary heart disease and,
201–2, 221–25
diabetes and, 229–31
life expectancy and, 49
obesity and, 235–37
osteoporosis and, 218
stroke and, 17
direct-to-consumer (DTC)
advertising, 150–59. See also
marketing
advertising agencies and research
companies, 109–10
Claritin, 152–54
Celebrex and Vioxx, 5–6, 28
as commercial speech, 157–59
FDA approval of, 150–52
FDA warnings about (see
warning letters, FDA)
health insurance and, 80
medical consumerism and, xx,